THE SELF IN TRANSITION

GERMAN MONITOR No. 75
General Editor: Pól Ó Dochartaigh

GDR/German Monitor founded by Ian Wallace in 1979

THE SELF IN TRANSITION

East German Autobiographical Writing Before and After Unification

Essays in Honour of Dennis Tate

Edited by

David Clarke and Axel Goodbody

Amsterdam - New York, NY 2012

ISBN: 978-90-420-3593-5
E-Book ISBN: 978-94-012-0868-0
©Editions Rodopi B.V., Amsterdam - New York, NY 2012
Printed in the Netherlands

Table of Contents

Ian Wallace

Foreword

It is an immense privilege and pleasure to have the opportunity in this brief foreword to celebrate the outstanding contribution to German Studies both in the UK and at large of a widely admired friend and colleague, Dennis Tate.

Dennis is undoubtedly best known for the high quality of the published research on GDR literature which he has consistently produced since the early 1980s. I well remember the pioneering paper he presented in Dundee in 1983 at a time when GDR studies were still in their infancy, and his many contributions since then were a major factor in establishing work on the previously neglected GDR as a major field of research in the UK. This also earned him a richly deserved international reputation, not least for his important work on the East German novel, on Franz Fühmann and, more recently, on autobiography – an appropriate theme for a volume conceived in his honour. It is no exaggeration to say that his publications will remain essential reference points for researchers in the field for many years to come.

Those who have worked most closely with Dennis know that, in addition to being a distinguished research scholar, he is also a gifted and dedicated teacher. As student questionnaires confirmed year after year, the various courses he taught at the University of Bath were always among those best received by a student body never afraid to express its views in the clearest terms. Above all, Dennis never lost sight of the fact that, in the face of multiple and often conflicting claims on his attention, the interests of his students always came first, and generations of Bath students owe him a real debt of gratitude for that. This is true not least of his doctoral students, to whose supervision he devoted a quite extraordinary amount of time and care.

Having begun his career at the University of Ulster in his native Northern Ireland, Dennis moved to Bath in 1978. Appointed as a Lecturer in German, he was subsequently promoted to Senior Lecturer, then Reader, and finally Professor of German Studies before retiring in August 2008 after 30 years of service to the University. Anyone who has ever worked closely with him knows him as an unfailingly considerate and congenial colleague and an always reliable source of good sense. He unfailingly exercised a calming influence in the kinds of storms which can assail academic life in times of stress, and I am not alone in having good reason to be grateful to him for that.

Like all the contributors to this splendid volume, his many friends in the academic world and beyond will join me in wishing Dennis and his wife Sylvia a long, fruitful and fulfilling retirement.

David Clarke and Axel Goodbody

Introduction

The essays collected here are offered in honour of, and thanks to Dennis Tate, who has been sorely missed as a colleague at the University of Bath since his retirement in 2008, although he remains an active researcher as Professor Emeritus. The enthusiastic response to our proposal to put together the volume which we received from colleagues with whom he has worked, in one capacity or another, over the last thirty years, is, however, an indication of gratitude not only for support and guidance received, but also for inspiration derived from his studies of the literature of the German Democratic Republic.

Dennis established his reputation with *The East German Novel: Identity, Community, Continuity* (1983),[1] a work which identified themes which would become central to the study of East German literature in the UK. In this book he investigated the struggles of a range of authors in the GDR, all committed to the project of socialism, to come to terms with the failings of the regime of the Socialist Unity Party (SED) and preserve the utopian possibility of a true socialist community in the face of their own disillusionment. Since the early 1990s, his research has focused on the exploration of the notion of 'subjective authenticity', a poetic principle first proposed by Christa Wolf in her essay 'Lesen und Schreiben' of 1968.[2] Dennis has identified subjective authenticity as a key concept characterising the mode of writing of GDR authors, particularly those who came to question their commitment to the SED regime and its ideological interpretation of contemporary and historical realities. In his monograph on Franz Fühmann (1995), his many articles and edited volumes, and in his latest book, *Shifting Perspectives: East German Autobiographical Narratives Before and After the End of the GDR* (2007), Dennis has examined the struggle of socialist writers to stay true to their own subjective experience in the face of political dogma, shifts in SED cultural policy, and latterly the collapse of the GDR and German reunification. Here Dennis has highlighted the significance of autobiography and other forms of 'life-writing', including autobiographical fiction and biographies whose depiction of historical subjects serves to throw light on the situation of the writing subject, as a means by which East German writers have sought to make sense of the past, and establish and maintain their personal identity in the context of the political struggles of their times, in ways which reson-ated with the lives of readers.

At the same time, Dennis's work is informed by that shift in the understanding of identity and in scholarship on life writing which, since the 1980s, has questioned the notion of autobiography as the discovery of an authentic and coherent self across the span of a lifetime, foregrounding instead the ways in which the self is constructed and repeatedly reconstructed in narratives responding to changing circumstances. What is given prominence in accounts of the past is determined by the social, political and psychological needs of the moment.[3] A further insight conveyed by the nuanced analyses contained in *Shifting Perspectives* is that, while individuals have been driven by the need to express a 'subjectively authentic' self in many forms of text (interviews, letters, diaries, memoirs, and essays, fiction and poetry as well as autobiography proper[4]), literature (with its special attention to the psychological developments accompanying political and social change, its complex narrative structures enabling it to juxtapose different positions and embrace contradictions and ambivalences, and its ability to reflect on the process of remembering through the voice of the narrator) has served, in the GDR at any rate, as the principal medium for sophisticated reappraisals and redefin-itions of the self.[5]

If, as Dennis points out, cultural policy makers in the SED long harboured a suspicion of autobiographical writing and its 'subjective' bias,[6] it is in part because the question of defining one's individual identity in relation to the past has been of such significance in East German society (and in other socialist countries in Central and Eastern Europe).[7] For the generation which had grown up under National Socialism and, in many cases, offered that regime its youthful enthus-iasm, the possibility of shaping their personal biographies in response to the discourse of the ruling party had particular benefits. In practical terms, this was a generation which, as Mary Fulbrook has demon-strated, was able to profit from the structural advantages afforded by the sweeping away of old elites in the GDR, rising rapidly to positions of responsibility and prominence at a young age.[8] State socialism allowed them to re-narrate their own past in terms of betrayal by one ideology and salvation by another. In the nineteen-fifties and sixties, this model was drawn on not merely by career-driven opportunists, but also by a number of significant GDR writers whose youth fell in the Third Reich and the war years, including Christa Wolf (whose autobiography *Kindheitsmuster* is discussed in contributions by Georgina Paul and Renate Rechtien to this volume). Even for those who, like Günter de Bruyn (discussed in Owen Evans' chapter) had maintained an ideological distance to Nazism, the conversion narrative held its attractions at the time as a means of distancing themselves from the horrors of the recent past. Political developments in the nineteen-seventies and eighties were, of course, to lead de Bruyn and other writers to repudiate this interpretation of the historical caesura of 1945, and to engage in reinterpretations of the past well before re-unification and the second great reversal of political and cultural values which it precipitated.

The autobiographies examined in the essays in the first section of this volume are, however, the work of an older generation, born between 1890 and 1910.[9] Hans Marchwitza, Greta Kuckhoff, Rudi Goguel and Elfriede Brüning had been members of the resistance in the Third Reich, and they chose to live in the Soviet Zone after the war. As Helmut Peitsch and Martin Kane show, such veterans of the communist movement were by no means exempt from reframing their personal history in response to the dominant ideology in the GDR. Communist survivors of concentration camps, former combatants in the Spanish Civil War, resistance fighters and wartime émigrés had to present their past actions and commitments in such a way that these chimed with the grand narrative of the Party. At the height of the GDR's own version of Stalinism in the 1950s, possession of the 'wrong' biography, for example being Jewish or having worked outside the Soviet Union during the Second World War, could spell the end of the career of even the most loyal SED member, as the case of ousted Politburo member Paul Merker demonstrates, for example.[10] External political control was compounded by a self-censorship resulting from what Wulf Kirsten has described as 'deformierende Angst-Abhängigkeit', a 'verschleppte Angstpsychose, die mit der Doppel-züngigkeit und der Lüge in Personalunion lebte'.[11] However, as Joanne Sayner's analysis of Greta Kuckhoff's postwar activities in promoting the history of 'Die Rote Kapelle' resistance group shows, not even all SED members re-interpreted their past lives exclusively according to this narrative. In fact, as Kuckhoff's life demonstrates, there were also individuals who were compelled by personal experience to seek to preserve the memory of suppressed aspects of the past.

Nevertheless, even in the GDR's later period of relative stability, the willingness of the individual to narrate a life-story conforming to the official view of the past as evidence of loyalty to the socialist project, for example in the autobiographical statements demanded of young people at various points in their careers, was an important factor in the relationship of citizens to the state. So familiar was this situation in the GDR that it has become the subject of parody since German unification: For example, in Leander Haussmann's *Sonnenallee* (1999), where the young hero Micha, after years presumably spent parroting the necessary clichés in school, re-writes his distinctly apolitical life as an *oppositional* autobiography in order to impress his new girlfriend; or in Uwe Tellkamp's *Der Turm* (2008), in which the very un-socialist protagonist Christian Hoffmann gets so carried away relating the long history of his personal commitment to defending peace against Western militarism that his recruiting officer for the *Nationale Volksarmee* starts to glance at the clock in sheer boredom.[12] In fact, Christian feels no such commitment: it is simply that he knows that such an autobiographical statement is necessary for him to achieve his goal of eventually studying medicine.

Such pressures may explain the fact that the autobiographical writing of the generation born in the 1930s which is examined in essays in the second section of this volume is typically oblique and complex. Ricarda Schmidt shows how Christa Wolf moulds her portrait of Heinrich von Kleist in *Kein Ort. Nirgends* into an identity narrative reflecting her own alienation in the GDR in the 1970s, Alongside the deterritorialisation observable in *Kein Ort. Nirgends* and other writings of Wolf's, which stemmed from her loss of belief in the GDR as a historical territory committed to realising harmonious human community, Georgina Paul traces sees Wolf's disillusionment with GDR socialism from the Biermann affair on reflected in a shift away from temporal anchoring of the utopian in the time depicted in her narratives to a timeless sphere, culminating in the author's latest novel, *Stadt der Engel*. Axel Goodbody shows how Wulf Kirsten also engages in exploration of the self through depiction of the lives of others. Kirsten's poetic idealisation of the world of his childhood as, for all the hardship suffered by the rural poor, one of unalienated labour and community, raises questions about the circumstances under which nostalgia can serve as a productive resource, preserving an awareness of utopian possibilities against which developments in the present can be measured. Heinz-Peter Preußer shows how the figures of both Hinze and Kunze in Volker Braun's *Hinze-Kunze-Roman* are projections of aspects of the author's self, and how Braun's loss of hope for realisation of unalienated existence in a reformed socialism is reflected in the difference between the vitalist Kunze and the post-*Wende* identification figure of the stoic philosopher emperor Marcus Aurelius. Christine Cosentino shows how Braun's portrait of his father in the late work *Das Mittagsmahl* is a form of self-exploration – his father's name, Erich, is construed as a combination of 'er' and 'ich' – which poses questions about his own historical and political consciousness and responsibility.

In the final section of the book, post-*Wende* reassessments of the past, mainly the 40 years of socialism, but also the Second World War and in the case of younger writers, life in post-unification Germany, are presented and evaluated. In the recasting of personal histories necessitated by the implosion of the GDR, those formerly loyal or acquiescent to the system sought to re-interpret their actions in the light of post-*Wende* political realities. Peter Barker discusses the Sorbian writer Jurij Brězan's autobiography written in the second half of the 1980s and the revisions he made to his account of events ten years later, after the *Wende*, showing how the author sought to justify the role he played as a writer who remained loyal to the SED long after his original political hopes had became illusions, and to demonstrate his continuing commitment to defending Sorbian culture.

While not every citizen of the GDR sought to retrospectively present themselves, like Klaus Ultzsch in Thomas Brussig's novel *Helden wie wir* (1995), as personally responsible for the fall of the Berlin Wall, the end of the GDR prompted a glut of autobiographical writing from people of all walks of life: authors, politicians, theologians, historians, actors, soldiers, singers, scientists, as well as ordinary citizens and victims of the regime. Ute Hirsekorn's reading of the autobiographical texts of SED politician Günter Schabowski provides an insight into the pressure to make new sense of one's life after the historical caesura of 1989 and the sometimes contorted reasoning which could result: Schabowski explains his misguided allegiance to the SED in psychological terms, presenting himself as quasi-innocent victim of a 'utopian syndrome'.

That this pressure has also applied to writers who have experienced the demise of *two* different ideological systems is shown in essays in the first two sections of this volume, for instance in Sara Jones' reading of the work of Elfriede Brüning and Heinz-Peter Preußer's and Christine Cosentino's chapters on Volker Braun. In the context of the self-reflection and, in some cases, dubious re-invention of the self after the end of the GDR, some of the more complex and interesting autobiographical writing reveals a loss of confidence in the ability of the writer to bring an authentic subject to light through excavation of the past: Renate Rechtien shows how the labyrinth and the spectral come to dominate in Christa Wolf's *Leibhaftig*, replacing her earlier conception of the work of the author as archaeological investigation of memories. Younger East German authors who have come to prominence since unification, for example Ingo Schulze and Reinhard Jirgl (analysed in this volume by Andrew Plowman and David Clarke respectively), express a distinct scepticism towards life writing. Elements of Schulze's biography are refracted through multiple personas in *Neue Leben,* and the self-serving nature of his protagonist's autobiographical self-presentations is exposed, while Jirgl rejects the notion of autobiography as the subject's search for identity within society, seeing authentic subjectivity and social existence as radically opposed.

Many of the contributions to this volume are concerned with literature as a medium for the critical exploration of the relationship between personal history and social history. As the recent boom in 'Memory Studies' has amply demonstrated, it is a feature of human social existence that we come to understand our past in communication with other people, and through the institutions and media which play a key role in our socialisation. This 'communicative memory', as Harald Welzer has termed it,[13] is in many cases naïve: we do not necessarily recognise ourselves that our view of our past, which we subjectively feel to be authentic, is conditioned by social factors. Cultural memory, however, operates on a different terrain. Literature in particular interrogates memory, highlights its contradictions and obfuscations, throws it open to reinterpretation, and, in doing so, challenges dominant narratives about the past. Indeed, as Hannes Krauss' semi-autobiographical essay, which closes the volume, demonstrates, critical engagement with literature is itself an activity through which we interpret and subsequently re-interpret our own relationship to our past and to the history of the societies which shape our lives.

This is the function of literature which, in the context of East Germany, has held a central place in the work of Dennis Tate, and it is therefore highly appropriate that a volume in his honour should take this issue as its focus.

Notes

[1]   For full details of Dennis Tate's publications, see the bibliography at the end of the current volume.

[2]   Christa Wolf, 'Lesen und Schreiben', in: *Werke*, ed. by Sonja Hilzinger, 12 vols, Munich: Luchterhand, 1999-2001, IV, pp. 238-82.

[3]   See Jeffrey K. Olick, Vered Vinitzky-Seroussi and Daniel Levy, 'Introduction' in Olick, Vinitzky-Seroussi and Levy, eds, *The Collective Memory Reader*, Oxford: Oxford University Press, 2011, pp. 1-62, especially p. 37; also Astrid Erll, 'Cultural Memory Studies: An Introduction', in: Astrid Erll and Ansgar Nünning, eds, *Cultural Memory Studies. An International and Interdisciplinary Handbook*, Berlin and New York: de Gruyter, 2008, pp. 1-18.

[4]   The defining feature of autobiography is generally accepted to be the 'autobiographical pact' between author and reader, i.e. the tacit assurance given by the author that the story which he relates is that of his own real life, narrated as authentically as possible – see Philippe Lejeune, 'The Autobiographical Pact', transl. by Katherine M. Leary, in Paul John Eakin, ed., *On Autobiography*, Minneapolis: University of Minnesota Press, 1989, pp. 3-30.

[5]   Astrid Erll provides an overview of research on literature as a medium of cultural memory in the last two chapters of her book, *Kollektives Gedächtnis und Erinnerungskulturen. Eine Einführung*, Stuttgart and Weimar: Metzler, 2005, pp. 143-193. See also Erll and Ansgar Nünning, 'Where Literature and Memory Meet: Towards a Systematic Approach to the Concepts of Memory Used in Literary Studies', in: Herbert Grabes, ed., *Literature, Literary History, and Cultural Memory* (REAL. Yearbook of Research in English and American Literature 21), Tübingen: Gunter Narr, 2005, pp. 262-94.

[6]   Dennis Tate, *Shifting Perspectives: East German Autobiographical Narratives Before and After the End of the GDR*, Rochester, NY: Camden House, 2007, p. 31.

[7]   James Mark, *The Unfinished Revolution: Making Sense of the Communist Past in Central-Eastern Europe*, New Haven and London: Harvard University Press, 2010, p. xxvi.

[8]   Mary Fulbrook, 'Histories and Memories: *Verklärung* or *Erklärung?*' in David Clarke and Ute Wölfel, eds, *Remembering the German Democratic Republic: Divided Memory in a United Germany*, Basingstoke: Palgrave Macmillan, 2011, pp. 91-101.

[9]   The essays are arranged simply by date of birth of the writer discussed. However, they are grouped in sections corresponding to the three distinct phases of remembering which emerged.

[10]   Jeffrey Herf, 'East German Communists and the Jewish Question: The Case of Paul Merker', *Journal of Contemporary History*, 29:4 (1994), 627-61.

[11]   Wulf Kirsten, 'Dankrede zur Verleihung des Schillerrings', in: *Brückengang. Essays und Reden*, Zurich: Ammann, 2009, p. 109.

[12]   Uwe Tellkamp, *Der Turm: Geschichte aus einem versunkenen Land*, Frankfurt/Main: Suhrkamp, 2008, pp. 330-1.

[13]   Harald Welzer, *Das kommunikative Gedächtnis: Eine Theorie der Erinnerung*, Munich: Beck, 2008.

Part One:

**The Third Reich in
Socialist Autobiographies**

Martin Kane

Omissions and Revisions:
Hans Marchwitza's Autobiographical Writing

Hans Marchwitza typifies those communist writers who returned to the SBZ after 1945 determined to see the political vision for which they had suffered made reality. This often meant in his autobiographical writing about the precarious years in exile a process of selective omission. He turns a blind eye to aspects of the cultural politicking of KPD émigrés in France which would have made awkward reading for the SED, and, while offering a vivid account of his arduous existence in the USA, he provides a picture of the rapacity of American capitalism which exactly fitted what was required of writers in East Germany in the immediate postwar period.

Those writers who had been forced into exile by Hitler and then opted to return to East Germany after 1945 were unconditionally supportive of the GDR. They were invariably prepared, particularly during the *Aufbau* period of 1949-61, to turn a blind eye to the defects and often harsh realities of the new society. Should they have needed any reminding about what was required of their writing, however, they would have found it in the promptings of cultural tsars such as Alexander Abusch:

> [E]s wäre sehr gut, wenn wir einige Schriftsteller haben würden, die nach der Methode Upton Sinclairs (ohne seine ideologischen Schwankungen) sehr schnell Romane über die Bodenreform, den Wiederaufbau der zerbombten Betriebe, den heroischen Kampf zur Überwindung des ganzen Hitlererbes in der Wirtschaft unseres Landes schreiben könnten.[1]

Where this preposterous suggestion might lead is demonstrated by early *Betriebsromane* such as Karl Mundstock's *Helle Nächte* (1952) or Hans Marchwitza's *Roheisen* (1955), which depict the construction of Eisenhüttenstadt, an industrial city carved out of forest land near the Polish border. Character and setting in these novels are made to carry wider significance. The building site arising from wild and virgin territory, and populated by purposeful *Helden der Arbeit*, strives to become an inspirational metaphor for the wider revolution underway. Action and plot resemble clips from propaganda newsreels, characters would not be out of place in the cruder form of political poster. As scenes of prodigious toil and productivity flow one to the next, we

learn nothing of the vicissitudes experienced by ordinary workers at
this time. Everyday grievances about output norms, housing, food and
clothing shortages, which would lead to the workers' uprising of 17
June 1953, are not on the agenda of these novels. Those elements
which lend Erik Neutsch's *Spur der Steine* (1964) its, for officialdom,
awkward plausibility (Frank Beyer's film version was rapidly
banished from East German cinemas) – the fleshing out of human
failings, the recognition that not all GDR citizens shared the
commitment of the idealised activist worker – are absent or merely
hinted at.

The catalogue of shortcomings in these prolix and didactic works
might easily be extended. However, no amount of caustic judgement
would answer the question of why their authors should have written in
this fashion. While it might seem tempting to describe Mundstock,
Marchwitza, and others of their ilk as scribbling in the shadow of
Party obligation, their political biographies demonstrate that they
required no directives to urge them on. *Altkommunisten* who had
fought and been persecuted for their beliefs, they yearned to see their
travails vindicated by the new world emerging. Reluctant to acknowledge that utopian aspirations might not always coincide with developing reality, they preferred to present a picture – at least for public
consumption – in tune with what they fervently hoped the GDR would
become, rather than what it actually was. When confronted with crises
such as the events of June 1953 it was unsurprising that they should
sink into 'beredtes Schweigen'.[2]

At this point engagement with Dennis Tate beckons, and specifically with his remarks about returning exiles who constructed 'a version of the past to fit their own needs at a given time',[3] and failed to
attempt the 'serious memoir that might have countered the simplifica-
tions of their earlier ostensibly autobiographical writing'.[4] Dennis
mentions Hans Marchwitza here, but not three of his autobiographical
works which seem to invite analysis in terms of his comments: *Meine
Jugend*, *In Frankreich* and *In Amerika*.

Franz Hammer has noted that Hans Marchwitza's work 'wurde
zumeist aus dem Autobiographischen gespeist'.[5] *Meine Jugend*,
written in the USA and published in 1947 in the Soviet Occupied
Zone, is a lightly fictionalized chronicle of Marchwitza's development
– the 'Prozeß eines sehr schweren Autodidaktentums'[6] – as a proletarian writer. It dramatizes in graphic detail his becoming a miner at

the age of fourteen in 1904, then moving from Upper Silesia to the Ruhr in search of better working conditions, thereby exchanging one variety of wage-slavery for another. At the heart of *Meine Jugend*, and indeed of everything Marchwitza wrote dealing with the world of work prior to returning to East Germany, are the oppressive lives of working people – in Germany of steelworkers and miners of coal and iron ore, in the USA of jobbing painters and labourers. He depicts not merely the horrors of a range of industrial milieux, along with their grim domestic backdrop of grinding poverty, but also locates them in a clear economic and political context. If his protagonists are initially oblivious to the ruthless mechanisms responsible for the circumstances in which they live, the development they undergo is towards an increasingly militant awareness of the capitalist system driving their exploitation and deprivation.

The life of Johann Thomek, the central character in *Meine Jugend*, closely parallels Marchwitza's own. The book concludes with his surviving, and having been politicized by, the horrors of the Western Front from 1915 to 1918. The autobiographical thread may be picked up in the figure of Franz Kreusat in Marchwitza's earlier, and first major work, *Sturm auf Essen* of 1930, the novel which established his reputation as the 'Kumpel-Dichter', the 'echteste Dichter der revolutionären Bergarbeiter'.[7] Kreusat's involvement in the struggle against the Kapp *Putsch* in the Ruhr of March 1920 mirrors that of Marchwitza, with one important exception: Kreusat falls victim to Gustav Noske's 'Freikorps' in the aftermath of the putsch. Marchwitza lived to fight another day, with his experience, from a KPD standpoint, of the political struggles between Left and Right into the early 1930s finding literary reflection in the first and second parts of his Kumiak trilogy, *Die Kumiaks* (Zürich, 1934) and *Die Heimkehr der Kumiaks* (Berlin, 1959). Unlike the eponymous hero of this second volume, however, Marchwitza evaded the concentration camp in which Peter Kumiak found himself on Hitler's coming to power. He escaped to Switzerland in April 1933,[8] was expelled and sought refuge in France in November 1934 before being sent by the Party to agitate on its behalf in the Saar plebiscite of January 1935. Marchwitza is conspicuously reticent about this episode in his life, and what was, in effect, a tactical fiasco for the KPD. After pressing, absurdly, for a 'rotes Saargebiet in Sowjetdeutschland',[9] the Party opted belatedly for a campaign alongside the SPD in favour of the status quo. This brought them a meagre 8.8% of the vote, with 90.7% going in support of the Saar becoming part of Germany.[10] From 1936 to 1938 Marchwitza was an officer in the Tschapaiew Battalion in the Spanish Civil War, before finding uncomfortable refuge, again in France and subsequently in the USA. In 1947 he returned to Germany and, via Stuttgart, to Babelsberg in East Berlin.

While Marchwitza wrote at length about the years from 1938 to 1946 in France and the USA, he gives us virtually nothing about his first period in France from 1934 to 1936, and just three short stories – 'Vor Teruel', 'Araganda', and 'Die Uniform', published in *Das Wort* in Moscow 1938/1939 – are set in Spain. *In Frankreich* contains two somewhat romanticized episodes about his experiences in Spain, but nothing of consequence on the Civil War itself. As an ever-loyal Party member, Marchwitza was clearly wary of ideologically touchy subjects. Ludwig Renn remarked in 1952:

> I hear it rumoured that at the moment speaking about Spain is unwanted, and that everything connected with it is cancelled. Supposedly this is happening because there were too many traitors in Spain. I don't understand such points of view.[11]

It is ironic, in view of this, that Renn's own Spanish memoir[12] 'wieder und wieder "gesäubert" und "überarbeitet" worden [war]' to become a 'konforme Propagandaschrift' for the official SED version of the International Brigades.[13] Renn was not alone in this. In the paranoid atmosphere engendered by the show trials of the 1950s his fellow veteran *Spanienkämpfer* were regarded with suspicion for their international and varied political connections in previous decades. This made them extremely circumspect about how they presented their experiences: 'aware of the boundaries and taboos of East German historical discourse, the majority [...] ended up censoring their own memories much more effectively than the SED could ever have done'.[14] What, specifically, had to be censored was the nature of Soviet policy in Spain. As Gerald Brenan puts it, the Communists were, for strategic reasons – the Soviet Union did not wish to alienate its French and British potential allies in Western Europe[15] – 'doing their utmost to damp down the revolutionary impulses of the peasants and factory workers'.[16] This led to bitter hostility between the Communists and revolutionist groups such as the Trotskyist POUM, culminating in Barcelona in April 1937 in a 'small-scale civil war within the civil war',[17] and the ruthless purging by the NKVD, the

Soviet secret police, of thousands of socialist and anarchist opponents of Franco. Marchwitza would undoubtedly have been aware of tragic and deeply contentious episodes such as this, but chose to add nothing to the debate, his silence espousing the official SED version of events.

Hans Marchwitza's two most immediately autobiographical works, *In Frankreich* and *In Amerika* have received scant critical attention.[18] As already noted, Dennis Tate makes no reference to them, nor do they feature in Wolfgang Emmerich's compendious survey of East German literature.[19] In Martin Mauthner's book on German writers exiled in France Marchwitza's name is not even mentioned.[20] This neglect deserves to be rectified, not least for the ways in which both texts fashion past personal experience into an instrument of justification for the present. The dedication which prefaces *In Frankreich*, 'Für die Jungen' – the last line of a poem Marchwitza wrote in the USA – he uses again in *In Amerika* when pressed to record for posterity what he and those who have shared his fate had gone through: 'Für die Jungen! [...] Sie müssen es lesen, die Jungen, sie müssen den Weg unserer grausamen Vergangenheit erleben' (369).

In Frankreich appeared in 1949, *In Amerika* in 1961. Issued as one volume in 1971 and constituting a continuous, chronological account, the two works are nevertheless very different in their ideological and political emphasis. *In Amerika* is sharper to the point of polemic than the earlier volume. It is clearly the work of a writer whose years in the GDR have taught him to be alert to present requirements. Instructive here is an anecdote about Arnold Zweig, who was persuaded in 1948 to rewrite parts of *Der Streit um den Sergeanten Grischa*. Zweig was encouraged not only to expunge all references to Trotsky and psychoanalysis, but also to remove a passage showing American soldiers weeping at the sight of starving concentration camp inmates – this on the grounds that 'Kapitalisten solcher Emotionen nicht fähig sind'.[21] Zweig colluded quite willingly in this act of distortion, demonstrating that, like Marchwitza, he had become 'der gereiftere, wissendere [...] Schriftsteller',[22] a writer who knows, who has learnt, or is only too willing, to deliver what is required of him.

In Frankreich begins in December 1938, making only fleeting reference to Marchwitza's first stay in France from 1934 to 1936. He informs us merely that he and other 'einsam gewordene Menschen' had congregated in 'kleinen, illegalen Hotels' in Paris, before going off to Spain, either to die there, or return as cripples (17). From other

sources we know that there was much more to Marchwitza's life at
that time. It is not difficult to ascertain that he had been very active,
politically and culturally, during both of his stays in France. He was,
according to Ralph Schock, one of that group of activist KPD writers
whose participation in the futile Saar campaign had left the Party's
resources in Paris, to quote Johannes R. Becher, 'außerordentlich
geschwächt'.[23] We learn, furthermore, that he was part of the rich cultural life generated by the German exiles in Paris, and one of those
writers who had performed more than once ('sprachen [...]
mehrfach'[24]) at the lively weekly meetings of the SDS (*Schutzverband
Deutscher Schriftsteller*) held in the Cafe Mephisto on the Boulevard
St. Germain. At the celebrated first international writers' conference
in defence of culture held in Paris in 1935 he had given a talk, 'Wir
schreiben nur unsere Erfahrungen' which was listened to 'mit Ach-
tung'.[25] It is therefore curious that none of this finds its way into his
memoirs. Could it be that there were too many individuals at the Paris
conference who had since fallen from favour, and with whom Marchwitza did not wish his name to be associated? Or was it that apart from
a jargon-free greeting from Wilhelm Pieck and a poem from Becher,
'niemand von denen, die später die Kulturpolitik in der DDR
dirigierten'[26] were among the array of distinguished writers – *inter
alia* Thomas Mann, Stefan Zweig, Franz Werfel – who contributed to
the *Sonderheft* assembled in November 1938 to celebrate the fifth
anniversary of the SDS in exile. As early as this, it seems, the more
inflexible elements within the KPD leadership in Paris were beginning
to draw their narrow cultural boundaries, and Marchwitza's retrospective silence in the GDR was an endorsement of them.

One further, less agreeable aspect of his activities in Paris merits
attention, demonstrating as it does a brand of loyalty to the Comintern
on Marchwitza's part which, one speculates, would later serve him
well on his return to East Germany. This, again from Kantorowicz:

> [E]s stellte sich durch B[redel]s Bericht über die 'Stimmung' gegen uns heraus,
> daß unser lieber H.M[archwitza] tückische Beschwerden über uns nach drüben
> [i.e. Moscow, M.K.] gesandt hat. Er fühlte sich nicht genügend in den Vorder-
> grund geschoben, er, den wir so in die Mitte der Veranstaltungen beim S.D.S.
> gerückt haben. Niemand wußte etwas bisher von seiner Beschwerde. Es kam erst
> durch B[redel] heraus. Ein heimtückischer und eitler Schwätzer also. Er sollte
> seine autobiographische Serie von d[en] Kumiaks umtaufen: die 'Schubiaks'
> würde besser passen.[27]

By 1938, France had long abandoned any pretence of hospitality towards its German visitors. A wave of sympathy in the early months of 1933, along with an initially 'liberales Asylrecht'[28] which had enabled the establishment of émigré publishing houses (Editions du Carrefour) and newspapers (*Pariser Tageblatt*) had ebbed away, with traditional animosities towards Germany dating back to 1870 reasserting themselves. Alfred Kantorowicz had written in December 1935: 'Die psychische Not ist furchtbar und die physische nicht minder. Alle hungern, alle laufen beschäftigungslos und vereinsamt herum'.[29] June 1936 finds him in even more despairing vein, and providing devastating comment on the heartless 'Je-m'en-foutisme'[30] of the French, and particularly of French officialdom at this time:

> Ich ziehe mir das Fazit dieser unerträglichen Jahre. Es ergibt, daß in keinem Land so viel moralisches Pathos über Gastfreundschaft ertönte, in keinem Land aber de facto so wenig für uns getan wurde wie in Frankreich. ... Man will uns nicht hören und nicht sehen ... wir [wurden] kalt und verächtlich behandelt.[31]

There were further aggravations in the mix: an inability of the majority of the French to distinguish between genuine German political refugees and Nazis, along with a covert admiration for Adolf Hitler which bred suspicion of his opponents. This, and the 'zunehmende Faschisierung der französischen Regierung'[32] with the coming to power in April 1938 of Edouard Daladier and his policy of appeasing Hitler and curbing all anti-Nazi activity, shattered the émigrés' self-image as a 'moralische Macht, eine Elite, die den besseren [...] Teil ihres Volkes vertrat'.[33] Any really effective anti-fascist efforts were, moreover, severely hampered by destructive schisms and conflict within the various exile groups, the main culprit here being the KPD, in thrall to Moscow and with its 'verdeckte, mit zahlreichen unerfreulichen taktischen Manövern verfolgte Führungsanspruch'.[34]

In Frankreich studiously avoids all mention of these problematical aspects of KPD politicking.[35] On the other hand, it is a graphic and vivid account of the consequences of the government decree of 12 November 1938 ordering the rounding-up and internment of all German émigrés. It opens with the author and other *Spanienkämpfer* being transported to the 'Bourbonenstadt M.' (Moulins), where, with war and invasion imminent, they find themselves under surveillance from a largely hostile provincial populace suspicious of their activities in Spain, uncomprehending of their reasons for fleeing Germany, and

– in Marchwitza's case – paranoid about a writer in receipt of modest royalties from a Moscow publisher. Incarcerated for three months in the chateau of the Dukes of Bourbon, still a prison to this day, the exiles are then despatched on a grim odyssey which takes them via a series of internment centres to the infamous former tile factory, Les Milles, some thirty kilometres from Marseilles, and second only to Le Vernet and Gurs in its notoriety.

Perhaps because of the toughening effect of his austere proletarian origins, Marchwitza seems to have been less affected than others – Kantorowicz, for instance – by the brutish squalor of Les Milles and other internment way-stations. His tale is vividly told, and enlivened by a wealth of incident and detail of the day-to-day struggle to survive in an alien and increasingly threatening environment. This, and the ability to recall lengthy slabs of dialogue and conversation, some of which could only have been in French – a language he claims not to know – lends ostensibly autobiographical writing the feel, in places, of fictional narrative. This would not matter if we did not sense that the account has been doctored and depoliticized for GDR consumption. We know, from a characteristically bilious piece by Marcel Reich-Ranicki – one of his legendary *Verrisse* – that Marchwitza in the GDR was 'von Sekretären und Lektoren unterstützt und kontrolliert'.[36] What the reader misses in *In Frankreich*, due, perhaps to the influence of these interfering hands, is an authentic and honest account of how Marchwitza the *Altkommunist*, the dedicated Party activist, had reacted at the time to the passage of historical and political events. Just as, for reasons already stated, he gives us no sense of his involvement in the émigré political and cultural life of Paris, so, for instance, is there reaction in only the vaguest of terms to events such as the Hitler/Stalin Pact of August 1939: 'Ging es wirklich nicht anders? Warum dieser sonderbare und unerwartete Pakt?' (99). Inevitably, we compare the feebleness of this response with the lengthy and tortured analysis to be found in Kantorowicz's *Nachtbücher*,[37] or with the seismic 'Schock des Hitler-Stalin-Paktes' registered by Wolfgang Leonhard in his definitive account of the waves of horrified disbelief which this alliance sent throughout all sections of the European Left.[38] Again, one feels, Marchwitza has chosen to gloss over a potentially problematic subject.

One can sense polemical interference, or emphasis, even more strongly in *In Amerika*. The circuitous route of the boat taking Marchwitza to the USA is the opportunity for a gesture, while anchored in Oran, in support of those whom 'der Teufel Profit mißhandelt' (287), the stopover in Trinidad yields a glimpse of the 'Knechte und Sklaven der Kolonialherren' and their 'britischen Bedrücker'(295), while the sight of sharks in the water provides him with an anticipatory image for what awaits him in New York: 'Es gibt schlimmere Raubtiere [...] das sind die Tresorbesitzer in Manhattan!' (296). Unmistakable here the Cold War politics of the 1950s, and the need, in the GDR, to demonize and pillory 'dieses eisige, herzlose Amerika' (390).

Once in New York, Marchwitza leads a curious double life 'inmitten der riesigen Betontürme' (305), the towering symbols of a rapacious capitalism. The would-be writer is forced into a round of harsh, menial, and often dangerous jobs – painter, steel-fixer, labourer – and is under constant harassment, for a pittance, from a succession of ruthless taskmasters. The solace and support of Hilde, the widow of a an émigré German professor and her family, and financial help from Mother Russia – 'Die Mutter denkt an uns'(360) – enables him to punctuate this remorseless routine with intermittent bouts of writing: some poems, work on *Meine Jugend* and his 'Frankreichbuch'. But never for a moment are we allowed to forget the icy heartlessness of American society.

To what extent external ideological pressures and the editorial controls described by Reich-Ranicki influenced the final versions of *In Frankreich* and *In Amerika* and the negative image which emerges of the two countries is hard to assess precisely. Sundry comments from within the GDR, however, offer some clues. On the occasion of the *Trauerfeier* for Hans Marchwitza on 20 January 1965 Alexander Abusch noted: '[Du] hast mit einer unermüdlichen Selbstkritik alle Deine früheren Werke überprüft, überarbeitet, neugestaltet'.[39] The political dimension to Marchwitza's zealous revisions emerges – somewhat ominously – in Werner Ilberg's analysis of the first, 1930, version of *Sturm auf Essen*: 'Eine zweite, nach 1945 entstandene Fassung des Romans enthält viele der hier verdeutlichten Mängel nicht mehr'.[40] It is clear that these so-called 'defects' stem from Marchwitza's failure fully to acknowledge the role of the KPD in the GDR version of the upheavals in the Ruhr and to recognise that it was by then, in the early 1920s, already (supposedly) a 'Massenpartei'. If this could be seen as a telling example of how, in the GDR, history might be tweaked to suit present purposes, then it is hardly speculative to assume that the same holds particularly true for *In Amerika*, in which Marchwitza is quite clearly enlisting and shaping his experience of the USA in the battle against capitalism and all it stands for.

After the harrowing years of forced emigration, the move to the SBZ was a kind of salvation and recompense for what Hans March-witza had suffered as a consequence of Hitler, and in exile: like many other returning communist writers and intellectuals he was well-rewarded materially and in terms of official honours. But all this came at a price, and one he was seemingly only too willing to pay – quies-cent consent to the official line, on both past and present. While his autobiographical accounts of France and the USA are highly reveal-ing, and rich in graphic detail of the daily tribulations and struggle for survival of a German communist writer who lacked the international celebrity of a Thomas Mann, an Ernst Toller or a Lion Feuchtwanger, they disappoint in what they fail to give us: the perspective of a genuinely proletarian, staunchly communist writer on the political, ideological and cultural interaction and tensions within the exiled German intelligentsia during the Nazi period. To return briefly to the subject of editorial interference, we know from Willi Meinck, *Cheflektor* with the Verlag Tribüne, that suggesting too many changes to one of his manuscripts could induce blind rage in Marchwitza: 'ich merkte, wie die Zornesadern an seinen Schläfen anschwollen. Er schrie mich an, sprang plötzlich von seinem Stuhl auf und stürzte sich auf mich'.[41] We may reasonably speculate that outbursts on occasions such as this were triggered more by a fundamental insecurity – Marchwitza could be sensitive about his background, and confessed on occasion to feeling uncomfortable in the presence of better edu-cated fellow intellectuals – about his status and abilities as a writer rather than by differences over this or that political position. Knowing what we do of his at all times unswerving loyalty to the Party, it would surely have been the reminder of his stylistic, rather than of any of his political shortcomings, which touched a raw nerve.

Notes

[1]   Alexander Abusch, *Literatur im Zeitalter des Sozialismus. Beiträge zur Literaturgeschichte 1921 bis 1966*, Berlin and Weimar: Aufbau, 1967, p. 570.

[2]   Günther Rüther, *'Greif zur Feder, Kumpel'. Schriftsteller, Literatur und Politik in der DDR 1949-1990*, 2nd edn, Düsseldorf: Droste, 1992, p. 64.

[3]   Dennis Tate, *Shifting Perspectives: East German Autobiographical Narratives before and after the End of the GDR*, Rochester, NY: Camden House, 2007, p. 2.

[4]   Tate, *Shifting Perspectives*, p. 154.

[5]   Franz Hammer, 'Die bitteren Exiljahre', in: Fritz Matke, ed., *'Kamst zu uns aus dem Schacht'. Erinnerungen an Hans Marchwitza*, Berlin: Verlag Tribüne, 1980, p. 34.

[6]   Hans Mayer, *Zur deutschen Literatur der Zeit. Zusammenhänge, Schriftsteller, Bücher*, Reinbek bei Hamburg: Rowohlt, 1967, p. 348.

[7]   Abusch, *Literatur im Zeitalter des Sozialismus*, p. 449.

[8]   This episode in his life was fictionalised in R. J. Humm's novel *Carolin. Zwei Geschichten aus einem Leben*, Zurich: Büchergilde Gutenberg, 1944, where he appears as the writer Pirasch.

[9]   See Horst Duhnke, *Die KPD von 1933 bis 1945*, Wiener Neustadt: Räteverlag, 1974, p. 160.

[10]   Ibid., p. 161.

[11]   Letter of 8 May 1952 to H[ermann] Duncker, quoted in: Catherine Epstein, *The Last Revolutionaries. German Communists and their Century*, Harvard: Harvard University Press, 2003, pp. 205-6.

[12]   Ludwig Renn, *Der Spanische Krieg*, Berlin: Aufbau, 1955.

[13]   Alfred Kantorowicz, *Politik und Literatur im Exil*, Munich: DTV, 1983, p. 193.

[14]   Josie McLellan, *Antifascism and Memory in East Germany. Remembering the International Brigades 1945–1989*, Oxford: Clarendon Press, 2004, p. 62. Using archive material to great effect, Josie McLellan brilliantly analyses the subjection of 'Spanienkämpfer' such as Willi Bredel, Ludwig Renn and Eduard Claudius to the processes of censorship and self-censorship.

[15]   See Chapter 5 of George Orwell, *Homage to Catalonia*, Harmondsworth: Penguin, 1964.

[16]   Gerald Brenan, Foreword to Franz Borkenau, *The Spanish Cockpit*, Ann Arbour: University of Michigan, 1963, p. vii.

[17] Paul Preston, *A Concise History of the Spanish Civil War*, London: Fontana, 1996, p. 185.

[18] Subsequent quotations from Hans Marchwitza, *In Frankreich. In Amerika*, Berlin and Weimar: Aufbau, 1971. Page numbers appear in parentheses.

[19] Wolfgang Emmerich, *Kleine Literaturgeschichte der DDR. Erweiterte Neuausgabe*, Leipzig: Gustav Kiepenheuer, 1997.

[20] Martin Mauthner, *German Writers in French Exile 1933–1940*, Edgeware: Vallentine Mitchell, 2007.

[21] Herbert Wiesner, 'Zensiert – gefördert – genehmigt. Oder wie legt man Literatur auf Eis?', in: Ernst Wichner and Herbert Wiesner, eds, *'Literaturentwicklungs-prozesse'. Die Zensur der Literatur in der DDR*, Frankfurt/Main: Suhrkamp, 1993, pp. 7-17 (here: p. 11).

[22] Werner Ilberg, *Hans Marchwitza*, Leipzig: VEB Bibliographisches Institut, 1971, p. 57.

[23] Ralph Schock, ed., *Haltet die Saar, Genossen! Antifaschistische Schriftsteller im Abstimmungskampf 1935*, Berlin and Bonn: J.H.W. Dietz Nachf., 1984, p. 19.

[24] Kantorowicz, *Politik und Literatur im Exil*, p. 162.

[25] Ibid., p. 223.

[26] Ibid., p. 172.

[27] Alfred Kantorowicz, *Nachtbücher. Aufzeichnungen im französischen Exil 1935 bis 1939*, ed. by Ursula Büttner and Angelika Voss, Hamburg: Christians, 1995, p.116.

[28] Patrik von zur Mühlen, 'Exil und Widerstand', in: Wolfgang Benz and Walter H. Pehle, eds, *Lexikon des deutschen Widerstandes*, Frankfurt/Main: Fischer, 1994, pp. 128-40 (here: p. 129).

[29] Von zur Mühlen, 'Exil und Widerstand', p. 111.

[30] Lion Feuchtwanger, *Der Teufel in Frankreich*, 3rd edn, Berlin: Aufbau, 2008, p. 44.

[31] Kantorowicz., *Nachtbücher*, pp. 157, 159 and 160.

[32] Feuchtwanger, *Der Teufel in Frankreich*, p. 265.

[33] Kantorowicz, *Nachtbücher*, p. 9.

[34] Von zur Mühlen, 'Exil und Widerstand', p. 133.

[35] For a detailed account of this, see Hans Albert Walter, 'Der Pariser KPD-Sekretariat, der deutsch-sowjetische Nichtangriffsvertrag und die Internierung deutscher Emigranten in Frankreich zu Beginn des zweiten Weltkrieges', *Vierteljahresschrift für Zeitgeschichte*, 36 (1988), pp. 483-528.

[36] Marcel Reich-Ranicki, 'Hans Marchwitza. Eine peinliche Legende', in: Reich-Ranicki, *Ohne Rabatt. Über Literatur in der DDR*, Stuttgart: Deutsche Verlags-Anstalt, 1991, pp. 19-23 (here: p. 23).

[37] Kantorowicz, *Nachtbücher*, pp. 271-5.

[38] Wolfgang Leonhard, *Der Schock des Hitler-Stalin-Paktes. Erinnerungen aus der Sowjetunion, Westeuropa und USA*, Freiburg/Breisgau: Herder, 1986.

[39] Alexander Abusch, 'Ansprache in der Trauerfeier', in: Fritz Matke, ed., *'Kamst zu uns aus dem Schacht'*, pp. 80-87 (here: p.113).

[40] Werner Ilberg, *Hans Marchwitza*, p. 22.

[41] Willi Meinck, 'Meine Begegnung mit Hans Marchwitza', in: Fritz Matke, ed., *'Kamst zu uns aus dem Schacht'*, pp. 112-4 (here: p.113).

Joanne Sayner

Verehrter Gen. Ulbricht:
Negotiations of Self and Socialist Identity
in Greta Kuckhoff's Letters

In 1955 Greta Kuckhoff, a survivor of the anti-Nazi resistance group 'Die Rote Kapelle', wrote to Walter Ulbricht about the representation of antifascism in his recently published *Zur Geschichte der neuesten Zeit*. This chapter investigates the ways in which she challenged Ulbricht with her alternative narrative. It examines the significance of the letter as a form of autobiography, literature, and memory. It suggests that the dialogical nature of the genre allowed Kuckhoff to reiterate her socialist identity while at the same time confronting the head of state.

> Sehr geehrter Gen. Ulbricht –
> aus politischer Disziplin habe ich 10 Jahre lang – nach einem ersten gescheitertem [sic] Versuch – nichts dazu getan, die Besonderheit unserer Widerstandsarbeit (Dr. Harnack, Schulze-Boysen) aufgrund meiner Kenntnisse darzulegen und auf die damit verbundenen Probleme hinzuweisen. Ich war überzeugt, dass die Partei eines Tages nach dem Studium der sicherlich vorhandenen Unterlagen und auch nach einer gründlichen Aussprache mit mir, eine Einschätzung vornehmen und die Haupterkenntnisse aus dem 9 Jahre lang geführten Kampf im richtigen Augenblick für den jetzigen Kampf einsetzen werde. Nachdem nunmehr Dein Buch über die deutsche Arbeiterklasse während des Faschismus erschienen ist, habe ich die dort gegebene Darstellung anhand meiner Erfahrungen geprüft und gefunden, dass ich dazu Stellung nehmen muss. [1]

Greta Kuckhoff wrote these words to Walter Ulbricht in 1955 in her capacity as one of the few surviving members of the anti-Nazi resistance group 'Die Rote Kapelle'. She was responding to his portrayal of antifascism in the recently published *Zur Geschichte der neuesten Zeit*.[2] Her archived papers contain both a handwritten draft of the letter (see Figure 1) and an amended typescript, from which the passage above is quoted, and which slightly reframes her experiences.[3] This chapter highlights the rhetorical strategies of Kuckhoff's portrayal of her resistance group. It examines the significance of the letter-writing genre both in relation to these memories of the Nazi past and the construction of socialist personalities. First, however, it considers the letter within the broader context of sources about Kuckhoff's life.

Born in 1902 to a working class family, Greta Lorke trained as an economist, spending time in North America as a student. During the

Nazi regime she worked as a translator, co-translating Hitler's *Mein Kampf* and other Nazi propaganda into English.[4] From 1933 she was involved in resistance activities within a group that the Nazis were later to label 'Die Rote Kapelle'. The group disseminated anti-Nazi leaflets, organised meetings, and provided financial support for those persecuted by the regime. Some members of the group were involved in transmitting military details to the Soviet Union. This large, politically and socially diverse group were arrested in 1942.[5] Fifty executions followed, including that of Adam Kuckhoff, whom Greta had married in 1937. Initially condemned to death, Greta's sentence was commuted to ten years' imprisonment and she was liberated by the Red Army in 1945. After the war Kuckhoff joined the Communist Party and the SED and held a series of institutionally important positions in the Soviet Zone. In 1950 she became head of the GDR state bank. She held this position until 1958 when she retired 'due to health reasons'. She then performed various roles in the GDR Peace Council and German-British Society. She wrote prolifically throughout her life and her papers contain thousands of texts which can be classified as 'life writing'.[6]

The volume of her correspondence is extensive, and it is characterised both by historicity and heterogeneity.[7] The archived letters include those dating from the Weimar Republic and from her time in North America, from her imprisonment during fascism, and from the immediate postwar period until her death in 1981. They include letters to and/or from over twelve hundred different addressees, including well-known names from the political sphere (in addition to Walter Ulbricht, Otto Grotewohl, Erich Honecker, Wilhelm Pieck, Franz Dahlem), literary and cultural figures from East and West (including Anna Seghers, Elfriede Paul, Elfriede Brüning, Stefan Heym, Wolf Biermann, Ingeborg Drewitz, Günter Weisenborn) and academics and historians, particularly those in East and West engaged in writing on the 'Rote Kapelle' group (Georg Lukács, Jürgen Kuczynski, Heinrich Scheel, Gerald Wiemers, Heinz Höhne, Gerhard Ritter, Wilhelm Flicke), as well as many of the surviving members and relatives of the resistance to Nazism (Falk Harnack, Hans Coppi, Harald Poelchau, Martha Dodd Stern).[8] As Kuckhoff often kept carbon copies of her side of the correspondence, a significant number of exchanges can be reconstructed, albeit with the 'inevitable displacement in time' of their responses.[9] Many of these letters are, in addition, annotated with later comments ('leicht verändert abgesandt', 'geschah nicht', 'nicht genehmigt', 'nicht abgeschickt' or, quite often, 'Quatsch'). Whether these notes are the result of her decision in 1981 to give her papers to the GDR state archive and the re-reading that she did at that point or whether they were written contemporaneously to their original composition is no longer discernable. What such comments and the draft letters reiterate, however, is the constructed nature of the genre. Despite a persisting aura of spontaneity, letter-writing is no less contrived than any other form of autobiographical expression.

In this chapter, letters are read as autobiography, as literature, and as memory. As Helmut Peitsch and Michaela Holdenried have shown, including letters within relatively recent and broadly conceptualised understandings of the autobiographical genre not only deepens our understanding of past events and constructions of the self, but also has significant implications in terms of gender, since women's life writing often does not conform to autobiography as traditionally defined.[10] In contrast, whether letters can be understood as *literary* constructs has long been debated.[11] The following chapter draws on Janet Gurkin Altman's assertion that it is possible to engage in 'literary readings' of letters, to examine the ways in which such texts are 'autobio-graphically undressed [...] and rhetorically addressed'.[12] In addition, it focuses on the 'Umweltanspruch' of the 'private' letter; that is, it considers the ways in which letters construct their own broader relevance even though, as in Kuckhoff's case, they were never intended for publication.[13] This chapter examines what Kuckhoff's choice of the letter genre to confront Ulbricht can tell us about the memory of this literary genre (or 'genre memory') and suggests how this letter and others in Kuckhoff's papers can shape our under-standing of past and present processes of cultural remembering (that is, the ways in which it is a 'memory genre').[14] As Detlev Schöttker reminds us in relation to the letter: 'Sein Zweck ist [...] nicht nur Information, sondern Gedächtnisbildung.'[15]

Framing Memory

> Keine literarische Gattung ist so sehr mit der Erwartung individueller Präsenz im Medium der Schrift verbunden wie der Brief.[16]

Letters are often characterised by a rhetoric of self-reflexivity and Kuckhoff's text is no exception. Indeed, the genre allows, firstly, for the focus on the writing self but also, secondly, demands a reciprocity through the construction of an addressee. A dialectic of 'self conceal-ment and self construction'[17] begins at the very start of the letter with the reference to a 'politische Disziplin' which has prevented Kuckhoff from speaking. Such self-discipline is also the closing trope of the letter, with reference to 'die 10 Jahre disziplinierten Schweigens'. Self-characterisation as an honest witness to the events which she de-scribes is repeatedly reinforced through reference to individual experi-ence. The letter thereby constructs a first person authority to challenge Ulbricht: 'aufgrund meiner Kenntnisse'; 'anhand meiner Erfahrung'; 'Übrigens bin ich der einzige Überlebende, der darüber Bescheid weiss'. At the same time, comparison between the handwritten draft and typescript shows that Kuckhoff reduces the emotional content of the letter while maintaining the personal involvement. She deletes her response to Ulbricht's text, 'Ich war erschüttert', replacing it with the more distanced, 'Nachdem nunmehr Dein Buch [...] erschienen ist'.

Within such a framework, Kuckhoff then outlines the key problem she perceives in Ulbricht's representation of the resistance group, that is, the emphasis on the leadership of the KPD:

> Ich bin mir darüber im Klaren, dass man historische Fakten darstellen kann und muss von einem festen Standpunkt aus und diese Tatsache die historische Wahr-heit nur stärker und klarer herausarbeiten lässt. Dass es um die Festigung des Vertrauens der Arbeiterklasse in ihre eigene Kraft, um die Anerkennung der führenden Rolle der kommunistischen Partei dabei geht, ist auch mir klar. Ander-erseits kann jedoch nicht jede Einzelheit eines historischen Gesamtvorganges so betrachtet werden, dass in ihm nun sich alle grundsätzlich richtigen Zusammen-hänge auch konkret nachweisen lassen. So trifft für den Gesamtwiderstandskampf sicherlich zu, dass die Arbeiterklasse unter Führung der KPD die führende Rolle hatte. Bewährte, der Partei verbundene Genossen haben sicher die höchste Ein-satzbereitschaft, die grösste Disziplin, das höchste Bewusstsein gezeigt und vielleicht auch die beachtlichsten Überzeugungsfolge nachweisen können. Gerade darum, aus dieser feststehenden historisch gültigen Wahrheit, lissen [sic] sich bestimmte Erscheinungen, wie die besonderen unserer Widerstandsgruppe dar-stellen — ja, den Besonderheiten gerecht zu werden ist notwendig, um des heuti-gen Kampfes willen. Insbes. was Westdeutschland angeht.

Within this confrontation are recurrent tropes of clarity, firmness and strength. These occur throughout the letter, with various colloca-tions of 'fest', 'klar' and 'Kraft' suggesting an unequivocal belief in the basic tenets of a Marxist approach to history and, in the eyes of her addressee, Kuckhoff's solid political credentials. The challenge to

Ulbricht's application of such belief is mitigated through the portrayal of 'der Partei verbundenen Genossen' as being characterised by superlatives. 'Die Partei' is in fact personified throughout the letter as an active, thinking entity, which both serves to link the positive traits to the addressee but at the same time distance him from the harshest criticism. Before introducing the more specific aspects of Ulbricht's text that Kuckhoff finds problematic, the letter reasserts the introductory equation of the past and present 'Kampf', of the battle for memory with West Germany. In fact, it is the battle with the historiography of the FRG that is a recurrent theme:

> Es hat Jahre gegeben, wo ich glaubte, der Zeitpunkt ist noch nicht gekommen, wo man dazu eine klare Stellung beziehen kann. Aber wenn man diesen besonderen wichtigen Teil der Arbeit und dieses Problem einzig den Feinden überlässt, dann kann das doch nur heissen: die Partei sieht diese Tätigkeit nicht als Unterstützung des Kampfes um eine sozialistische Entwicklung auch für Deutschland an. Die Tatsache, dass sie kein Wort dafür findet bedeutet Missbilligung oder aber, es fehlt ihr an geschichtlich gültigen Argumenten für die Erklärung unseres – beweisbaren – Verhaltens. Hart gesprochen überlässt sie dann das Feld denen, die heute unsere Todesurteile für rehtens [sic] erachten und heute noch z.B. die Vollstreckung des Urteils gegen Prof. Kraus und mich fordern.
>
> Das Nicht-Erwähnen schafft die Angelegenheit doch nicht aus der Welt. Ein so infamer und dennoch international angesehener Historiker wie Prof. Ritter hat ebenso Stellung dazu genommen, wie Dulles, Dallin und ein Dutzend Autoren in neofawschistischen [sic] Zeitschriften.[18] Nicht nur in Deutschland, auch in Frankreich und der Schweiz wurde ausführlich darüber berichtet. M.W., hat der frühere Generalrichter Manfred Röder, unser Ankläger, ausreichend dokumentarisches Material.[19] Aus der Welt schweigen kann man die Vorgänge also nicht. Man muss sie einordnen in einen historisch hart und begründet gesehenen Zusammenhang mit dem Kampf der Arbeiterklasse in DL und mit den Fronten im gerechten Krieg. Es handelt sich keinweses [sic] um eine 'getartnte Ausflugsgesellschaft' [sic] – der Kern arbeitete weniger romantisch und das Gewicht der Tätigkeit liegt keineswegs dort wo es in Deinem Buch liegt.

Pointing to the transnational nature of these memories, the letter draws upon the Cold War context in order to prompt a response from the addressee. The repeated reference to fascists in the present, including those still demanding her execution[20] and the former Nazi judge Manfred Roeder, suggests Kuckhoff's awareness that 'memory is always a dimension of political practice'.[21] Historical reconstruction of the events of the resistance is, she insists, both a 'Gefahrenquelle' and something 'der durchaus positiv genutzt werden kann'. Her insistence on the necessity of confronting difficult issues is something that she repeats throughout her correspondence.[22]

In redressing 'das Gewicht der Tätigkeit', Kuckhoff's letter takes issue with the individuals named by Ulbricht in connection with the group and then goes on to state what an accurate history of the work of the 'Rote Kapelle' should instead emphasise. It was not the case, Kuckhoff writes, 'dass die Funktionäre der KPD, die Gen. Husemann und Coppi "die aktivsten" Mitglieder der Gruppe waren'. While in no way doubting the willingness of these people to sacrifice their lives, she points to other figures who undertook 'die entscheidende Arbeit'. In the typescript she emphasises the role of Dr. Arvid Harnack and Harro Schulze-Boysen, having decided to delete most of a list of other resisters mentioned in the handwritten draft. She criticises Ulbricht's decision to mention, 'als einen der wenigen', Communist Wilhelm Guddorf and claims that his testimony in the Nazi legal process had unnecessarily harmed both her and other members of the group. Guddorf had, she argues, 'den moralischen Halt verloren'. In contrast, there follows a list of traits which are, according to Kuckhoff, important for characterising the group:

> 1. Die Kontinuität und Gründlichkeit der Arbeit von 33-42, die allein eine so umfassende Widerstandtätigkeit auf vielen Gebieten ermöglichte. Beweis: Systemat. Besetzung wichtiger, informationssicherer Stellen im Partei- und Verwaltungsapparat der Nazis.
> 2. Systematisches Studium der Praxis im Licht der marxist. Erkenntnisse, die planvoll gelehrt und miteinander geprüft wurden.
> Herausgabe von Schriften zu ökonomischen, politischen, kulturellen und militärischen Fragen. Weitergabe regelmässiger Wirtschaftsanalysen, Flugblätter, Flugschriften, eine Zeitung 'Die Innere Front'.
> Beginn der Arbeit mit 'Fremdarbeitern'.
> Hervorzuheben ist die Sammlung und Weiterleitung entscheidender Informationen an die SU, Organisation eines schlecht unterrichteten, aber an Initiative reichen Apparates.
> Es gelang, Vertreter der verschiedensten Schichten der Bevölkerung zu aktiver Betätigung zu gewinnen und breitere Kreise zu neutralisieren (Idee der Volksfront ab 1933, Mai, Einfluss Dimitroff).

Within the context of past and present historiography of the 'Rote Kapelle' group such emphases are significant. That the resistance work began in 1933 is something which Kuckhoff stressed throughout her writing, along with the unusual longevity of their actions.[23] The numerous practical activities the group were involved in are accentuated through the listing and also encapsulated in the processual nomenclature chosen to describe their work: 'Widerstandsarbeit',

'Widerstandstätigkeit', 'Gesamtwiderstandskampf', and 'Widerstands-
gruppe' are used instead of the more abstract noun 'Widerstand'. Such
vocabulary also serves to emphasise both the communality of their
work and the diversity of their membership. The Marxist foundation
of their resistance is stressed but is not unequivocal:

> Eine solche weitreichende Wirkung – gewiss blieb auch sie viel zu gering – hatte
> wohl sonst keine Gruppe in DL. Diejenigen, die diese Arbeit leisteten waren
> häufig erst auf dem Wege zu richtigen marxistischen Erkenntnissen, aber sie leg-
> ten denjenigen, mit denen sie zu tun hatten, die Gefahren des Krieges und der
> Unterdrückung oft besser, verständlicher, für bestimmte Entwicklungsphasen
> wirksamer dar als einige routinerte Genossen. Ich denke, dass die Wahrheit der
> marxistischen Erkenntnisse auch heute wieder – richtig und lebendig dargelegt –
> viel breiter zur Wirkung gebraucht werden könnte als es heute geschicht [...].
> Dieser – richtigen Darlegung könnte eine Werbekraft gegeben werden, die unserm
> Kampf um ein einheitliches demokratisches Deutschland nur von Nutzen wäre.

This letter encapsulates Kuckhoff's 'Wertehierarchie',[24] that is, her
understanding of antifascism both past and present, as reiterated
throughout her enormous body of life writing. For Kuckhoff, political
beliefs must constantly be worked at, must adapt to changing situa-
tions, and can always be enriched through discussion with those who
think differently.[25] Within this context, the letter draws a thematic
parallel between the group's educational work during the Nazi regime
and the possibility of such work in the GDR present. This becomes
particularly visible in the redrafting, where emphasis is placed on
those resisters without training in Marxist thought: the sentence 'Von
den führenden Genossen und Kameraden sah jeder das zugleich als
seine sozialistische und patriotische Pflicht an' becomes 'Von den
Kameraden – auch den nicht marxistisch Gebildeten – sah jeder das
zugleich als seine patriotische Pflicht an'.
    A dialogical imperative is at the heart of Kuckhoff's political un-
derstanding and is stressed in a final appeal to Ulbricht to meet with
her and talk about the way he represented the 'Rote Kapelle' group.
Her selection of genre to confront Ulbricht is one which emphasises
the reciprocity of the process of remembering and also its constructed
nature. In choosing to write to her addressee in this way, Kuckhoff
draws on the 'genre memory' of this type of text.[26] Both writer and
addressee have certain expectations of this act of writing; the reader
knows that s/he will be addressed directly, at least at the start of the
letter, and interpellated throughout. The writer knows that such con-

ventions matter, as encapsulated in Kuckhoff's uncertainty about exactly how to proceed: there is a delicate linguistic balance inherent in her move from 'Verehrter Gen. Ulbricht' to 'Sehr geehrter Gen. Ulbricht' during the drafting process. Kuckhoff's use of the letter to confront this institutional figure of authority – and, presumably, her assumption that she could alter both significant power relations and dominant narratives of GDR history in doing so – convey a certain belief in the persuasiveness of the epistolary text. In fact, her correspondence throughout her life with the relatives, witnesses and historians from East and West related to the resistance of the 'Rote Kapelle' group is testament to this continued conviction. It is certainly the case for Kuckhoff that 'the letter is above all an extension of daily life', of the work she believes is integral to being a committed, thinking socialist.[27] She confronts public narratives and sometimes public figures through a genre associated with intimacy, individuality and confession. In doing so, she arguably puts herself in a position of assumed subordination from which she then directs the harshest of criticism. But, for Kuckhoff, the power of the letter is not merely a formal one; the correspondence between Kuckhoff and her husband during their imprisonment, and the last letters written by Adam Kuckhoff and her other friends are among some of the most moving writings in the archive.[28] The 'genre memory' of Kuckhoff's collection of letters suggests that when something important needs to be said then a letter, with its aura of immediacy and potential rhetorical strength, is a powerful way to do it.

At the same time, the archived letters are also a 'memory genre' with the power to shape cultural remembering at the time(s) of reading. While the letter to Ulbricht shows how international political constellations of 1955 undoubtedly affected the way that resistance to Nazism was framed, the emphasis on personal experience and continuing political agency mitigates against purely constructivist understandings of memory (that is, a belief that memory is constructed only by the political contingencies of the present).[29] The reference to the battles over memory between East and West remind us that such narratives were 'constantly at war with one another'.[30] No less conflicted, however, are contemporary re-readings, particularly in the light of dominant, monolithic conceptualisations of antifascism in the GDR.[31] Literary studies have, particularly since the early 1990s, begun to pay more attention to letters and, within the context of East Germany, there have been several published collections of correspondence previously only available in archives.[32] There are many hundreds of letters still to be explored in Kuckhoff's papers alone which testify to the complicated and contradictory discourses of remembering resistance to Nazism in the GDR. The letter to Ulbricht is one example of an individual who challenged the realities of socialism in a country that she had been prepared to die for. The extent to which she and others were successful can be debated, but the presence of such voices undoubtedly enriches our understanding of the cultural histories of the GDR.

Communicating the Message?

While the memory of the literary genre assists in the process of communication and shapes Kuckhoff's personal memories through the conventions of letter writing,[33] the letter of course invites a response. Such a response goes beyond a mere exchange of paper, especially where considerable emotional investment is involved. Kuckhoff's memories of resistance formed a fundamental part of her identity, as shown in nearly forty years of life writing. As John Paul Eakin has stressed, all identity, and therefore all autobiographical writing, is relational,[34] but arguably nowhere more so than in the genre of letter-writing. After all, 'every assertion of individual autonomy is dependent on the recognition of that autonomy by others'.[35] It is not known whether Ulbricht replied to this letter as no response exists among Kuckhoff's papers. Indeed, as there is also no copy of this letter in the SED archives in Berlin it cannot be unequivocally asserted that it was ever sent.[36] There is an exchange of letters from 1971 when Kuckhoff gave Ulbricht a copy of her volume in honour of her husband's work (albeit twenty-five years after its original publication) but this contains no reference to any previous correspondence.[37] However, rather than remain with this Derridian quandary,[38] the contemporary reader can do worse than attempt what Ulbricht would have had to do in 1955, that is, be 'obliged to seek to measure the sincerity of the letter'.[39] It concludes:

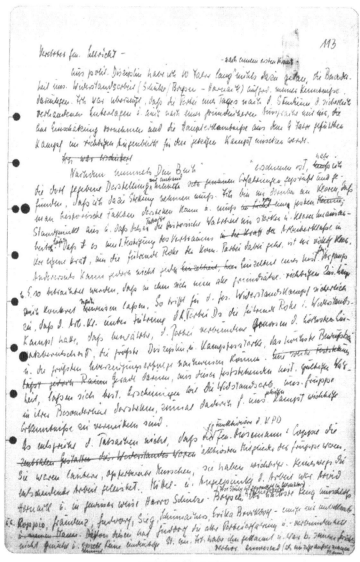

Kopie aus dem Bundesarchiv

Figure 1 Kuckhoff's Letter to Ulbricht (BArch N2506/58)

Es hat mich [sic] eine grosse Überwindung gekostet, Dir dazu zu schreiben. Nichts ist mir grässlicher als der Gedanke, man könnte diese Darlegung als Wunsch nach Geltung auffassen, sei es für meine Freunde oder gar für mich. Aber die 10 Jahre disziplinierten Schweigens sollten für mein ehrliches Bemühen Zeugnis ablegen, der Sache zu dienen.

Throughout her life, Kuckhoff followed up the political philosophy she advocated in her writings and radio work with educational talks and meetings.[40] It was through these face-to-face contacts that she conveyed her own experiences and challenged people's understandings of antifascism and anti-Nazi resistance. Letters often facilitated and responded to such meetings, opening dialogues that sometimes lasted for years. Kuckhoff's relationship to Ulbricht, in contrast, remained somewhat fraught, ultimately resulting in her losing her position as head of the state bank in 1958. Memories of the 'Rote Kapelle' group continued to cause controversy up to, and well beyond, Kuckhoff's death in 1981. While her memory work continued throughout her life it seems that Ulbricht did not respond as she had hoped to her closing question and explicit appeal for further dialogue:

Vielleicht kenn ich nicht alle Motive, die Dich zu Deiner Darstellung bewegten — sollte man dann nicht zu einer Aussprache kommen?

Notes

[1] Greta Kuckhoff's papers are held at the Bundesarchiv Berlin-Lichterfelde (BArch N2506). Thanks are due to to Ulf Rathje for his help and support during the research for this chapter. BArch N2506/58 Typescript of letter to Walter Ulbricht 1955. My text follows the orthography of Kuckhoff's letter.

[2] Walter Ulbricht, *Zur Geschichte der neuesten Zeit*, Berlin: Dietz, 1955.

[3] BArch N2506/58. Handwritten draft of letter to Walter Ulbricht (see Figure 1).

[4] Adolf Hitler, *Mein Kampf*, trans. James Murphy, London: Hurst Blackett, 1939.

[5] Jan Foitzik, 'Gruppenbildung im Widerstand', in Hans Coppi, Jürgen Danyel and Johannes Tuchel, eds, *Die Rote Kapelle im Widerstand gegen den Nationalsozialismus*, Berlin: Hentrich, 1994, pp. 68-78.

[6] This article is part of a larger project on Kuckhoff's life writing entitled *Reframing Antifascism: Memory, Genre and the Life Writings of Greta Kuckhoff* (Palgrave, forthcoming).

[7] Peter Bürgel, 'Der Privatbrief. Entwurf eines heuristischen Modells', *Deutsche Vierteljahrsschrift für Literaturwissenschaft und Geistesgeschichte*, 50 (1976), 281-97 (here: pp. 282-3).

[8] BArch N2506.

[9] Mireille Bossis, 'Methodological Journeys Through Correspondences', *Yale French Studies*, 71 (1986), 63-76 (here: 64).

[10] Michaela Holdenried, 'Einleitung', in: Holdenried, ed., *Geschriebenes Leben: Autobiographik von Frauen*, Berlin: Schmidt, 1995, pp. 9-20 (here: p. 10); Helmut Peitsch, *"Deutschlands Gedächtnis an seine dunkelste Zeit": zur Funktion der Auto- biographik in den Westzonen Deutschlands und Westsektoren von Berlin 1945 bis 1949*, Berlin: Edition Sigma, 1990, p. 24.

[11] Bürgel, 'Der Privatbrief', p. 290; Bossis, 'Methodological Journeys'.

[12] Janet Gurkin Altman, 'The Letter Book as a Literary Institution 1539–1789: Toward a Cultural History of Published Correspondences in France', *Yale French Studies*, 71 (1986), 17-62 (here:18-19).

[13] Bürgel, 'Der Privatbrief', p. 287. Such letters can be differentiated from those written by canonised authors who know that such texts are likely to become part of their oeuvre: Detlev Schöttker, ed., *Adressat: Nachwelt. Briefkultur und Ruhm- bildung*, Munich: Fink, 2008.

[14] Jeffrey K. Olick, 'Genre Memories and Memory Genres: A Dialogical Analysis of May 8, 1945 Commemorations in the Federal Republic of Germany', *American Sociological Review*, 64 (1999), 381-402; Astrid Erll and Ansgar Nünning, 'Concepts and Methods for the Study of Literature and/as Cultural Memory', in Ansgar Nünning, Marion Gymnich and Roy Sommer, eds, *Literature and Memory: Theoretic- al Paradigms – Genres – Functions*, Tübingen: Franke, 2006, pp. 11-28 (pp. 13-18).

[15] Detlev Schöttker, 'Vorwort', in: Schöttker, ed., *Adressat: Nachwelt*, pp. 7-8 (here: p. 7).

[16] Schöttker, 'Vorwort', p. 7.

[17] Dennis Tate, *Shifting Perspectives: East German Autobiographical Narratives Before and After the End of the GDR*, Rochester, NY: Camden House, 2007, p. 11.

[18] Allen Welsh Dulles, *Germany's Underground*, New York: The MacMillan Company, 1947; Gerhard Ritter, *Carl Goerdeler und die deutsche Widerstands- bewegung*, Stuttgart: Deutsche Verlagsanstalt, 1954. Two series of articles on the group appeared in *Der Fortschritt* called 'Das Geheimnis der Roten Kapelle' (1950) and in *Der Stern*, 'Rote Agenten unter uns' (6 May 1951-1 July 1951). No authors are

named for the articles. Friends of Kuckhoff sent her the articles, copies of which are preserved in the archive, BArch N2506/55.

[19] Manfred Roeder, *Die Rote Kapelle: Aufzeichnungen*, Hamburg: Siep, 1952.

[20] The fifth article from the series, 'Das Geheimnis der Roten Kapelle', is framed by an image of someone hanging from the gallows in 1942 and is juxtaposed with another image which implies that the gallows of the 1950s are still waiting to be filled.

[21] Popular Memory Group, 'Popular Memory: Theory, Politics, Method', in Richard Johnson et al., eds, *Making Histories: Studies In History-Writing and Politics*, London: Hutchinson, 1982, pp. 205-52 (here: p. 205).

[22] For example, in her letter to Eberhard Poppe, Rector of Halle University, she writes: 'Probleme sind nun einmal stets "heiße Eisen", aber schmieden wir sie nicht zu Werkzeug, das unserer Sache dient, schmiedet der Feind daraus Waffen'. BArch N2506/54, 23 January 1973.

[23] See, for example, her correspondence in relation to an exhibition she helped to curate on the 'Rote Kapelle': Joanne Sayner, 'The Personal and the Political: Remembering Adam Kuckhoff, Remembering Resistance', in: Carola Hähnel-Mesnard, ed., *Antifaschismus Revisited: Geschichte – Ideologie – Erinnerung*, Paris: Éditions Kimé, 2009, pp. 122-36.

[24] Bürgel, 'Der Privatbrief', p. 283.

[25] For further details, see Joanne Sayner, 'Living Antifascism: Greta Kuckhoff's writings in *Die Weltbühne*', in Meesha Nehru & Sara Jones, eds, *Writing Under Socialism*, Nottingham: Critical, Cultural and Communications Press, pp. 71-95.

[26] Erll and Nünning, 'Concepts and Methods', p. 13.

[27] Bossis, 'Methodological Journeys', p. 64.

[28] BArch N2505/198, N2506/142, N2506/143, N2506/210, N2506/250.

[29] Susanna Radstone, ed., *Memory and Methodology*, Oxford: Berg, 2000, p. 10.

[30] Popular Memory Group, 'Popular Memory', p. 207.

[31] Herfried Münkler, 'Antifaschismus und antifaschistischer Widerstand als politischer Gründungsmythos der DDR', *Aus Politik und Zeitgeschichte*, B 45 (1998), 16-29.

[32] For two examples among many, see Anna Seghers, *'Hier im Volk der kalten Herzen.' Briefwechsel 1947*, Berlin: Aufbau, 2000; Elfriede Brüning, *'Ich mußte*

einfach schreiben, unbedingt...' Briefwechsel mit Zeitgenossen 1930-2007, ed. by Elenore Sent, Essen: Klartext, 2008.

[33]   Erll and Nünning, 'Concepts and Methods', pp. 17-18.

[34]   John Paul Eakin, *Touching the World: Reference in Autobiography*, Princeton N.J and Oxford: Princeton University Press, 1992.

[35]   Marijke Huisman, 'Living History: The Reception of Autobiographies in Three Dutch Journals, 1850-1918', in Ansgar Nünning, Marion Gymnich and Roy Sommer, eds, *Literature and Memory: Theoretical Paradigms – Genres – Functions*, Tübingen: Franke, 2006, pp. 155-66 (p. 158).

[36]   BArch DY 30.

[37]   Greta Kuckhoff, ed., *Adam Kuckhoff zum Gedenken: Novellen, Gedichte, Briefe*, Berlin: Aufbau, 1946. BArch N2506/50 Letter from Greta Kuckhoff to Walter Ulbricht, 7 February 1971; BArch N2506/158 Letter from Walter Ulbricht to Greta Kuckhoff, 24 March 1971.

[38]   Derrida writes of letters that never arrive and of those that, on arriving, are not understood. Jacques Derrida, *The Post Card: From Socrates to Freud and Beyond*, trans. Alan Bass, Chicago: University of Chicago Press, 1987.

[39]   Charles A. Porter, 'Foreword', *Yale French Studies*, 71 (1986), 1-4 (here: 4).

[40]   On Kuckhoff's postwar radio work, see Joanne Sayner, 'The Organic Intellectual: The Public and Political Impact of Greta Kuckhoff 1945-1949', in Rebecca Braun and Lyn Marven, eds, *Cultural Impact: Theoretical and Practical Issues of Reception in the German-Speaking World*, Rochester, NY: Camden House, 2010, pp. 227-42.

Helmut Peitsch

'Ein Kommunist kann nicht die Politik seiner Partei vom Blickwinkel seines Einzelschicksals her begreifen': Rudi Goguels Schreiben über das eigene Leben

Rudi Goguel's *Es war ein langer Weg* (1947) made a distinctive contribution to early depictions of communist resistance and life in the Nazi concentration camps. Characterised by unusual openness in reflecting on the past and integrating elements of fiction in the record of events, it contradicts the assumption that initial, fact-oriented accounts were only later followed by more complex representations of resistance in the Third Reich, written by people who were children at the time. Goguel also deserves to be remembered for breaking taboos in GDR historiography in the 1970s, when he introduced a broader understanding of religiously motivated and other forms of resistance, and challenged the doctrine that only West Germans need feel guilt.

Als ein 'Journalist […], den man als Komponisten des Liedes von den "Moorsoldaten" kannte',[1] erscheint Rudi Goguel auf einer Liste 'viele[r] prominente[r] Namen' wie denen der Schriftsteller Heinar Kipphardt, Wolf Biermann und Peter Hacks, mit der der Historiker Bernd Stöver illustriert, dass zwischen 1949 und 1989 'die DDR für ungefähr eine halbe Million Menschen eine gewisse Anziehungskraft hatte':[2] Goguel gehörte unter den Übersiedlern von West nach Ost zu der – insbesondere nach dem Verbot der KPD in der Bundesrepublik zeitweilig stark anwachsenden – Gruppe derer, die sich der politischen Strafverfolgung durch die Übersiedlung in die DDR entzogen, so dass 1957 die Zahl der Übersiedlungen von West nach Ost über 50.000 lag. Am Fall Rudi Goguel, der von den zwölf Jahren Faschismus elf in Gefängnis, Zuchthaus und Konzentrationslager erlebt hatte, lässt sich eine zentrale These von Dennis Tates großer Studie zum autobiographischen Erzählen in der DDR belegen, dass 'making personal sense of the relationship that they as Germans had to the Third Reich' den 'core of personal experience' bilden konnte,[3] auch wenn der in die DDR übergesiedelte Journalist Goguel im Unterschied zu Christa Wolf, Franz Fühmann, Günter de Bruyn und Brigitte Reimann nicht Schriftsteller, sondern Wissenschaftler wurde.

1947 veröffentlichte Rudi Goguel in Düsseldorf einen Erlebnisbericht über Widerstand und Verfolgung mit dem Titel *Es war ein langer Weg. Ein Roman unserer Zeit*, dessen Neuauflage 1949 einen

geänderten Untertitel erhielt: *Ein Bericht. Ein notwendiges Nachwort
– vier Jahre später*. 1974 begründete er seinem westdeutschen Freund
Karl Schabrod, der aus Goguels Buch in seinem eigenen, im
Röderberg-Verlag der bundesrepublikanischen Vereinigung der Verfolgten des Naziregimes 1969 erschienenen *Widerstand an Rhein und
Ruhr 1933-1945* zitiert hatte,[4] seine Verweigerung einer Neuausgabe
von *Es war ein langer Weg*:

> Vieles, was im Jahre 1946 verständlich war, kann heute so nicht mehr gesagt
> werden, bezw. [sic] es müßten ausführliche Kommentare eingefügt werden, die
> dann allerdings die Lesbarkeit des Buches stark einschränken. […] Also, lassen
> wir es bei dem Zeitdokument von 1946, das seine Berechtigung hatte, das aber
> heute bei vielen Beteiligten (z.B. unseren Neuengammer Kameraden!) Wider-
> spruch hervorgerufen hat und hervorrufen würde.[5]

Die Ablehnung der Wiederveröffentlichung eines im Westdeutschland
der Besatzungszeit geschriebenen Erlebnisberichts in der DDR der
siebziger Jahre unter Hinweis auf das Unverständnis der Leser und
den Widerspruch der Kameraden bestätigt und modifiziert einen
Befund von Dennis Tates Untersuchung:

> Cultural policymakers on the pro-communist side had a deeply ingrained
> suspicion that autobiography was a medium for dangerously uncontrolled confess-
> ional writing. This meant that there was a noticeable gap after the appearance of
> the early postwar writing on specific, ideologically uncontroversial aspects of the
> Third Reich period (the Spanish Civil War in Alfred Kantorowicz's *Spanisches
> Tagebuch* of 1948 or the communist experience of concentration camp suffering
> as depicted in Willi Bredel's *Die Prüfung* of 1946 and Wolfgang Langhoff's
> *Moorsoldaten* of 1947) before the subject could be broached again by the new
> generation of authors who had been children and young adults of the Third
> Reich.[6]

Goguels Beispiel zeigt einerseits, dass schon in dem frühen Erlebnisbericht eines kommunistischen Verfassers 'ideologisch kontroverse
Aspekte des Dritten Reiches' thematisiert wurden, andererseits dass
sich dieser Verfasser das 'Misstrauen' gegen 'unkontrolliertes
Bekennen' zu eigen machte: 'Ein Kommunist kann nicht die Politik
seiner Partei vom Blickwinkel seines Einzelschicksals her begreifen,
sondern er muß in Zusammenhängen denken', erklärte Goguel in
seiner Selbstkritik, die er als der örtliche Spitzenkandidat zur ersten
Bundestagswahl auf der Mitgliederversammlung der Konstanzer KPD
am 3.12.1949 übte, nachdem die Stadtkreisleitung in einer Wahl-
analyse gefordert hatte, die Positionen der Partei zur Kriegsge-

fangenenfrage und zur Oder-Neiße-Grenze zu korrigieren.[7] Keine drei
Jahre später kehrte der auf den Posten des kaufmännischen Leiters des
Freien Verlags der KPD nach Düsseldorf versetzte Goguel von einem
Kuraufenthalt in der DDR nicht in die Bundesrepublik zurück,
nachdem der im Parteivorstand für den Verlag verantwortliche
Funktionär wegen 'angestrebter Vorbereitung von Hoch- und Landes-
verrat'[8] verhaftet worden war und Goguel somit eine 'Strafe zwischen
drei und fünf Jahren' erwartet hätte.[9]

Goguels Erlebnisbericht unterscheidet sich durch die Einbeziehung
der Vor- und der Nachgeschichte der Haft von der – in der zeitgenössischen Literaturkritik so genannten – 'KZ-Literatur',[10] zu der die
von Dennis Tate ebenso wie von Carsten Wurm für die sowjetische
Besatzungszone in den Vordergrund gerückten bereits im Exil publizierten Texte Langhoffs, Bredels und Bruno Heiligs gezählt wurden.[11] Aber in der SBZ erschienen auch z.B. über das von Goguel
dargestellte Konzentrationslager Sachsenhausen nach 1945 verfasste
Erlebnisberichte wie der von Theodor Feuerlein (1945) oder die von
Lucie Grosser herausgegebenen *KZ Sachsenhausen* (1946), für die
gilt, dass das Lager den aus dem eigenen Leben exklusiv berichteten
Ausschnitt bildete.[12] Von den zahlreicheren in den Westzonen pub-
lizierten Erlebnisberichten über Sachsenhausen erschien einer in der
SBZ in Lizenz; der VVN-Verlag Berlin/Potsdam druckte 1949 Arnold
Weiß-Rüthels in München 1946 herausgekommenen Erlebnisbericht
Nacht und Nebel nach, in dem der Kommunist Harry Naujoks, der den
Verfasser vor einem Blockältesten gerettet habe,[13] als der beste
Lagerälteste erschien, der sich zusammen mit anderen namentlich
genannten, später in der DDR Prominenten wie Karl Schirdewan,
Fritz Selbmann und Wilhelm Girnus 'verdient gemacht' habe.[14] Inner-
halb des Ausschnitts Lager gewichteten die meisten in Westdeutsch-
land veröffentlichten Erlebnisberichte, abgesehen von denen, deren
Verfasser nach Dachau oder Mauthausen verlegt worden waren,[15] das
Ende der Haft in Sachsenhausen, den auch 'Hungermarsch' und 'To-
tentanz' genannten 'Todesmarsch',[16] ebenso stark wie die von Lucie
Grosser in der Publikation des Berliner Hauptausschusses der Opfer
des Faschismus abgedruckten Erlebnisberichte von Ferdinand Ab-
romeit, Karl Raddatz und Wolfgang Szepansky, die mehr als die
Hälfte der Broschüre *KZ Sachsenhausen* ausmachten.[17]

Die Konzentration der erzählten Zeit auf die Tage um das Ende des
April 1945 kennzeichnete insbesondere einen ohne Genrebezeichnung

1948 im Ostberliner Verlag Volk und Welt erschienenen Text über Sachsenhausen, Gunther R. Lys' *Kilometerstein 12,6*, der von den Rezensenten in der SBZ übereinstimmend als Dichtung gewertet wurde. 'Menschheitsdichtung und KZ-Roman' überschrieb *Neues Deutschland* seine Besprechung,[18] ebenso urteilte Stephan Hermlin im Berliner Rundfunk.[19] In Willi Bredels Zeitschrift *Heute und Morgen* verglich Erich Fabian Lys' Buch mit Bredels, Heiligs, Langhoffs und Petersens Darstellung von 'Gestapo und KZ':

> Zum erstenmal hat hier ein Überlebender, der ein Dichter ist, auch die dem gräßlichen Erleben angemessene starke Sprache gefunden. […] Ein Buch von jener deutschen Scham, die alle noch Schwankenden aufrüttelt zu aktivem Kampf, ohne Aufruf, ohne Tendenz, nur mit der allmächtigen und gestalteten Wahrheit.[20]

Fabian grenzte *Kilometerstein 12,6* als Roman ausdrücklich vom 'Dokumentarische[n]' ab,[21] um den höheren Wert der 'Gestaltung' zu betonen, obwohl er einräumte: 'Es war und ist immer noch bitter notwendig, die Zweifel der Schuldflüchtlinge durch wahrheitsgetreue Berichte über die viehischen Grausamkeiten und kaltblütig technisierten Massenvernichtungen zu zerstreuen.'[22]

Der politische Häftling Lys vermied, als Autor den autobiographischen Pakt mit dem Leser einzugehen, indem er einen Erzähler wählte, der abwechselnd aus der Sicht von vier jeweils im Mittelpunkt stehenden Protagonisten den Todesmarsch erzählt, der für alle mit dem Tod endet (und dem 1944 ins Außenlager Lieberose verlegten Autor erspart geblieben war); nicht nur der russische Kriegsgefangene R 74284, der ungarisch-jüdische Arzt UJ 86595 und der französische Widerstandskämpfer F 120963, sondern auch der deutsche politische Schh 10233 sterben, für den der Autor in einem späteren Interview auf das Vorbild Harry Naujoks verwies,[23] der allerdings überlebte und 1965 als Mitglied der illegalen KPD mit Lys, der 1950 die DDR verlassen hatte, zusammenarbeitete an Egon Monks NDR-Fernsehspiel *Ein Tag – Bericht aus einem deutschen Konzentrationslager 1939*.[24] Statt auf ein apokalyptisches Ende fokussierte Monks Film auf den alltäglichen Faschismus, vor Kriegsbeginn, aber nach dem Novemberpogrom. Er suchte, den Zuschauer 'zum Suchen nach Zusammenhängen [zu] bewegen', indem er 'das Konzentrationslager […] als ein Spiegelbild der Gesellschaft, die es erbaut hatte', zeigte, und deshalb ohne eine zentrale Figur, mit der Identifikation möglich wäre, auf 'den Eindruck' des Zuschauers zielte, 'jetzt weiß ich, wie das war, in einem deutschen Konzentrationslager gewesen zu sein'.[25] Am Schluss des von Lys als 'eine Art Universalgeschichte'[26] konzipierten Sachsen-hausen-Buchs stand dagegen das in allen ostdeutschen Rezensionen zitierte Bild des Märtyrers. In den letzten Sätzen über den toten Paul Rothkegel heißt es dort: 'Die ihn aufhoben – es waren Gefährten [...]; aber das Lächeln, das auf seinem Gesicht stand, hielten sie für den Spiegel des Schmerzes. In Wirklichkeit aber war es das Glück über das Bild eines anderen Lebens in einer anderen Zeit.'[27]

In Alfred Kantorowicz' Zeitschrift *Ost und West* formulierte Wolfgang Joho die Bindung dieses humanistischen Deutungsmusters an einen Literaturbegriff, der den autobiographischen Pakt ausschließt:

> Dies Buch [...], [...] von einem geschrieben, der dabei war, und der mit Hiob sagen kann: 'Ich blieb übrig, daß ich Euch's ansagte', ist nicht einfach Reportage des Furchtbaren, es ist Dichtung; es ist nicht nur erschütternd und bis zum letzten Satz wahr und echt, es ist außergewöhnlich; es spiegelt nicht nur sinnlose Vernichtung und Grausamkeit, sondern auch sinnvollen Widerstand und Glauben an den endlichen Sieg des Guten. Es ist das Buch eines Dichters, der eigenes furchtbares Erleben soweit objektiviert hat, daß es zum Erleben einer barbarisch geknechteten, weil fortschrittlichen Menschheit wurde und darum Gültigkeit und Wert gewinnt über den Bereich des nur Persönlichen. Es ist ein Universum eingefangen in diesem schmalen Band.[28]

Dass die von Meike Hermann vorgeschlagene Periodisierung der Funktionen von Erlebnisberichten in einem Spannungsfeld zwischen Literatur und Geschichtswissenschaft fragwürdig ist, kann eine Rezension von Goguels Erlebnisbericht belegen, in der die von Hermann in eine zeitliche Abfolge gebrachten Funktionen der Information (unmittelbar nach 1945), der 'Anrührung und Erschütterung'[29] (in den 1960er Jahren) und der Vielstimmigkeit (seit den 1980er Jahren) zeitgleich 1947 begegnen:

> Wir wissen, daß leider die Wertung in literarischen Kreisen nicht die unsrige sein wird, daß man gerade dort, wo schwere Schuld lastet, das offene Wort und das Rühren an das Versagen einer Intelligenz am wenigsten wird ertragen können. Zur Tarnung des schlechten Gewissens wird man wie immer nach 'echter Kunst' rufen, nach harmonisierenden Floskeln, mit zartem Stift geschriebenen Arabesken um unsere Katastrophe.[30]

Der kontroverse, 'vielstimmige' Charakter von Information über das Geschehen in den faschistischen Konzentrationslagern sowie seiner Deutung und Wertung zeigte sich schon in den ersten Nachkriegsjahren in der Rezeption nicht nur von Erlebnisberichten, sondern auch von Eugen Kogons Buch *Der SS-Staat*, das beanspruchte, 'ein vorwiegend soziologisches Werk' zu sein:[31] 'Nicht Teile, Erlebnisse, dies und das, sondern das ganze System',[32] auch wenn der Anspruch auf wissenschaftliche Objektivität mit dem subjektiven Erleben auf bezeichnende Weise verknüpft wurde:

> Denn unter den Wenigen, die dem höllischen System lebend entkommen sind, bin ich als religiöser und politischer Mensch, als Soziologe und Schriftsteller einer der ganz Wenigen, die von vornherein die Voraussetzungen mitgebracht und sich durch besondere Umstände in die Lage versetzt haben, bei aller Entwürdigung zum bespienen Objekt innerlich in souveräner Subjektstellung verharrend, kritisch zu erleben, was ihnen widerfuhr.[33]

In der Münchener KPD-Zeitschrift *Die Nation*, in der die zitierte Rezension von Goguels 'Roman' erschien, verteidigte dieser 1948 Kogons *Der SS-Staat* gegen die scharfe Kritik eines seiner Genossen, ebenfalls eines ehemaligen KZ-Häftlings. Während Karl Feuerer Kogon vorwarf, den SS-Staat zu einem 'Tummelplatz niedriger kommunistischer Praktiken zu machen',[34] brach Goguel 'Eine Lanze für Kogons "Der SS-Staat"'. Goguel verteidigte Kogons Buch mit vier Begründungen: Erstens sei 'bis zum heutigen Tage kein Buch erschienen, das das KZ-Problem so gründlich auf seine psychologischen, soziologischen und ökonomischen Wurzeln hin untersucht'; zweitens habe kein Buch 'eine annähernde Wirkung erzielt', nämlich 'Aufklärung [...] in die Massen der Gleichgültigen und Unwissenden gebracht'; drittens seien Kogons 'abfällige Ansichten über kommunistische Lagerfunktionäre' selbstkritisch aufzunehmen: 'ich hätte es lieber gesehen, wenn die notwendige Kritik [...] aus unsern eigenen Reihen zuerst eingesetzt hätte', viertens erkläre sich die einzige 'Schwäche' von Kogons Buch – 'daß der subjektive Faktor, die Geschichte der Widerstandsorganisation [...] zu kurz kam' – daraus, dass 'er sie ganz einfach nicht kannte'. Goguels positive Beurteilung des *SS-Staats* schloss eine harsche Kritik der meisten Erlebnisberichte ein, die gerade von kommunistischen Verfassern in den ersten beiden Jahren nach Kriegsende veröffentlicht worden waren; die Ausnahme – und der einzige Verfassername, den er nennt – ist Walter Pollers *Arztschreiber in Buchenwald*, der Bericht eines Sozialdemokraten: 'So gutgemeint die zahllosen "Tatsachenberichte" und "Erlebnisschilderungen" unserer KZ-Kämpfer auch sein mögen, sie bleiben restlos an der Oberfläche hängen'.[35]

So kann die im Untertitel von Goguels im selben Jahr wie die Verteidigung von Kogons informierender und wertender Untersuchung erschienenem Buch *Es war ein langer Weg* gegebene Genrebezeichnung *Ein Roman unserer Zeit* zunächst überraschen. Dem Rezensenten der kommunistischen Zeitschrift *Das neue Wort* allerdings war diese Zuordnung nicht problematisch. In seinem Vorwort dagegen spricht der Autor von seinem 'Rechenschaftsbericht', den er vom 'Tagebuch' einerseits, von der 'erfundene[n] Geschichte' andererseits abgrenzt.[36] Die Verpflichtung auf Nachprüfbarkeit der Darstellung erstreckt Goguel ausdrücklich auch auf die 'Figuren des Dramas', die 'ohne Maske erscheinen' (W, 6) sollen. Nachdem er versichert hat, ausschließlich 'aus der Erinnerung' zu schreiben, abgesehen von einigen Dokumenten wie Briefen und offiziellen Akten, nimmt er einen möglichen Einwand des Lesers vorweg, der sich gegen die Schreibweise richten könne und der erklärt, weshalb der 'Rechenschaftsbericht' als Roman bezeichnet werden kann:

> Ihr mögt euch wundern, daß ich Einzelheiten anführe, die so lange zurückliegen. Aber wie sollte ich jemals Ereignisse wie meine Verhaftung, den Sturz ins Ungewisse, den Prozeß, das Blutbad in Hameln oder den Untergang der 'Cap Arcona' vergessen? Und jene Gespräche, die einen zu entscheidenden Einfluß auf den Gang der Ereignisse genommen haben – sie klingen mir heute noch, während ich dies niederschreibe, in den Ohren! Wie könnte ich sie je vergessen? (W, 6)

Goguels Aussagen zur Gegenwärtigkeit der Erinnerung im Gedächtnis entsprechen die erzählerischen Techniken der auf Illusion zielenden Vergegenwärtigung, die als Fiktionalisierung auslegbar sind: die Benutzung des Präsens und der Erlebten Rede wie der Vorrang der Szene, vor allem der hohe Grad der Dialogisierung des Textes. Zugleich macht Goguels Selbstkommentar aber deutlich, dass die Zeitebenen der selbsterlebten Vergangenheit und der Erzählergegenwart in eine sehr betonte Beziehung gesetzt werden sollen. Insbesondere die Methode, kurze Abschnitte zu reihen, fördert die explizite wie die implizite Kommentierung und damit die Reflexion.

Wie wirksam dieses Illusion und Reflexion verbindende Verfahren war, belegt nicht zuletzt die bereits zitierte Rezension, die das Verfahren am Beispiel der Justiz thematisiert:

> Die Schilderung der Verhandlung vor dem Sondergericht brandmarkt die Justizmethoden des Dritten Reiches – und wir erfahren dabei auch, daß der Senatspräsident, der damals die schwersten Strafen verhängte, heute 'entnazifiziert' ist.[37]

Für die Verbindung der Nachkriegswirklichkeit der Westzonen mit
den Jahren des Nationalsozialismus benutzt Goguel auf beiden Zeitebenen das Zitat von Dokumenten, sei es, dass er aus der Urteilsbe-
gründung von 1935 zitiert (W, 21-2), sei es, aus den Freisprüchen für
den Richter und die Gefängnisbeamten 1946 (W, 117-20) oder aus
dem Brief eines Gefängnisdirektors, der um einen 'Persilschein' für
sein Entnazifizierungsverfahren bittet (W, 139-41). Anlässlich des
eigenen Prozesses lehnt es der Verfasser ausdrücklich ab,

> sich mit der Schilderung der Justizzeremonie aufzuhalten. Sitten und Gebräuche
> der Rechtswahrer und ihrer Lakaien gleichen sich auf der ganzen Welt. Die des
> Dritten Reiches zeichnen sich bestenfalls durch eine besondere Paarung von
> Zynismus und offener Brutalität aus. (W, 25)

Auch Goguel stellt auf einigen Seiten die allgemeine, bürokra-
tische Seite der Haft dar, wendet in solchen Passagen sowohl das
Mittel des ebenso auf Identifikation zielenden wie verallgemeinernden
'Du' als Erzählpronomen an, und benutzt den entsprechenden Unmit-
telbarkeitstopos: 'Nur wer sie erlebt hat...' (W, 72). Es ergibt sich aber
aus der Ablehnung des unspezifischen Haft-Themas eine gegenüber
den meisten Erlebnisberichten, auch denen politischer Häftlinge,
veränderte Gewichtung der Vorgeschichte. Während in vielen Erle-
nisberichten die Verhaftung als die eines Unschuldigen dargestellt
wird, berichtet Goguel die Situation der Verhaftung als eine der
Selbstkritik. Gerade weil er sich in dieser Lage seiner schon früher
geäußerten Kritik erinnere, gelange er zu keiner Desillusionierung, die
in Resignation münden würde, sondern zu 'Selbstkritik' (W, 49), die
einmal die KPD bzw. deren Führung, dann aber auch ihn selbst als
Mitglied dieser Partei betrifft. Die Gewissheit, 'trotz aller Fehler blieb
die Partei der große Motor' (W, 18), wird als sein Denken und Handeln bis in die KZs Sachsenhausen und Neuengamme bestimmend
eingeführt: 'Ich will zeigen, mit welch unerhörten Schwierigkeiten die
Organisation Tag für Tag zu kämpfen hatte. Für uns war die Partei die
einzige Kraftquelle. Organisiere dich oder gehe unter – das war der
Wegweiser im KZ.' (W, 161)
　　Diese Identifizierung mit der Partei schließt für Goguel Kritik
durchaus ein. In der Situation der Verhaftung, des 'Sturz[es] ins
Ungewisse' (W, 6), wird diese Kritik an der Politik der KPD-Führung
zwischen der Machtübertragung an Hitler, 1933, und 1935 besonders
scharf formuliert:

Die Fiktion eines baldigen Volksaufstandes gegen die Nationalsozialisten beherrschte das Denken unserer führenden Funktionäre. [...] Man sprach vom Terror der Faschisten, vom Schwindel der Arbeitsbeschaffung. Man erklärte, daß auch Hitler die kapitalistische Krise nicht beheben könne. Man war überzeugt, daß die Wahlen gefälscht seien und bereits die Mehrheit des Volkes in Wirklichkeit gegen Hitler eingestellt war. Man fühlte sich als Exponent einer Millionenbewegung, nein: des gesamten werktätigen Volkes und sah nicht die täglich stärker zutagetretende Isolierung unserer Aktivisten, die täglich solider werdende Fundierung der Hitlerpartei bis tief in die Massen der Arbeitschaft hinein. (W, 12-13)

Goguel vergegenwärtigt dem Leser seine in erbitterten Diskussionen vorgebrachten Einwände, die teilweise in dem Dialog mit Mitgefangenen noch weitergehen: 'Ich sehe nur passive, indifferente Arbeiter, die zu irgendwelchen Widerstandshandlungen nicht zu bewegen sind.' (W, 12)

Aus Goguels in der Erzählergegenwart unterstützter früherer Einschätzung der faschistischen Massenbasis ergeben sich Probleme im Umgang mit dem Adressaten: Der Wechsel von 'Ihr' und 'Wir' zeigt an, dass dem Autor sein Anspruch auf Repräsentanz für die deutsche Arbeiterklasse bzw. für das deutsche werktätige Volk nicht unproblematisch ist. Als antifaschistischer Kämpfer und Opfer der Verfolgung schreibt er 'Ihr', so wenn er einem Außenstehenden das Recht abspricht, 'über einen Lagerfunktionär zu Gericht zu sitzen. Das möge er uns, den Ueberlebenden, überlassen' (W, 162). Als derjenige, der ein neues demokratisches und friedliebendes Deutschland mit aufbauen will, schließt er in einem 'Wir' den Erzähler und den Leser zusammen, wenn er ankündigt, dass 'wir' einige aus den Scharen 'namenloser Helden' der Antifaschisten 'kennenlernen' (W, 13) werden.

Im Laufe des Berichts wird der Adressat in den Leseranreden immer deutlicher als einer porträtiert, der zur Veränderung seiner Einstellungen bereit sei. So heißt es einmal über seine Vorkenntnisse, die eine Abkürzung eines bestimmten Teils des Berichts erlauben:

Ich darf aber bei euch voraussetzen, daß ihr den Film 'Todesmühlen' gesehen habt, daß ihr die Mörderprozesse von Auschwitz, Dachau, Belsen, Mauthausen und Neuengamme in den Zeitungen verfolgt habt und daher über den Charakter und die politische Rolle der SS im Bilde seid. (W, 160)

Die so als lernbereit gekennzeichneten Leser, die der Konfrontation mit der eigenen Mitschuld nicht ausweichen und sich der Aufklärung durch die alliierten und lizenzierten Medien aussetzen, werden deshalb von Goguel als 'Freunde' (W. 143; vgl. auch W, 51, 53, 59, 64, und 149) angesprochen und in der verallgemeinernden Selbstanrede des 'Du' (W, 45; vgl. W, 162) zur Identifikation mit dem antifaschistischen Widerstandskämpfer angehalten.

Aus der Kritik an den falschen politischen Einschätzungen der Führung der KPD ergibt sich auch noch ein anderer Adressat: ein 'Ihr', das sich ausschließlich an die organisierten Kommunisten wendet und zwar vor allem an die, die sich weigern, Selbstkritik zu üben.

Goguel wurde am Tag der Volksabstimmung im Saargebiet verhaftet, deren Ergebnis ihm seine Kritik bestätigte. So berichtet er, wie er die 'Sinnlosigkeit' und das 'Umsonst' der bisherigen KPD-Politik 'hinausschreien' wolle:

> Hört ihr's, die ihr nur vom 'Terror' redet? Hört ihr's, die ihr die Nazis eine Bande krimineller Abenteurer nennt? Hört ihr's alle? Habt ihr euren Feind nicht unterschätzt? Heute bricht eine neue Epoche an: Wir müssen umlernen. Wir müssen um die Seele unseres Volkes kämpfen, um die deutsche Arbeiterschaft, die das Banner Bebels und Liebknechts achselzuckend über Bord warf und sich [...] dem Henker selbst ausliefert. (W, 24)

Dass Goguels 'Rechenschaftsbericht' die Probleme, die die Mitschuldigen betreffen, wie die seiner Genossen jeweils auch dem anderen Adressaten unterbreitet, trug ihm das Lob der 'Offenheit' ein.[38] Anlässlich der Darstellung von 'Einzelbeispielen' für die 'Demoralisierung' 'auch aufrechte[r] und anständige[r] Genossen' reflektiert er die damit gegebene Möglichkeit der Ausnutzung seines Berichts durch politische Gegner:

> Ich bin mir dabei vollkommen im klaren, daß unsere Gegner die Schilderung eines demoralisierten Kommunisten mit Behagen aufgreifen werden. Sie mögen nicht vergessen, diesen Absatz meines Berichtes jeweils zu zitieren. [...] Es ist billig, ein Heldenepos vom KZ zu singen und die Rollen einseitig zu verteilen. Wollte man totschweigen, daß auch aufrechte und anständige Genossen im Lager im Laufe der Jahre der Demoralisierung verfallen sind, so würde man ein Märchen Tausendundeinenacht erzählen, aber keine Tatsachen berichten. (W, 161)

Die 'Offenheit' wehrt eine existentiell-moralische Heroisierung der Opfer als Widerstandskämpfer ab und verweist auf die Verhältnisse, unter denen die Häftlinge zu leben und zu kämpfen gezwungen seien, statt auf die Individuen als Träger von Idealen oder moralischen Werten. Deshalb unterscheidet der Erzähler verschiedene Reaktionsformen, wie das gesamte KZ-System sich auf den einzelnen Häftling auswirkte, auch wenn er betont, dass die 'Mehrzahl' (W, 160) der Kommunisten 'durch den moralischen Sumpf zu immer neuem Widerstand angestachelt' (W, 161) worden sei.

Aus der Orientierung auf das 'System' (W, 160) der Konzentrationslager folgt für Goguels Erlebnisbericht die Darstellbarkeit der Korruption, sowohl der materiellen, die den einzelnen politischen Häftling, der eine Funktion übernahm, zum 'Büttel' (W, 124) der SS machen konnte, als auch der ideologischen (W, 153-54, 168-70, 175, und 180), die er vor allem im Nationalismus aufdeckt, der auch die Beziehungen zwischen Kommunisten verschiedener Nationalität bestimmen konnte:

> Die Kapos reißen Holländern und Russen die Hemden vom Leib, Latten und Peitschen sausen durch die Luft auf nackte Körper. Ich sehe Julius Baumgarten aus Dachau, der sich selbst mit Vorliebe als 'alter Bolschweik' bezeichnet, bei der Arbeit. 'Ihr verdammten Schweine', gröhlt Julius. 'Ihr wollt euch nicht waschen! Herunter mit den Klamotten! Euch wollen wir Ordnung beibringen!' (W, 152)

Goguel vertritt sehr eindeutig den Begriff der 'Kollektivschuld' (W, 136). Aufgrund seiner in Deutschland gemachten Erfahrungen sieht er sich als Vertreter einer revolutionären Strömung, die sich von der unterscheidet, die die deutschen politischen Emigranten vertreten, denen er 1944 in Sachsenhausen begegnet.[39] Während er diese 'stets in Verbindung mit irgendwelchen zentralen Parteistellen' und im Besitz 'praktische[r] Schulung vor allem in Spanien' sieht, meint er zunächst, dass die in Deutschland gebliebenen Genossen 'abseits vom großen politischen Strom gelebt haben' (W, 143). Dieses Urteil kehrt sich ihm dann um, als es um die Beurteilung der deutschen Situation geht, und das bedeutet für Goguel im Wesentlichen: um das Begreifen der 'deutsche[n] Mentalität' (W, 143).

Goguels Offenheit verdankt sich nicht nur seinem Ernstnehmen der Adressaten und seinem Blick auf das System des Konzentrationslagers, das die Individuen Verhaltensweisen in den Verhältnissen entwickeln lässt, sondern auch einem moralischen Selbstbild, das militante Züge trägt. Offenheit folgt gerade aus der Härte. Militärische Vergleiche sind keineswegs selten, so wenn Goguel vom 'Schlachtfeld' (W, 13) oder der 'Schlacht' (W, 16) spricht, wo er das Gebiet des politischen Kampfes gegen den Faschismus meint. Der Widerstandskämpfer versteht sich zwar als Soldat, aber die eigentümlichen Züge einer Männlichkeitsideologie fehlen, denn er kann die wesentlichen

Merkmale des Kämpfers eben auch an einer Frau wahrnehmen; so
heißt es nach einer Vorausdeutung auf den späteren 'elend[en]' Tod
einer im Verhör standhaft gebliebenen Genossin:

> Ich glaube aber nicht, daß dieser Gedanke sie sonderlich erschüttert hätte.
> Menschen wie Tilde Klose – so ähnlich habe ich mir Vera Figner, die russische
> Revolutionärin vorgestellt – gehen ihren Weg unbekümmert um Einzelschicksale.
> Auch wenn es das eigene ist. (W, 34)

Dem politischen Ziel das eigene Leben unterzuordnen macht in
Goguels Sicht die Besonderheit des Widerstandskämpfers aus. Er
schildert aber nicht nur Kommunisten, die diesem Persönlichkeitsideal
entsprechen, sondern auch solche, deren Überordnung des Privaten,
vor allem der Familie, sie zu Verrätern an der politischen 'gemeinsamen Sache' werden lasse. In der Darstellung derselben Gerichts-
verhandlung ironisiert er in der Figur des Peter einen Kommunisten,
der auf die Linie der Pflichtverteidiger einschwenkt:

> Seht, da ist der arme Peter mit rundem Gesicht und großen erschrockenen
> Kinderaugen. Er breitet die Arme aus, dicke Tränen rollen über seine Backen,
> während er beschwörend ausruft: 'Meine Frau verlangt nach mir, meine Kinder
> schreien nach mir – geben Sie mich meiner Familie wieder!' Das wird man zwar
> nicht tun, guter Peter, aber du wirst deine drei Jahre nicht absitzen, sondern zur
> gegebenen Zeit wegen Wohlverhaltens ein halbes Jahr geschenkt bekommen. So
> wie Peter machen es nur wenige. (W, 35-6)

Goguel vertritt jedoch trotz der Ironie gegen eine privat-familiäre
Empfindsamkeit kein asketisches, das Private ausklammerndes Selbstbild. Er berichtet, wie sehr ihn und die anderen Mithäftlinge die
'Geschichte' von Tünnes und Viktoria 'quälte' (W, 126). Die Frau
verlangte die Scheidung von dem Gefangenen, weil 'Vicky als aufrechte deutsche Frau nicht länger den Namen eines wegen Hochver-
rats bestraften Zuchthäuslers tragen könne' und 'seit Monaten ein
Verhältnis mit einem SA-Mann hatte' (W, 126). An dieser Stelle
zitiert Goguel aus einem privaten Brief, obwohl dies dem 'Prinzip
unserer Geschichte' (W, 98; vgl. auch W, 59) nicht entspreche. Im
Brief an seine Frau Lydia reflektiert er die 'Gefahr des Auseinanderlebens' (W, 127), weil die alltägliche Gegenwart keine gemeinsame
mehr sei; auf die Schilderung der Gefahr lässt er die eines Gegen-
mittels folgen, das in seiner Verbindung von Orientierung auf die
Zukunft und auf Kampf in der Gegenwart seinem Persönlichkeitsideal

auch in der privaten Beziehung zum Ehepartner Geltung verschaffen soll.

'Die tausend Dinge des Alltags', schreibt Goguel seiner Frau, 'die man früher gemeinsam zu beraten pflegte, machst Du heute mit anderen Leuten ab, ebenso wie auch ich, und Leben besteht nun einmal zum großen Teil aus solchen Alltäglichkeiten' (W, 127). Der Gefahr des Auseinanderlebens setzt er 'nur ein Mittel' entgegen: 'das ganz bewußte Hinarbeiten auf ein gemeinsames Ziel. Weißt Du: getrennt marschieren, vereint schlagen.' (W, 128) Was er damit meint, kann er selbst in der durch die Briefzensur bedingten Sklavensprache deutlich machen: 'Du zum Beispiel kennst ganz gewiß meine Lebensziele, meine Auffassungen von dem, was man mit "Recht" und "Unrecht" bezeichnet, und mehr als das, was ich für meine Pflichten halte. Dies ist immer ein ganz bestimmter Wegweiser.' (W, 128) Seine 'Zuversicht' für die Zukunft gründet sich einmal auf seine Anstrengung, die Beeinflussung der Ansichten seiner Frau durch die veränderten Verhältnisse sich vorzustellen, dann auf seine Überzeugung von der Notwendigkeit der 'schweren Opfer, die wir nun einmal bringen mußten', und auf ihre über die Ehe hinausreichende Gemeinsamkeit: 'Vergiß nie, daß Du das Los von vielen ungezählten Frauen teilst' (W, 128).

Das Verhältnis von Privatem und Öffentlichem, von Offenheit und Härte, das den 'Rechenschaftsbericht' Rudi Goguels bestimmt, wird vom Verfasser an sich selbst als etwas beschrieben, das er sich aneignen musste und das sich bewährte. Erworben wurde diese 'nüchterne, pflichtgetreue Ueberlegung', 'daß du auch auf diesem, deinem jetzigen Posten deine revolutionäre Pflicht zu erfüllen hast', in der Isolation der Haft:

> Erbarmungslos wird deine Selbstkritik, ebenso schonungslos wird deine Kritik an anderen. Die Jahre der Einzelhaft waren es, die mich später befähigt haben, das Massensterben in den 'Todesmühlen' zu erleben, ohne weich zu werden. (W, 73)

Goguels Unterordnung der privaten und emotionalen Momente unter die politischen und rationalen schließt das Ernstnehmen von Widersprüchen ein. Sein Bekenntnis zur 'Liebe zu meiner Partei' bedeutet deshalb auch eine Absage an einen 'gewissen Unfehlbarkeitswahn', der es ablehne, 'über die vergangenen Fehler [zu] sprechen' (W, 76).

Auf die Außerkraftsetzung einer privaten Perspektive auf das Leiden reagierten die – bemerkenswert prominenten – Rezensenten, die
Goguels 'Rechenschaftsbericht' 1947/48 fand, indem sie entweder die
Grenze zur Literatur scharf zogen oder dem 'Dokument' einen unbe-
stimmten 'Wert des Menschlichen' zuschrieben.[40] So billigte der
frühere Literaturkritiker der *Kölnischen Zeitung* Detmar Henrich Sarnetzki, der sehr nachdrücklich betonte, dass 'kein Roman' vorliege
und das Buch nur einen 'zeitpolitischen Wert' besitze, Goguel zwar
das 'Bestreben' zu 'sachlicher Nüchternheit' zu, tadelte aber die über
die 'Erlebnistreue' hinausgehende 'Absicht, gerade aus der sachlichen
Darstellung heraus durch beiläufig eingeschaltete politische Betrachtungen propagandistisch zu wirken'.[41] Die sozialdemokratische Päda-
gogin und Publizistin Hildegard Wegscheider stellte Goguels Buch
in eine Reihe mit sehr unterschiedlichen 'dokumentarische[n] Berichte[n] aus den Jahren des Schreckens', die gleichermaßen als 'eine
Mahnung zur schnelleren Rückbesinnung auf die Würde und den Wert
des Menschlichen' gewertet wurden: nicht nur 'vor allem' Kogons
und Pollers Buchenwald-Bücher, sondern auch der Erlebnisbericht des
sogenannten Ehrenhäftlings Isa Vermehren über Ravensbrück, *Reise
durch den letzten Akt*, sowie der des Offiziers Gerhard Boldts aus der
Reichskanzlei, *Die letzten Tage* (1947).[42]

Alle vier neben *Es war ein langer Weg* genannten Erlebnisberichte
sind in den folgenden Jahrzehnten in der Bundesrepublik mindestens
einmal (so Pollers) wieder gedruckt worden, doch nicht nur Kogons,
sondern auch die durch Nationalismus, Militarismus und Rassismus
höchst fragwürdigen Bücher Vermehrens und Boldts wurden Long-
seller und sind auch heute lieferbar. Goguels Buch dagegen, das Franz
Ahrens 1948 in seinem für die VVN-Hamburg erstellten 'Querschnitt
durch die Literatur über die Verfolgungen und den Widerstand' auf
den vierten Platz 'eine[r] Kernbibliothek' gesetzt hatte, wurde nicht
einmal in den Bibliographien genannt, die zum Thema Widerstand
und Verfolgung bezeichnenderweise an der Wende von den 1950er zu
den 1960er Jahren von Autoren entweder im Umfeld der infolge des
KPD-Verbots bedrohten VVN oder jüdischer Herkunft herausgebracht
wurden. Joseph Melzer nahm 1960 Lucie Grossers in der SBZ erschienene Sammlung von Sachsenhausen-Berichten auf in *Deutsch-
jüdisches Schicksal in dieser Zeit*;[43] Heinz Brüdigam nannte in *Wahrheit und Fälschung* 1959 zu Sachsenhausen nur Arnold Weiß-Rü-
thel,[44] und Ursel Hochmuth verzeichnete 1960 in *Wächst Gras dar-*

über? die Erlebnisberichte Weiß-Rüthels und Franz Ballhorns, um Gunther Lys' *Kilometerstein 12,6* als Darstellung von 'Leiden und Größe antifaschistischer Häftlinge im KZ Sachsenhausen' hervorzuheben.[45]

Auch in der DDR wurde Lys' Buch, trotz der Übersiedlung des Verfassers in die BRD, in einer an der Gewerkschaftshochschule erarbeiteten 'Literaturauswahl', die darauf zielte, 'jungen Menschen', die 'oft nur annähernde Vorstellungen von der furchtbaren Zeit des Faschismus und seinem zutiefst inhumanen Wesen haben', zu 'helfen, die Probleme jener Zeit besser zu verstehen',[46] deutlich gegenüber der gleichfalls genannten Sammlung Grossers hervorgehoben: '1945. Die Rote Armee rückt näher. Das KZ Sachsenhausen wird evakuiert. Unter den Hunderten, die unterwegs zugrunde gehen, sind es vier, deren Leben am Kilometerstein 12,6 zu Ende ist. Wir erleben mit ihnen noch einmal ihr Schicksal.'[47] Goguels Buch musste fehlen, weil sich die Auswahl auf in der SBZ/DDR veröffentlichte 'Belletristik' und 'Sachliteratur (Dokumente, Berichte, Protokolle)' beschränkte; bezeichnend war aber, dass 211 Seiten zur Belletristik, worunter Lys' Titel erschien, nur 14 zur Sachliteratur folgten, wo Grossers *Konzentrationslager Sachsenhausen* aufgelistet war.[48] Allerdings räumte der Bearbeiter ein, dass 'Literatur mit Doppelcharakter – sowohl belletristisch als auch dokumentarisch, z.T. auch unter Belletristik verzeichnet' worden sei.[49]

In einer am Institut für Marxismus-Leninismus 1959 erstellten internen 'Literaturübersicht der in der DDR und in Westdeutschland erschienenen Veröffentlichungen zur Geschichte des zweiten Weltkrieges' wurde die Erwartung formuliert, dass die 'biographische[n] Arbeiten und Erlebnisberichte sowie selbstbiographische[n] Skizzen', die '[e]inen breiten Raum in der veröffentlichten Literatur des antifaschistischen Widerstandskampfes [ein]nehmen', 'abgelöst' würden von 'größere[n], umfassendere[n] Arbeiten'. Nur ein Beispiel für die 'überholten "Erinnerungsberichte"' über Konzentrationslager wurde genannt, Robert Leibbrands 1945 in Stuttgart erschienener 'Tatsachenbericht' *Buchenwald*, dessen Verfasser 1950 in die DDR übergesiedelt war und 1956 stellvertretender Leiter der Abteilung Geschichte am IML wurde; das Beispiel für die geforderten 'umfassendere[n] Arbeiten' stammte auch von einem Übersiedler: Erika Buchmann, die 1946 in Stuttgart *Frauen im Konzentrationslager* veröffentlicht hatte, wurde die Autorschaft von *Die Frauen in*

Ravensbrück (1959) zuerkannt, bemerkenswerterweise aber nicht im
Buch selbst.[50] Das zur Eröffnung der Gedenkstätte erschienene Buch
wurde zum Muster der offiziellen, auch für die beiden anderen zentralen Gedenkstätten der DDR verfassten Darstellungen. In dem 1961
erschienenen *Damals in Sachsenhausen. Solidarität und Widerstand
im KZ Sachsenhausen,* dessen Untertitel auf den kollektiven Protagonisten verweist, von dem das auch Historiker, die nicht Häftlinge
gewesen waren, umfassende 'Autorenkollektiv' berichtet, wurde nur
an drei Stellen, aber sehr ausführlich aus publizierten Erlebnisberichten zitiert, zwei in Westdeutschland erschienenen, zur Einlieferung
aus Lienaus und zu öffentlichen Exekutionen und zum 'unmensch-
lichen Arbeitsregime' aus Weiß-Rüthels, nicht aus Goguels.[51] Das
Zitat aus Lienaus Erlebnisbericht wurde damit begründet, dass es
'erkennen [lasse], was ein Mensch empfand, wenn sich hinter ihm das
Lagertor mit der Inschrift "Arbeit macht frei" für Jahre oder für immer
schloß'.[52]

In der 'Literaturübersicht' des IML wurde nicht nur negativ
bewertet, dass die Veröffentlichungen über den Zweiten Weltkrieg in
der BRD von der 'Memoirenliteratur der Hitlergenerale, Nazidiplo-
maten und anderer aktiven Stützen des Hitlerfaschismus beherrscht'
seien, sondern auch, dass die sozialdemokratische Literatur zum
Widerstand 'im wesentlichen aus Lebenserinnerungen' bestehe; beiden Arten von Autobiographik wurde vorgeworfen, dass 'die
grundlegenden Lehren des zweiten Weltkrieges geleugnet' würden.[53]

Mit diesen begann sich Rudi Goguel nach seiner Übersiedlung in
der DDR wissenschaftlich zu beschäftigen. Am Ende der 1950er Jahre
erschien die von Goguel redigierte 'Dokumentation' *Polen, Deutschland und die Oder-Neiße-Grenze,*[54] die in der 'Literaturübersicht' des
IML sehr gelobt wurde, weil sie 'anhand einer vielzahl [sic] von Dokumenten die Ziele und Hintergründe der aggressiven Politik des
deutschen Imperialismus gegenüber Polen seit 1934 bloslegt [sic]'.[55]
Auch als selbstkritische Auseinandersetzung mit seinen 1949 vertre-
tenen Positionen zu Polen und der Sowjetunion kann seine wissenschaftliche Arbeit 'als Historiker' verstanden werden.[56] Zunächst
arbeitete Goguel am Deutschen Institut für Zeitgeschichte,[57] dann als
Kommissarischer Leiter der Abteilung für Geschichte der imperial-
istischen Ostforschung an der Humboldt-Universität,[58] die – nachdem
Goguel dort 1964 'Über die Mitwirkung deutscher Ostforscher am
Okkupationsregime in Polen im 2.Weltkrieg' promoviert hatte – als

Forschungsgruppe Westdeutsche Ostpolitik dem Deutschen Wirt-
schaftsinstitut eingegliedert wurde.[59] Schließlich – als Invalidenrent-
ner seit 1968 – war er auch 'freiberuflich publizistisch' tätig,[60] vor
allem für den Deutschen Verlag der Wissenschaften, dem er 1965
vorgeschlagen hatte, aus Helmut Eschweges seit 1958 entstandenem
Manuskript einen 'Dokumentenband gesondert erscheinen zu lassen':
'Die Tatsache', so Goguel, 'daß bis heute keine wissenschaftliche
Darstellung der Ausrottung der Juden durch das Naziregime in der
DDR vorhanden ist, ist beschämend.'[61] Goguel unterstützte die Publi-
kation von Eschweges *Kennzeichen 'J'. Bilder, Dokumente, Berichte
zur Geschichte der Verbrechen des Hitlerfaschismus an den deutschen
Juden* (1966), zu dem er eine Einleitung schrieb, und wurde selbst
Koautor der sieben Jahre später erscheinenden 'wissenschaftlichen
Darstellung' *Juden unterm Hakenkreuz. Verfolgung und Ausrottung
der deutschen Juden 1933–1945*.

   Die in Goguels Konstanzer Selbstkritik programmierte Ersetzung
des autobiographischen 'Blickwinkel seines Einzelschicksals' durch
wissenschaftliches 'in Zusammenhängen [D]enken'[62] konnte dazu
führen, dass in den Institutionen, in denen er tätig war, gegen seine
Beschäftigung mit dem Drang des deutschen Imperialismus nach
Osten der Vorwurf des 'Objektivismus' erhoben wurde. Goguel selbst
beschrieb 1967 den 'Zwiespalt' der wissenschaftlichen Arbeit seiner
Abteilung im DWI zwischen der von der Leitung geforderten 'Kon-
zentrierung auf Fragen der Tagespolitik' und 'der historischen Forschung, die für die Analyse langfristiger ideologischer Prozesse
unerläßlich ist'.[63] Bei einem Deutsch-polnischen Historikergespräch
über die Oder-Neiße-Grenze 1957 kritisierte Goguel in seinem Einlei-
tungsreferat nicht nur 'Tendenzen bei uns, daß es schädlich sei, über
eine Sache zu diskutieren, die ein historischer Fakt geworden ist',
sondern vor allem 'zu den vielen Fragen der Umsiedler zu schweigen'. Die 'Auseinandersetzung mit allen Argumenten, die die Vertreter des Revisionismus ins Treffen führen und die auf einen großen
Teil der Umsiedler und andere Bevölkerungsteile im Westen und
teilweise auch noch im Osten Deutschlands einen Einfluß ausüben',
bedürfe 'einer exakten Beweisführung sowie der wissenschaftlichen
Erläuterung solcher Begriffe wie "Kollektivschuld", "Kriegsverbre-
chen", u.a.m.'[64]

   Christoph Kleßmann, der Goguels Arbeiten u.a. über die Rolle der
Nord- und Ostdeutschen Forschungsgemeinschaft und der 'Reichs-

universität Posen'[65] in der faschistischen Okkupationspolitik 'diskutable wissenschaftliche Substanz' zugesprochen hat, obwohl er die 'Prämissen' einer 'ungebrochene[n] Kontinuität' vom Kaiserreich über Weimarer Republik und Faschismus in die BRD als 'ideologische' missbilligt, hat eine Feststellung Goguels 'berechtigt' genannt:[66] 'daß keiner der in Westdeutschland tätigen an den Nazi-Greueln in Polen mitschuldigen "Ostforscher" bis heute sich zu einem Eingeständnis seiner Schuld bereit gefunden hat'.[67] Die Frage der Schuld richtete Goguel in seiner Einleitung zu *Kennzeichen "J"* auch an die Bevölkerung der DDR. Auch wenn er einräumte, dass es 'keine vorbehaltlose Zustimmung der deutschen Bevölkerung' zur Verfolgung und Vernichtung der Juden gegeben habe, betonte er 'die Schuld und die Verantwortung jedes einzelnen Bürgers'.[68]

Der Wechsel vom autobiographischen zum wissenschaftlichen Schreiben eröffnete Goguel eine Möglichkeit, das aus dem 'Blickwinkel eines Einzelschicksals' Geschriebene 'in Zusammenhänge' zu bringen: Als Bibliograph leistete er einen Beitrag zur Ausweitung und Vervielfältigung der Perspektiven auf Verfolgung und Widerstand.

Nachdem er 1972 über den am Ende seiner Haft im KZ Neuengamme stehenden 'Untergang der Häftlingsflotte in der Lübecker Bucht' im Frankfurter Röderberg-Verlag einen 'Report' publiziert hatte, für den das Literaturverzeichnis, dessen Umfang vom 'Verzeichnis der archivalischen Quellen' wesentlich übertroffen wird, den Erlebnisbericht *Es war ein langer Weg* als nur einen der 'Zeugenberichte ehemaliger Häftlinge sowie von Neustädter Bürgern und Angehörigen der Schiffsbesatzungen' ausweist, 'aus deren Mosaik der objektive Tatbestand rekonstruiert werden mußte',[69] erarbeitete Goguel zwei Bibliographien; während die erste, vom KAW herausgegebene sich auf in der DDR erschienene Titel beschränkte, enthielt die zweite, deren Erscheinen Goguel nicht mehr erlebte, auch in der DDR nicht gedruckte Literatur. Die zugrundegelegte Definition des antifaschistischen Widerstands wurde entsprechend erweitert; richtete sich 1974 der bibliographisch erfasste Widerstandskampf 'gegen Unterdrückung und Ausbeutung, gegen Rassenhetze und Völkermord. Einen bevorzugten Platz nehmen die Lebensbeschreibungen hervorragender Widerstandskämpfer ein',[70] so hieß es 1976:

gegen die faschistische Diktatur, gegen Unterdrückung und Ausbeutung, gegen Krieg und Völkermord, gegen Chauvinismus und Rassenhetze. Einen bevorzugten Platz nehmen die Lebensbeschreibungen hervorragender Widerstandskämpfer aus der revolutionären Arbeiterbewegung, aus dem christlichen Widerstand und aus der bürgerlichen Opposition ein.[71]

Übernommen wurde die dem autobiographischen Pakt entsprechende Unterscheidung von 'Biographien, Memoiren, Tagebücher[n] und Erlebnisberichte[n]'[72] 'nach der dargestellten Persönlichkeit': 'Memoiren und Erlebnisberichte sind als autobiographische Beiträge anzusehen. Hier ist also Autor und dargestellte Person identisch und entsprechend alphabetisch eingeordnet.' Weggelassen wurde hingegen der Abschnitt VI der ersten Bibliographie 'Belletristik. Auswahl', in dem – unter besonderer Berücksichtigung 'ausländische[r] Autoren' – 'jeweils von einem Autor einige der profiliertesten Titel zu unserer Thematik aufgeführt' wurden.[73]

Auffällig oft fand sich in dieser Rubrik die Titelergänzung 'Judenverfolgung' oder 'Auschwitz', in der Regel zu Büchern, die in der BRD nicht in Übersetzung erschienen, von Jan Dobraczynski 1960, Ladislav Fuks 1966, Anatoli Kusnezow 1968, Jozef Lanik 1968, Robert Merle 1957, Gustav Morcinek 1965, Theun de Vries 1965, Maria Zarebinska-Broniewska 1949. Die Zahl der aufgeführten selbständigen biographischen und autobiographischen Veröffentlichungen wurde 1976 mehr als verdoppelt gegenüber 1974, als ein Sechstel der fast 300 Titel Memoiren, Erlebnisberichte und Tagebücher von nichtkommunistischen politisch und rassistisch Verfolgten waren. Zu Sachsenhausen verzeichnete die Bibliographie von 1976 sehr viel mehr Erlebnisberichte, darunter in Luxemburg, der Schweiz und Österreich publizierte; unter den zwanzig Titeln waren viele, die heute auf der Literaturliste der Website der Gedenkstätte nicht verzeichnet sind, wo in den 1990er Jahren geschriebene 'Erinnerungsberichte' dominieren und von den in den ersten drei Nachkriegsjahrzehnten publizierten nur Ballhorns, Lienaus und Weiss-Rüthels als 'survivors' testimonies' aufgeführt werden, allerdings auch Lys' *Kilometerstein 12,6*.

In einer in seinem Todesjahr 1976 maschinengeschriebenen 'Kurzvita' vermerkte Goguel nicht nur als Mitglied der Zentralleitung des Komitees der Antifaschistischen Widerstandskämpfer und dessen zentraler Geschichtskommission 'propagandistische Tätigkeit unter der Jugend', sondern auch: 'Begonnen: Autobiografie (2 Kapi[t]el)'.[74]

Anmerkungen

[1] Gerhard Leo, *Frühzug nach Toulouse*, Berlin: Verlag der Nation, 1988, S. 222.

[2] Bernd Stöver, *Zuflucht DDR. Spione und andere Übersiedler*, München: Beck, 2009, S. 11.

[3] Dennis Tate, *Shifting Perspectives: East German Autiobiographical Narratives Before and After the End of the GDR*, Rochester, NY: Camden House, 2007, S. 10.

[4] Karl Schabrod, *Widerstand an Rhein und Ruhr 1933–1945*, Frankfurt/Main: Röderberg, 1969, S. 63-4.

[5] Joachim Arndt, 'Rudi Goguel – eine politische Biographie', Politologische Diplomarbeit, FU Berlin, 1998, S. 40.

[6] Tate, *Shifting Perspectives*, S. 31.

[7] Arndt, 'Rudi Goguel', S. 61.

[8] Vgl. Alexander von Brünneck, ‚Politik und Verfolgung der KPD seit 1948', in: Bernhard Blanke u.a., Hg., *Die Linke im Rechtsstaat. Bd.1: Bedingungen sozialistischer Politik 1945-1965*. Berlin: Rotbuch, 1976, S.211-35 (hier: S. 225); Georg Fülberth, *KPD und DKP 1945-1990. Zwei kommunistische Parteien in der vierten Periode kapitalistischer Entwicklung*, Heilbronn: Distel, 1990, S. 85-6.

[9] Arndt, 'Rudi Goguel', S. 62.

[10] Hans Mayer, 'Bilanz der Widerstandsliteratur (II)', *Unser Appell*, 1:2 (1947), 6-7 (hier: S. 7).

[11] Vgl. Carsten Wurm, 'Die Autobiographik', in: Ursula Heukenkamp, Hg., *Deutsche Erinnerung. Berliner Beiträge zur Prosa der Nachkriegsjahre (1945-1960)*, Berlin: Schmidt, 2000, S.239-94 (hier: S. 252).

[12] Meike Hermann, 'Historische Quelle, Sachbericht und autobiographische Literatur. Berichte von Überlebenden der Konzentrationslager als populäre Geschichtsschreibung?', in: Wolfgang Hardtwig und Erhard Schütz, Hg., *Geschichte für Leser. Populäre Geschichtsschreibung in Deutschland im 20. Jahrhundert*, Stuttgart: Steiner, 2005, S.123-45 (hier: S. 139).

[13] Arnold Weiss-Rüthel, *Nacht und Nebel. Aufzeichnungen aus fünf Jahren Schutzhaft*, München: Kluger, 1946, S. 84.

[14] Arnold Weiss-Rüthel, *Nacht und Nebel*, S. 156.

[15] Hermann Riemer, *Sturz ins Dunkel*, München: Funck, 1947, S. 185. Wilhelm Zarniko, *Neun Jahre lebendig begraben. Ein Tatsachenbericht aus der Hölle der Nazi-KZ*, Hamburg: Morawe und Scheffelt, 1946, S. 11.

[16] Fritz Müller, 19633. *Wozu im KZ?*, Düsseldorf: Sauren, 1946, S.22. Heinrich Lienau, *Zwölf Jahre Nacht. Mein Weg in das 'Tausendjährige Reich'*, Flensburg: Nielsen, 1949, S. 193. Franz Ballhorn, *Die Kelter Gottes. Tagebuch eines jungen Christen 1940–1945*, Münster: Quell, 1946, S. 168-74.

[17] Lucie Grosser, Hg., *KZ Sachsenhausen*, Berlin: OdF, 1946, S. 21-36.

[18] *Neues Deutschland*, 3. November 1948, 3.

[19] Michael Rohrwasser, 'Nachwort', in: Gunther R. Lys, *Kilometerstein 12,6. Roman*, Frankfurt/Main: Stroemfeld/Roter Stern, 1988, S.215-31 (hier: S. 229).

[20] Erich Fabian, 'Gestapo und KZ', *Heute und morgen*, (1949), 55-56 (hier: 56).

[21] Fabian, 'Gestapo and KZ', S. 56.

[22] Ebd., S. 55.

[23] Rohrwasser, 'Nachwort', S. 228.

[24] Egon Monk, 'Über die Genauigkeit', in: *Egon Netenjakob: Liebe zum Fernsehen und ein Portrait des festangestellten Fernsehregisseurs Klaus Wildenhahn*, Berlin: Spiess, 1984, S. 157-64 (hier: S. 191).

[25] Monk, 'Über die Genauigkeit', S. 192, 194 und 162.

[26] Rohrwasser, 'Nachwort', S. 227.

[27] Lys, *Kilometerstein 12,6*, S. 212-13.

[28] Wolfgang Joho, 'Günther R. Lys: "Kilometerstein 12,6"', *Ost und West*, 3:1 (1949), 84-5 (hier: S. 84-5).

[29] Hermann, 'Historische Quelle', S. 143.

[30] O.F., 'Bis zum Ziel', *Die Nation*, 1:9 (1947), 28-9 (hier: S. 29).

[31] Eugen Kogon, *Der SS-Staat. Das System der deutschen Konzentrationslager*, Berlin: Verlag des Druckhauses Tempelhof, 1947, 2. Aufl., S. 18.

[32] Kogon, *Der SS-Staat*, S. 8.

[33] Ebd., S. 8.

[34] Karl Feuerer, 'Kogonsche KZ.-Betrachtung', *Die Nation*, 1:1 (1947), 31.

[35] Rudi Goguel, 'Eine Lanze für Kogons "Der SS-Staat"', *Die Nation*, 1:6 (1947), 22.

[36] Rudi Goguel, *Es war ein langer Weg. Ein Roman unserer Zeit*, Düsseldorf: Komet, 1947, S. 6. Zitate im Text mit der Sigle W bezeichnet.

[37] 'Es war ein langer Weg', *Das neue Wort*, 2:18 (1947), 32.

[38] Hermann Langbein, *...nicht wie die Schafe zur Schlachtbank. Widerstand in den nationalsozialistischen Konzentrationslagern*, Frankfurt/Main: Fischer, 1980, S. 132.

[39] Vgl. zu solchen Differenzen später in der DDR Simone Barck, *Antifa-Geschichte(n). Eine literarische Spurensuche in der DDR der 1950er und 1960er Jahre*, Köln u.a.: Böhlau, 2003, S. 93.

[40] Siehe Wgd. [d.i. Hildegard Wegschneider], 'Von neuen Büchern', *Horizont*, 2:26 (1947), 21.

[41] Detmar Henrich Sarnetzki, 'Rudi Goguel: Es war ein langer Weg', *Welt und Wort*, 3 (1948), 80.

[42] Siehe Wgd., 'Von neuen Büchern'.

[43] Joseph Melzer, *Deutsch-jüdisches Schicksal in dieser Zeit. Wegweiser durch das Schrifttum der letzten 15 Jahre*, Köln: Melzer, 1960, S. 108.

[44] Heinz Brüdigam, *Wahrheit und Fälschung. Das Dritte Reich und seine Gegner in der Literatur seit 1945*, Frankfurt/Main: Röderberg, 1959, S. 33.

[45] Ursel Hochmuth, *Wächst Gras darüber? 400 Literaturhinweise zum Thema unbewältigte Vergangenheit*, Jugenheim/Bergstraße: Weltkreis, 1960, 2. Aufl., S. 39.

[46] Albert Kroh, *Faschismus und Widerstand. Eine Literaturauswahl Belletristik und Sachliteratur über die Zeit des Faschismus und des Widerstandskampfes in Deutschland und den okkupierten Ländern*, Bernau: Hochschule der Deutschen Gewerkschaften „Fritz Heckert", 1963, 'Vorwort' (ohne Seitenangabe).

[47] Kroh, *Faschismus und Widerstand*, S. 48.

[48] Ebd., S. 228.

[49] Ebd., S. 212.

[50] 'Literaturübersicht der in der DDR und in Westdeutschland erschienenen Veröffentlichungen zur Geschichte des zweiten Weltkrieges', Typoskript o.J. [1959] im Nachlass von Simone Barck, ZZF, Potsdam, S. 18-20. Vgl. zur 'Enteignung der

Buchmannschen Autorschaft mit dem Segen des KAW' Barck, *Antifa-Geschichte(n)*, S. 96.

[51] *Damals in Sachsenhausen. Solidarität und Widerstand im KZ Sachsenhausen*, Berlin: Kongreß-Verlag, 1961, S. 62.

[52] *Damals in Sachsenhausen*, S. 13.

[53] 'Literaturübersicht', S. 32, 45 und 57.

[54] Rudi Goguel, Hg., *Polen, Deutschland und die Oder-Neiße-Grenze*, Berlin: Rütten und Loening, 1959.

[55] 'Literaturübersicht', S. 13.

[56] Erwin Geschonneck, *Meine unruhigen Jahre*, Berlin: Aufbau, 1997, 4. Aufl., S. 127.

[57] Arndt, 'Rudi Goguel', S. 63-7.

[58] Christoph Kleßmann, 'DDR-Historiker und "imperialistische Ostforschung". Ein Kapitel deutsch-deutscher Wissenschaftsgeschichte im Kalten Krieg', *Deutschland Archiv*, 35:1 (2002), 13-31, S. 17.

[59] Christoph Kleßmann, 'Das MfS und die "imperialistische Ostforschung" – ein kurzer Nachtrag', *Deutschland Archiv*, 35:6 (2002), 1002-6 (hier: S. 1004).

[60] Arndt, 'Rudi Goguel', S. 86.

[61] Helmut Eschwege, *Fremd unter meinesgleichen. Erinnerungen eines Dresdner Juden*, Berlin: Links, 1991, S. 204 und 203.

[62] Arndt, 'Rudi Goguel', S. 61.

[63] Kleßmann, 'Das MfS und die "imperialistische Ostforschung", S. 1004 und 1005.

[64] 'Deutsch-polnisches Historikergespräch über die Oder-Neiße-Grenze', *Dokumentation der Zeit*, 135 (1957), Sp. 88-91 (hier: Sp. 88-90).

[65] Rudi Goguel, 'Die Nord- und Ostdeutsche Forschungsgemeinschaft im Dienste der faschistischen Aggressionspolitik gegen Polen (1933–1945)', *Wissenschaftliche Zeitschrift Humboldt-Universität Berlin*, 15 (1966), 663-74. Rudi Goguel, 'Die Bedeutung der "Reichsuniversität Posen" für die Germanisierungspolitik im zweiten Weltkrieg', *Wissenschaftliche Zeitschrift Humboldt-Universität Berlin*, 17 (1968), 189-95.

[66] Christoph Kleßmann, 'DDR-Historiker und "imperialistische Ostforschung"', S. 25.

[67] Zitiert nach Christoph Kleßmann, 'DDR-Historiker und "imperialistische Ostforschung", S. 24.

[68] Helmut Eschwege, *Kennzeichen "J". Bilder, Dokumente, Berichte zur Geschichte der Verbrechen des Hitlerfaschismus an den deutschen Juden*, Berlin: Deutscher Verlag der Wissenschaften, 1966, S. 13 und 9.

[69] Rudi Goguel, *'Cap Arcona'. Report über den Untergang der Häftlingsflotte in der Lübecker Bucht am 3.5.1945*, Frankfurt/Main: Röderberg, 1972, S. 4.

[70] Rudi Goguel, *Antifaschistischer Widerstandskampf 1933 bis 1945. Bibliographie*, Berlin: Komitee der Antifaschistischen Widerstandskämpfer, 1974, S. 2.

[71] Rudi Goguel, *Antifaschistischer Widerstand und Klassenkampf. Die faschistische Diktatur 1933 bis 1945 und ihre Gegner. Bibliographie deutschsprachiger Literatur aus den Jahren 1945 bis 1973*, Berlin: Militärverlag der Deutschen Demokratischen Republik, 1976, S. 22.

[72] Goguel, *Antifaschistischer Widerstand und Klassenkampf*, S. 323.

[73] Goguel, *Antifaschistischer Widerstandskampf 1933 bis 1945*, S. 3-4.

[74] Arndt, 'Rudi Goguel', S. 86.

Sara Jones

Why Stay?
Shifting Perspectives on 'Inner Emigration' and
Resistance in the Works of Elfriede Brüning

This chapter examines the shifting perspectives on 'inner emigration' and resistance to fascism in the works of the East German writer, Elfriede Brüning. Focusing on two fictional texts, *...damit du weiterlebst* (1949) and *Septemberreise* (1974) and one explicitly autobiographical work, *Und außerdem war es mein Leben* (1994), the chapter analyses Brüning's presentation of different forms of opposition to Nazism. Drawing on statements by the author external to the primary texts, the position of these three works in Brüning's autobiographical project is considered. In particular, the chapter examines tensions in Brüning's presentation of female resistance to fascism across the three works and the conflict between narrative identities based on political commitment to antifascism and those based on a gendered commitment to familial ties. It is argued that a comparison of autobiography and self-reflexive fiction can elucidate tensions in the author's self-understanding by highlighting the ways in which she explores different aspects of her identity and experience across different narrative personae.

In his analysis of autobiographical narratives by East German writers both before and after the *Wende*, Dennis Tate argues that in the GDR the development of *Prosa* and the concept of subjective authenticity, which 'combines the awareness of the potential of multi-level narrative provided by modernist fiction with the integrity of self-analysis to which autobiography has traditionally aspired', make sharp divisions between autobiography and fiction problematic.[1] Tate highlights the shifting perspectives in the 'autobiographical projects' of the works of well-known GDR writers as evidence of an 'intimate long-term relationship between autobiographically based fiction and explicit autobiography'.[2]

Fluid boundaries between different modes of self-representation have also been considered by feminist critics of autobiography. As Leigh Gilmore argues, the delimitations of what has traditionally been considered autobiography have been developed on the basis of canonical works of famous male authors.[3] The traditional theoretical framework for interpreting and defining autobiography is thus based on a particular subject position, which may exclude individuals who have undergone a different process of socialisation, for example, on the basis of gender.[4] Women's self-portraits are often characterised by features that would traditionally place them outside of the genre of autobiography, such as an 'episodic and anecdotal' style, 'nonprogressive narratives', a 'focus on others' and 'lack of heroic self-assertion'.[5] As Susan Stanford Friedman argues, this need not be an essentialist conception of 'male' or 'female' writing, but can be based on an understanding of different socialisation mechanisms and group cultural identities.[6] Thus a broader definition of 'life-writing', which may include fictional forms, might permit a more inclusive examination of strategies of self-representation.

Nonetheless, this does not mean that the distinction between life writing and fiction must be collapsed completely: following Dorrit Cohn, autobiography can be considered referential in that there is a claimed identity between author and narrator. This does not, however, guarantee that the author does not lie or fantasise about his or her life.[7] The writer of autobiography creates a particular face, which he or she posits as being identical with him or herself. This identity might be an illusion or even a lie, but the form of the illusion can reveal much about its creator. In works marked as fiction, referentiality in this sense does not exist; however, as will be seen, statements by an author external to the primary text may blur this distinction where they assert that their fictional forms are based on their own life experiences, that is, that the text both reveals and conceals its author.

Based on this theoretical approach, this chapter analyses selected autobiography and (auto)biographical fiction of the East German author, Elfriede Brüning. Through consideration of writings outside of the texts themselves, their place in Brüning's autobiographical project is assessed. In turn, the chapter examines the shifting perspective of the narrators within these works on the issue of 'inner emigration' and resistance to fascism and what these perspectives can reveal about Brüning's relationship to this part of her past.

Born in 1910, Brüning joined the Communist Party in 1930 and the *Bund proletarisch-revolutionärer Schriftsteller* (BPRS) in 1932.[8] She remained in Germany throughout the 12 years of Nazi rule and, before the war, took part in illegal activities on behalf of the BPRS, including smuggling documents to Prague for publication in the emigrant press. In the war years, she largely withdrew from political activity and, in her autobiography, describes herself as having been in 'inner emigration'.[9] Nonetheless, her involvement in antifascist resistance is, as noted by Joanne Sayner, a fundamental part of her self-understanding.[10] As will be seen, the experience of staying in Germany during the Nazi period and the possibility of resistance to fascism are central to many of Brüning's texts.

...damit du weiterlebst

The first novel Brüning produced after the war on the subject of antifascist resistance was her 1949 work *...damit du weiterlebst*. The text focuses on the anti-Nazi activities of a handful of individuals. In her afterword, Brüning states that, although the text is described as a novel, she is not certain if this is quite the right word: 'Die Hauptträger der Handlung haben wirklich gelebt und die geschilderten Leiden erdulden müssen, bis zum bitteren Ende'.[11] She explains that the main figures in the novel, Hans and Hilde Steffen, are based on Hans and Hilde Coppi – members of the resistance group surrounding Harro Schulze-Boysen – and that the text includes transcripts of letters the couple sent to each other during their imprisonment (ud, 255). In this way, Brüning attributes to the text a clear biographical dimension. Nonetheless, at the same time, she makes no claim to the accuracy of the picture she paints of these individuals: 'Wieweit das Bild, das sich mir aus dem Mosaik der Schilderungen über Hans und Hilde zusammenfügte, einem Porträt der wirklichen Coppis entspricht, kann ich nicht entscheiden. Es scheint mir auch nicht wichtig' (ud, 256).

Brüning thus places the novel in the space between biography and fiction, claiming referentiality for the work without claiming identity between the text and an external reality. Moreover, in an interview in 1984, she adds a further dimension to this interaction between fiction and biography when she states that she could not have written the book, 'wenn ich nicht die zwölf Jahre im Nazi-Deutschland gelebt und erlitten hätte. In dieses Buch sind auch meine persönlichen Erlebnisse in jener Zeit eingeflossen'.[12] Although she was not part of this resistance group, Brüning suggests that the novel is a re-working of her own experiences of life under the Third Reich. She thereby encourages her readers to approach the text as, in some respect, referential to the life of the author.

What then is the view of the reasons for remaining in Germany and participating in antifascist resistance in this semi-biographical text?

Notably, the work offers a gendered division between the motives of the two protagonists, Hans and Hilde Steffen. Both are politically committed to the defeat of the Nazi dictatorship; however, Hilde's commitment is seen to have a second, familial, dimension. When the heavily pregnant Hilde begins to have doubts about the potential success of their resistance, the couple argue: Hans cannot understand how someone can risk their life for a cause when they are not completely certain that it will be worth the sacrifice. Hilde responds: 'Ich tue es Hans […], weil du es doch auch tust. Natürlich lasse ich dich nicht im Stich' (ud, 104). Hans fiercely criticises her apparent subjugation to her husband and insists that his wife must have a mind of her own; he cannot understand how she can risk her life unless she believes it will work. Hilde counters that their political work, based on a mutual hatred of the war and the government that has caused it, can never be senseless: even if every last one of them is killed, they must do it for the future generations, particularly for their own child:

> Wenn unser Kind von uns wissen will, ob wir an der Barbarei dieser Zeit teilgehabt haben, dann können wir ihm klar in die Augen sehen und ihm ohne zu erröten sagen: Wir haben unsere Pflicht getan. Wir sind uns selber treu geblieben. (ud, 106)

Hans gradually begins to understand her point of view, attributing it to the fact that she is pregnant: 'Hans verstand, daß Hilde jetzt in erster Linie als Mutter empfand, die von dem Gedanken beherrscht war, dem kommenden Kind Vorbild zu sein' (ud, 106). This mixture of political motivations with an emotive response founded on thoughts of their son is thus portrayed as a gendered response, based on the physical experience of carrying a child. Where male resistance is presented as being motivated purely by politics, female resistance is motivated by a combination of political conviction and private familial ties to husband and child. As will be seen, this duality is particularly interesting in light of a similar tension in Brüning's explicitly autobiographical text, *Und außerdem war es mein Leben*.

Septemberreise

Nonetheless, the experience of active resistance to fascism during the war years was not one shared by the author. A work in which the life of the narrator has superficially much more in common with that of the author is Brüning's short story, *Septemberreise*. This text was first serialised in *neue deutsche literatur* in 1967, but not published in book form until 1974.[13] The narrative is constructed in the form of a letter from the narrator, Vera, to her dead lover, only referred to as 'Du'. The narrator reflects on her relationship with this man: from the early days of revolutionary politics in the Weimar Republic, through his emigration and her marriage to a member of the bourgeoisie in the Third Reich, to his death in the GDR in the 1960s.[14] In her comments on Ruth Eberlein's thesis, which focused on Brüning's works,[15] Brüning states in October 1984 that in her literature she always drew from reality and that in *Septemberreise* her intention was to criticise the cowardly 'Spießer', a persona which came to the fore in the private lives of many comrades who had otherwise proved themselves in class warfare.[16] Brüning thus once again encourages a reading of the text as a reworking of her own experiences during the Third Reich and in the early years of the GDR.

The gendered division in the reasons of the male and female characters for remaining in Germany during the Third Reich which is seen in ...*damit du weiterlebst* is echoed in this later text. When the narrator's lover, the 'Du' to whom her letter is addressed, leaves Germany for Prague, she is desperate to stay with him in exile and fears arrest by the Gestapo on every return journey (SR, 41), but he insists that she must return: it was not morally justifiable to leave Germany without urgent political necessity: 'ein paar von uns müßten ausharren, und dazu gehöre auch ich' (SR, 42). He convinces her that her point of view is 'spießig' and 'kleinbürgerlich', they cannot think about love in such times (SR, 44). Once again the female 'inner emigrant' is seen to subjugate her personal happiness to the political aims of the male resister of fascism.

Nonetheless, what is interesting in this text is that the male antifascist's political motives are seen to be muddied by a bourgeois attachment to appearance and restrictive moral values. When in Germany, before being forced into exile, the lover is described as 'konsequent', 'entschlossen' and 'unbestechlich' in his political convictions; it was these characteristics which first attracted the narrator to him (SR, 128). However, Vera begins to realise that her lover's actions in his private life do not appear to match these purported political principles. Particularly on his return to Germany at the end of the war and in their involvement in the building of the socialist state, the

narrator begins to see that her lover has not truly escaped his bourgeois background. Their relationship is marred by his concern that
their extra-marital affair should not become public.[17]

This criticism of the male communist's 'bourgeois' approach to his
personal relationships is particularly highlighted in the text by the
female protagonist's focus on the private, and the absence of
substantial discussion of his (or her) political actions. The little the
reader does learn of his political work is set in the context of her
recollections of their intimate relationship. She is angry when he fails
to appear for their first meeting after sleeping together: his excuse is
that he was delivering political pamphlets (SR, 18). When he is
occupied with approaching elections, she is preoccupied with fears
that she is pregnant (SR, 20). When he arranges for rooms in her
parents' ice café to be used for meetings of leading Communists, she
portrays her parents as acquiescing to his demands without really
understanding the political dimension of what was being asked of
them and places herself in the position of passive observer (SR, 28).
Whereas both male and female protagonists in ...*damit du weiterlebst*
are involved in political action against Nazism (for example, writing
and distributing flyers and broadcasting on an illegal radio station),
the narrator of *Septemberreise*, whilst admiring the courage and
commitment of her partner, does not appear to be involved in resistance activities herself. Particularly after her marriage to the bourgeois
Olaf, the focus is on private concerns relating, in particular, to familial
life.

The narrator's motives are seen to be based on love for the male
protagonist and subjugation to his political action. Although she
shares his belief in Communism and antifascism, she is not seen to
take part in any active resistance to Nazism, but to withdraw into the
private space of marriage. It is only after the end of the war, when she
is required to decide whether to leave with her husband and daughter
for the Western zone of occupation or stay in the East that the reader
sees her make an explicitly political decision. Nonetheless, this
political decision is bound intimately to her private attachment to the
lover: she chooses, 'Dich und unser Land' (SR, 40). Again, this is
particularly interesting when compared to tensions in the author's
presentation of her own life regarding her experiences in Nazi
Germany.

Und außerdem war es mein Leben

As Wagner-Egelhaaf notes, many critics see the differentiation of public and private life as constitutive of autobiographies by women in that they undertake a fundamental separation – ascribing the male autobiographical self to the public sector and the female to the private. Wagner-Egelhaaf notes that a conflict can be observed in autobiographies by women between the public and private and that this conflict calls into question the division of art and life – a division inherited by an aesthetic paradigm propagated by men: 'Die Irritierung der männlich sanktionierten Differenz "öffentlich/ privat" bildet also einen autobiographischen Impuls, der aus nahe liegenden Gründen bevorzugt in Autobiographien weiblicher Provenienz zum Tragen kommt.' [18]

If this concept is extended to include texts with (auto)biographical dimensions, an interesting pattern begins to emerge. While this differentiation between public and private is clearly called into question in *...damit du weiterlebst*, since the female protagonist's political action is bound to her subject position as wife and mother, in *Septemberreise* the female narrator sets her autobiographical self almost exclusively within the private sphere, whereas the male protagonist appears to define himself by his political function, at least in the Nazi period. What then does this pattern look like with regard to a text that is explicitly autobiographical? In *Und außerdem war es mein Leben* (1994), through the subtitle, *Aufzeichnungen einer Schriftstellerin*, an explicit link is made between the narrator and the author. [19] Thus, unlike *Septemberreise* and *...damit du weiterlebst*, this text is autobiographical in the traditional sense, in that the paratext asserts referentiality to the life of the author. [20]

Turning first to the question of the protagonist's reasons for staying in Germany during the Third Reich, interesting tensions can be seen between the presentation of this decision in *Und außerdem* and Brüning's work marked as fictional. After the refusal of her first novel for publication by the Malik-Verlag, the narrator reflects on the reasons behind this – conceding that Wieland Herzfelde's position as an exile publisher had been too precarious to publish the work of an unknown author. She describes herself as 'unbekannt, vorläufig auch unbelastet' and adds that it was better for her to return to Germany and take part in illegal resistance work there (UA, 49). She thus presents her decision as being based on her unknown status and, therefore, the lack of immediate threat to her physical well-being. Parallels can be drawn here between this motivation and that of the female protagonist of *Septemberreise*. However, in *Septemberreise* this reason for staying is imposed on Vera by her lover, rather than being the result of independent moral and political reasoning. In her self-presentation, Brüning thus portrays active political engagement on the part of the female antifascist, as is also seen in ...*damit du weiterlebst,* rather than subjugation to male political action.

This contrast between active resistance and subjugation to male authority is similarly highlighted in descriptions of group belonging, particularly among members of the BPRS and the KPD. As Sayner notes, in Brüning's presentation of group experiences of the Communist Party in *Und außerdem*, the narration shifts from the first-person singular to the first-person plural:[21]

> In Zirkeln studierten wir Marx und Engels. Wir gingen auf die Straße und demonstrierten. Wir verteilten Flugblätter. Abends diskutierten wir uns in der Wohngruppe oder auch zu Hause, im Kreis von Genossen, die Köpfe heiß. (UA, 23)

Through the use of 'wir', the narrator thus presents herself as part of this political group and as engaged actively in political action. As seen above, although referring to the quite different context of antifascist resistance during the war, Hilde uses the first-person plural in a similar fashion to explicitly include herself in the political resistance to Nazism: 'Wir haben unsere Pflicht getan' (ud, 106). In contrast, in *Septemberreise,* the narrator's use of language both includes and excludes herself from the active Communist group. In her recollect-ions of the Weimar period she describes the police suppression of demonstrations with water canons, 'um *Dich* und *Deine* Genossen (und meist auch mich) von der Straßen zu spülen, auf denen *wir* uns immer neu formierten' (SR, 27, my emphasis). She thus suggests that these were not her comrades, but rather part of a political world that she only participated in as part of her relationship with the lover, but simultaneously includes herself in this group of political activists.

Nonetheless, as the narrative of *Und außerdem* moves chrono-logically through the Nazi period, this picture of active political action on the part of the female protagonist becomes more complicated. Sayner argues in reference to the chapter 'Mein Doppelleben als

Illegale' that the protagonist's resistance work is 'the basis upon which her subsequent antifascist self-understanding is built and is of primary significance within the autobiography as a whole', but that there are 'tensions on the level of the narrating present', resulting in part 'from a need to justify a lack of the protagonist's resistance from 1937 onwards'.[22] As Sayner notes, Brüning's literary resistance to fascism is subject to marginalisation within the text, in that there is limited detail given on the content of the work she wrote and published in the emigrant press. The focus instead is on Brüning's 'practical, and dangerous, acts of resistance', notably posting illegal flyers and working as a courier for the emigrant press in Prague.[23] These activities are furthermore presented as being independent decisions of the narrator: she states that as soon as she first saw the protocols of meetings in the propaganda ministry, she thought immediately that these must be passed to the émigré journalists in Prague (UA, 55).

However, this portrayal of active resistance is complicated by the presence in the text of the underground communist resistance groups, including the individuals whose life story forms the basis of ...*damit du weiterlebst*. The narrator states that she did not know of these resistance groups at the time, and acknowledges that they 'ungleich Wichtigeres geleistet haben' (UA, 63), thereby reducing the impact of her own acts of resistance. However, she adds that their work was, nonetheless, not useless: 'Gibt sie doch den nach uns Geborenen Kunde davon, daß es selbst in der finstersten Zeit unserer Vergangenheit Menschen gab, die sich bemühten, die Wahrheit zu schreiben.' (UA, 63) As Sayner argues, she thus recognises the debate over 'inner emigration' in West German academic discourse, but takes a 'defensive stance'.[24] Moreover, the linguistic parallels with the reasoning of Hilde Steffen for continuing resistance, despite a sense of futility, cloud the boundaries between this form of 'inner emigration' and active resistance, as Brüning places words into the mouth of her female resister that she also attributes to her self-representation.

The defensive stance taken in this passage also manifests itself as a tension between the desire to be involved in resistance on the part of the protagonist and subjugation to her male partner in the later years of the Third Reich. After her arrest by the Gestapo in 1935 and subsequent release, the protagonist marries Joachim Barckhausen in 1937 and gives up her resistance work. As Sayner argues, the description of the remaining time until 1945 'focuses largely on the familial sphere', but 'is pervaded by a need to justify the lack of any further involvement in resistance'.[25] Personal memories begin to outweigh the political in the narrator's description of this period,[26] and there are evident parallels with the narrator's withdrawal to the private estate of her bourgeois husband in *Septemberreise*. The effects of war are narrated primarily through the position of the narrator as wife and mother and her description of her relationships in this period are marked by 'subordination and repression'.[27] For example, the protagonist does not object to the announcement of her marriage by Barckhausen's father, even though she has not been asked and is against marriage on political grounds (UA, 69).

Moreover, part of the process of self-justification is based on the objections of her husband to any form of resistance, which he considers futile (UA, 80).[28] The protagonist hopes that a communist friend, Martin, will put her in contact with communists living in Germany. When Martin passes her a report on the seventh congress of the Communist International, Barckhausen flushes it down the toilet: the protagonist is portrayed as helpless to prevent her husband's actions: 'J.B., noch ehe ich begriff, was er tat, [ging] mit den bedruckten Seiten zur Toilette' (UA, 79). There is a tension between this sense of helplessness and the admission of responsibility contained in the statement '*wir* vernichteten sie [the pages] wie wertlose Fetzen Papier' (UA, 79, my emphasis). This assertion is followed by the recollection that this event resulted in their first real marital fight, based on the narrator's realisation of their different attitudes towards resistance. She states that Barckhausen viewed such activities as pointless, but does not explain her own position in this argument, acknowledging only, 'in der Tat war die Lage verzweifelt' (UA, 80). The implication is thus that she (reluctantly) accedes to her husband's position. Parallels can again be drawn between this discussion of the futility of active resistance and the fight between Hans and Hilde Steffen discussed above. In ...*damit du weiterlebst*, however, it is the female protagonist who voices Barckhausen's views and this attitude is combined with thoughts of the 'Nachgeborenen', which outweigh her sense that little can be achieved by their efforts.

Conclusion

In his analysis of Stefan Heym's writing, Tate argues that comparison of the author's ostensibly fictional works with his autobiographical text, *Nachruf* (1988), reveals a 'fascinating dialectic of self-concealment and self-construction', in which Heym divides his personal experiences between his fictional narrators in order to both confront and avoid sensitive aspects of his past.[29] A similar dialectic can be observed in the works discussed in this chapter. The analysis of the presentation of the Third Reich in *Und außerdem* reveals tensions in the self-representation of the author between her identity as an antifascist, based on memories of her illegal political activities, the desire to justify the decision to remain in 'inner emigration', and her gendered identity as wife and mother.[30] These tensions in the author's self-understanding are explored in her works marked as fiction through the division of personal experiences between different narrative personae. Hilde, the active female resister of fascism, voices views the protagonist of *Und außerdem* claims for herself. Brüning thereby examines her reasons for not being involved in active resistance groups through a focaliser who responds quite differently to these pressures. The narrator of *Septemberreise* focuses almost exclusively on the private sphere and is at the fringes of the communist movement. She thus represents an exploration of this part of Brüning's experience of fascism and from the point of view of an individual barely involved in political action. In this respect, Vera's regret at her subjugation to her lover is particularly interesting in light of the tension between political action and the passivity in life-changing decisions seen in Brüning's portrayal of her own life. In this way, comparison of autobiography and self-reflexive fiction elucidates further the tensions in this author's self-understanding. A complex interplay of different narrative subject positions can be observed and these shifting perspectives on lived experience attest, in turn, to the absence of a single, coherent, version of the self, which calls into question the dominance of traditional autobiography over other subjective accounts of the past.

Notes

[1]   Dennis Tate, *Shifting Perspectives: East German Autobiographical Narratives before and after the End of the GDR*, Rochester, NY: Camden House, 2007, p. 22.

[2]   Tate, *Shifting Perspectives*, pp. 9-10.

[3]   Leigh Gilmore, *Autobiographics: A Feminist Theory of Women's Self-Representation*, New York: Cornell University Press, 1994, p. 2.

[4]   Cf. Gilmore, *Autobiographics*, p. 6 and Estelle C. Jelinek, *The Traditions of Women's Autobiography: From Antiquity to the Present*, LaVergne TN: MacMillan, 2003, p. 265.

[5]   See Jelinek, *The Traditions of Women's Autobiography*, p. 265.

[6]   Cited in Martina Wagner-Egelhaaf, *Autobiographie*, Stuttgart: Metzler, 2000, p. 96.

[7]   Dorrit Cohn, 'Fictional versus Historical Lives', in: Cohn, *The Distinction of Fiction*, Baltimore: Johns Hopkins University Press, 1999, p. 31.

[8]   See Christoph M. Hein, *Der Bund proletarisch-revolutionärer Schriftsteller Deutschlands: Biographie eines kulturpolitischen Experiments in der Weimarer Republik*, Münster: Lit, 1991 for a comprehensive history of this organisation.

[9]   First published as Elfriede Brüning, *Und außerdem war es mein Leben: Aufzeichnungen einer Schriftstellerin*, Berlin: Elephantenpress, 1994. Further editions appeared in 1996 and 1998, published by Agimos and dtv respectively, under the title, *Und außerdem war es mein Leben: Bekenntnisse einer Zeitzeugin*. The 2004 edition, *Und außerdem war es mein Leben: Erinnerungen*, published by dtv, has been heavily revised by the author, who has removed several chapters. A further edition of the text, with the title of the 1996 and 1998 editions, was published by Neues Leben in 2010. Subsequent references are to the 1994 edition (UA followed by page number in parenthesis in the text).

[10]   Joanne Sayner, *Women without a past: German Autobiographical Writings and Fascism*, Amsterdam: Rodopi, 2007, p. 249.

[11]   Elfriede Brüning, *...damit du weiterlebst*, Halle: Mitteldeutscher Verlag, 1958, p. 253. First published in Berlin in 1949. Subsequent references are to the 1958 edition (ud followed by page number in the text).

[12]   Elizabeth Simons, 'Interview mit Elfriede Brüning', *Weimarer Beiträge*, 30:4 (1984), 610-19 (here: p. 613).

[13] For further discussion of the criticism of this text in *neue deutsche literatur* and the delay in publication, see Sara Jones, *Complicity, Censorship and Criticism: Negotiating Space in the GDR Literary Sphere*, Berlin: de Gruyter, 2011, pp. 157-70.

[14] Elfriede Brüning, *Septemberreise*, Halle: Mitteldeutscher Verlag, 1974, p. 149. Subsequent references refer to this edition (SR followed by page number in parenthesis in the text).

[15] Ruth Eberlein, *Untersuchungen zur Darstellung der Persönlichkeitsentwicklung und des Ringens um Gleichberechtigung der Frau in den Büchern Elfriede Brünings und zu deren Aufnahme durch die Literaturkritik und die Leser der DDR 1950–1983*, unpublished doctoral thesis, Pädagogische Hochschule Magdeburg, 1985.

[16] Fritz-Hüser-Institut (FHI), Bestand Brüning (BRÜ), Ablieferungsliste 13.

[17] This disappointment with antifascists returning from exile to take power in the GDR is explored in more detail in Sara Jones, 'Sex and Socialism: the Antifascist Hero in the Life and Works of Elfriede Brüning', *glossen*, 26 (2007), at: http://www.dickinson.edu/glossen/heft26/article26/jones.html (last accessed 27 July 2011). See also Jones, *Complicity, Censorship and Criticism*, pp. 188-95.

[18] Wagner-Egelhaaf, *Autobiographie*, p. 96.

[19] As noted above, the text has been published with three different subtitles, all of which imply an identity of narrator and author (see Note 9 above). For a discussion of the implications of the different wording see Sayner, *Women Without a Past*, p. 250.

[20] This is the basis of Philippe Lejeune's 'autobiographical pact'. See Philippe Lejeune, 'Der autobiographische Pakt', in: Günter Niggl, ed., *Die Autobiographie: Zu Form und Geschichte einer literarischen Gattung*, 2nd edn, Darmstadt: Wissenschaftliche Buchgesellschaft, 1998, pp. 214-57.

[21] Sayner, *Women Without a Past*, p. 254.

[22] Ibid., p. 258.

[23] Ibid., pp. 260-1.

[24] Ibid., p. 260.

[25] Ibid., p. 263.

[26] Cf. Ibid., p. 267.

[27] Ibid., pp. 267-8.

[28] Cf. Ibid., p. 263.

[29] Tate, *Shifting Perspectives*, pp. 11-12.

[30] Sayner similarly notes the 'intersection of familial, political and gender constellations' in this text. See *Women without a Past*, p. 256.

Part Two:

**Writing the Self in the
German Democratic Republic**

Ricarda Schmidt

Heinrich von Kleist in Christa Wolfs *Kein Ort. Nirgends*

Applying Eakin's term 'identity narrative' to the portrayal of the Kleist figure in Christa Wolf's *Kein Ort. Nirgends*, this chapter explores how Wolf projects her own political interests and aims, and her philosophy of history onto this historical figure. It is argued that quotations from Kleist's letters are transformed from a personal into a political context, making the fictional Kleist figure's attitude to the state more consistent and more oppositional than that of the historical Kleist, while eliminating some of his moral ambiguities. By focussing on the assumed psychological motivation of the historical Kleist's restrictive pronouncements on gender norms, rather than their manifestations in the protagonist's behaviour, the text shifts the reader's attention away from the negative effects of these repressive norms towards their function for the constitution of subjectivity, and thus encourages empathy with the protagonist. Finally this chapter compares the aesthetics of Wolf's text on Kleist with the aesthetics of texts by Kleist.

In seinem Buch *Shifting Perspectives. East German Autobiographical Narratives Before and After the End of the GDR* macht Dennis Tate darauf aufmerksam, dass die wachsende Zahl und die Vielfalt von autobiographischen Ansätzen in der Literatur der letzten Jahrzehnte die Grenze zwischen Fiktion und Autobiographie immer mehr in Frage stellen.[1] In seiner Untersuchung der wechselnden Formen 'subjektiver Authentizität' im Werk Christa Wolfs spannt er den Bogen von der Entwicklung des Begriffs 'subjektive Authentizität' in Wolfs Aufsatz 'Lesen und Schreiben' über die Analyse seiner literarischen Erscheinungsformen in den autobiographischen Texten *Nachdenken über Christa T.* (1968), *Kindheitsmuster* (1976), *Sommerstück* (1989) und *Leibhaftig* (2002), also in Werken von den 60er Jahren bis ins neue Millenium.[2] Als gemeinsames Merkmal dieser ästhetisch sehr verschiedenen Texte identifiziert er die Reflexion von Aspekten des Selbst von Erzählerin und Autorin in anderen und das Verwischen der Grenzen zwischen Autor, Erzähler und Protagonist. Dies sind auch Aspekte, die Wolfs 1979 erschienene Erzählung *Kein Ort. Nirgends* charakterisieren.

Nun hat aber Christa Wolf mit *Kein Ort. Nirgends* bewusst *keinen* autobiographischen Text schreiben wollen. Um Distanz zu gewinnen von den repressiven Strukturen in der DDR, die mit der Ausbürgerung von Wolf Biermann im November 1976 und dem nachfolgenden Exo-

dus von Künstlern nur zu offenbar geworden waren,[3] versucht sie vielmehr, ihre persönlichen Erfahrungen von Entfremdung in zwei historisch entfernten Figuren zu reflektieren: den Dichtern Karoline von
Günderrode und Heinrich von Kleist. Deren historisch nicht belegte
Begegnung wird in dieser Erzählung in einem geselligen Kreis an
einem Sommernachmittag im Jahre 1804 imaginiert. Die Erzählerin,
die am Anfang und am Ende des Textes durch den expliziten Verweis
auf die zeitliche Differenz zwischen sich und den Protagonisten in den
Vordergrund tritt und die durch ihre schriftstellerische Tätigkeit
sowohl mit der Autorin Christa Wolf als auch mit Kleist und Günderrode verbunden ist, setzt diese Autoren zu sich selbst in Beziehung als
'Vorgänger',[4] deren weiteres Schicksal, nämlich das im Selbstmord
kulminierende Scheitern ihres Versuchs, einen Lebens- und Wir-
kungsbereich zu finden, ihr (und den Lesern) bekannt ist: 'Wir wissen,
was kommt.' (KON, 151). Mit der Wahl dieser Autoren als Vorgänger
betritt Wolf sowohl Neuland als auch wohl vorbereitetes Terrain.
Günderrode war vor Christa Wolfs Wiederentdeckung und Heraus-
gabe ihrer Schriften unbekannt und galt als unbedeutend. Dagegen
war eine Revision gegen die Verdikte von Georg Lukács und Bertolt
Brecht, die Kleist als reaktionären Junker abgestempelt hatten,[5] bereits
seit den frühen 60er Jahren in der Literaturwissenschaft der DDR im
Gange.[6] In der ersten Hälfte der 70er Jahre begannen Literaten in der
DDR verstärkt, sich Kleist zuzuwenden, und Peter Goldammer gelang
es, für seinen Sammelband *Schriftsteller über Kleist* Originalbeiträge
von so bekannten DDR-Autoren wie Elke Erb, Wulf Kirsten, Heinz
Czechowski, Joachim Seyppel, Rolf Schneider und Gerhard Wolf zu
bekommen.[7]

Mit der Selbstreflexion in anderen – durch Zeit, Lebensumstände
und Geschlecht von der Erzählerin unterschiedenen – Menschen,
deren Werk zu ihren Lebzeiten nicht von Erfolg gekrönt war und
deren Wert von der Nachwelt umstritten blieb, praktiziert Wolf im
Medium der Fiktion ein Konzept von Identität, das der Autobio-
graphieforscher Paul John Eakin auf die These '*all* identity is relational' brachte.[8] Die Verlagerung vom Konzept der Autonomie zur
Relationalität des Subjekts hat zur Folge, dass Eakin den Begriff der
Autobiographie neu und viel weiter fassen will, besonders im Konzept
von Autobiographie Texte einschließen will, 'in which the focus is,
paradoxically, on someone else's story'.[9] Um dieser Relationalität
Rechnung zu tragen, ersetzt Eakin den Begriff der Autobiographie

durch den von 'identity narrative', der die prägenden Erfahrungen des Subjekts durch Familie und Gemeinschaft stärker in den Vordergrund stellen will, oder das Subjekt durch die Darstellung eines nahen Anderen porträtiert.[10]

Ohne hier *Kein Ort. Nirgends* als Ganzes unter das Genre der Autobiographie oder auch nur des 'identity narrative' im Sinne Eakins subsumieren zu wollen, sollen hier doch einige Elemente von 'Identitätsnarration' an Hand der Gestaltung der Kleistfigur herausgearbeitet werden. Denn die Gestaltung der beiden historischen Protagonisten, 'die als Ideenträger ihrer Zeit funktionieren' und eine 'Kondensation einer Epoche'[11] darstellen, in denen die Erzählerin ihre eigenen Erfahrungen im 20. Jahrhundert spiegelt, lässt Schlussfolgerungen über die Wahrnehmung von Konflikten sowie über die angestrebten Lösungsformen der mit der Autorin Christa Wolf eng verwobenen Erzählfigur dieses Textes zu. Insbesondesoll untersucht werden, welche Aspekte von Kleists Leben, Werk und Briefen in diesem Text in den Vordergrund gestellt und welche ausgeblendet werden, wie sie ästhetisch gestaltet werden, kurz, was sich aus der spezifischen Konstruktion der Kleist-Figur des Wolfschen Textes als Projektionsfigur auf die politischen Interessen und Ziele und das Geschichtskonzept der Erzählerin, in der Wolf sich selbst thematisiert, schließen lässt.

Hilda Brown datiert Wolfs Faszination mit Kleist vor allem auf die Jahre 1977-83 und beurteilt *Kein Ort. Nirgends* als denjenigen Text Wolfs, in dem ihr Kleistbild 'am weitesten und tiefgründigsten entwickelt' sei,[12] verglichen mit Kleist-Bezügen in Wolfs Interviews, aber auch der Erzählung *Kassandra* sowie den begleitenden Vorlesungen in *Voraussetzungen einer Erzählung: Kassandra* von 1983 und Wolfs Aufsatz über 'Penthesilea' von 1982.

Im Mittelpunkt der Erzählung steht das Verhältnis des männlichen und des weiblichen Künstlers zur Gesellschaft. Bei Kleist kontrastiert vor allem seine Kritik an den utilitaristischen Tendenzen seiner Zeit mit seinem Idealismus und seinem Perfektibilitätsstreben in einem emphatischen Bildungsbegriff. Des weiteren sind die Klage über mangelnde soziale Anerkennung und Wirkung des Künstlers und seine aus dieser Spannung zwischen sich und der Umwelt erwachsenden psychischen Probleme von Ambivalenz und Zerrissenheit zentrale Themen.

Wolf hat in *Kein Ort. Nirgends* Zitate aus über zwanzig Briefen
von Kleist eingefügt, vornehmlich aus der Zeit von 1800 bis 1801,
aber auch aus zwei Briefen von 1805 und 1807,[13] und zwar so, dass
der Sprachstil der Erzählerin und der des (aus Originalzitaten sich
entwickelnden) inneren Monologs oder Dialogs des Protagonisten
miteinander verschmelzen und die Grenzen zwischen den Figuren und
der Erzählerin verwischt werden. Das Personalpronomen 'wir' in-
diziert die angestrebte Verklammerung der Perspektiven des frühen
19. und des späten 20. Jahrhunderts.[14] Ute Brandes bemerkt zu der
Verwendung von Zitaten in *Kein Ort. Nirgends* treffend, dass Zitate
zwar vollständig in den fiktiven Text eingehen, aber im Sinn 'durch
ihre neue Umgebung pointiert und erweitert' werden, nämlich bei der
Kleist-Figur oft vom Persönlichen zum Staatspolitischen.[15]

Als Beispiel für solch eine staatspolitische Pointierung von Zitaten
Kleists möge die fiktive Umsetzung seiner brieflichen Rechtfertigungen für seine Weigerung, ein Amt in der preußischen Regierung
anzutreten, dienen. So bekennt Wolfs Kleist öffentlich im Gespräch
mit dem bürokratischen Vertreter des Status quo, Savigny: 'Ich trage
eine innere Vorschrift in meiner Brust, gegen welche alle äußern, und
wenn sie ein König unterschrieben hätte, nichtswürdig sind.' (KON,
86). Dies ist ein wörtliches Zitat aus Kleists Brief vom 10. Oktober
1801 an seine Verlobte Wilhelmine von Zenge,[16] in dem er sich
während seines Paris-Aufenthaltes dafür rechtfertigt, nicht ein für die
finanzielle Absicherung einer Ehe unabdingbar notwendiges Amt
antreten zu wollen. Durch die Veränderung des Ansprechpartners und
des Kontextes erhält diese Äußerung mehr den Charakter einer
grundsätzlichen Kampfansage gegen den Staat auf der Basis eines
extremen Individualismus als den einer bloß persönlichen Rechtfertigung für eine Berufswahl. Überdies scheint die Genese dieser inneren Vorschrift außerhalb der Grenzen des Sozialen zu liegen, und
das Innere scheint einer repressiven sozialen Hierarchie als unbe-
fleckter absoluter Gegenpol entgegenzustehen. Obwohl das Zitat bis
auf das Wort genau ist, blendet der Kontext, in den es gestellt wird,
doch viel von Kleists zeitgleichen Reflexionen und auch seiner
weiteren Entwicklung aus, wie sie sich in seinem literarischen Werk
manifestiert. Denn die Sicherheit des Gefühls als Erkenntnismedium
und Leitfaden für moralisches Handeln stellt Kleist sowohl in einem
etwas früheren Brief an Wilhelmine von Zenge vom 15. August 1801

als auch in seinen späteren Dramen und Erzählungen immer wieder in
Frage. An Wilhelmine schreibt Kleist:

> Man sage nicht, daß eine Stimme im Innern uns heimlich u deutlich anvertraue,
> was Recht sei. Dieselbe Stimme, die dem Christen zuruft, seinem Feinde zu ver-
> geben, ruft dem Seeländer zu, ihn zu braten u mit Andacht ißt er ihn auf – Wenn
> die Überzeugung solche Taten rechtfertigen kann, darf man ihr trauen? (Kleist,
> Briefe, S. 261).

Aus den vielen Beispielen in Kleists Werken für das irrende Gefühl
des Menschen sei hier nur an Alkmene erinnert, die ihren Ehemann
Amphitryon nicht von dem als Amphitryon posierenden Gott Jupiter
unterscheiden kann und deshalb eine tiefe Erschütterung ihrer Identität
erleidet, die auf der Gefühlssicherheit der Liebe zu ihrem Manne
beruhte. Weder Kleists Briefe in ihrer Gesamtheit noch sein nach
1804 verfasstes Werk vertreten also so eine klare Dichotomie zwischen Individualität und sozialer Struktur und eine Privilegierung des
Individuums als Garant von Wahrheit wie der Wolfsche Kleist, der ein
authentisches privates Zitat in einen proklamativen öffentlichen
Kontext stellt. Der historische Kleist war auch keineswegs ein so
grundsätzlicher Kritiker des preußischen Staates, wie es in *Kein Ort.
Nirgends* den Anschein hat. Trotz seiner punktuell scharfen Kritik am
preußischen Staat hat er ja wiederholt versucht, in diesem Staat eine
Anstellung zu finden oder vom König Unterstützung zu erbitten.
Gerade um die Zeit der Handlung von *Kein Ort. Nirgends*, nämlich
am 24. Juni 1804, berichtet Kleist – in indirekter Rede genau, doch
distanziert – seiner Schwester Ulrike von seinem demütigend verlau-
fenen Versuch, seine Dienste dem preußischen König anzubieten: er
habe um die Erlaubnis gebeten, in seinem 'Vaterlande bleiben zu
dürfen. Ich hätte Lust *meinem Könige* zu dienen, keinem Andern;
wenn er mich nicht gebrauchen könne, so wäre mein Wunsch im
Stillen mir und den Meinigen leben zu dürfen.' (Kleist, Briefe, S.
324).
    Ebenfalls im geselligen Gespräch verwendet der Wolfsche Kleist
ein Zitat aus jenem Brief Kleists vom 15. August 1801 an seine Verlobte, in welchem er die Diskrepanz zwischen der 'höchsten Sit-
tenlosigkeit bei der höchsten Wissenschaft' (Kleist, Briefe, S. 259)
reflektiert, die er in Paris vorfindet. Er verallgemeinert seine von den
französischen Zuständen ausgelösten Überlegungen in dem Verdacht,
dass der Staat nicht um der Ausbreitung der Gelehrsamkeit und der

Wahrheit, sondern um des materiellen Vorteils willen in das Er-
ziehungswesen investiere. Wolfs Kleist verwendet diesen Passus in
leichter Abwandlung:

> Ein Staat kennt keinen andern Vorteil, als den er nach Prozenten berechnen kann.
> Die Wahrheit will er nur soweit kennen, als er sie gebrauchen kann. Er will sie
> anwenden. Und worauf? Auf Künste und Gewerbe. (KON, 88; vgl. auch Kleist,
> Briefe, S. 260).

Diesem fast wörtlichen Kleist-Zitat folgt in *Kein Ort. Nirgends* ein
Plädoyer des Wolfschen Kleist für die Freiheit der Künste von staatlicher Beeinflussung:

> Aber die Künste lassen sich nicht wie militärische Handgriffe erzwingen. Künste
> und Wissenschaften, wenn sie sich selbst nicht helfen, so hilft ihnen kein König
> auf. Wenn man sie in ihrem Gang nur nicht stört, das ist alles, was sie von
> Königen begehren. (KON, 88)

Damit wird der Riss zwischen Künstler und Gesellschaft, den Wolf
zur Zeit der Biermann-Ausbürgerung empfand, auf die historische
Figur Kleists projiziert, und die Künste werden moralisch über den
utilitaristischen und repressiven Staat gestellt. Der Wolfsche Kleist
wird so zum Sprachrohr von Staatskritik und zum Träger einer moralischen Sicherheit, die dem historischen Kleist und seinem Werk oft
fehlen. Vor allen Dingen jedoch steht das Zitat von der
Unmöglichkeit, die Künste durch den Staat zu regulieren, bei Kleist in
einem ganz anderen Kontext. Denn in seinem Brief an seine
Schwester Ulrike vom 25. November 1800, aus dem das Zitat stammt,
beziehen sich Künste und Wissenschaften nicht auf die schönen
Künste und die reine Wissenschaft, sondern vielmehr auf die Künste,
die zum Aufbau einer blühenden Industrie notwendig sind. Kleist
wohnte nämlich den Sitzungen der Technischen Deputation des
Manufaktur-Kollegiums, das für die Überwachung des Fabrikwesens
zuständig war, bei, weil er sich ein Bild vom Fach machen wollte,
bevor er sich entschied, hier eventuell ein Amt anzutreten. Ulrike
gegenüber begründet er seine Ablehnung, ein Amt in diesem Kolle-
gium anzunehmen, mit seiner Kritik an der allzu starken Reglemen-
tierung der Industrie durch den Staat. Unmittelbar vor dem oben von
Wolf verwendeten sentenzhaften Zitat artikuliert Kleist ein Plädoyer
dafür, dem Kapitalismus Freiraum zur Entfaltung zu lassen:

Übrigens ist, so viel ich einsehe, das ganze preußische Commerziensystem sehr *militairisch* – u ich zweifle, daß es an mir einen eifrigen Unterstützer finden würde. Die Industrie ist eine Dame u man hätte sie fein u höflich aber herzlich einladen sollen, das arme Land mit ihrem Eintrit zu beglücken. Aber da will man sie mit den Haaren herbei ziehen – ist es ein Wunder, wenn sie schmollt? Künste lassen sich nicht, wie die militairischen Handgriffe erzwingen. Aber da glaubt man, man habe Alles gethan, wenn man Messen zerstört, Fabriken baut, Werkstühle zu Haufen anlegt – Wem man eine Harmonika schenkt, ist der darum schon ein Künstler? Wenn er nur die Musik erst verstünde, so würde er sich schon selbst ein Instrument bauen. Denn Künste u Wissenschaften, wenn sie sich selbst nicht helfen, so hilft ihnen kein König auf. Wenn man sie in ihrem Gange nur nicht stört, das ist Alles, was sie von den Königen begehren. (Kleist, Briefe, S. 169)

Interessanterweise steht auch das oben in *Kein Ort. Nirgends* verwendete Zitat vom staatlichen Anwenden der Wahrheit in Kleists Brief an seine Verlobte in einem ganz anderen Kontext. Ihm folgt nämlich eine grundsätzliche Reflexion über die gegenläufige Bewegung innerhalb des Geschichtsverlaufs, wie ihn Rousseau konzipiert hat. Kleist referiert hier, dass Rousseau in der geschichtlichen Entwicklung vom Naturzustand zum gesellschaftlichen Menschen Perfektibilität und Korruptibilität unauflöslich verstrickt sieht. Mit der Entwicklung weg vom Naturzustand gehe laut Rousseau zwar ein Gewinn an Wissenschaftlichkeit und die Überwindung des Aberglaubens einher, aber auch ein moralischer Verfall, der sich im Hang zu Luxus und Sinnlichkeit sowie sozialer Ungerechtigkeit manifestiere. Kleist artikuliert seine Beunruhigung über die mangelnde Eindeutigkeit moralischer Kategorien in einem so begriffenen gegenläufigen Geschichtsverlauf (wenn denn Rousseau recht hätte) folgendermaßen:

Auch ist immer Licht, wo Schatten ist, u umgekehrt. Wenn die Unwissenheit unsre Einfalt, unsre Unschuld u alle Genüsse der friedlichen Natur sichert, so öffnet sie dagegen allen Gräueln des Aberglaubens die Thore – Wenn dagegen die Wissenschaften uns in das Labyrinth des Luxus führen, so schützen sie uns vor allen Gräueln des Aberglaubens. Jede reicht uns Tugenden u Laster, u wir mögen am Ende aufgeklärt oder unwissend sein, so haben wir dabei so viel verloren, als gewonnen. – Und so mögen wir denn vielleicht am Ende thun, was wir wollen, wir thun recht –. Ja, wahrlich, wenn man überlegt, daß wir ein Leben bedürfen, um zu lernen, wie wir leben müßten, daß wir selbst im Tode noch nicht ahnden, was der Himmel mit uns will, wenn niemand den Zweck seines Daseins u seine Bestimmung kennt, wenn die menschliche Vernunft nicht hinreicht, sich u die Seele u das Leben und die Dinge um sich zu begreifen, wenn man seit Jahrtausenden noch zweifelt, ob es ein *Recht* giebt – – kann Gott von solchen Wesen

Verantwortlichkeit fordern? […] Was heißt das auch, etwas Böses thun, der
Wirkung nach? Was ist *böse*? *Absolut böse*? Tausendfältig verknüpft u ver-
schlungen sind die Dinge der Welt, jede Handlung ist die Mutter von Millionen
andern, u oft die schlechteste erzeugt die beßten – (Kleist, Briefe, S. 261)

Manches, was Kleist in dem hier zitierten Brief vom 15. August 1801
an Wilhelmine schrieb, wird vom Wolfschen Kleist in einem späteren
Gespräch vorgebracht (vgl. KON, 103). Doch in jenem Gespräch werden Perfektibilität und Korruptibilität nicht als prinzipielle, stets
gleichzeitig vorhandene Komponenten des geschichtlichen Verlaufs
begriffen, sondern die Korruptibilität wird ins Reich der Magie
gerückt, wenn Wolfs Kleist sagt: 'Doch sobald wir in das Reich des
Wissens treten, scheint ein böser Zauber die Anwendung, die wir von
unsern Kenntnissen machen, gegen uns zu kehren.' (KON, 103)

Der historische Kleist oszilliert also zwischen der provokanten
Zurückweisung staatlicher Ansprüche aus einer Position individueller
moralischer Unbedingtheit einerseits und dem beunruhigenden Verdacht, dass alle moralischen, geschichtsphilosophischen und epistemi-
schen Kategorien von grundsätzlicher Ambiguität seien, andererseits.
Ausgehend vom optimistischen Bildungsbegriff der Aufklärung, der
in Wilhelm von Humboldts neuhumanistischer Konzeption vom
wahren Zweck des Menschen als der 'höchste[n] und proportionir-
lichste[n] Bildung seiner Kräfte zu einem Ganzen'[17] kulminiert und
damit die anvisierte idealistische Ganzheit des Individums mit gat-
tungsgeschichtlicher Vervollkommnung verschränkt, stellt Kleist nach
seiner Kant-Krise gerade den Anspruch dieser geschichtsphilosophischen Doktrin auf allseitige Vervollkommnung in Frage. Sein Re-
kurs auf Rousseau trägt entscheidend dazu bei, die anfangs naiven
geschichtsphilosophischen Prämissen Kleists für Widersprüchlichkeit
und Konflikt zu öffnen.[18]

Dem Wolfschen Kleist dagegen ist zwar eine formale Offenheit
eigen, indem sein innerer Monolog oft nicht eindeutig ihm zuzu-
schreiben ist, sondern sich zur fiktiven Günderrode als auch der
Erzählerin und den Lesern hin öffnet. Doch inhaltlich artikulieren die
obigen Zitate im inneren Monolog und Dialog des Wolfschen Kleist in
Form von Sentenzen eine viel eindeutigere Staatskritik, als sie der
historische Kleist in Werk und Briefen entwickelt hat, und zwar vom
Standpunkt einer dem Künstler privilegiert zugänglichen Wahrheit
und einer unhintergehbaren Individualität her. Der Ende des 18. Jahrhunderts entwickelte Bildungsbegriff, dem Kleist vor der Kant-Krise

angehangen hatte, wird hier reaktualisiert für ein Insistieren auf einer Gesellschaftsutopie, die als Kritik am real existierenden Sozialismus fungiert. Diese Kritik aber speist sich aus den gleichen Quellen wie der implizit kritisierte Marxismus und hält, wie der Marxismus, am Konzept der teleologischen Entwicklung fest.

Wird der Wolfsche Kleist also einerseits zum Sprachrohr für die Staatskritik der Erzählfigur, so dient er andererseits zur Reflexion der innerpsychischen Konflikte im Künstler. Soziales Außenseitertum, innere Zerrissenheit, Einsamkeit, Empfindsamkeit scheinen über die Jahrhunderte hinweg die Figur Kleist und die Erzählerin im Topos der mangelnden sozialen Wirkung ihres künstlerischen Anliegens zu verbinden. In der Metapher des Gelächters manifestiert sich das subjektive Empfinden der Wirkungslosigkeit des Künstlers:

> Jahrhundertealtes Gelächter. Das Echo, ungeheuer, vielfach gebrochen. Und der Verdacht, nichts kommt mehr als dieser Widerhall. Aber nur Größe rechtfertigt die Verfehlung gegen das Gesetz und versöhnt den Schuldigen mit sich selbst.
> Einer, Kleist, geschlagen mit diesem überscharfen Gehör, flieht unter Vorwänden, die er nicht durchschauen darf. Ziellos, scheint es, zeichnet er die zerrissene Landkarte Europas mit seiner bizarren Spur. Wo ich nicht bin, da ist das Glück. (KON, 6)

Hinter der kafkaesk anmutenden Formulierung 'Verfehlung gegen das Gesetz' verbirgt sich ein Psychogramm der Ambivalenz des Außenseiters. Einerseits übertritt der Außenseiter wissentlich gesellschaftliche Normen, die hier im Begriff 'Gesetz' abstrahiert, kodifiziert und erhärtet werden. Andererseits jedoch bedarf er der Anerkennung durch die Gemeinschaft, um sich selbst das als Schuld empfundene Anderssein zu vergeben, um den eigenen 'Zweifel an seiner Bestimmung' (KON, 14-15) zu übertönen. Dies ist jedoch nicht einfach eine Anerkennung seiner Differenz im Sinne von Gleichwertigkeit, sondern im Sinne von Überlegenheit. D.h. erst wenn sein Anderssein zur gesellschaftlich bewunderten 'Größe' geworden ist, also wenn er selbst eine neue Norm konstituiert, kann der Außenseiter sein eigenes Abweichen von der alten Norm akzeptieren. Mit dieser apodiktischen Feststellung über die Internalisierung von Normen durch den Oppositionellen verklammert die Erzählerin ihre eigene Befindlichkeit einer Außenseiterin in der DDR des späten 20. Jahrhunderts, deren humanistische Einwände von einer repressiven Gesellschaft nicht gehört werden, mit der supponierten Ambivalenz Kleists gegenüber der preußischen Gesellschaft Anfang des 19. Jahrhunderts.

Worin nun mag des historischen Kleist 'Verfehlung gegen das Gesetz' bestehen? In welchem Sinne mag er sich als 'Schuldiger' emp-
funden haben und was davon kommt in Wolfs literarischer Gestalt
zum Ausdruck? Beim historischen Kleist lässt sich das Leiden des
gegen das bestehende Gesetz verstoßenden Außenseiters zugleich auf
ästhetischer als auch auf sozialer Ebene erkennen. Als sein Versuch,
mit seinem *Guiscard*-Drama eine neue Form des Dramas zu finden,
die Antike und Moderne vereint, scheitert, gerät Kleist in eine tiefe
Krise. Sie resultiert in langer Krankheit und in Selbstmordversuchen,
auf die die Erzählung besonders durch Hofrat Wedekind, den Arzt,
anspielt. Der historische Kleist schreibt am 5. Oktober 1803 an seine
Schwester Ulrike über das Scheitern seines *Guiscard*:

> Das Schicksal, das den Völkern jeden Zuschuß zu ihrer Bildung zumißt, will,
> denke ich, die Kunst in diesem nördlichen Himmelsstrich noch nicht reifen lassen.
> […] Ich trete vor Einem zurück, der noch nicht da ist, und beuge mich, ein Jahr-
> tausend im Voraus, vor seinem Geiste. Denn in der Reihe der menschlichen Er-
> findungen ist diejenige, die ich gedacht habe, unfehlbar ein Glied, und es wächst
> irgendwo schon ein Stein für den, der sie einst ausspricht. (Kleist, Briefe, S. 320)

Hier führt der historische Kleist also überpersönliche sozialhis-
torische Gründe für sein Scheitern an und misst der Erfindung ästhetischer Formen eine Objektivität und logische Folgerichtigkeit zu,
die der Entdeckung naturwissenschaftlicher Tatsachen analog ist.
Doch weit davon entfernt, seinen auf dieser geschichtsphilosophischen
Basis imaginierten größeren potentiellen Nachfolger gelassen zu erwarten, reagiert der historische Kleist narzisstisch gekränkt mit Destruktion und Selbstdestruktion. Seiner Schwester Ulrike schreibt er:

> Ich habe in Paris mein Werk, so weit es fertig war, durchlesen, verworfen, und
> verbrannt: und nun ist es aus. Der Himmel versagt mir den Ruhm, das größte der
> Güter der Erde; ich werfe ihm, wie ein eigensinniges Kind, alle übrigen hin. Ich
> *kann* mich deiner Freundschaft nicht würdig zeigen, ich kann ohne diese Freund-
> schaft doch nicht *leben*: ich stürze mich in den Tod. (Kleist, Briefe, S. 321)

Dieser Brief macht deutlich, dass für Kleist literarische Größe
durchaus einen Aspekt von Macht hatte, durch die sich das Ich in der
Welt behauptet, ja die Welt prägt. Seine Unfähigkeit, ein Amt
anzunehmen, sich also in den für seine Schicht üblichen sozialen
Bahnen zu bewegen, kontrastiert mit seinem Ehrgeiz, dennoch durch
sein Schreiben seiner Familie Ehre machen, also innerhalb seiner
Schicht etwas gelten zu wollen. In Briefen an seine Schwester Ulrike

artikuliert Kleist immer wieder sein Begehren nach schriftstel-
lerischem Ruhm. So versucht er, Ulrike dazu zu motivieren, ihn
weiterhin finanziell zu unterstützen, indem er ihr seine Absicht mitteilt, durch seine schriftstellerische Arbeit 'mir den Kranz der Un-
sterblichkeit zusammen zu pflücken' (Kleist, Briefe, S. 317). Am 5.
Oktober 1803 gesteht Kleist über die außerästhetische Motivation
seines *Guiscard*-Projektes: 'Ich habe nun ein Halbtausend hinter
einander folgender Tage, die Nächte der meisten mit eingerechnet, an
den Versuch gesetzt, zu so vielen Kränzen noch einen auf unsere
Familie herabzuringen' (Kleist, Briefe, S. 320).

Für den historischen Kleist zur Zeit der Handlung von Wolfs 1804
situiertem Text geht es also sowohl bei dem ästhetischen Ehrgeiz des
Guiscard-Dramas als auch dem sozialen Begehren nach Ruhm durch
literarische Leistungen um die persönliche Anerkennung seines
Wertes, um die Rechtfertigung seiner von der Norm abweichenden
Existenz vor seiner Familie und seinen Mitmenschen, weniger um
einen politischen Einfluss auf die Gesellschaft seiner Zeit. Dieser
primär narzisstische Antrieb kontrastiert mit dem explizit humani-
sierenden Einfluss auf die Gesellschaft, den Wolf als Schriftstellerin
anstrebt.[19] Erst vier oder fünf Jahre nach der in *Kein Ort. Nirgends*
imaginierten Begegnung zwischen Kleist und Günderrode versucht
der historische Kleist in seiner nationalen Phase von 1808 bis 1810,
durch sein Schreiben direkt auf die Gesellschaft seiner Zeit einzu-
wirken. In dieser Phase jedoch vertritt Kleist, besonders in *Die
Herrmannsschlacht* und 'Ode an Germania', eine macchiavellistische
Politik, in der brutalste Mittel vorgeschlagen werden, um ein libertäres
Ziel zu erreichen (Deutschland zu einigen, um den Unterdrücker Napoleon abzuwerfen). Indem sich Wolfs Erzählung auf die vornationale
Phase Kleists beschränkt, werden also die eher problematischen
politischen Aspekte des historischen Kleist eliminiert. Die Konzentration auf den frühen, pränationalen Kleist und die Verwendung der
Begriffe Größe und Schuld in einem stark abstrahierenden Gestus
erlauben es, dass Kleist als literarische Figur zur Projektionsfläche für
die Erzählerin/Autorin wird, obwohl ihr humanistisches Konzept von
Größe und literarischem Wirken zum Wohle der Gemeinschaft durchaus anderes meint als die offenen persönlichen Machtphantasien des
pränationalen Kleist.

Wenn auch die gewalttätige nationale Komponente aus Kleists
Werk durch die gewählte Handlungszeit der Erzählung ausgespart ist,

so thematisiert der Text aus der Innenperspektive des Protagonisten doch etwas vom persönlich-egoistischen Element von Kleists Suche nach Größe und Ruhm, in der das literarische Werk als Waffe fungiert, die dem Autor Macht verleiht: 'Es zerreißt ihn, daß er denen nichts gilt. Das Werk ist nicht geschrieben, mit dem er auch diesen hier einst Schläge versetzen wird, daß sie in die Knie gehn sollen.' (KON, 42) Und gegenüber Goethe schreibt die Erzählung Kleist, mittels innerem Monolog und Dialog, Zweifel und vor allem Rachegelüste zu: 'Wenn es mir nicht gelänge, ihm [d.i. Goethe] meine Leiden heimzuzahlen. Ich werde ihm den Lorbeer von der Stirne reißen.' (KON, 127) Und: 'Eines Tages, Günderrode, wird er [Goethe] sich vor mir fürchten.' (KON, 130).[20]

Diesem persönlichen Ehrgeiz, den Wolfs Kleist als Furie apostrophiert, widerspricht Günderrode mit dem Ausruf: 'Wollen Sie Ihr Leben von Furien gejagt durchlaufen!' (KON, 127). Da Günderrode als Frau selbst nicht die Möglichkeit hat, gesellschaftlichen Ehrgeiz durch ihr Schreiben zu befriedigen, macht sie durch diese Entgegnung Kleists Ehrgeiz als Aspekt einer destruktiven, sozial produzierten Maskulinität kritisch kenntlich.

Die sexistischen Rollenvorstellungen, die der historische Kleist in seinen Briefen formulierte, werden zwar bei Wolfs Kleist evoziert, doch nur schwach, etwa in seinem Unbehagen gegenüber Günderrodes Selbstbewußtsein ('Soll eine Frau so blicken?', KON, 12, und 'Soll eine Frau so sprechen?', KON, 119) sowie in der herablassenden Frage in erlebter Rede, ob sie es nötig habe zu dichten: 'Kennt sie nichts Besseres, sich die Langeweile zu vertreiben?' (KON, 26). Manche der traditionellen Rollenvorstellungen des Protagonisten werden durch kleine distanzierende Einschübe der Erzählerin ironisch in Frage gestellt, wie etwa in der Bemerkung: 'Über die Ausbildung der Frauen hat er eine feste, wie er glaubt, gegründete Ansicht' (KON, 94).

Kleists massivere Artikulationen tradierter Geschlechternormen in seinen Briefen dagegen bleiben in dieser Erzählung unerwähnt. Hier seien einige seiner Geschlechterstereotype zitiert, die in *Kein Ort. Nirgends* nicht verwendet werden: 'Kannst Du Dich dem allgemeinen Schicksal Deines Geschlechtes entziehen, das nun einmal seiner Natur nach die zweite Stelle in der Reihe der Wesen bekleidet?' (Kleist, Briefe, S. 43); Frauen haben die 'heilige[...] Pflicht Mütter u Erzieherinnen des Menschengeschlechtes zu werden' (Kleist, Briefe, S.

43-4); 'die Bestimmung des Weibes ist wohl unzweifelhaft u unver-
kennbar [...], *Mutter zu werden, u der Erde tugendhafte Menschen zu
erziehen'* (Kleist, Briefe, S. 130; vgl. auch S. 141); 'Keine Tugend ist
doch weiblicher, als Sorge für das Wohl Anderer', dagegen mache
Eigennutz das Weib häßlicher und der Katze ähnlicher (Kleist, Briefe,
S. 136); Kleist setzt als Faktum seiner Verlobten gegenüber voraus,
dass das höchste Bedürfnis des Weibes 'die Liebe ihres Mannes' sei
(Kleist, Briefe, S. 277), und er geht von festen in der Natur
verankerten Sphären aus: 'Durch Euch will die Natur nur ihre Zwecke
erreichen, durch uns Männer auch der Staat noch die seinigen' (Kleist,
Briefe, S. 130); 'den Mann erkennt man an seinem Verstande; aber
wenn man das Weib nicht an ihrem Herzen erkennt, woran erkennt
man es sonst?' (Kleist, Briefe, S. 235). Kleists Bedürfnis, Wilhelmine
auszubilden und zu formen wie ein Mundstück zu seiner Klarinette
(vgl. Kleist, Briefe, S. 106, 123, 152, 154, 156, 159, 163, 172, 175)
oder wie einen Edelstein (vgl. Kleist, Briefe, S. 178) sowie ihre
Veredlung zu seinem Genuss (vgl. Kleist, Briefe, S. 220) zieht sich als
Basso continuo durch seine Briefe. Kleists harsche Kritik an der
mangelnden Weiblichkeit seiner Schwester Ulrike als Missgriff der
Natur (vgl. Kleist, Briefe, S. 253) und der Vorwurf, 'an ihrem Busen
läßt sich doch nicht ruhen' (Kleist, Briefe, S. 240), werden ebenfalls
nicht in *Kein Ort. Nirgends* zitiert, doch wird abstrahierend auf sie in
Kleists 'Widerwillen gegen Zwitterhaftes' (KON, 26) angespielt.

Das in seinen Briefen zum Ausdruck kommende Bestehen des
historischen Kleist auf strikten Geschlechternormen und die Ablehnung der Androgynität seiner Schwester Ulrike wird vom Wolfschen
Kleist dagegen psychoanalytisch unterminiert, wenn er der Günderrode gegenüber ein Geständnis macht, für das ich keinen Beleg in
Kleists Briefen gefunden habe: 'manchmal ist es mir unerträglich, daß
die Natur den Menschen in Mann und Frau aufgespalten hat' (KON,
133). Günderrodes Erklärung, dass Kleist in Wirklichkeit unter dem
Konflikt zwischen männlichen und weiblichen Anteilen in sich selbst
leide (KON, 133), beleuchtet Kleists 'gender trouble' von der psychologischen Perspektive des 20. Jahrhunderts her und lässt so sein
briefliches Beharren auf essentialistischen Geschlechternormen[21] als
Projektion eines internen Konfliktes nach außen erscheinen. Durch die
Fokussierung auf diese angenommene psychologische Motivation für
Kleists Bestehen auf strikten Geschlechternormen gegenüber Wilhelmine und Ulrike wird die Aufmerksamkeit des modernen Lesers von

der Manifestation dieser repressiven Normen selbst weg und auf deren Funktion für die Subjektkonstituierung des Protagonisten hin gelenkt und so einem einfühlenden Verstehen nahegebracht.

Dem 20. Jahrhundert wird Wolfs Kleist vor allem auch durch die Thematisierung seiner inneren Zerrissenheit nahegerückt. So wird die Unvereinbarkeit der widerstrebenden Teile Kleists in einem Traum, in dem er ein Tier jagt und erschießt, das einen Teil seiner selbst symbolisiert (vgl. KON, 37), psychoanalytisch universalisiert und zugleich als bildliche Antizipation seines Selbstmordes in Szene gesetzt. In direkter Rede beklagt Kleist gegenüber seinem Arzt, Wedekind, sein Unglück, 'von Bindungen abzuhängen, die mich ersticken, wenn ich sie dulde, und die mich zerreißen, wenn ich mich löse' (KON, 52). Kleists Gemütskrankheit wird von der Erzählerin psychoanalytisch als Verdrängung einer unerträglichen Wahrheit motiviert:

> Kleist beginnt die Gründe für seine Irrfahrt zu vergessen, die Einsicht in seine Handlungen, die er einmal besessen haben muß, schwindet ihm. [...] Gemütskrank, das Wedekindsche Stichwort, unbestimmt und geheimnisvoll genug, alles das zu decken, auch vor ihm selbst. Denn kein Mensch kann auf die Dauer mit der Erkenntnis leben, daß, so stark wie sein Widerstand gegen das Übel der Welt, der Trieb in ihm ist, sich diesem Übel unbedingt zu unterwerfen. Und daß der Name, den er dem Übel leiht, ein Ersatzname ist, den uns die Furcht vor andren Benennungen eingibt. Napoleon. Kleist spürt, wie das gräßliche Wort anschwillt, sich vollsaugt mit seinem ganzen Haß, seiner ganzen Mißgunst und Selbstmißachtung. Und er spürt auch – das aber darf nicht wahr sein –, wie alle trüben Ströme seiner Seele von diesem Namen angezogen werden, ihm gierig zutreiben als dem Ort, der ihnen bereitet ist. (KON 69-70)

Wolfs Kleist stellt seinem Arzt Wedekind (der wiederum später der Gesellschaft das Gleichnis mitteilt) seine Zerrissenheit im Gleichnis vom Hund dar, der sich vor der für ihn unlösbaren Aufgabe, zwischen zwei entgegengesetzten Befehlen zu entscheiden, in den Schlaf flüchtet (vgl. KON, 72, 78-81). Der Protagonist bezieht das Gleichnis in expliziter Selbstreflexion auf den Widerspruch zwischen seiner inneren Bestimmung und dem ökonomischen und sozialen Zwang, ein Amt anzunehmen, das seiner Bestimmung widerspräche (vgl. KON, 80-1). In Traum, Parabel und Reflexion des Protagonisten sowie der Erzählerin wird also das Thema der Zerrissenheit durch verschiedene ästhetische Mittel umkreist, die über das authentische Zitat hinausgehen.

Aus Kleists brieflich verbürgter Beobachtung bei seinem Paris-Aufenthalt, dass jedes vierte Wort der Franzosen Rousseau sei, doch zwischen dem Denken Rousseaus und der französischen Gegenwart eine Kluft klaffe, leitet die Erzählung ab, das er als positiven Wert eine Umsetzung des Ideals in die Wirklichkeit erwarte oder anstrebe. Dieser idealistischen Position, die offensichtlich von der Erzählerin geteilt wird, steht innerhalb der Fiktion der Realist Savigny entgegen, der behauptet:

> Daß man die Philosophie nicht beim Wort nehmen, das Leben am Ideal nicht messen soll – das ist Gesetz. […] Es ist das Gesetz der Gesetze, […] auf dem unsere menschlichen Einrichtungen in ihrer notwendigen Gebrechlichkeit beruhn. Wer dagegen aufsteht, muß zum Verbrecher werden. Oder zum Wahnsinnigen. (KON, 63-4)

Unter Bezugnahme auf Rousseaus berühmten Aufsatz, ob der Fortschritt in Wissenschaft und Kunst sich wohltätig oder verderblich auf die Menschheit ausgewirkt habe, wird eine Diskussion über geschichtsphilosophische Konzepte geführt, in der Kleist die Rolle hat, gegen einen einseitig rationalistischen Fortschrittsglauben zu polemisieren ('Ach, wie traurig ist diese zyklopische Einseitigkeit!', KON, 102; vgl. Kleist, Briefe, S. 257) und statt dessen auf der ganzheitlichen menschlichen Entwicklung zu beharren, zu deren Fürsprecher der Dichter gemacht wird.

Wolfs Kleist wird zum Hoffnungsträger, zum Wegbereiter der Freiheit in der folgenden erlebten Rede:

> Ein Maß war ihm gesetzt, das zu erfüllen er anstreben mußte, eine Verheißung, daß es im Menschen, auch in ihm lag, eine Gangart zu finden, die ins Freie führt; denn was wir wünschen können, muß doch im Bereich unsrer Kräfte liegen, dachte er, oder es ist nicht ein Gott, der die Welt regiert, sondern Satan […]. (KON, 125-6)

Doch entgegen diesem Beharren auf der Verwirklichbarkeit des Ideals akzeptiert Wolfs Kleist gegen Ende der Erzählung in einem Austausch mit Günderrode, in dem die Sprecherpositionen kunstvoll verschwimmen, die prinzipielle Differenz zwischen Ideal und Wirklichkeit innerhalb der Grenzen seines eigenen Lebens:

> Daß die Zeit unser Verlangen hervorbringt, doch nicht, wonach uns am meisten verlangt.
> Die niedergehaltenen Leidenschaften.
> Wir taugen nicht zu dem, wonach wir uns sehnen.

Wir müssen verstehen, daß Sehnsucht keiner Begründung bedarf.
Die Zeit scheint eine neue Ordnung der Dinge herbeiführen zu wollen, und wir
werden davon nichts als bloß den Umsturz der alten erleben. (KON, 139)

In diesen Dialog sind Zitate von Günderrode und Kleist eingebaut,
und zwar so, dass die Aussagen von beiden akzeptiert werden können
und einen Konsens zwischen ihnen herstellen. Der letzte Satz stammt
aus Kleists Brief vom Dezember 1805 an Otto August Rühle von
Lilienstern, in dem Kleist sich über den mangelnden Widerstand des
preußischen Königs gegen Napoleon beklagt, der im Begriff sei, ganz
Europa zu überrennen und dabei die deutsche Reichsverfassung
aufzuheben und die Verwaltung der deutschen Länder an von ihm
abhängige Dynastien zu geben (vgl. Kleist, Briefe, S. 352) – eine
übrigens bemerkenswert genaue Antizipation der politischen Entwicklung für den kurzen Rest von Kleists Lebenszeit, von der aber in der
Erzählung nur die abstrakte Sentenz zitiert wird, die sich auch auf das
20. Jahrhundert anwenden lässt.

Später teilt der Wolfsche Kleist Günderrode seine grundsätzlichen
Zweifel am gesamten Geschichtsverlauf mit: 'Oft denk ich: Wenn der
erste Idealzustand, den die Natur hervorrief und den wir zerstören
mußten, nie zu jenem zweiten Idealzustand führte, durch die Organisation, die wir uns selber geben?' (KON, 148)

Doch die psychische Zerrissenheit, die beim historischen Kleist im
Selbstmord kulminierte, wird in *Kein Ort. Nirgends* zwar gestaltet,
aber am Ende durch die, wenn auch nur auf einen Augenblick
beschränkte, utopische Seelenverschmelzung zwischen Kleist und
Günderrode in Harmonie überführt. Durch das in der Wir-Form aus-
gedrückte Bekenntnis der Erzählerin zur neuhumanistischen Bildungs-
utopie wird dieser harmonische Moment ausgeweitet zum Wiedergewinnen der Hoffnung auf einen letztlich dennoch progressiven
Geschichtsverlauf – eine Hoffnung, die im Plural der ersten Person
des Personalpronomens sowohl Kleist und Günderrode, als auch die
Erzählerin, die Autorin Christa Wolf und potentiell die Leser dieser
Erzählung umfassen kann:

Begreifen, daß wir ein Entwurf sind – vielleicht, um verworfen, vielleicht, um
wieder aufgegriffen zu werden, darauf haben wir keinen Einfluß. Das zu belachen,
ist menschenwürdig. Gezeichnet zeichnend. Auf ein Werk verwiesen, das offen
bleibt, offen wie eine Wunde. [...] Unser unausrottbarer Glaube, der Mensch sei
bestimmt, sich zu vervollkommen, der dem Geist aller Zeiten strikt zuwiderläuft.
(KON, 150-1)

Die sich in Kleist spiegelnde Erzählerin artikuliert hier die Hoffnung, dass die Distanz zwischen ihr selbst und der Gesellschaft einmal überwunden wird, indem ihre Vorstellungen irgendwann einmal von der Gesellschaft als Leitideen angenommen werden. Diese Leitideen werden subjektiv-emphatisch in Form eines Glaubensbekenntnisses artikuliert, das dem am Anfang der Erzählung zitierten pervertierten Glaubensbekenntnis nun etwas Positives entgegensetzt. Der vom Negativen zum Positiven sich entwickelnde Glaube der Erzählerin wird als grundsätzlich oppositionell deklariert, weil er im tatsächlichen Geschichtsverlauf nie verwirklicht wurde, doch basiert er konzeptionell auf der um 1800 entwickelten Zielvorstellung von der Interdependenz und Ergänzung von individueller und sozialer Perfektibilität im Begriff der Bildung.

Zusammenfassend lässt sich sagen, dass in *Kein Ort. Nirgends* Zitate von Kleists Kritik an staatlichen Institutionen sowie sein in Briefen bekundetes individuelles Bildungs- und Perfektibilitätsstreben zu einer viel allgemeineren, grundsätzlichen Kritik am Staat kombiniert werden, als sich dem Kontext von Kleists Briefen oder seinem tatsächlichen Verhalten gegenüber dem preußischen Staat entnehmen lässt. Eine solche Zuspitzung des vorhandenen kritischen Potentials einer historischen Figur ist ein legitimes Mittel literarischer Gestaltung. Doch kritisch zu reflektieren bleibt zweierlei: Inwiefern unterscheidet sich die Ästhetik dieser Kleist als Protagonist verwendenden Erzählung von der Ästhetik des literarischen Autors Kleist – trotz der extensiven Nutzung von Originalzitaten aus Kleists Briefen? Inwiefern weist die spezifische Form der Pointierung der Kleistschen Staatskritik in dieser Erzählung eine Perspektive auf, die an ihre Entstehungszeit gebunden ist oder über sie hinaus Geltung beanspruchen kann?

Obwohl der historische Kleist sicher eine Perfektibilisierung der Gesellschaft wünschte, liegt die anhaltende Faszination seines literarischen Werkes jedoch gerade darin, das zu erforschen, was einer Perfektibilisierung der Gesellschaft entgegensteht (besonders etwa in 'Erdbeben', 'Die Verlobung in St. Domingo', 'Michael Kohlhaas' und *Penthesilea*). Dies tut er vor allem, indem er den Konflikt zwischen Individuum und Gesellschaft bis zum schlimmstmöglichen Punkt treibt, d.h. seine Plots kulminieren meistens – mit Ausnahme der beiden letzten Dramen, der Komödien und der Erzählungen 'Die Marquise von O...' und 'Der Zweikampf' – nach vielen dramatischen

Handlungsumschlägen und Verkennungen in einem gewaltsamen Tod oder im Wahnsinn der Protagonisten. *Kein Ort. Nirgends* dagegen ist durch Handlungsarmut (ein geselliger Nachmittag bei Tee und Gespräch), Introspektion, Verschmelzung der Protagonisten und das schließliche Wiedergewinnen einer utopischen Perspektive nach dem Durchgang durch eine scharfe Staatskritik und persönliche Verzweiflung charakterisiert. D.h. aus der Gegenüberstellung der Zerrissenheit und dem Abgrundhaften im historischen Kleist mit den geschlechtsspezifischen Begrenzungen aber auch Stärken der Dichterin Karoline von Günderrode gewinnt Wolfs Text ästhetisch und politisch eine neue Harmonie und eine utopische Perspektive. Die klassischen Tendenzen von Christa Wolf, auf die wiederholt hingewiesen worden ist,[22] gewinnen am Ende die Oberhand über die romantischen Protagonisten in *Kein Ort. Nirgends*.

Kleists Verhältnis zum Staat wird in der Wolfschen Erzählung seiner problematischen nationalistischen Töne entkleidet. Seine Staatskritik wird pointiert von der Perspektive des neuhumanistischen Bildungsbegriffs, der hier als Hebel gegen die verkrustete Bürokratie des DDR-Staates eingesetzt wird. Dieser Bildungsbegriff verschränkt individuelle und soziale Perfektibilität und belebt so die teleologische geschichtsphilosophische Perspektive des in der Realität bankrotten Sozialismus von den gleichen Idealen aus der Zeit um 1800 her, von denen sich auch der Marxismus als libertäre Ideologie herleitet. Die Offenheit im Bezug der inneren Monologe (die auf Kleist, Günderrode, die Erzählerin, die Leserin, oder eine Kombination dieser Positionen referieren kann oder auf alle gleichzeitig zusammen) lädt zur Identifikation der Leserinnen und Leser mit einer Position ein, die eine radikale Staatskritik zu artikulieren sucht, ohne jedoch die utopisch-teleologische Basis des sozialistischen geschichtsphilosophischen Denkens aufzugeben. Dies wäre, so scheint mir, jedoch eine Herausforderung des 21. Jahrhunderts.

Anmerkungen

[1] Vgl. Dennis Tate, *Shifting Perspectives: East German Autobiographical Narratives Before and After the End of the GDR*, Rochester, NY: Camden House, 2007, S. 1-15. Ich danke Steven Howe herzlich für anregende Kommentare zum ersten Entwurf dieses Aufsatzes.

² Vgl. Tate, *Shifting Perspectives*, S. 194-235. Zur Durchlässigkeit der Grenzen zwischen Autorin, Erzählerin und Protagonisten vgl. auch Helga G. Braunbeck, *Autorschaft und Subjektgenese*, Wien: Passagen Verlag, 1992, die darin eine Dekonstruktion des überlieferten Konzepts der Autorschaft sieht. Braunbeck liest die fluktuierende Referenz von Personalpronomen in *Kein Ort. Nirgends* als Betonung der Spaltung und Heterogenität des Subjektes, die das 'auf immer Prozeßhafte der Subjektgenese und die Konstitution des Ichs durch den andern' verweise (S. 154). Zur Verwischung der Grenzen zwischen Autobiographie und Biographie in Wolfs *Kindheitsmuster* und *Kein Ort. Nirgends* vgl. Sandra Frieden, '"Falls es strafbar ist, die Grenzen zu verwischen": Autobiographie, Biographie und Christa Wolf', in Angela Drescher, Hg., *Christa Wolf. Ein Arbeitsbuch. Studien – Dokumente – Bibliographie*, Berlin und Weimar: Aufbau, 1989, S. 121-39.

³ Vgl. zum historischen Kontext der Entstehung dieser Novelle u.a.: Dennis Tate, *The East German Novel*, Bath: Bath University Press, 1984, S. 214. Peter F. Teupe, *Christa Wolfs Kein Ort. Nirgends als Paradigma der DDR-Literatur der siebziger Jahre*, Frankfurt/Main: Lang, 1992, S. 7-48. Jörg Magenau, *Christa Wolf. Eine Biographie*, Reinbek bei Hamburg: rororo, 2002, S. 267-314.

⁴ Christa Wolf, *Kein Ort. Nirgends*, Darmstadt und Neuwied: Luchterhand, 1980, S. 5. Alle weiteren Verweise auf diesen Text werden in Klammern nach der Sigle KON gegeben.

⁵ Vgl. Georg Lukács, 'Die Tragödie Kleists' (1937), in: Helmut Sembdner, Hg., *Heinrich von Kleists Nachruhm. Eine Wirkungsgeschichte in Dokumenten*, München: dtv, 1997, S. 434; vgl. auch Bert Brecht, 'Über Kleists Stück *Der Prinz von Homburg*', in: Sembdner, Hg. *Heinrich von Kleists Nachruhm*, S. 535.

⁶ Vgl. Ernst Fischer, 'Heinrich von Kleist', *Sinn und Form*, 13 (1961), S. 759-844. Hans Mayer, *Heinrich von Kleist: Der geschichtliche Augenblick*, Pfüllingen: Neske, 1962. Siegfried Streller, 'Heinrich von Kleist und Jean-Jacques Rousseau', *Weimarer Beiträge*, 8 (1962), 541-61.

⁷ Vgl. Peter Goldammer, Hg., *Schriftsteller über Kleist*, Berlin und Weimar: Aufbau-Verlag, 1976; vgl. besonders S. 322-401 für Meinungen von Literaten in der DDR zu Kleist seit 1957.

⁸ Paul John Eakin, 'Relational Selves, Relational Lives: Autobiography and the Myth of Autonomy', in: Eakin, *How Our Lives Become Stories. Making Selves*, Ithaca and London: Cornell University Press, 1999, S. 43-98 (hier: S. 43).

⁹ Eakin, 'Relational Selves', S. 56.

¹⁰ Eakin, 'Relational Selves', S. 74; vgl. auch S. 86-98.

¹¹ Ute Brandes, *Zitat und Montage in der neueren DDR-Prosa*, Frankfurt/Main und Bern: Lang, 1984, S. 71 und 79.

[12] Hilda Brown, 'Authentizität und Fiktion. Christa Wolfs Kleistbild', *Kleist-Jahrbuch* (1995), 167-82 (hier: S. 167).

[13] Vgl. Brown, 'Authentizität und Fiktion', S. 171.

[14] Vgl. die Analyse der Wolfschen Montagetechnik bei Brandes, *Zitat und Montage*, S. 61-100.

[15] Brandes, *Zitat und Montage*, S. 74.

[16] Vgl. Heinrich von Kleist, *Sämtliche Werke und Briefe in vier Bänden*, hg. von Ilse-Marie Barth, Klaus Müller-Salget, Stefan Ormanns und Hinrich C. Seeba, Bd. 4: Briefe, Frankfurt/Main: Deutscher Klassiker Verlag, 1997, S. 272. Weitere Verweise auf diesen Briefband werden im Text gegeben als: Kleist, Briefe, gefolgt von der Seitenangabe.

[17] Wilhelm von Humboldt, 'Ideen zu einem Versuch, die Gränzen der Wirksamkeit des Staates zu bestimmen (1792)', in: Wilhelm von Humboldt, *Werke in fünf Bänden*, hg. v. Andreas Flitner und Klaus Giel, Stuttgart: Cotta'sche Buchhandlung, 1969, Bd. 1, S. 64.

[18] Vgl. zum Rousseau-Bezug Kleists die bisher unveröffentlichte Dissertation von Steven Howe, 'Philosophical Inspirations for Violent Fiction and Drama: Heinrich von Kleist and Jean-Jacques Rousseau', University of Exeter, Juni 2010.

[19] Vgl. dazu Christa Wolf, *Die Dimension des Autors: Essays und Aufsätze, Reden und Gespräche 1959–1985*, Darmstadt und Neuwied: Luchterhand, 1987. Im Gespräch mit Therese Hörnigk weist Christa Wolf darauf hin, dass die Wurzeln ihres Konzepts von der gesellschaftlichen Aufgabe von Literatur in der 'frühen Aufklärung' liegen. Therese Hörnigk, *Christa Wolf*, Göttingen: Steidl, 1989, S. 35. Vgl. auch die Untersuchung von Wolfs Selbstverständnis des Schriftstellers als moralische Instanz an Hand der Verwendung religiöser Metaphorik in ihrem Werk, die um Schuld und Sühne kreist, in Ricarda Schmidt, 'Religiöse Metaphorik im Werk Christa Wolfs', in: Ian Wallace, Hg., *Christa Wolf in Perspektive*, Amsterdam: Rodopi, 1994, S. 73-106; vgl. zu *Kein Ort. Nirgends* bes. S. 87-90.

[20] Zur anti-klassischen Wende in der DDR-Literatur der 70er Jahre vgl. Tate, *The East German Novel*, S. 1-11.

[21] Vgl. zu den verschiedenen Konzeptionalisierungen von Geschlecht in Kleists Werk Ricarda Schmidt, 'Performanz und Essentialismus von Geschlecht bei Kleist: eine doppelte Dialektik zwischen Subordination und Handlungsfähigkeit', *German Life and Letters* 64:3 (2011), 374-88.

[22] Vgl. Ricarda Schmidt, 'Truth, Language and Reality in Christa Wolf', in: Martin Kane, Hg., *Socialism and the Literary Imagination. Essays on East German Writers*, New York und Oxford: Berg, 1991, S. 107-123 (hier: S. 121): 'Her optimism, her

need for harmony, her view of women's humanising potential (though argued historically, not biologically), as well as her universally acknowledged great role in contemporary literature, have, paradoxically, brought Wolf closer to the classical Goethe than to the Romantic writers whose insoluble conflicts she has portrayed so sympathetically.' Vgl. auch Tate, *Shitfing Perspectives*, 2007, S. 225-6, der darauf hinweist, dass Wolf sich ihr Leben lang immer wieder Trost von den Klassikern Goethe und Thomas Mann geholt hat, nicht von Büchner, Kleist oder Günderrode, und dass Wolfs *Leibhaftig* sich selbst durch klassische Balance auszeichne.

Georgina Paul

'Aber erzählen läßt sich nichts ohne Zeit': Time and Atemporality in Christa Wolf's Subjectively Authentic Narratives

Starting from Dennis Tate's observations on the increasing complexity of the handling of narrative temporality in Christa Wolf's later fictions, this essay explores the relationship between Wolf's authorial commitment to the time and place in which she lived and the atemporal psychological dimension of 'Tiefe' as characteristic of her 'subjektive Authentizität'. While her fictions up to *Kassandra* characteristically address their own limitations as temporally-bound narratives, they are, I argue, premised upon a dialectical relation between imaginative 'Unbegrenztheit' (Kant) and the coordinates of the real-historical world which is the site of her striving for the realisation of socialist community. With her growing disillusionment vis-à-vis socialism after 1976, the sense of a real-historical site in which the psychic energies associated with 'Tiefe' might be harnessed recedes, and the dimension of atemporality in her narratives becomes dominant.

Dennis Tate's major work on East German autobiographical prose, *Shifting Perspectives* (2007), features a notably lucid account of Christa Wolf's '"subjective authenticity" in practice'.[1] In this context, Tate notes the increasing complexity of Wolf's handling of temporality in her later fictions. While *Kindheitsmuster* (1976) is famously intricate in its treatment of time, the narrative is nonetheless structured as a precise and intelligible interweaving of three temporal planes: the childhood and youth of the figure Nelly from the early 1930s to her release from a TB sanatorium aged seventeen in 1946, the narrator's journey to her home town, now in Poland, over forty-six hours in July 1971, and the composition of the novel in the period between 3 November 1972 and 2 May 1975. By contrast, the temporality of *Sommerstück* (1989) is, Tate observes, less precise. The 'Jahrhundertsommer' treated in the text emerges as an 'amalgam of three summers, 1975, 1976, and 1977' (SP, 218), less a real time than a narrative 'Zeit-Gelände'[2] in which 'everyday rhythms and rituals' in the rural community are posited against the 'time-obsessed futility of the outside world' (SP, 218). *Leibhaftig* (2002) is more disorientating still. The events related within the text take place during a period of crisis spent by the narrator in hospital in 1988 (SP, 222), corresponding to

Wolf's real-life stay in hospital that year for a series of operations for a burst appendix, further complicated by a collapse of her immune system (SP, 220). The text is narrated, however, in a 'timeless present tense' (SP, 222) which reproduces the 'zeitlose[..] Gegenwart'[3] of the narrator's sickness-blighted (semi-)consciousness. The temporal point from which this aetiology of an illness is narrated remains unresolved. The only indication is the temporally imprecise '[v]iel, viel später' and the reference to this time as 'eine Zeit, in der das Wort "Zeit" wieder einen Sinn haben [...] wird' (L, 68), which is the prerequisite for narration to take place at all since 'erzählen läßt sich nichts ohne Zeit' (L, 70). This 'fundamental point about narration' (SP, 223) – that it is a necessarily temporal phenomenon – provides the starting-point here for a series of reflections on time and narrative in Wolf's work which will, building on Tate's observations of 'Zeitlosigkeit' in the later narratives, look in particular at the significance of atemporality within her authorial project.

Wolf's oeuvre can be seen as a continuous struggle with and against time, understood in a range of different ways. In the first place, the 'vierte Dimension der modernen Prosa', the 'Dimension des Autors' (W, IV, 427), which was key to her concept of 'subjektive Authentizität', is, as she describes it in 'Lesen und Schreiben' (1968) by analogy with the fourth dimension in relativity theory, also a temporal dimension. It is the dimension 'der Zeitgenossenschaft, des unvermeidlichen Engagements' (W, IV, 265) through which the author commits herself to the historical situation in which she finds herself, in other words to the place and the time in which she lives: 'Der geographische Ort, an dem ein Autor lebt und *der zugleich ein geschichtlicher Ort ist*, bindet ihn.' (W, IV, emphasis added) This authorial commitment translates into an ethical demand to create a fusion of self with the most difficult and challenging aspects of the times. For her great model, Georg Büchner, writing is, she claims, the medium 'sich mit der Zeit zu verschmelzen in dem Augenblick, da beide ihre dichteste, konfliktreichste und schmerzhafteste Annäherung erfahren' (W, IV, 265) and it is this that guarantees the continuing energy of his work. At the time of writing this major poetological essay, Wolf was optimistic about the compatibility of her technically innovative and subjectively motivated *Prosa* and the socialist society of the GDR whose teleological politics determined a particular relationship to historical time:

Der Autor also, der hier skizziert wird, nutzt die Vorteile unserer Gesellschaft, deren größter es für ihn ist, daß sein Denken nicht von einem Leben in einer antagonistischen Klassengesellschaft geprägt wurde: das heißt, er hat eine wichtige Freiheit, die es ihm zur Pflicht machen sollte, sich weiter in die Zukunft vorauszuwerfen als sein Kollege, der in der Klassengesellschaft lebt. (W, IV, 277)

Over the course of the years, however, her conviction of the 'tiefe Übereinstimmung zwischen dieser Art zu schreiben mit der sozialistischen Gesellschaft' (W, IV, 269) was to be severely tested. By the closing stages of her work on *Kindheitsmuster*, she writes of her 'Grundangst davor, zuviel zu erfahren und in eine Zone der Nichtübereinstimmung gedrängt zu werden' (W, V, 545-6) as far as the socialist society of the GDR is concerned, and her later works, notably *Sommerstück*, the post-unification novel *Leibhaftig*, but also her volume of diary texts, *Ein Tag im Jahr* (2003), reveal her progressive self-distancing from the socialist regime, in particular in the aftermath of the Biermann crisis of November 1976. The existential crisis of the period of the late 1970s is an indication of how fundamentally her sense of historical mission had been shaken. At the same time, her writing, in closely documenting her subjective state over the course of the GDR's last decade, made of her an intellectual figurehead inextricably entwined with a particular era in German literary and public history, not least in her own self-definition – a point to which I shall return below.

When Wolf composed 'Lesen und Schreiben', she was already thinking of writing as an activity directed against time in a more precise way, in so far as the passage of time promotes forgetfulness: 'Sich-Erinnern ist gegen den Strom schwimmen, wie schreiben – gegen den scheinbar natürlichen Strom des Vergessens, anstrengende Bewegung.' (W, IV, 257) Her interest in writing as a medium of personal and collective recollection is related to a third characteristic of the 'Dimension des Autors', alongside 'Zeitgenossenschaft' and 'Engagement', namely 'Tiefe'. This is an explicitly psychological category, and refers, as the opening section of 'Lesen und Schreiben' makes clear, to the potential of the human psyche radically to increase the density of time through mental activity: remembering, anticipating, thinking, making links.

Es ist eine Alltagssituation der modernen Psyche, eine Relativierung und vorübergehende *Aufhebung der objektiven Zeit*, eine durchschnittliche Erfahrung: daß der Augenblick fast unendlich dehnbar ist, daß er eine enorme Menge und

Vielschichtigkeit an Erlebnismöglichkeiten in sich trägt, während fünf Minuten
doch schlichte fünf Minuten geblieben sind. (W, IV, 242, emphasis added)

This interest in the activity of the human psyche – and in a narrative
form which can convey it – corresponds closely to that of modernist
writers such as Virginia Woolf, notably analysed by Erich Auerbach
in the final chapter of his 1953 study, *Mimesis*.[4] Importantly, Wolf
links psychic activity of this kind to a utopian impulse to reach beyond
current circumscribing limitations to self-fulfilment: '[Tiefe] ist das
Resultat von unbefriedigten Bedürfnissen, daraus entstehenden
Spannungen, Widersprüchen und unerhörten Anstrengungen des
Menschen, über sich selbst hinauszuwachsen oder, vielleicht: sich zu
erreichen.' (W, IV, 243) In other words, it is in the mind's depths – not
only in memory, but also in the impetus of desire which informs *what*
memories surface in relation to any given historical moment or
contemplated subject-matter – that the energy source is to be found
which will propel the individual forward on her or his historical path.
In this sense, to engage with psychic complexity is, for Wolf, a moral
imperative for the committed writer and an aspect of 'Zeitgenossenschaft' and 'Engagement': 'Wenn die Gesellschaft diese massenhaft
auftretende Fähigkeit nicht genügend zu nutzen weiß, langweilen wir
uns. Und das wäre nicht nur langweilig, sondern besorgniserregend.'
(W, IV, 242)

Precisely the engagement with the 'Vielschichtigkeit an Erlebnismöglichkeiten' within any limited temporal span poses a key challenge for Wolf's narrative project. In the 1973 conversation with Hans
Kaufmann, which together with 'Selbstinterview' and 'Lesen und
Schreiben' forms the third text in a triad of poetological statements
following the breakthrough to the form of *Nachdenken über Christa
T.*, Wolf speaks with palpable excitement (and in language borrowed
from her reading of theoretical physics) about her discovery of an
'eingreifende Schreibweise' in which the writer does not construct a
mechanistic plot ('Fabel'), but rather opens herself to the movement
both of her subject-matter and of her own subjectivity in the course of
writing:

Plötzlich hängt alles mit allem zusammen und ist in Bewegung; für 'gegeben'
angenommene Objekte werden auflösbar und offenbaren die in ihnen vergegen-
ständlichten gesellschaftlichen Beziehungen (nicht mehr jenen hierarchisch
geordneten gesellschaftlichen Kosmos, in dem Menschenpartikel auf soziologisch

oder ideologisch vorgegebenen Bahnen sich bewegen oder von dieser erwarteten Bewegung abweichen) [...]. (W, IV, 409)

It is important for Wolf that her form of writing be understood as a dynamic *process* rather than judged as an end-product; she wants it to be seen as a 'Vorgang, der das Leben unaufhörlich begleitet, es mitbestimmt, zu deuten sucht; als Möglichkeit, intensiver in der Welt zu sein, als Steigerung und Konzentration von Denken, Sprechen, Handeln' (W, IV, 408-9). This dynamic, processual aspect is central to all of Wolf's writing from *Nachdenken* on and must be taken into account if one is to do justice to her project. However, in moving beyond conventional plot-construction to an attempted reproduction in narrative form of the dynamics of the human psyche ('Tiefe'), she is confronted by the problem of how to represent what is potentially boundless. As Peter Brooks has noted, '[plot] is the very organizing line, the thread of design, that makes narrative possible because finite and comprehensible'.[5] By contrast, the dynamic interaction of the psyche's functions at any given moment tests the possibilities of representation in finite narrative form. As Wolf's narrator exclaims in *Nachdenken über Christa T.*: 'Wie man es erzählen kann, so ist es nicht gewesen. [...] Allein, daß man trennen muß und hintereinanderreihen, um es erzählbar zu machen, was in Wirklichkeit miteinander vermischt ist bis zur Unlösbarkeit.' (W, II, 77) In *Kindheitsmuster* there is a similar acknowledgement of the limitations of linear narrative:

> Im Idealfall sollten die Strukturen des Erlebens sich mit den Strukturen des Erzählens decken. Dies wäre, was angestrebt wird: phantastische Genauigkeit. Aber es gibt die Technik nicht, die es gestatten würde, ein unglaublich verfilztes Geflecht, dessen Fäden nach den strengsten Gesetzen incinandergeschlungen sind, in die lineare Sprache zu übertragen, ohne es ernstlich zu verletzen. (W, II, 396)

By the time Wolf came to write *Kassandra* (1983), she was explicitly seeking the ideal of the narrative 'Gewebe' (W, VII, 12). In this work, the simultaneity aspired to is reflected at least in part in the relational construction of the different components of the text (the *Voraussetzungen einer Erzählung* and the narrative *Erzählung*) which can be apprehended as 'deepening' the linear narrative of the *Erzählung* itself through cross-referencing, counter-thoughts, and, again, acknowledgement of the shortcomings of the narrative form: 'Empfinde die geschlossene Form der Kassandra-Erzählung als Widerspruch zu der fragmentarischen Struktur, aus der sie sich für mich eigentlich zusammensetzt. Der Widerspruch kann nicht gelöst, nur benannt werden.' (W, VII, 154)

Interestingly, these recurrent moments in Wolf's texts where the limitations of the narrative form are addressed have the rhetorical function of imaginatively extending the text beyond the stated limits. Her readers, encouraged to consult their own psychological complexity by analogy with the processes of remembering and forgetting set out in her works, can begin to apprehend what the temporally bound narrative, constrained by the linearity of language, has not been able to say. These moments act as incitements to think beyond the text, to recreate and also to substitute its operations with the operations of the readers' own individual psyches. They behave, then, like the 'Wortgemälde' described by the theoretical physicist Werner Heisenberg and cited by Wolf in 'Lesen und Schreiben' whose task it is 'im Geist des Hörenden durch Bild und Gleichnis gewisse Beziehungen hervorzurufen, die in die gewollte Richtung weisen, ohne ihn durch eindeutige Formulierungen zum Präzisieren eines bestimmten Gedankengangs zwingen zu wollen' (W, IV, 267).

A similar function, albeit more radical, can be attributed to the moments in Wolf's texts where temporality breaks down altogether. The most striking of these is the closing paragraph of *Kindheitsmuster*, as the narrator – having finally emerged as an 'Ich' after over five hundred pages in which she has been split between the second- and third-person pronouns – paradoxically renounces the bounded unified state which the first-person pronoun implies in favour of a waking dream of figural shift and change:

> Nachts werde ich – ob im Wachen, ob im Traum – den Umriß eines Menschen sehen, der sich in fließenden Übergängen unaufhörlich verwandelt, durch den andere Menschen, Erwachsene, Kinder, ungezwungen hindurchgehen. Ich werde mich kaum verwundern, daß dieser Umriß auch ein Tier sein mag, ein Baum, ein Haus sogar, in dem jeder, der will, ungehindert ein und aus geht. Halbbewußt werde ich erleben, wie das schöne Wachgebilde immer tiefer in den Traum abtreibt in immer neuen, nicht mehr in Worte faßbare [sic] Gestalten, die ich zu erkennen glaube. Sicher, beim Erwachen die Welt der festen Körper wieder vorzufinden, werde ich mich der Traumerfahrung überlassen, mich nicht auflehnen gegen die Grenzen des Sagbaren. (W, V, 594)

This passage rewards analysis in the larger context of Wolf's oeuvre. The dynamism of the 'Umriß eines Menschen [...], der sich in fließenden Übergängen unaufhörlich verwandelt' is reminiscent of the images of perpetual transformation endorsed in *Nachdenken über Christa T.*:

> Daß alles, was erst einmal 'dasteht' – dieses Wort schon! –, so schwer wieder in Bewegung zu bringen ist, daß man also schon vorher versuchen muß, es am Leben zu halten, während es noch entsteht, in einem selbst. Es muß andauernd entstehen, das ist es. Man darf und darf es nicht dahin kommen lassen, daß es fertig wird. (W, II, 187)

That the 'Umriß' is also capable of changing shape to become 'ein Tier [...], ein Baum, ein Haus sogar' recalls the similarly positively connoted 'Himmelslandschaften' of *Juninachmittag*, 'denn dort oben hatten sie den Trick heraus, eins aus dem anderen hervorgehen, eins ins andere übergehen zu lassen: das Kamel in den Löwen, das Nashorn in den Tiger und [...] die Giraffe in den Pinguin' (W, III, 91) which in context alludes also to the stream-of-consciousness narration and its creative connectivity from one idea and scene to the next. Also very striking in the *Kindheitsmuster* passage is the permeability of the boundaries of the self, as other people or even 'jeder, der will' pass 'ungezwungen' and 'ungehindert' through the lines of the 'Umriß' or in and out through the self-conceived-as-house. It therefore reads as a fantasy of not being exclusively self-contained as an individual any more. It is emphatically not a bad dream about invasion by others – the 'Wachgebilde' is registered not as nightmarish, but as 'schön' – and as such it presupposes not feeling vulnerable in being open to others. Is it then a vision of achieved community, with the permeable psyche as a living space – 'Haus' – in which others are accommodated? This vision is complemented by Kassandra's red-and-black dream, a similarly fluid moment which follows immediately upon Kassandra's attainment finally of a sense of belonging in the 'Wir' of the Skamander community. Here, life and death interpenetrate one another in a way which is not antagonistic, but 'schön', in a manner likened to the element which figures eternal flux and unboundedness, the sea:

> Farben sah ich, rot und schwarz, Leben und Tod. Sie durchdrangen einander, kämpften nicht miteinander, wie ich es, sogar im Traum, erwartet hätte. Andauernd ihre Gestalt verändernd, ergaben sie andauernd neue Muster, die unglaublich schön sein könnten. Sie warn [sic] wie Wasser, wie ein Meer. (W, VII, 369)

The final phrase of *Kindheitsmuster*, 'mich nicht auflehnen gegen die Grenzen des Sagbaren', reads as an expression of relief and release. Coming at the end of a long text which took many years and a very considerable self-discipline to write and yet which apparently fails in its original aim of attaining psychic completeness, this waking dream figures not closure, as might be expected, but the expansion of the psychic energies outwards, beyond the limitations of the 'sayable' and thus also beyond the constraints of temporality as the domain of linear narrative language. As such, it figures the movement of the psychic energy beyond the compass of the real-existing, now completed writing project, reaffirming a commitment to the continuing 'unerhörten Anstrengungen [...], über sich selbst hinauszuwachsen' which Wolf associates with the atemporal dimension of 'Tiefe'.

It is also notable, though, that the narrator of *Kindheitsmuster* only allows herself to drift off into the waking dream in the confident knowledge 'beim Erwachen die Welt der festen Körper wieder vorzufinden'. Presupposed is, then, an oscillating movement or dialectical relation between the vision of the waking dream and the 'Welt der festen Körper' in a manner reminiscent of the structure of the Kantian sublime. The experience of the sublime, in Kant's account, is an imaginative projection into 'Unbegrenzheit' beyond the reach of what can be apprehended by the senses,[6] but from which the 'Vernunft' returns enriched by the idea of a non-sensible totality, for Kant a moral category.[7] This is helpful for thinking about the goal of Wolf's writing. The imagined totality towards which it is directed is the attainment of 'Selbsterkenntnis' or self-knowledge, in turn conceptualised as the moral basis for achieving harmonious human community, as set out most clearly in the trajectory of the *Kassandra-Erzählung*. While Wolf's texts characteristically address the extent to which they fall short of the goal, they are nonetheless to be understood as a thought-challenge played out in a temporally-bound narrative language which both potentially extends the imagination of the reader to encompass the *idea* of this totality *and* refers the 'Vernunft' thus extended back to the coordinates of the palpable historical world (space and time) which is the site of the striving for the realisation of its vision.

Thinking about Wolf's project in these terms illuminates both how idealist it was, in the philosophical meaning of the term, at least before her disillusionment with the regime set in, and also, at the same time,

how predicated it was on Wolf's commitment to the GDR as a historical territory (time and place) at least notionally committed to the
realisation of harmonious human community. The 'Welt der festen
Körper' (W, V, 594), in so far as it is a *political* world in which it is to
be imagined that one day real bodies will live together in harmonious
community in real time, becomes less tangible as Wolf's original
sense of unity with the goals of socialist society goes into abeyance
after 1976 and very markedly after the writing of *Kassandra*, in
which, under cover of the allegory, she explored her own movement
away from the 'Übereinstimmung mit den Herrschenden' (W, VII,
298). This in turn begins to point towards an explanation as to why the
handling of time becomes more complex in the works of the 1980s
and after. The energy generated by the text becomes less directed as
the coordinates of time and space within which its force might be
recontained and therefore harnessed become less specific.

   The deterritorialisation of Wolf's project is signalled by the title of
Kein Ort. Nirgends (1979), Wolf's initial response to her falling-out
with the Party after the Biermann protest. The text seeks to retrieve its
relation to historical time by projecting into an unknown future when
its vision might be taken up again, the narrative 'wir' asynchronically
bracketing the 19th century writers Kleist and Günderrode with the
modern narrator: 'Begreifen, daß wir ein Entwurf sind – vielleicht, um
verworfen, vielleicht, um wieder aufgegriffen zu werden.' (W, VI,
105) In the *Kassandra-Erzählung*, it is its mythical status which
allows for the exploration of the attainment of harmonious human
community in the Skamandros caves at the narrative close, but notably
this is only realisable in a 'Zeitloch' (W, VII, 369) on the margins of a
warring society in the period immediately prior to its collapse. The
hope for a future society which would write the values of this
community on its banners now seems very fragile. *Sommerstück*
focuses on Wolf's real-life model for this community, the circle of
friends and family who gathered in the Mecklenburg countryside in
the late 1970s as a form of retreat from the vicissitudes of the political
present in Berlin. Tate, as quoted above, sees in the diffuse and
unspecific temporality of the narrative the positing of 'everyday
rhythms and rituals' against the 'time-obsessed futility of the outside
world' (SP, 218). But it could equally well be seen as a representation
of the suspension of real-historical time in Wolf's utopian
imagination, a reiteration of the idea that community is only possible

within a 'Zeitloch'. For the idyll of the fictional summer under blue skies and bright sunshine is tempered from the outset by the retrospective awareness of its temporal boundedness:

> Aber wirklich geglaubt haben wir nicht, daß unsere Zeit begrenzt war. Jetzt, da alles zu Ende ist, läßt sich auch diese Frage beantworten. Jetzt, da Luise abgereist, Bella uns für immer verlassen hat, Steffi tot ist, die Häuser zerstört sind, herrscht über das Leben wieder die Erinnerung. (W, X, 11)

The past-tense narration of *Sommerstück* emanates from a standpoint in a sober and disillusioned future following the destruction of the constituent elements of the summer idyll it depicts – the hospitable houses, the circle of friendship – but it also, from that disillusioned standpoint, examines the destructive potential already contained within the supposedly idyllic moment, the jealousies and tensions between the characters and the weaknesses within them which mirror on the personal psychological level the disintegrative tendencies observed in the larger village community. Wolf's historical pessimism is gathering pace in this book.

Leibhaftig, which deals with events in Wolf's biography from the year 1988, but from a post-unification perspective, is the most radical of Wolf's texts in terms of its handling of narrative temporality. It is also the work which engages most uncompromisingly with her psychological investment in the GDR. While the narrative trajectory reproduces the progress of an illness, from delivery into hospital by ambulance in the opening pages to recovery at the close, so that it retains a sense of temporal progression for the reader, this real-historical aspect is of lesser importance than the focus of the present-tense narration on the suffering narrator's disengagement from the temporal dimension: 'Alle meine Zeitlichkeit ist in Zeitlosigkeit versunken' (L, 69). Metaphorically collapsing the underground spaces of the hospital in which the operation theatres are located, the subterranean passageways beneath the city into which the narrator ventures in her anaesthetic-induced dreams, the diseased inner organs of the narrator's body, and classical images of the labyrinth and Hades (L, 178), the text is a complex account of an 'Abfahrt' (L, 6) into the depths of memory in which 'die Zeitebenen einander heillos durchdringen' (L, 59). 'Tiefe', the perennial concern of Wolf's narratives, in this work becomes 'bösartig' (see L, 132), and the venture into atemporality now figures not as a moment of vision and a source of psychic energy for the continuing transformation of the real world so much as a withdrawal from the real world altogether, a drive towards self-dissolution (L, 129) and death. The reason for this is to be found in its historical orientation. According to Wolf's 1968 description, 'Tiefe', although concerned with memory, is utopian and forward-looking; it is 'das Resultat von […] unerhörten Anstrengungen des Menschen, über sich selbst hinauszuwachsen oder, vielleicht: sich zu erreichen' (W, IV, 243). In *Leibhaftig*, by contrast, Wolf's orientation is backward-looking. This is a late work of lament for the life lived, amongst other things expressing the fear that the life has been lived in vain because invested in the wrong object. The GDR, not just as territory, but in terms of Wolf's image of it as a society whose goals she had once supported, is here profoundly mourned. It is described as the 'Hoffnungs- und Menschheitsstadt' which was or was to become the narrator's 'eigentliche Heimat' (L, 136), but of course signally failed to live up to the hopes invested in it. It is, in words derived from Goethe, something once dearly prized ('Ich besaß es doch einmal / was so köstlich ist') and never to be forgotten ('Daß man doch zu seiner Qual / Nimmer es vergißt', L, 99) which is nevertheless both devilish ('ob es auch einen Teufel gibt, der stets das Gute will und stets das Böse schafft?', L, 119) and a 'Vergiftung' which must be purged from the body (L, 93). The process of healing which the text ultimately records is premised on the acceptance of life itself as the purpose of living (L, 164) and so by implication the renunciation of all historical teleology.

The closing sentences of *Leibhaftig* allude to Ingeborg Bachmann's poem 'Enigma', the opening lines of which read: 'Nichts mehr wird kommen'.[8] In many respects *Leibhaftig* has all the hallmarks of closure in terms of Wolf's oeuvre. But there was the unfinished business of the novel which was to deal with the disclosure of Wolf's involvement with the Stasi as an IM, promised in 1993 and finally published in 2010 under the title *Stadt der Engel oder The Overcoat of Dr. Freud*. This long autobiographical work ends with a dream-like flight above the bay of Los Angeles accompanied by the guardian angel Angelina, not dissimilar to the dream of flying above the city of Berlin with the 'Botin' Kora Bachmann in *Leibhaftig* with its implication of achieved aloofness from the messy processes of history. There is a note of finality here: 'Das unvergleichliche Gefühl des Fliegens, Angelina neben mir. Eine Arbeit ist getan, Angelina […].

Eine vorläufige Arbeit ist zu einem vorläufigen Schluß gekommen.'[9] Wolf is, it seems, signing off her oeuvre here with a flight into the atemporal boundlessness of the ocean and the sky, definitively beyond the 'Grenzen des Sagbaren'.

Notes

[1] Dennis Tate, *Shifting Perspectives. East German Autobiographical Narratives Before and After the End of the GDR*, Rochester, N.Y.: Camden House, 2007, Chapter 6. Subsequent references follow the abbreviation SP in parentheses.

[2] Christa Wolf, *Sommerstück*, in *Werke*, ed. Sonja Hilzinger, Munich: Luchterhand, 1999-2001 (12 vols.), x, p. 84. See SP, 218. Unless otherwise stated, all subsequent references to texts by Wolf will be from *Werke*, indicated by the abbreviation W and followed by the relevant volume and page number(s) in parentheses.

[3] Christa Wolf, *Leibhaftig*, Munich: Luchterhand, 2002, p. 76. Subsequent references follow the abbreviation L in parentheses.

[4] See Erich Auerbach's analysis of Virginia Woolf's handling of time in relation to consciousness in *To the Lighthouse* in Auerbach, *Mimesis. The Representation of Reality in Western Literature*, trans. Willard R. Trask, Princeton and Oxford: Princeton University Press, 2003, pp. 525-53. Jochen Vogt cites the passage from Woolf's novel analysed by Auerbach as exemplary of narrative 'Zeitdehnung' – Jochen Vogt, *Aspekte erzählender Prosa. Eine Einführung in Erzähltechnik und Romantheorie*, Opladen: Westdeutscher Verlag, 1990, pp. 102-3.

[5] Peter Brooks, *Reading for the Plot. Design and Intention in Narrative*, Cambridge, MA: Harvard University Press, 1984, p. 4.

[6] Immanuel Kant, *Kritik der Urteilskraft*, 1. Teil, 1. Abschnitt, 2. Buch 'Analytik des Erhabenen', paragraph 23, at: http://gutenberg.spiegel.de/buch/3507/32 (accessed 12 July 2011).

[7] 'Diese Idee des Übersinnlichen aber, die wir zwar nicht weiter bestimmen, [...] sondern nur *denken* können, wird in uns durch einen Gegenstand erweckt, dessen ästhetische Beurteilung die Einbildungskraft bis zu ihrer Grenze [...] anspannt, indem sie sich auf dem Gefühle einer Bestimmung desselben gründet, welche das Gebiet der ersteren gänzlich überschreitet (dem moralischen Gefühl), in Ansehung dessen die Vorstellung des Gegenstandes als subjektiv-zweckmäßig beurteilt wird.' Kant, *Kritik der Urteilskraft*, 'Allgemeine Anmerkung zur Exposition der ästhetischen reflektierenden Urteile', at: http://gutenberg.spiegel.de/buch/3507/39 (accessed 12 July 2011).

[8]   Ingeborg Bachmann, 'Enigma', in *Werke*, ed. Christine Koschel, Inge von Weidenbaum and Clemens Münster, Munich, Zurich: Piper, 1978 (4 vols.), I, p. 171.

[9] Christa Wolf, *Stadt der Engel oder The Overcoat of Dr. Freud*, Berlin: Suhrkamp, 2010, p. 413.

Renate Rechtien

From *Vergangenheitsbewältigung* to Living with Ghosts: Christa Wolf's *Kindheitsmuster* and *Leibhaftig*

This chapter examines two works of Christa Wolf that engage with Germany's history at different points in the author's life: *Kindheitsmuster* (1976) explores the country's fascist past with a view to conducting *Vergangenheitsbewältigung*, a project that ultimately fails. *Leibhaftig* (2002) re-engages with memory of fascism, but places it in relation to how the GDR and its demise are to be remembered from a post-unification perspective. A complex memory text that probes the material as well as the psychological foundations on which East German society rested, *Leibhaftig* portrays East Berlin as an uncanny underground world of unacknowledged and repressed memories. Pervaded by imagery of human pain and suffering, the narrative re-constructs GDR history as a 'Krankheitsfall', confronting the reader with questions about the denials, displacements, and deformations that contributed to the state's demise.

Anne Fuchs has argued that the normative framework of *Vergangenheitsbewältigung* which dominated postwar West German collective memory discourses until recent years ultimately established a 'false dichotomy between repression and mastery'. Often based on a simplified version of the Freudian model to 'remember, understand, and integrate' a repressed past, West Germany's canonised discourse of contrition sanctified the duty to remember, but it 'demonised forgetting'.[1] By contrast, on the basis of the doctrine of antifascism, East Germans tended to be exculpated of their guilt as early as the 1950s, with collective remembrance foregrounding images of the antifascist hero as victim.[2] Since unification, such divergent memories have of course been negotiated and renegotiated alongside memory of the GDR and of unification. In combination with issues arising from memories of the suffering of Germans themselves during the war, a veritable memory boom has, since the early 1990s, resulted in the pluralisation of German memory discourses, but also in an intensification of highly politicised debates about the status of some memories in relation to others.[3]

In literary remembering since the early 1990s, questions about literature's capacity to provide an alternative space for the representation, negotiation and mediation of historical experience have assumed a new significance. One manifestation of this has been a paradigm shift in contemporary German culture from the forward-looking literary perspectives associated with the older discourse of contrition to a preoccupation with death, decay, the uncanny, and the spectral.[4] Especially members of the older generation of writers who are about to be absorbed into history have tended to brush politicised memory discourses aimed at achieving normalisation against the grain, exploring that which history has forgotten and left unresolved. Two works by Christa Wolf that engage with Germany's national history at very different points in the author's life illustrate this paradigm shift in a number of important regards, and these will be explored in this chapter.

With her major autobiographical work *Kindheitsmuster* (1976), Wolf was one of the first authors in the GDR to accept responsibility for the burden of history by way of *Vergangenheitsbewältigung*. Aesthetically complex and a hybrid text that blurs the boundaries between autobiography proper and fiction, *Kindheitsmuster* infringed on significant taboos in GDR culture and society at the time of its publication,[5] but it also questioned the inherent optimism of West Germany's model of contrition. After all, the project of integrating the forgotten childhood self into the writing subject's present identity fails; for a variety of reasons, including self-censorship, self-rejection and above all self-alienation, the gulf that separates present from past self ultimately proves to be unbridgeable.

Wolf's *Leibhaftig* (2002), written twenty-six years later, re-engages with memory of fascism, but this is now placed in relation also to issues of how the GDR and its demise are to be remembered from a post-unification perspective. Set around the time when GDR socialism collapsed, the leitmotif of this narrative is that of a journey into the underworld, into Hades. Transported through a life-threatening illness into a labyrinthine world where dreams, hallucinations, and fantasies have replaced all certainties about herself and the historical events unfolding around her, the narrator is now confronted at the ultimate threshold between life and death no longer with a Freudian project, namely that of gaining self-understanding and identity, but with the utterly existential question of the survival of the subject. With its emphasis on topographical motifs that revolve around ruins, decay and destruction, its labyrinthine structure, and a pervading sense of suffering and corporeality, Wolf's narrative re-envisions the history of twentieth-century Germany as an age of hell. Following the emphasis on image constellations or 'Denkbilder' in Walter Benjamin's topographical model of historical representation, *Leibhaftig* is an allegorical text that traces human experience as it becomes manifest in memories that, as fleeting moments or fragments, permit only a fractured sense of historical insight and understanding.[6] Multivalent and multiperspectival, the process of remembering is here envisioned as one that is involuntary and contingent, characterised by ambivalence, uncertainty, and ambiguity.

Where the history of the GDR is concerned specifically, it is argued here, *Leibhaftig* constructs alternative images to those which have been predominant in German cultural memory and in particular in the media since the early 1990s. Especially in German television, representations of the GDR have consisted of a polarised and unchanging repertoire. On the one hand, these are pictures of euphoric Germans celebrating the fall of the Wall, and on the other hand images of the GDR as an 'Unrechtsstaat' (illegitimate state) that is part of an 'evil empire' in the grasp of the Stasi.[7] As a result of Germany's unification processes, furthermore, the history of the GDR has increasingly been erased also from the topography of united Germany, where it has in many instances been ranked alongside the 'burdened landscapes' of the fascist past.[8] Hence, Wolf is clearly also concerned in *Leibhaftig* with an anchoring of the GDR in united Germany's history as a concrete place that was home to its citizens; as a consequence, its loss is declared the subject of mourning.

When Wolf embarked on her major autobiographical project to reconstruct her childhood during the Third Reich, she was realising a long-held desire. As Sonja Hilzinger has noted, work on this aspect of her biography may in fact be traced back to the mid-1950s,[9] but had persistently been postponed as a result of the vagaries of GDR cultural policy and resulting processes of self-censorship. By the early 1970s, the project appeared to assume a new urgency for the author who was concerned about ongoing processes of alienation and self-alienation in the GDR that she believed were the result of the continuing obfuscation of the past by members of her generation and the delegation of responsibility for German fascism to the Federal Republic of Germany.[10] On account of the regime's tight grip on cultural production, writers of her generation had a moral duty to fulfil insofar as they could play a role in promoting an honest dialogue between the generations. Hence *Kindheitsmuster* was conceived not as a work whose subject matter is the past, but rather the present: Wolf thought of it as a 'Gegenwartsbuch'[11] that would acknowledge the 'Riß, der durch die Zeit geht' by fostering a 'Gedächtnis an uns selbst', 'an das, was wir getan haben, an das, was uns zugestoßen ist' (KM, 14). As one of the media of memory, literature can play a fruitful role in such an undertaking, since, as Helmut Peitsch has observed, its specific quality is an ability, 'on the one hand, to cut through other forms and practices of remembering and, on the other, to make these forms and practices of social memory its object of study.'[12]

The complexity and aesthetic sophistication of Wolf's *Kindheitsmuster* certainly reflect intentions of this kind. The narrative comprises a complex mixture of personal memories, critical self-observations and self-reflections alongside carefully researched historical facts and essayistic observations about the nature of memory and the intricacies of conveying its vagaries through the inadequate medium of language. As a text, it defies conventional genre boundaries and has been variously designated as novel, autobiographical novel, fictional autobiography, or a hybrid autobiographical form. In contrast to classical autobiography, the narrator of *Kindheitsmuster*, who is closely based on the author herself, but not identical with her, no longer acts as a guarantor of truth who tells her life-story chronologically and who avails herself of history as material that can be moulded by a bounded, coherent and self-knowing subject. Influenced in particular by Ingeborg Bachmann's dismissal of literary forms that locate the subject in history rather than tracing history within subjectivity,[13] Wolf's construction of her life-history makes subjectivity problematic, substituting her principle of 'phantastische Genauigkeit' (KM, 396) for the self-knowing and self-assured author of classical autobiography and his or her assertion of veracity. As her narrator explains, 'phantastische Genauigkeit' aimed at developing the narrative means that would transpose lived experience into literature, resulting '[i]m Idealfall' in a text where 'die Strukturen des Erlebens sich mit den Strukturen des Erzählens decken' (KM, 396).

The memory landscape constructed in *Kindheitsmuster* is indebted to the modernist figurations of memory developed by Freud in his *Das Unbehagen in der Kultur* and by Walter Benjamin in his *Berliner Kindheit um neunzehnhundert*, and Wolf here clearly first experimented with memory work which is conceived of in topographical terms as an excavation of layers of experience with a view to interpreting, understanding and re-integrating a forgotten or repressed past for the sake of healing. As the very opening lines of *Kindheitsmuster* assert, following William Faulkner's famous idea that the past is never dead: 'Das Vergangene ist nicht tot; es ist nicht einmal vergangen. Wir trennen es von uns ab und stellen uns fremd' (KM, 13). In accordance with Freud and Benjamin's psychotopographical and fragmentary approach to the past, Wolf makes use in *Kindheitsmuster* of geological imagery, making reference to 'verkapselte Höhlen', 'gut versiegelt[e] Hohlräume' the walls of which may become 'morsch und brüchig' over time, and which the individual spends much energy sealing and resealing over time (KM, 109), as well as to 'Abgründe der Erinnerung' (KM, 109), which her narrator aims 'auf den Grund zu gehen' (KM, 32), and 'Gesteinsmassen' that have to be moved (KM, 224). In her essay 'Lesen und Schreiben', Wolf had four years earlier already used similar imagery when she coined the term 'Medaillons' of memory that in her view foster a tendency to trade in clichés and neat fables where individual as well as collective memory is concerned. Such ossified images of the past, she had warned there,

> sind für die Erinnerung, was die verkalkten Kavernen für den Tuberkulosekranken, was die Vorurteile für die Moral: ehemals aktive, jetzt aber durch Einkapselung stillgelegte Lebensflecken [...] man muß viel vergessen und viel umdenken und umdeuten, ehe man sich immer und überall ins rechte Licht gerückt hat [...]. Auch ich habe meine Medaillons.[14]

It is clear, then, that the work of Benjamin provided at least some inspiration for Wolf's undertaking to work up the history of the Third Reich from an aesthetic and moral perspective which was to go against the grain of collective forgetting in German culture. As Lutz Köpnick has pointed out, this dimension has hitherto been grossly neglected in criticism of the work, resulting in insufficient attention being paid to its decidedly modernist ambition to rescue 'Erfahrungsspielräum[e] in einer von fatalem Erfahrungsverlust geprägten Zeit'.[15]

Nevertheless, the basic underlying premise of her childhood autobiography remained indebted to the Freudian idea of rescuing a forgotten self with a view to integrating her into an identity in the present. For this purpose, the subject is split into three 'selves' who each represent a crucial stage in the life to be unearthed, 'Ich, du, sie, in Gedanken ineinanderschwimmend, sollen im ausgesprochenen Satz einander entfremdet werden' (KM, 13). These three layers of self correspond to a division of the spatio-temporal dimensions of the text into three phases marking the process of self-excavation. An evocation of both the Proustian *mémoire volontaire* and *mémoire involontaire* in the course of a journey back to the place of childhood are further dimensions of the text that, in the words of Barbara Kosta, have made it into 'a working station, a fabric, an arrangement of dialogues with herself; the author becomes a post-modern *bricoleur*'.[16] As Elizabeth Dye has observed, 'within this complex interplay of distant and recent past and the narrative present, it is the fallibility of memory itself which drives the plot.'[17] At the same time, however, Wolf's notion of the subject by no means sits comfortably with postmodernist conceptions of an utterly fragmented subjectivity. Rather, it is the very tension created in the text between the fragmentation of the subject for the sake of gaining self-understanding through distance from personal memories on the one hand, and the hope that the remembered and the remembering self may eventually become reunited in a coherent and authentic subjectivity in the present on the other, which sustain the inner drama of the text.

The decision to write autobiographically about her childhood during the Third Reich was evidently beset for Wolf by fears, but also by a good measure of resentment over what she refers to as 'Entblößung der Eingeweide' (KM, 264) for the sake of remembrance. Her narrator bemoans as an unjust fate or a poisoned chalice 'diese Zeit, da der Schreibende, ehe er zur Beschreibung fremder Wunden übergehen darf, die Wunde seines eigenen Unrechts vorweisen muß' (KM, 251). But the moral task of conducting memory work from the perspective of personal experience is understood as constructing an important counter-site to historical meta-narratives and national memory projects that, so the author asserted already in the 1970s, instrumentalise memory for the purpose of political identity projects, processes which are viewed by Wolf as fostering collective 'forgetting' (KM, 19). The site of both personal and cultural memory, she declares, must consequently be the individual, not the collective: 'Es ist der Mensch, der sich erinnert – nicht das Gedächtnis' (KM 177).

The self-imposed task of conducting what amounts to an archaeological excavation of herself through a dialogue with her own consciousness was clearly seen as a hazardous one that forced Wolf to confront what were then deep-seated and deeply internalised social and cultural as well as personal taboos. Following her commitment to the principle of subjective authenticity, it meant that the author had to carry the burden of history representatively for the nation as whole, whilst straddling the fine line between public self-exposure and preservation of her own and her family's integrity. Wolf's narrative bears witness to the challenges which confronted her at the time in this regard:

> Man kann entweder schreiben oder glücklich sein. In der Nacht vor diesem Hitzetag, vor dem kurzen Morgenschlaf, als dir alles klar war, sahst du auch ein, daß man unerschrocken und zugleich behutsam würde vorgehen müssen, um die geologischen Schichten […] abzutragen. Mit 'kundiger Hand', dachtest du ironisch, die sich nicht fürchten dürfte, Schmerz zuzufügen, wohl aber, es überflüssigerweise zu tun. Und daß nicht nur diese Hand: daß auch die Person, der sie angehört, aus der Schutzfarbe werde heraustreten müssen und sichtbar sein. Denn man erwirbt sich Rechte auf ein so beschaffenes Material, indem man sich mit ins Spiel bringt und den Einsatz nicht zu niedrig hält. (KM, 233)

Aesthetically, Wolf's autobiographical memory project has without doubt been a success, and a sizeable body of criticism in Germany and beyond has testified to this over time. But as a writer in the communist half of the divided German nation, she was clearly in considerable tension during the early 1970s between her commitment to the socialist cause and her desire to break taboos and communicate more openly, especially about the longer-term implications of childhood socialisation under fascism for the foundations on which the GDR state rested. In dialogue with herself, Wolf's narrator shows an acute awareness of the moral rigour she ought to show for the sake of her children and grandchildren in this regard:

> Was heißt das: sich verändern? Ohne Wahn auskommen lernen. Den Blicken der Kinder nicht ausweichen müssen, die unsere Generation treffen, wenn – selten genug – von 'früher' die Rede ist: Früher, in den dreißiger, früher, in den fünfziger Jahren (KM, 218).

However, whilst she tests the boundaries between what can be said now and what has to remain 'sealed' or silenced memory in this respect, she fails to resolve what presents itself to her as a paradox: 'Falls es strafbar ist, die Grenzen zu verwischen… Falls es strafbar ist, auf die Grenzen zu pochen… Falls es stimmt, daß es niemandem gelingt, das eine zu tun und das andere nicht zu lassen…' (KM, 110).

One of the obstacles to remembrance turns out to be the realisation that her commitment to 'authenticity' and moral integrity is considerably undermined by the fact that the indoctrination she experienced as a child in a totalitarian fascist state with its authoritarian patterns of behaviour and thought ran so deep that an 'authentic' self in the present who is free from the lasting impact of this socialisation is not available; hence the 'Hang zur Authentizität' (KM, 240) of the narrator in the present is ultimately outweighed by her realisation that the child she might have become, one she might have been able to love in the present, was irretrievably lost a long time ago:

> Vielleicht sollte es dir leid tun um das Kind, das sich damals verabschiedete: von niemandem gekannt und als dasjenige geliebt, das es hätte sein können. Das sein Geheimnis mitnahm: das Geheimnis von den Wänden, in die es eingeschlossen war, die es abtastete, um jene Lücke zu finden, die ihm etwas weniger Angst machte als die anderen – aber doch auch noch Angst genug. (KM, 339)

Ultimately, furthermore, it proves impossible from the perspective of the moral integrity the narrator covets in the present to associate the person she wants to have become with the horrors of the Holocaust: 'Weil es […] unerträglich ist, bei dem Wort "Auschwitz" das kleine Wort "ich" mitdenken zu müssen' (KM, 337).

A dimension of *Kindheitsmuster* that is of particular relevance to post-unification German memory discourses is its focus in the second half of the text on the experience of flight and expulsion. As Elizabeth Dye has observed, it is interesting that this theme, which constitutes a substantial part of Wolf's autobiography, has hitherto been ignored in most critical analyses.[18] This suggests that although in different historical circumstances and for different reasons, the issue of the flight was subject to forgetting in both Germanys until the 1970s for different reasons. In West Germany it did exist as part of communicative memory, but was not integrated into cultural or collective memory discourses until recent years. In the GDR, this subject constituted a particularly deeply entrenched taboo. It is only very recently for instance that historians have revealed details about the rape of German women by soldiers of the Red Army.[19] However, during the GDR's existence such revelations were unthinkable. In *Kindheitsmuster* the final five chapters are devoted to the topic of the trek westwards, in addition to which it features throughout as a kind of fugal motif that at once frames and interrupts the memory process.[20] The child Nelly in *Kindheitsmuster* is clearly traumatised by the experience of the flight, a factor which is the result not least of her mother's decision to send her children away with their grandparents, whilst remaining behind herself in order to look after the family home and property. As Nelly witnesses the most horrendous suffering on the trek, she increasingly loses touch with reality. Initially suffering from profound numbness of feeling, she gradually descends into a condition that is described in the language of trauma:

> Wenn Nelly irgendwann in der Gefahr schwebte, den Boden unter den Füßen zu verlieren, dann in jener Nacht. Verzweiflung wäre der Ausdruck nicht, verzweifeln zu können bedeutet, man hängt mit der Ursache der Verzweiflung zusammen. Nelly hing mit nichts mehr zusammen. Wo sie jetzt ging […] wo sie ging, stolperte, steckenblieb, war der äußerste Rand der Wirklichkeit. Der Umkreis dessen, was sie noch denken durfte, war auf einen Punkt zusammengeschrumpft: durchhalten. Erlosch der Punkt, das war ihrem Körper stärker bewußt als ihrem Gehirn, stürzte sie über den Rand (KM, 455).

Criticism has generally interpreted the fact that Nelly eventually recovers from a complete physical and emotional breakdown as an indication that the experiences of the flight did not result in a lasting trauma. The text itself, however, speaks a different language.

For instance, when the narrator endeavours to portray the traumatic experiences of displacement, memory interferes in unexpected ways with her intention of providing an authentic account of these events. In contrast to the moral resistance which stood in the way of her accepting as an authentic self the child she had been as a willing and loyal supporter of Hitler, it is now her body which ruptures the memory project. The fact that one of the chapters about the flight is entitled 'Ein Kapitel Angst' already points to the predominant emotion the narrator associates with this part of her life. Furthermore, she defines her personal memory as an 'Angst- und Gefühlsgedächtnis' (KM, 26). Approaching this part of her life again, in fact, turns increasingly into a story of illness. Not only does she now resist and resent her self-imposed task more vehemently than before, but she is also under increasing physical and emotional strain, suffering from irritation, listlessness, nausea, choking fits, and problems with her heart. She even has to take an extended break from her work at some point in order to recover from the pressures of her task, which leaves her feeling permanently overtaxed and exhausted. At one point, she has to spend weeks in hospital to recover from the impact of over-exertion. In contrast to the hardened, sealed, and ossified memory caverns she is confronted with in her endeavours to unearth her childhood self, the narrator's body during the process of writing vociferously speaks the language of displaced memory and hysteria. However, it is a language the narrator of *Kindheitsmuster* has not learned to understand. The focus on 'durchhalten' which ensured her survival as a child during the flight has in her adult self turned into a deeply internalised mechanism of self-control, of seeing things through, no matter what personal price she has to pay.

Critical assessments of *Kindheitsmuster* have tended to appreciate the aesthetic qualities of the text, but have accused the author of being insufficiently candid when it comes to assessing the foundation years of the GDR in the light of the experiences of her generation in the 1930s. In my view an observation of Walter Benjamin's in the *Passagen-Werk* is pertinent in this regard, namely that forgetting is an inevitable aspect of remembrance, but that memory invoked with a specific intent can only promote remembering if it is free of constraints.[21] In the case of *Kindheitsmuster*, these very constraints have been inscribed into the text as a leitmotif.

In the end, the narrator of *Kindheitsmuster* declares her memory project a failure, exercising self-censorship:

> Die Linien – Lebenslinien, Arbeitslinien – werden sich nicht kreuzen in dem Punkt, der altmodisch 'Wahrheit' heißt. Zu genau weißt du, was dir schwerfallen darf, was nicht. Was du wissen darfst, was nicht. Worüber zu reden ist und in welchem Ton. Und worüber auf immer zu schweigen [...]. (KM, 401)

The paradoxes that go to the heart of the experiences of authors like Wolf could clearly not be resolved in the context of the Cold War and national division. Rooted in the guilt she had incurred as a child of the Third Reich, she adopted the burden of history in the context of the polarities created by the Cold War with the illusory notion that the writer in the morally superior socialist state must, in a manner of speaking, singlehandedly 'rescue' history from its uncanny tendency to repeat itself. It soon follows that such a perspective not only represses the wartime suffering of Germans like Wolf themselves, but such morally principled thinking also places her at an emotional distance from the real victims of the Holocaust, namely the Jews. What remains, as her autobiography observes, is the phantom pain of a displaced and self-alienated self: 'Der Schmerz – vielleicht vergißt man ihn jetzt – ist noch zu benennen, zu fühlen nicht mehr. Dafür [...] der

Schmerz über den verlorenen Schmerz... Zwischen Echos leben, zwischen Echos von Echos...' (KM, 401)

A decade after the collapse of the GDR and German unification, Wolf returned to core issues which *Kindheitsmuster* had left unresolved. The fact that the narrator of *Leibhaftig* is rushed into hospital with a life-threatening abdominal infection which, so her surgeon tells her, has developed 'jahrzehntelan[g]', a 'Vergiftung' that requires an 'Entgiftung, eine Reinigung, ein Purgatorium', creates an immediate link back to the earlier memory project.[22] The text also makes it explicit early on that the central figure in Wolf's first major post-unification engagement with Germany's national history is the now much older self of *Kindheitsmuster*. Significantly, the two figures are connected by reference to the experience of flight and displacement at the end of the World War Two. A literary fragment which was later incorporated into *Kindheitsmuster* portrays the experience of the flight as one that results in profound and lasting self-estrangement:

> Vertauscht war ich nicht, aber ich selbst war ich auch nicht mehr. Nie vergaß ich, wann dieser Fremdling in mich gefahren war, der mich inzwischen gepackt hatte und nach Gutdünken mit mir verfuhr. [...] Gegen dieses Urteil gab es keine Berufung.[23]

In *Leibhaftig*, a similar experience is described: 'Tief in mir kicherte jemand mit mir über mich', 'Jemand grinst in mir' (LH, 9, 82). Clearly then, the collapse of the GDR has reawakened the older, unresolved trauma of displacement which has now come to haunt the self in a way that is life-threatening. Although the political constraints which prevented the autobiographical self in the earlier text from exploring the traumatic experience of the displacement with greater honesty have now been removed, the narrator of the late 1980s can still not find the language that would give expression to it, since trauma has no language: 'Benennungen, Namen, Wörter [...] sind falsch. [...] sie sind falsch.' (LH, 83). It is therefore the body which takes centre stage in the process of remembering, with memory performatively rather than narratologically inscribed. Sigrid Weigel has explained in this regard that memory discourses in Western European culture as a whole have tended to marginalise corporeal memory, a factor she has attributed amongst other things to the significance that has been attached to psychoanalytical models of working through the past in order to understand and integrate it.[24] In *Leibhaftig,* this paradigm of meaning-making is called into question. In spite of the fact, for instance, that a veritable flood of images and messages from her unconscious virtually assault the narrator in her fever dreams, fantasies, and hallucinations, it is not self-analysis which produces healing. Rather, it is the persistent endeavours of the medical team and the means of modern science and technology placed at their disposal which save her life on the one hand, and the narrator's loss of (self-)control, of 'Selbstbeherrschung' through the illness, on the other, (LH, 80) that permit change and ultimately healing to occur. As she drifts in and out of consciousness, the central figure of *Leibhaftig* can only passively and fleetingly register fragments of her 'self' as body and as consciousness, but there is no self-knowing, unified subjectivity in charge of any kind of 'story' or self-construction: 'Das Bewußtsein zieht sich zurück, es geht zum Grund' (LH, 31).

Notions of a subject capable of making sense of itself have consequently been abandoned in favour of a subjectivity understood as multiple and fractured; what is more, this subjectivity is in the process of dissolving altogether as a result of the illness. In the final analysis, the only 'truth' or fact of subjectivity remaining is the existential truth of an eventual extinction of self; this is conveyed in the text by the play on the words 'zum Grund gehen' with 'zugrunde gehen' (LH, 31). The duty to carry the burden of history by remembering truthfully, by bearing her innermost self to the world, which in *Kindheitsmuster* had been resented as an 'Entblößung der Eingeweide' perceived as 'schauerlich' (KM, 264), has failed to produce the kind of self-knowledge needed to heal the wounds of (personal and collective) history. On the contrary, in an uncanny twist of fate, it has merely paved the way for the far more literal and immediate corporeal suffering produced by the surgeons having to cut into the flesh and bone of her body for healing to become possible. This procedure, it is clear, finally brings home the one inalienable existential truth about the subject: its existence as body, as 'Leib'.

Like all meaning in the text, its title, *Leibhaftig*, points to the ambiguous and uncertain nature of language itself as a medium of memory. On the one hand, it is associated in German with the authenticity or authority of the subject, alluding amongst other things to an association of the author of autobiography with a 'guarantor of truth' and with an 'authentic' self. But its meaning in psychopathology is exactly the opposite. Here it signifies illusions, hallucinations, deceptive memory, and pseudohallucinations.[25] As a subject who is transported through her illness into a variety of worlds, the self in Wolf's *Leibhaftig* is associated with the figure of the traveller between worlds, who in the cultures of modernity has made an appearance variously as a nomad or, following Walter Benjamin, as the *flâneur*. In Christa Wolf's *Leibhaftig*, notably, it is the female traveller or *flâneur* who, performatively, is able to mediate between dimensions of human experience we have become accustomed to thinking of as mutually exclusive: the world of the conscious and of the unconscious, life and death, remembering and forgetting, past and future, reality and fantasy, mind and body, communism and capitalism. More importantly still, compared to *Kindheitsmuster*, the direction of travel where memory is concerned has now been reversed from looking forwards towards the future (for instance by taking decisions about what to reveal and what to conceal) to looking backwards. Whilst the author of Wolf's autobiography aimed to rescue a forgotten self from a past which had become unfamiliar and uncertain through processes of forgetting, the self in Wolf's *Leibhaftig* is transported through illness from the world of assumed certainties to a world of fundamental ambiguity and confusion. Memory work is consequently no longer associated with an enlightenment project of rescuing aspects of the past for the sake of the future, but with not knowing, with uncertainty, with lack of orientation and intent, and with dissolution of the self as a knowing and comprehending subject.

It is immediately striking that the leitmotif of *Leibhaftig* and its structural principle is the labyrinth, a topos and a memory figure which is highly suggestive of the return in history of the ever-same of the past. In contemporary Western culture (in German culture specifically in the work of Thomas Mann, Hermann Hesse, or Franz Kafka), the labyrinth has functioned as a signifier of cultural crisis and confusion.[26] At the same time, it has been associated since ancient times with conceptions of history which connect it not with irrefutable truths and rationality, but rather with hybrid forms of historical remembering such as myth, allegory, fantasy, or storytelling. In the ancient world, furthermore, it was linked to the idea of a dangerous quest for survival, a journey into Hades which confronted questers entering the labyrinth with their corporeal existence and forced them to contemplate the reality of death. In the case of Wolf's *Leibhaftig*, all of these associations are, of course, relevant. But the motif of the labyrinth also

permits the author topographically to inscribe the history of the GDR
into the upper strata of a memory shaft (LH, 29) which leads downwards through historical layers and ruins into the past, into the ancient
world. As was the case with the memory figure of the *flâneur*, the
direction of movement of historical remembering is therefore again
reversed. In what was previously conceived of as excavation work, the
subject of history now moves backwards and downwards through
history, a history experienced as labyrinthine and hence unknowable
in its totality.

Such an understanding of history echoes that of Walter Benjamin
in his reconstruction of the prehistory of modernity in his *Passagen-
Werk*, suggesting that Wolf's more tentative exploration of Benjamin's conception of history in *Kindheitsmuster* has developed considerably over time. For Benjamin history is not understood as totality or
as a continuum, but as fragment. Memory, understood as concrete
trace, Benjamin believed, is structured topographically and revolves
around images that encapsulate and symbolise human experience.
Remembering is not retrieval from a storehouse, but the unearthing
and contemplation of images of historical 'Erfahrung' which are momentarily accessible as flashes of remembrance, but whose significance is rarely understood at the time. The past, Benjamin believed,
remains hidden from us 'beneath', in the ruins of history, but it is always present in the here and now, in the 'Jetztzeit', waiting to be discovered.[27] Conceiving of history as the return of the ever-same, Benjamin envisioned modernity as an age of hell.

Such spatialization of memory has opened up new dimensions for
an exploration of cultural memory which have clearly informed
Christa Wolf's *Leibhaftig*. In her volume of diary-like essays *Ein Tag
im Jahr* (2003), the author has recorded her fascination with Benjamin's notion of modernity as an age of hell and with the spatial motif
of the labyrinth as a structuring device for her narrative: 'Die Moderne
als Zeitalter der Hölle. – Dies ist, wie ich deutlich spüre, mein Thema.
Entfremdung, in ihrer heutigen Gestalt. In der Gestalt, in der ich sie
erlebt habe und erlebe: "sozialistische", kapitalistische Entfremdung.'[28]

Following Benjamin's *Passagen-Werk*, reality is represented in
Leibhaftig in three spatial, labyrinthine layers: the hospital in which
the narrator fights for her life after a physical collapse during the final
days of the GDR's existence in 1989; the cityscape of East Berlin

which is representative of GDR society in its death throes; and the subterranean underground world of Berlin, where the narrator in her fevered dreams and hallucinations is confronted with the ghosts of her personal history, which is also that of twentieth-century Germany. Each dimension of experience in these labyrinthine structures is pervaded by a sense of the Freudian uncanny, pointing to repressed memories and an unresolved past. The narrator, furthermore, is undergoing a series of operations to save her life, as a result of which she suffers torture-like agonies when she is conscious (LH, 19), but is also haunted during her hallucinations and dreams by the agonies of those who have suffered as victims of history: 'bei diesem höllischen Getöse peinigt mich die Geschichte des Schmerzes und der Folter' (LH, 20). Historical experience is represented consequently in corporeal terms, as material reality or trace, and as individual and collective memory. Fluid shifts between the first and the third person singular indicate that the self is understood as both subject and object of history: 'Untertauchen. Untergetauchtwerden'(LH, 6), 'Ich reg mich doch gar nicht auf. Sie hätte gar nicht die Kraft, sich aufzuregen.' (LH, 8) There is barely any plotline, and no narrator who is in any way capable of being in charge of any kind of a story: 'Das Erzählen habe ich aufgegeben' (LH, 70). In fact, language itself is constantly called into question. On the one hand, it is multivalent and ambiguous, as my reflections on the title have suggested. On the other, it is limited where representation of the complexity of human experience is concerned. In contrast to psychological suffering, as Elaine Scarry has pointed out, language cannot adequately express physical pain, since pain has no referent. This is why corporeal suffering has rarely been represented in literature and has remained a blind spot in our culture and civilization.[29] It is clear then that Wolf's *Leibhaftig* is indebted to the traditions of literary and philosophical modernism, but it also seeks to renegotiate some of the fundamental values and assumptions of modernity at the same time.

The collapse of the GDR, which here coincides – in a manner that alludes to the uncanny nature of history at its core – with the mortal illness of the narrator, is enacted in *Leibhaftig* as a crisis which is played out at the ultimate threshold of existence, on the boundary between survival and extinction. As a subject who lives in 'verschiedenen Wirklichkeiten', a 'Grenzgängerin' in a number of respects, Wolf's narrator bridges the rift between worlds, transporting the reader from the 'Welt der festen Körper' (KM, 594) to an experience of liminality, uncertainty, ambiguity, and confusion. Memory of the GDR is performatively reclaimed from homogenizing and objectifying discourses and inserted into the alternative discourse of literary remembering. In this domain, all certainties of the subject of history are fundamentally called into question, with remembering posited as an unreliable process which inevitably involves forgetting, and which is beyond the control of the individual. By definition, then, it cannot be placed in the service of any project involving intent.

Inviting the reader to reflect on a civilisational history that has, in association with Walter Benjamin's *Angelus Novus*, heaped 'Leid' upon 'Leid', Wolf seeks to foster the 'Leidensfähigkeit' of the subject by inserting the body as ultimate authority into the history of Western civilization. Described by Freud as the 'Austragungsort und Symbolisierungsfeld' of culture, where its permanent memory traces are inscribed, the body is here designated by Wolf, as in Kafka's paradigmatic text *In der Strafkolonie*,[30] as the site of cultural memory:

> Die Soldaten des Herodes, welche die kleinen Kinder auf die Spitzen ihrer Schwerter spießen. Die ersten Christen, in der Arena Auge in Auge mit den wilden Tieren, die sie unter gräßlichem Gebrüll zerreißen. Die Greueltaten der Conquistadoren, der Kreuzritter, der Fürsten nach den Bauernkriegen. Die Frau, die, geschunden, im Landwehrkanal treibt. Und da hat mein Jahrhundert erst angefangen. Schinden auf jede denkbare Weise. Das Martyrium und der Untergang der Leiber, mein Leib mitten unter ihnen. […] Dafür, daß in diesem Bett etwas endet und danach, falls es ein Danach gibt, etwas anderes anfängt, ist dieses schauerliche Getöse der Preis, und die Qual der Leiber, die mir aus irgendeinem Grund eingebrannt werden soll. (LH, 20)

But by placing the history of the GDR *en abyme* within the depth of the history of Western civilization more widely, she appears also to relativize it and its *raison d'être* as one manifestation amongst many others in the history of humankind of history's terrible tendency to repeat itself. This echoes, I suggest, Walter Benjamin's conception of the new as merely that which has always been there since ancient times.[31]

For Benjamin as a historical materialist, this presence of ancient history in the here and now, in the history of modernity, became manifest in the arcade within the city, which he considered the realization of the architecture of the ancients – the labyrinth – in modernity. Within and beyond the arcade, Benjamin envisioned further layers of history, further labyrinths, which, in a downward spiral, pointed the way through layers and ruins of historical matter, to the entrance to the underworld, to hell.[32] *Leibhaftig* comprises of a similar constellation, performatively inscribing the historical foundations of the GDR into the material history of modernity. Wolf draws in this regard in particular on Benjamin's understanding of memory as a site ('Schauplatz des Gedächtnisses') and of its 'Traumschrift'.[33] In Wolf's spatial memory constellation, history is conceived of by way of labyrinthine interconnected layers: the patient's dreamlike hallucinatory vision of the hospital, which is described as '[ein] Komplex von Gebäuden [...], die durch lange Betongänge miteinander verbunden sind' (LH, 39); the dream-like, ghostly vision of the cityscape of East Berlin in ruins, its topographical milestones reduced to rubble, to 'Steinhaufen' (LH, 146), a doomed city built not as a monument to the triumph of socialism over capitalism, but as a symbol of the futility of all great civilizational projects of human history, of their 'Vergeblichkeit' (LH, 145); and the labyrinthine subterranean uncanny world of the catacombs below the city of Berlin, where the ghosts of the forgotten victims of history are waiting for redemption alongside the remains of those who tortured and abused them (LH, 143). All three layers of this uncanny, dreamlike vision are interconnected by labyrinthine passageways of a variety of kinds, blurring the boundaries between past, present and future: the tubes and wires that keep the narrator's fragile body alive in hospital in the period just before the GDR collapsed (LH, 118) appear directly to bleed into the cables and pipes protruding from the dug-up Friedrichstraße in the immediate aftermath of unification, when the 'burdenend landscapes' of the communist past will be erased in order to construct an all-German future modelled on capitalist Western Germany.[34] Friedrichstraße station, in turn, imagined here as a 'Schlachthaus. Getarnt als Grenzübergangsstelle' (LH, 25), is connected by transit passages to the catacombs below the city of Berlin, to the uncanny world of repressed and unresolved memory. Hence Wolf has constructed a constellation in which the body as site of cultural memory is inextricably intermeshed with the material 'Schauplätze' of memory, echoing Benjamin's notion of 'body-and-image-space'.[35] Saturated at every level by images of pathology, decay, trauma, suffering and destruction, her narrative inscribes the memory spaces of the GDR into those of modernity, conceiving of memory work as an 'Archäologie der Zerstörungen' (LH, 143). Significantly, however, the memory spaces of East Berlin are connected at the foundations to those of the West, emphasizing that neither history can be understood without its 'other': 'die Gewißheit, daß ich nach dem Passieren des Mauerdurchbruchs in ein Terrain geraten bin, welches sich exakt spiegelbildlich zu dem verhält, in dem ich mich vor dem Mauerdurchbruch bewegt habe' (LH, 113). As a result, her construction suggests, if a 'Bloßlegen der Eingeweide' (LH, 143) is necessary for the purposes of fostering post-unification national identity constructions, this is memory work to be conducted on both sides of the former border.

It is, of course, significant that an anaesthetist by the name of Kora Bachmann accompanies the narrator of *Leibhaftig* during her hallucinations and fantasy-dreams of excursions through the cityscape of Berlin both above and below the ground. After all, Ingeborg Bachmann constructed capitalist West Berlin in the mid-1960s in her narrative *Ein Ort für Zufälle* (1964), as a doomed city that is pervaded by trauma and decay.[36] With *Leibhaftig*, Wolf is clearly paying tribute to Bachmann, and she extends the dystopian vision of her forebear belatedly across the border to the socialist half of the formerly divided city. In so doing, she clearly invites both former Germanys to re-engage with the past and to acknowledge the problematical historical foundations on which an all-German future inevitably rests. But there is clearly also an optimistic message which *Leibhaftig* is imparting; and this is the personal freedom the writer who once felt she had to shoulder the responsibility for German history has found in the new historical constellation. In spite of the destruction and doom that her narrative *Leibhaftig* portrays, her autobiographical self here finally gives herself permission to let go of the moral burden of Germany's history. In this regard *Leibhaftig* is a testimony to the narrative freedom and the new imaginative spaces which the collapse of the GDR has opened up.

Notes

[1] Anne Fuchs, 'From "Vergangenheitsbewältigung" to Generational Memory Contests in Günter Grass, Monika Maron and Uwe Timm', *German Life and Letters*, 59:2 (2006), 169-86 (here: 177).

2   Christa Wolf pointed out in this regard that in the GDR memory of fascism was externalised to the Federal Republic of Germany as early as the 1950s. At the same time cultural memory construction fostered images of the antifascist hero as victim of fascism. See Christa Wolf, 'Erfahrungsmuster. Diskussion zu Kindheitsmuster', in Christa Wolf, *Die Dimension des Autors*, II, Berlin and Weimar: Aufbau, 1986, 350-87 (here: p. 351). See also Herfried Münkler, 'Das kollektive Gedächtnis der DDR', in: Dieter Vorsteher, ed., *Parteienauftrag: Ein Neues Deutschland. Bilder, Rituale und Symbole der frühen DDR*, Munich and Berlin: Koehler & Ameland, 1997, pp. 458-68.

3   See Fuchs, 'From "Vergangenheitsbewältigung" to Generational Memory Contests'.

4   See Arne de Winde and Anke Gilleir, eds, *Literatur im Krebsgang. Totenbeschwörung und 'memoria' in der deutschsprachigen Literatur nach 1989*, Amsterdam and New York: Rodopi, 2008, pp. 13-21. See also Karen Leeder, 'Dances of Death: A Last Literature from the GDR', in: Renate Rechtien and Dennis Tate, eds., *Twenty Years On: Competing Memories of the GDR in Post-Unification German Culture*, Rochester NY: Camden House, forthcoming.

5   For a more extensive discussion of this dimension, see Renate Rechtien, 'Gelebtes, erinnertes, erzähltes und erschriebenes Selbst: Günter de Bruyns Zwischenbilanz und Christa Wolfs *Kindheitsmuster*,' in: Dennis Tate, ed., *Günter de Bruyn in Perspective*, Amsterdam and Atlanta: Rodopi, 1999, pp. 151-70.

6   See Sigrid Weigel, *Body- and image-space. Re-reading Walter Benjamin*, trans. Georgina Paul with Rachel McNicholl and Jeremy Gaines, London: Routledge, 1996, xv. See also David Frisby, *Fragments of Modernity: Theories of Modernity in the Work of Simmel, Kracauer, and Benjamin*, Cambridge MA: MIT Press, 1986, pp. 211-3.

7   See Dennis Tate's introduction to *Twenty Years On*.

8   See Renate Rechtien, 'Introduction. Cityscapes of the German Democratic Republic – An Interdisciplinary Approach,' *German Life and Letters*, 63:4 (2010): 369-74.

9   Sonja Hilzinger, afterword to *Kindheitsmuster*, in Christa Wolf, *Kindheitsmuster*, in *Werke*, ed. by Sonja Hilzinger, 12 vols, Munich: Luchterhand, 1999-2001, V, pp. 647-59 (here: p. 647). All subsequent references to *Kindheitsmuster* will relate to this edition and will be given as KM followed by the page number in brackets.

10   Christa Wolf, 'Erfahrungsmuster. Diskussion zu *Kindheitsmuster*', in *Werke*, VIII, pp. 31-72 (here: pp. 31-3).

11   Wolf, 'Erfahrungsmuster', p. 35.

¹² Helmut Peitsch, Charles Burdett, Claire Gorrara, eds, *European Memories of the Second World War*, Oxford and New York: Berghahn, 1999, p. xix.

¹³ See Ingeborg Bachmann, *Frankfurter Vorlesungen. Probleme zeitgenössischer Dichtung*, Munich: Piper, 2000.

¹⁴ Christa Wolf, 'Lesen und Schreiben', in *Werke*, IV, pp. 238-82 (here: p. 255).

¹⁵ Lutz Köpnick, 'Rettung und Destruktion: Erinnerungsverfahren und Geschichts-bewußtsein in Christa Wolfs *Kindheitsmuster* und Walter Benjamins Spätwerk', *Monatshefte*, 84 (1992), 74-90 (here: 75).

¹⁶ Barbara Kosta, *Recasting Autobiography: Women's Counterfictions in Contemporary German Literature and Film*, Ithaca, NY: Cornell University Press, 1994, p. 63.

¹⁷ Elizabeth Dye, 'Painful Memories. The Literary Representation of German Wartime Suffering', unpublished PhD thesis, University of Nottingham, March 2006, p. 238.

¹⁸ Dye, 'Painful Memories', pp. 248-72.

¹⁹ See for instance Anthony Beevor, *Berlin. The Downfall 1945*, London: Penguin, 2002.

²⁰ Dye, 'Painful Memories', p. 232.

²¹ See Sven Kramer, *Walter Benjamin*, Hamburg: Junius, 2003, 101-24.

²² Christa Wolf, *Leibhaftig*, Munich: Luchterhand, 2002. All subsequent references to this text will be to this edition and will be noted as LH followed by the page number in parentheses.

²³ Christa Wolf, 'Blickwechsel', in *Werke*, III, pp. 111-28 (here: p. 117).

²⁴ Sigrid Weigel, *Bilder des kulturellen Gedächtnisses*, Dülmen-Hiddingsel: Tende, 1994, 49-50. Elaine Scarry makes a similar point in *The Body in Pain. The Making and Unmaking of the World*, New York and Oxford: OUP, 1985 pp. 1-45

²⁵ See Karl Jaspers, *Allgemeine Psychopathologie*, Berlin, Heidelberg and New York: Springer, 1973, p. 66.

²⁶ See for instance David Kenosian, *Puzzles of the Body. The Labyrinth in Kafka's 'Prozeß', Hesse's 'Steppenwolf', and Mann's 'Zauberberg'*, New York, etc.: Peter Lang, 1995, pp. 2-4.

[27] David Frisby, *Fragments of Modernity: Theories of Modernity in the Work of Simmel, Kracauer, and Benjamin*, Cambridge, MA: MIT Press, 1986, pp. 211-213.

[28] Christa Wolf, *Ein Tag im Jahr. 1960–2000*, Munich: Luchterhand, 2003, p. 618. See also Dennis Tate's engagement with this aspect of Wolf's text in Tate, *Shifting Perspectives. East German Autobiographical Narratives Before and After the End of the GDR*, Rochester, NY: Camden House, 2007, p. 222.

[29] Scarry, *The Body in Pain*, p. 43.

[30] Ibid., pp. 49-51.

[31] Frisby, *Fragments of Modernity*, p. 208.

[32] Ibid., p. 193.

[33] Ibid., p. 86.

[34] See Rechtien, 'Introduction. Cityscapes of the German Democratic Republic'.

[35] Sigrid Weigel, *Body- and image-space*, pp. 16-29.

[36] See Andrew Webber, *Berlin in the Twentieth Century. A Cultural Topography*, Cambridge: CUP, 2008, p. 49.

Axel Goodbody

Poetic Reflections on Stunted Lives: Wulf Kirsten's Contribution to East German Autobiographical Writing

Memory has been recognised as a central concern in Wulf Kirsten's writing, but the autobiographical dimension of his work has not hitherto attracted attention. This article examines the account of his childhood (1939-47), *Die Prinzessinnen im Krautgarten*, passages in his speeches and essays on life in the GDR and the *Wende*, and autobiographical themes in his poetry. Kirsten's contribution to GDR life writing is shown to be distinctive in its regional and rural focus, its utopian heightening of childhood as a yardstick by which to measure the present both before and after the *Wende*, its foregrounding of landscape and place, and in its poetic language, imagery and echoing of literary tradition.

> die stille tropft wie blut aus einer wunde.
> ein engel sieht die dreifältige sonne.
> der sechsflügelige seraph *kündet vom tage,*
> *vom heute gewesenen tage* und schlingert
> mit schlagseite über die bruchstellen
> deiner und meiner gestutzten biografie.
> Wulf Kirsten, 'lebensspuren'

The autobiographical dimension in Wulf Kirsten's writing has not hitherto attracted much attention. He is generally regarded as a regional landscape poet, whose detailed depiction of rural life in Saxony during the GDR years was grounded in local belonging and empathy with the people, and who came to indict the neglect and mismanagement they experienced as a result of the socialist collectivisation of farming, in forms ranging from wistful elegy to apocalyptic visions of destruction. Kirsten breathed new life into twentieth-century German nature poetry through a distinctive combination of thematic concerns and formal elements from Theodor Kramer, Peter Huchel and Johannes Bobrowski, in irregular, unrhymed verses with frequent enjambment, structured by alliteration, internal rhyme and rhythmic patterns, employing chains of metaphors, resonating with echoes of passages from the Bible and literary tradition, and in a language characterised by laconic condensation in unexpected compounds, and use of unfamiliar dialect words and suggestive-sounding names.[1] In the last decade, however, a number of studies have explored the significance of memory in Kirsten's writing, and he has received honours and awards for a poetic and essayistic oeuvre increasingly perceived as a 'persistent work of remembering the historical caesurae of 1945 and 1989, enlightening contemporaries and reminding them of their responsibilities'.[2]

In the early poem 'satzanfang' Kirsten set out a poetic programme of acting as chronicler of local history, recording the biographies of the local people and witnessing to their achievements and the hardships and injustices they suffered:

> ans licht bringen
> die biografien aller sagbaren dinge
> eines erdstrichs zwischenein.
>
> inständig benennen: die leute vom dorf,
> ihre ausdauer, ihre werktagsgeduld,
> aus wortfiguren standbilder setzen
> einer dynastie von feldbestellern
> ohne resonanznamen[3]

Such statements have, however, masked an admittedly less prominent autobiographical concern, distracting attention from his asking, in prose writing and poems written throughout his life, but particularly in the second half of the nineteen-sixties and again in the late eighties and early nineties, who he himself is, and how he became what he is.

The end of the Second World War and the *Wende* are the two most important breaks, or rifts ('Bruchstellen') in Kirsten's 'stunted' biography – and indeed in the biographies of his GDR contemporaries, for much (but by no means all) of his personal experience is representative of his generation's.[4] The term 'stunted'[5] is taken from the poem 'lebensspuren' (traces of lives), written in 1981. In a bleak reflection on the political, economic and cultural stagnation of the time, Kirsten imagines the carved figures in a deserted village church swinging groggily into life, whispering the past like the restless springs in Mörike's 'Um Mitternacht', but no longer possessed of the power to give meaning to contemporary reality through the promise of a better world to follow. He has returned time and again to 1945 and 1989 as turning points in German history, remembering and interpreting them in the light of subsequent experience, and to other historical developments which have left their mark on him personally.

Childhood plays a central role in Kirsten's writing. This is in part because revisiting the past has enabled him to take stock of his social and cultural heritage, and to establish his own identity and poetic voice. However, it is also because, in what has been an at times painfully personal process, he sought first to reconcile childhood experience and feelings with official understandings of historical events, and later to challenge and correct public perceptions of these events with refutations and counter-narratives or images. This has involved confronting the powerful tug of nostalgia for a lost childhood world which came to an abrupt end in 1945, and making it productive for his poetic project. It has necessitated recognising on the one hand the hardships and injustices which characterised that world in reality, and on the other the ambivalences of the historical changes which followed, and locating these and later changes in the broader context of processes of modernisation and the cultural, political and moral challenges they pose.

The one extended work of Kirsten's which is explicitly autobiographical is *Die Prinzessinnen im Krautgarten*, first published in 2000.[6] Subtitled 'Eine Dorfkindheit', this is an account of his childhood from the age of five to thirteen. The period covered is 1939 to 1947, and the place Klipphausen in Saxony, a village with a mere 350 inhabitants at the time, situated in a side valley of the river Elbe between Dresden and Meissen. Kirsten grew up as the oldest in a family of five children. His father was a cottager, a stone mason by training, but dependent for a living on the produce of a small family farm. The eighth chapter of the book, 'Die Nacht im Rübenkeller', which describes the arrival of the Russian army on 7 May 1945, and constitutes the focal point of the narrative, had already been published in *neue deutsche literatur* in 1985,[7] fifteen years before the book was completed. Most of Kirsten's autobiography was therefore written when he was in his late fifties and sixties, at a time of life when it may be natural for thoughts to return to one's childhood. However, Kirsten was undoubtedly encouraged by the political upheaval of the *Wende* to reflect on the earlier experience of traumatic disruption which had marked the end of his childhood, both in order to reassess the past in the light of present developments, and to distance himself from these developments through historical contextualisation. Passages in the

book hinting at the challenges Kirsten faced in the early nineties include the following: 'An die Stelle des gewohnten, langsam dahin-
fließenden Nebeneinander war ein wüstes, wildes Durcheinander getreten. Nein, nicht "getreten" – wie eine Lavamasse kam es herange-
quollen, jede Ritze füllend, nicht aufzuhalten. Ohne Anfang, ohne
Ende, uferlos, unübersehbar, alles unter sich begrabend.' (PK, 147-8)

Die Prinzessinnen is then one work in the spate of autobiographies
which emerged in response to the sweeping away of social norms,
realignment of cultural values and challenge to personal identities
which resulted from the implosion of the East German communist
party and the dissolution of the state. It is clearly an example of the
emotional reflection on lost traditions and the rediscovery of long-
suppressed cultural roots triggered by the collapse of communism.
However, it differed from other products of such reflection in being
essentially a continuation of Kirsten's already existing poetic project.
In his poems, he had already sought for more than two decades to
challenge the hegemonic memory dictated by the state's value system
through a personal counter-remembering of the Third Reich, the
Second World War, and life in the despised provinces. However, he
now goes further than before in challenging the GDR's antifascist
myth of origin and describing the beginnings of the Republic in such a
way as to explain problems which were to lead to its demise. For
instance he describes the cowardly opportunism of a slightly older
contemporary, his group leader in the Hitler Youth, who feigned
injury in order to avoid being drafted in to defend the village against
the advancing Russians in the last weeks of the war, and went on to
become an officer and trainer in the GDR Volkspolizei (PK, 138). At
the same time, Kirsten explains the support which he (and his
generation) gave to the communist party in the GDR for so long,
despite growing disillusionment with real existing socialism, as a
consequence of the fear instilled in them by the draconian punishment
meted out to contemporaries who stepped out of line politically:

> Man war da nicht zimperlich. Gerade wenn es um Jugendliche ging. Nur weil ein
> vorwitziger Kleewunscher Junge einen die Ruhmestaten der Roten Armee glorifi-
> zierenden Film mit den Worten kommentiert hatte: 'Genau wie bei den Nazis!',
> durfte er fünf Jahre im Speziallager Mühlberg verbringen. […] Auf Erlebnisse
> dieser Art sollten sich generative Ängste gründen, die sich auch dann nicht mehr
> abbauen ließen, als man eine Lippe riskieren konnte, ohne Gefahr zu laufen, im
> Gelben Elend oder jenseits des Ural zu landen. Von jenen finsteren Zeiten her
> mag so manches Stillhalteabkommen mit Stiefvater Staat getroffen worden sein.

Sicher, es führte dann allmählich in eine Bequemlichkeit hinüber und hinein, die hinwiederum von Jüngeren leicht zu verspotten und zu verachten war. (PK, 227)

Kirsten depicts the daily grind of life for small farmers and artisans like his parents, refers repeatedly to the injustice and exploitation they suffered, and provides examples of poverty, homelessness, and social exclusion resulting from illegitimacy and mental illness. He describes the paramilitary training he reluctantly took part in as a member of the Hitler Youth, recounts the fate of boys only a few years older than himself who lost their lives after being called up, and writes of Polish prisoners of war and starving German refugees toward the end of the war. He mentions the bombing of Dresden, and requisitioning, rape, and suicides following the arrival of the Red army. However, these are all incursions of injustice, suffering and violence into what was up until 1945 essentially a secure and happy childhood, one spent playing in the farm's many outbuildings and ranging across the neighbourhood, without fear or restriction by adults:

In jeder Stallung war ich herumgekrochen. Was gab es nicht alles zu entdecken! Spreu- und Schirrkammern. Geheimnisvolle Bereiche in einem ewigen Halbdunkel, von deren stickiger Stille und verstaubter Dingfülle eine magische Anziehungskraft ausging. Jeder Winkel des Gehöfts war vertraut […]. Das den Hof umgebende Gelände war nicht minder Teil des Auslaufs, in dem ich mich frei und sicher bewegte wie in einer zusätzlichen Haut, ohne daß mich jemand daran hinderte und dabei störte. (PK, 144-5)

Life in the rural community in which he grew up was, as described in the earlier chapters of Kirsten's autobiography, less determined by Nazi ideology than by the timeless rhythms of traditional farming, and quasi-feudal structures of land ownership and authority. He writes as chronicler of a lost way of life, describing tools and trades which have gone. For all the drudgery of the adults, then, the war years emerge as a timeless period of harmonious dwelling for the child, of intimate familiarity with the surrounding nature: 'Kein Flurstück blieb unentdeckt. Wir liefen uns die Heimat an den nackten Fußsohlen ab.' (PK, 12)[8] It is, at least in the consciousness of the sixty-year-old recalling the scene, a form of being at home in the world which he has never regained:

Der Wiesenhang zwischen dem Mühlgraben und unserem Gartenzaun war ein Ort, an dem es sich wunderbar ungestört spielen ließ. Aber auch einfach dazusitzen, zu beobachten, ins Tal und ins Dorf zu blicken, dem blanken Müßiggang

zu obliegen, geriet, wenn ich es leibhaftig bin, den ich da in meiner Erinnerung
sehe, zu intensiver Weltbetrachtung aus eigenem Anchauen, wo nichts im Husch
vorüberflog, wo man vielmehr alles schön langsam in sich einziehen lassen konnte. (PK, 8)

Mindful of the tendency of memory to idealise the past, and of the
danger of sentimental falsification of the childhood 'Heimat', Kirsten
comments repeatedly on the factual unreliability of recall and the
selective reconstruction of the past unavoidably present in the process
of remembering: 'Meine Erinnerung bildet sich ein, [...]' (PK, 89), he
writes, 'Der Erinnerung kommt es so vor, als [...]' (PK, 106), 'wie ich
zu rekonstruieren wage' (PK, 135). However, the effect of such acknowledgement is precisely to permit him to bathe Klipphausen in the
golden glow of a long-vanished idyllic era: at one point he refers to it
as 'eine versunkene, überrollte, zugeschüttete Wirklichkeit, der gar
nichts anderes übrig bleibt, als zum Märchen zu mutieren' (PK, 49-
50). The book is characterised by a tension between critical realism
and nostalgic idealisation. The earlier chapters in particular hint at a
fairy-tale, pre-industrial epoch in which the child was free of the
regimentation of later life. Even the labour of peasants and artisans is
presented as essentially un-alienated. Here, as in Kirsten's poems (see
'welt unmittelbar' and 'textur', elb, 74 and 280), we find utopian
images of a way of life in immediate contact with reality, against
which the present is measured and found wanting.

Kirsten's autobiographical reflections in *Die Prinzessinnen im
Krautgarten* end in 1947. For the period after this, we have only scatt-
ered comments on his experience of life in the GDR and the *Wende* in
the essays and speeches collected in the volume *Brückengang* (2009).
As in the post-*Wende* writing of his contemporaries, mixed feelings
are expressed here: scornful dismissal of the corruption and hypo-
critical betrayal of socialist principles under the SED, but equally
regret over lost opportunities and disappointed hopes, and anger over
false promises, injustices and negative developments in the new Germany.

Kirsten writes scathingly for instance of the reappearance of the
opportunism he had witnessed in the years after the Second World
War, when 'der Blockwart zum Sekretär der Einheitspartei avanciert
war': '1989 konnte ich wieder erleben, wie rasch eine Farbe abzu-
blättern vermag. Drei Kniebeugen und die Farbe Rot blätterte ab. Zum
Vorschein kamen lauter heimliche Widerstandskämpfer und Verfech-

ter der freien Marktwirtschaft.' (Bg, 127) In the essay 'Weimar von innen', Kirsten recalls how the building stock in the city's historical centre had been allowed to decay to a state almost beyond repair under 40 years of socialism. But he is equally critical of the wholesale post-*Wende* dismantling of the GDR's social provision of accommodation. The property speculation which accompanied the wave of renovation and modernisation after 1990 is 'mit einschneidenden sozialen Ver-änderungen und räumlichen Umschichtungen verbunden' (Bg, 268).

Elsewhere he comments ruefully on the dumping of a million unsold books published in the GDR by publishers and bookshops in 1991, including all 2500 copies of a reprint of his own *Die Schlacht bei Kesselsdorf* (Bg, 124). However, this is not the main thrust of his speeches and essays since the *Wende*. In a speech about the novelist Horst Bienek delivered in 1999, Kirsten describes the bullying, denunciation and crushing punishment meted out to writers in the 'stalinomane Praxis' of the GDR's early years, and argues that such experiences led to cowardly conformity and compliance in his generation. (Bg, 99-100) He recounts in a speech before the Schiller-gesellschaft in 2002 how he was approached by the Stasi and subjected to observation when he declined to assist them. But not to lay claim to particular courage, for he comments self-critically on the many small compromises he entered into over the years, in his writing and his career, before eventually overcoming his timidity:

Auf dem Wege zur Selbstfindung, einer mit Mühe verbundenen Wort- und Textierungsarbeit, mischte viel zu lange das Wechselspiel von Angst und Mut mit. Spielräume, die kampagneweise mal größer, mal kleiner gehalten wurden, galt es auszuloten, um sie tatsächlich nutzen zu können. In diesem Umfeld agierten Vorsicht, Rücksichtnahme wie diverse Spielarten von Mimikry. Ein Katalog von Beispielen für Selbstverleugnung, Zurücknahmen, Zurückhaltungen, Verzichten, Verstellungen wäre aufzulisten. Viel zu spät habe ich Ängste abge-baut. Dies beschleunigte sich erst, als ich die Erfahrung machte, wie rasch man auch als Mitläufer im Sumpf der Korruption versinkt, weil ein fauler Kompromiß unweigerlich den nächsten nach sich zieht. (BG, 108)

Others have traced Kirsten's gradual development from the com-promises and self-contradictions of the poems collected in the volume *satzanfang* (1970) through the open criticism of pollution in *der bleibaum* (1977), to the apocalyptic pessimism and angry protest with which he expressed his growing ideological disillusionment in *die erde bei Meißen* (1986). He stood by the poet Reiner Kunze when the latter was subject to Stasi observation and increasing harassment by the authorities for his political views in the first half of the 1970s, and protested in writing against Kunze's exclusion from the 'Schriftstellerverband' in 1976 (a response to the publication of Kunze's *Die wunderbaren Jahre* in West Germany). He also played an active role in the Weimar 'Bürgerbewegung' in the late 1980s (he has lived in Weimar since 1965). Pfarrer Christoph Victor's diary of events in the city from 1988 to 1990[9] reveals how Kirsten joined the local group of *Demokratie Jetzt* in September 1989, and subsequently became a member of *Neues Forum*. As a speaker at public meetings in October and November, he was a vigorous advocate of political integrity, justice and democracy. Although he soon found himself in a rearguard of intellectuals pleading for a reformed socialism with a public increasingly set on reunification, and withdrew from politics, stung by accusations of being a 'selbsternannter Bürgerbewegter', he continued to work with Pfarrer Erich Kranz, the principal leader of the local 'Bürgerbewegung.' When the Weimar Stasi headquarters was occupied by demonstrators in early December, Kirsten assisted Kranz in setting up a citizens' committee, which worked up to the autumn of 1992, exposing cases of political injustice and corruption.

But it is Kirsten's poetry rather than his prose writing or essays on which his literary reputation principally rests, and if a claim is to be made for a significant autobiographical dimension in his writing, then it must hold true for his poems. Though we do not find analytical reflection on his inner development, a good dozen poems are centrally concerned with his childhood, while others look back at experiences in the post-war years, and reflect on his situation after the *Wende*.

As already mentioned, it has been assumed that Kirsten is more concerned with speaking for the local people than with self-portraiture. This is certainly the main thrust of the programmatic statement 'Entwurf einer Landschaft' which he published at the end of the volume *satzanfang*, asserting: 'Ich möchte den Werktag einer lokalisierten Agrarlandschaft, die für beliebig andere stehen mag, poetisieren (nicht romantisieren!), in einer aufgerauhten, "körnigen" Sprache, die ich dem Thema angemessen finde'.[10] Yet the 'Weltzugewandtheit' which he referred to as a principal aim included relating the self to the social and natural environment ('Sein Thema finden heißt zu sich selbst finden') and to historical developments ('ständige Auseinandersetzung zwischen dem lyrischen Ich und der

Zeit').[11] Reticence concerning the autobiographical dimension of his work may have been dictated by the political requirements of the time. There is in any case a clear autobiographical subtext in many of the poems in the volume (including self-portraits and portraits of members of his family): they sought to probe his personal past as well as that of the community, and to construct a poetic persona.

As in *Die Prinzessinnen im Krautgarten*, the freedom of the child from cares and responsibilities stands in the foreground, together with the child's unmediated contact with nature in idyllic natural surroundings, his wondering gaze, taking in colours, shapes and sensations, and his imagination, which turns every day into an adventure. The adult poet mourns the loss of the child's vivid ability to see, hear, smell, feel and taste things, and seeks to recapture his intimacy with the natural environment through poetic evocation:

> über die weizenstoppel zu dritt
> nachmittags, einst im september.
> barfuß einer mit wegfarbner sohle:
> 'es distelt, lauft nicht so schnell!' (elb, 31)

These opening lines of 'über die weizenstoppel' are typical in recalling a moment which epitomises his childhood as a time of simple living, companionship (he refers to 'redsames nebeneinander'), and freedom to roam the surrounding wheat fields and explore areas of wilderness, helping themselves to cherries and other fruit from the trees in season. The sense of distance from contemporary reality and irreparable loss is present again at the beginning of the poem 'das vorwerk', in which the subject is depicted as spending the summer in hermit-like seclusion, 'landstraßenfern', on an outlying farm:

> ehmals
> saß ich im gespinst der öde,
> da kroch mir das trugbild der zeit
> wie tagedieb und tunichtgut
> durch das einsiedelhaar (elb, 24)

However, as in *Die Prinzessinnen*, evocation of the childhood 'Heimat' (whose idyllic qualities are here already overshadowed by the terms 'gespinst der öde' and 'trugbild der zeit') and lament at its loss are juxtaposed with passages alluding to the daily toil, hardship and hunger of the adults, or references to harsh wartime realities. Three of the four sections of 'das vorwerk' are given over to the daily tasks of the farm labourers: 'das tagwerk des gesindes/ blieb randvoll gefüllt,/ war nichts als schund und plack' (elb, 25). Kirsten's poems 'über sieben raine', a portrait of his grandmother, who walked for two hours daily to sell local farmers' butter at the market in Dresden, and 'grabschrift', dedicated to his grandfather, a travelling journeyman who died of exposure sleeping rough on his way to Berlin in 1907, pay similar testimony to the tough lives of the poor.

Kirsten often introduces an undertone of ironic detachment which draws attention to the discrepancy between his idealising memory and historical reality. In the poem 'kindheit', for example, he stylises himself as a Grimmelshausian Simplicissimus, spending autumn days guarding the cattle herd outside the village:

> hinter dem dorf
> saß ich,
> eines bauern hütejunge,
> auf herbstnem graskleid
> im geruch der umwaldeten wiesen.
> ich war der kuhfürst
> sancta simplicitas
> im brombeerverhau. (elb, 30)

A similar balance between emotion-laden recollections and ironic detachment is found in 'das tal' and 'im häuslerwinkel'. In the latter the bombing of Dresden serves as a marker of the proximity of this timeless childhood world with wartime destruction (it performs a similar function in 'schulweg'):

> auf keiner karte verzeichnet,
> nicht aufzufinden mehr
> region einfältiger lehmkabachen,
> die wäldische kindheit
> im winkel der häusler,
> schlicht wie ein kalkbrennerleben,
> barfuß über distel und strunk.
> die satzzeichen zur biografie
> rochen nach lunte und
> fielen vom himmel als brandfackeln
> mit feuerschwänzen. (elb, 37)

Here, as in many of his other poems written in the sixties, Kirsten welcomes the arrival of socialism and the founding of the GDR ('in allen knechtskammern/ entsiegelt das geheimnis/ landläufiger demut'), and ends by expressing his intention to put the loss of his childhood behind him: 'ausgerollt habe ich den lebensfaden/ auf der lichtseite welt/ bei lebzeiten/ wie die waldrebe,/ zieh meiner straße,/ unmittelbar.' (elb, 37) However, the implication that state socialism has legitimately succeeded the destruction of a corrupt authoritarian regime suppresses memory of the pain and hardship of the postwar years, and the injustices incurred under the new repressive regime. These poems written in the sixties read as an unsuccessful attempt to reconcile personal experience with political expectations.

The comparatively few autobiographical references in the poems written between the early seventies and the late eighties, which were published in *der bleibaum* and *die erde bei Meißen*, are deeply pessimistic, and reflect Kirsten's political disillusionment. 'väterlich- erseits, mütterlicherseits' (1980) lists the professions of Kirsten's grandparents and other relatives (who were smiths, wheelwrights, carpenters, vagabonds, peddlers, weavers and farmers), concluding they were all short-changed by history, and implying it is natural that he should share their fate: 'bleichgesichtige/ hungerleider sie alle auf lebenszeit,/ denen der brotkorb immer um eine etage/ zu hoch hing', 'ein geschlecht von handwerkern/ und kleinbauern, nie aus dem dunkel/ getreten seiner und meiner leibeigenen/ geschichte' (elb, 189).

Kirsten's next poetry collection, *stimmenschotter* (1993), which comprises poems written between 1987 and 1992, was the first pub- lished after the *Wende*. Although many poems allude to the changed political circumstances, they are interspersed with the other, pre- *Wende* texts in such a way as to obliterate any sense of a break in 1990. In 'märchenhafte geschichte' Kirsten describes a trip in October 1990, in the company of the West German poets Peter Hamm and Michael Buselmeier, seeking out places associated with Friedrich Nietzsche (engagement with whose work had not been encouraged in the GDR). Having found the (decaying) house in Naumburg where the philosopher lived with his sister after he had lost his sanity, they search for the village of Pobles (today part of Muschwitz), where he spent the summer holidays with his grandparents and discovered his passion for reading. Night has fallen by the time they locate 'das sprachlose Pobles', which is 'grabesstill und gespenstisch zur nacht gebettet'. The village church stands in ruins, and the place, 'in sich versunken, erdwärts/ zusammengerutscht in die schuttkegel/ aller irdischen vergänglichkeit', is an image of the material disintegration and moral decay of the GDR.

The comment in a biography of Nietzsche, 'hier hat er wirklich gelebt', prompts Kirsten to ask: 'wo haben wir wirklich gelebt?' (elb, 227) This question, a central preoccupation of Kirsten's after 1990, is addressed in his poetry by looking back to a better time. But not, as in the writing of some contemporaries, through selective recall of the GDR years in a spirit of 'Ostalgie,' but rather through revival of his longstanding evocation of a more authentic, slower-paced way of life in the Klipphausen of his childhood. In half a dozen poems he speaks openly of the hardship of a 'kindheit auf rübenäckern/ und verqueckten feldern' (elb, 205) and describes wartime deprivation, suffering and the tragic loss of many young lives. But this aspect of the past is outweighed, as before, by a fairy-tale quality, symbolised in *Die Prinzessinnen im Krautgarten* by the mysterious walled kitchen garden of the local manor house, in which he imagines its two elderly princess owners walking slowly up and down, clad in black. Time stands still in this overgrown, secret garden, which tantalisingly recalls a lost age of security, order and plenitude, echoing the Rococo garden which appears in variations throughout Eichendorff's poems, fiction and autobiographical writings, and which derives in part from Eichendorff's memories of his childhood home in Lubowitz.

The poem 'selbst' (written 1991) describes a secret hide (possibly identical with the 'gespinst der öde' referred to in 'das vorwerk'), in which the young Kirsten would lie daydreaming, 'ein tagträumer, der ganze nachmittage lustvoll vertrödelte/ und begeistert den wolkenbildern nachsah,/ lag still für sich als fauler stauner in blutigen zeiten' (elb, 199). Moments of similar fulfilment are evoked in 'Mecklenburgischer sommer (1959)', which is one of the few poems from this period looking back at experiences during the forty years of socialism. It refers to a historical turning point of almost equal importance for Kirsten with 1945 and 1989, namely the compulsory collectivisation of agriculture which was carried out in 1960. The poem implies that Kirsten rediscovered the world of his childhood during a summer spent working on a family farm in Mecklenburg. It laments the sweeping away of a way of life involving traditional, seasonally determined rhythms of work by what he calls 'der große schlingschlang' (elb, 208) of agricultural modernisation. What Kirsten regrets above all is the disappearance of a primarily corporeal relationship with time and space, one of physical contact, meditative observation and knowledge of things derived from direct seeing and understanding.

If one of the key questions in *stimmenschotter* is: 'wo haben wir wirklich gelebt?', another is asked in the poem 'wie leb ich hier?' (elb, 243-4), in which changes in the landscape around Weimar reflect the political and social development since the *Wende*. The land has been divided up and sold, properties have been fenced off, and unwanted possessions, like the compromising aspects of people's past lives, have been swiftly disposed of:

die nackten tatsachen
über den zaun geworfen
ins herrenlose schwarzdorngestrüpp.
gartenplunder mit vorbedacht
entsorgt zum nulltarif.
das leben in die gleiche
gebracht.

Abandoned by the state, and excluded from places previously accessible to him, the poet no longer feels at home:

stiefvater staat hat sich
aus dem staube gemacht,
aufgeflogen, flügellos.
wer hat das scheitholz
geschichtet? wem gehört das flurband
vor der stadt?
mittendrin mein weg
über die schaftrift,
auf den schlittenberg hinauf,
flirrende schattenzüge neben mir her,
felderwärts gleitendes licht.
Wie leb ich hier? (elb, 243-4)

'vor der haustür' expresses his alienation in the new Germany more baldly: 'manchmal morgens,/ wenn ich vor die haustür trete,/ den stadtrand noch stille anwandelt/ für einen atemzug,/ umfängt mich herzbeklemmend die fremde. [...] ein fremdling bin ich/ mir selbst, landlos,/ dorfverloren, ausgesandt,/ das leben zu bestehn/ am hauseck, an das die hunde pissen.' (elb, 247)

Kirsten's preoccupation with Buchenwald, which begins around the time of the *Wende*,[12] is part of a concern with the gradual disappearance of traces of the past in the German landscape, and of memory of the past in the public sphere. In 'september am Ettersberg' he stands at the place where Russians desperately trying to escape were mown down by camp guards, and is prompted to think of the members of the Russian forces stationed in the GDR who are deserting before their units are withdrawn. He reflects on the responses of his companions to the change of circumstances after the *Wende*:

einer neben mir
weiß nichts mehr von sich, die erinnerungen sind ihm
davongelaufen. ein anderer schreibt
sein verflossenes leben um, bringt es nachträglich
in die passende form und fasson. einer hat den lieben gott
über die klinge springen lassen. einer trug den decknamen
Petrus und schrieb getreulich berichte. die boshaftigkeit
seiner verleumdungen sucht ihresgleichen,
wird mir berichtet. mehr begehr ich nicht zu wissen
von diesem tag, in wolkenlose geschichte getaucht. (elb, 229)

'feldwegs nach Orlamünde' brings together the past and the present in a melancholy review of Kirsten's own life and of socio-political developments. Gerhard Kaiser has shown in his detailed interpretation of the poem how the largely sober, unemotional tone is interrupted at two points, when the landscape through which the poet is walking suddenly opens up to a cosmic richness.[13] The sight of the ancient town in the evening sunshine and the song of the Oriole transport him back to his childhood, and it is momentarily 'als wär die dreimal gewendete zeit/ neunmal stehengeblieben' (elb, 250; the dates Kirsten is thinking of are probably 1933, 1945 and 1989). But Kirsten's habitual melancholy returns at the end of the poem, where he refers to the town as 'grown limp with rust and choked in mud' ('im rost verlummert/ und schlammstumm erstickt', elb, 250).

In Kirsten's most recent major volume, *wettersturz* (1999), the poem 'zeitgenossen' contains the formulation of Kirsten's poetic programme since the *Wende* as: 'auzuschreiben gegen das schäbige/ vergessen, das so viele leben einschließt,/ leben aus lauter vergangenheit' (elb, 295). The conception of remembering the past as a moral and political imperative is developed in a speech thanking the Konrad-Adenauer-Stiftung for the award of their literary prize in 2005. All his writing, he notes, has been 'im Grunde Lebensbeschreibung', or to be more precise, 'ein Abwälzen von Lebensstoff, der sich im Gedächtnis sedimentär abgelagert hat' (Bg, 111). Individual experiences are related to collective ones, and to historical causes and effects, in a process of literary work: 'nahezu bohrend schmerzhaft werden Erinnerungen abgefragt, reaktiviert, Vergessenes, Halbvergessenes durch Gedächtnistraining zurückzugewinnen gesucht'. In the face of the patent untruth of official versions of history in the GDR, it was the task of his generation of writers to engage in 'eigene Geschichtsfindung', and contribute to an unofficial counter-history of the GDR. Perhaps out of politeness to his CDU listeners, he does not expand on the ways in which he has continued this writing programme since reunification, addressing developments in East Germany as an inveterate 'schwarzseher' in times of 'epidemischer gedächtnis-/ schwund', in poems such as 'zeitgenossen', 'gesinnungswechsel' and 'frohe botschaft':

> laß die propheten stein und bein schwören,
> glänzende zeiten herbeireden, dich
> mit beglückungsprojekten eindecken,
> was auch immer sie heißen mögen,
> flügelschlag der geschichte erdenthoben,
> schwarzseher will man nicht dulden (elb, 372)

But Kirsten's provocative remembering in response to the *Wende* is only one aspect of a body of poetry which has sought since the 1960s to halt a forgetting which facilitates opportunism and destructive modernisation, by naming things, restoring them to being, and training readers to see and hear things themselves. Terms such as the 'grinding-stone of history' (elb, 105, 109, 132) and the 'shredder of progress' (elb, 187) allude to the danger of what he has called 'Verniemandung' in the processes of economic, social and cultural modernisation. (The term is adapted from the Mexican essayist Octavio Paz's concept of *ninguneo*, or 'no-one-ness', in *The Labyrinth of Solitude*, signifying a stripping away of identity.)

Kirsten's concern with the past must be understood in the context of the global boom in memory which began in the 1980s in response to the social and cultural changes associated with post- or late modernity. His preoccupation with his childhood corresponds to the revival of nostalgia identified by Svetlana Boym in *The Future of Nostalgia* as a potentially constructive response to developments in contemporary society. It is a manifestation of the longing for continuity in a fragmented world, a defence mechanism at a time of

historical upheavals and general acceleration of the pace of life.
'Unreflected nostalgia breeds monsters. Yet the sentiment itself, the
mourning of displacement and temporal irreversibility, is at the very
core of the modern condition,' Boym writes.[14] Although it is common-
ly dismissed as sentimental abdication of personal responsibility, the
wish for a guilt-free homecoming, and an ethical and aesthetic failure,
nostalgia can nevertheless perform a valuable function, in drawing
attention to unrealised possibilities. What the past might have been
has a bearing on what the future might become: 'Fantasies of the past
determined by needs of the present have a direct impact on realities of
the future'.[15]

Boym's distinctions between *melancholia*, which she defines as a
matter of purely individual consciousness, and *nostalgia*, which links
individual biographies with the fate of groups and nations, and between 'restorative' nostalgia (typically seeking to regain lost territory)
and 'reflective' nostalgia, which recognises the ambivalence of human
longing and the contradictions of modernity, show Kirsten firmly
aligned with the latter in both cases. Poems such as 'diktum' (elb,
282), which characterises the ambivalent temptation to indulge in
emotion-laden reflection on the past in the phrases 'der roggenseele
altes trugbild' and 'erinnerungs-/ sucht, du grünes holz des lebens',
can be seen as exemplifying the 'creative rethinking of nostalgia'
which Boym calls for, and her 'self-conscious exploration of longing',
not merely as an artistic device, but also as 'a way of making sense of
the impossibility of homecoming'.[16]

Kirsten's contribution to GDR autobiography is then an unusual
one in several respects. Firstly, it complements those depicted in other
essays in this volume, most of which are concerned with authors based
in Berlin, by being a regional (Saxon and Thuringian) remembering,
and a rural as opposed to an urban one. Secondly, there is also an
unusual class dimension to it, in that Kirsten describes himself as
'plebeian, not proletarian', and the community he speaks for is one of
agricultural labourers rather than the workers and farmers forming the
backbone of the socialist 'Arbeiter- und Bauernstaat'. Further distinctive features are that Kirsten's post-*Wende* yardstick is not 'Ostalgie' for the GDR, but his childhood, and the extent to which he
draws attention to the fact that this is a utopian construction, a construction of the remembering subject rather than reality. It is also
uncommon for landscape to stand in the foreground, as a sphere of

both autobiographical and collective remembering: it is simultaneously a 'cultural landscape' generated by centuries of human dwelling
and work and his personal home.

Finally, Kirsten's is a distinctly poetic remembering, one working
with images of the past rather than reflecting discursively, and paying
particular attention to language. It responds allergically to official
pronouncements and the ready-made phrases of ideology, and turns
away from abstract ideas in general to the sensual qualities of things,
incorporating dialect words and place names, and deautomatising
reading by condensing words into expressive compounds. Kirsten
seeks to preserve the memory of disappearing ways of life by reviving
linguistic repertoires associated with them, words discarded by history: 'wegrandworte, zu den gärten hinaus-/ geworfelt, dem distelpur-
pur eingeblasen, ausgestorbene/ wahrheiten, flurbereinigte flurnamen
die fülle,/ zugetragen vom auge der erinnerung' (elb, 284).

Notes

[1]   See for instance Bernhard Rübenach, ed., *Peter-Huchel-Preis. Ein Jahrbuch.*
1987. Wulf Kirsten. Texte. Dokumente. Materialien, Moos and Baden-Baden: Elster
Verlag, 1987; Wolfgang Emmerich, 'Von der "durchgearbeiteten Landschaft" zur
nature morte: Alte und neue Landschaftslyrik von Volker Braun, Wulf Kirsten und
anderen', *literatur für leser*, 1990 (2), 69-83; Axel Goodbody, 'Veränderte
Landschaft: East German Nature Poetry Since Reunification', *gfl-journal*, 2 (2005),
at: www.gfl-journal.de/2-2005/goodbody.html (last accessed 27 July 2011).

[2]   The honorary doctorate he received from the University of Jena in 2003 was
awarded for 'sein herausragendes lyrisches, erzählerisches und essayistischesWerk',
acknowledging his enrichment of the German language, his poetic appropriation of
the landscape and culture of Saxony and Thuringia, and his interventions on behalf of
suppressed and misunderstood literary traditions, but stressing in particular his 'den
Zäsuren von 1945 und 1989 gewidmete hartnäckige Arbeit aufklärend-verpflichtender
Erinnerung'. Gerhard R. Kaiser, ed., *Landschaft als literarischer Text. Der Dichter
Wulf Kirsten. Festschrift anlässlich der Ehrenpromotion durch die Friedrich-Schiller-
Universität Jena, 27. Mai 2003*, Jena: Glaux, 2004, 6-7. See also Anke Degenkolb's
monograph *'Anzuschreiben gegen das schäbige vergessen'. Erinnern und Gedächtnis
in Wulf Kirstens Lyrik*, Berlin: Logos, 2004, and Manfred Osten's eulogy 'Erinnerte
Gegenwart und lyrisches Gedächtnis bei Wulf Kirsten', in Günther Rüther, ed., *Verleihung des Literaturpreises der Konrad-Adenauer-Stiftung e.V. an Wulf Kirsten.
Weimar, 22. Mai 2005. Dokumentation*, Sankt Augustin: Konrad-Adenauer-Stiftung,
2005, 12-17, at: http://www.kas.de/wf/doc/kas_7788-544-1-30.pdf?051230110348
(last accessed 27 July 2011).

[3]   For convenience, Kirsten's poems are cited in the following from the comprehensive anthology *erdlebenbilder. gedichte aus 50 jahren. 1954-2004*, Zurich: Ammann, 2004 (here: p. 17), rather than from the individual volumes in which they
originally appeared. References to this volume are given in parantheses as 'elb', followed by the relevant page numbers.

[4]   Kirsten has elsewhere described 20th-century German history as 'geschichts-
befrachtete Wechselbäder', i.e. a succession of hot and cold baths into which his generation has been plunged, each leaving its historical legacy – *Brückengang. Essays
und Reden*, Zurich: Ammann, 2009, 122-30. References to this volume are given in
parentheses as 'Bg', followed by the relevant page numbers.

[5]   'gestutzt' is literally translated as 'pruned', 'trimmed', 'cropped' or 'docked', but
I have chosen 'stunted' because it seems close enough in meaning, and retains the
concentration of plosive consonants underlining the violent curtailing of biographies.

[6]   Wulf Kirsten, *Die Prinzessinnen im Krautgarten. Eine Dorfkindheit*, Munich and
Zurich: Piper, 2003. References to this text are given in parentheses as 'PK', followed
by the relevant page numbers.

[7]   Wulf Kirsten, 'Die Nacht im Rübenkeller', *neue deutsche literatur*, 33.4 (1985),
19-28.

[8]   *Die Prinzessinnen im Krautgarten* was preceded by two other prose works which
relate obliquely to his childhood home and possess thematic parallels. The first is his
affectionately ironic 'Portrait of a Provincial Town', *Kleewunsch* (Kleewunsch is a
fictional entity combining aspects of the village Klipphausen and the nearby town
Wilsdruff). The second, his 'Historical Report', *Die Schlacht bei Kesselsdorf*, describes the impact on the community of a previous bloody battle (Prussian troops
inflicted a crushing defeat on the Saxon army in the Battle of Kesselsdorf in 1745).
Die Schlacht bei Kesselsdorf and *Kleewunsch* were published in 1984 and reprinted in
1987, but they have been largely ignored by the reading public, whereas the more
accessible *Prinzessinnen im Krautgarten* was warmly received in reviews in *Die Zeit*,
the *Süddeutsche Zeitung*, the *Spiegel*, the *Neue Zürcher Zeitung*, and the *Frankfurter
Rundschau*, and was recommended to listeners on *Deutsche Welle*.

[9]   Christoph Victor, *Oktoberfrühling. Die Wende in Weimar 1989. Mit einer
Betrachtung zwanzig Jahre danach 'Der Himmel über uns' von Wulf Kirsten*, 2nd
edn, Weimar: Stadtmuseum Weimar, 2009.

[10]   Wulf Kirsten, *satzanfang. gedichte*, Berlin and Weimar: Aufbau, 1970, pp. 94-5.

[11]   Ibid., p. 94.

[12]   See for instance the poems 'der bärenhügel' (elb, 221), 'september am Ettersberg'
(elb, 229) and 'rauher ort' (elb, 368-9); Holm Kirsten and Wulf Kirsten, eds, *Stimmen
aus Buchenwald. Ein Lesebuch*, Göttingen: Wallstein, 2002; and Kirsten's text in

Wulf Kirsten and Harald Wenzel-Orf, *Der Berg über der Stadt. Zwischen Goethe und Buchenwald*, Ammann: Zurich, 2003.

[13] Gerhard R. Kaiser, 'Endzeit, Jahreszeit, Menschenzeit. Thüringer Landschaft in Wulf Kirstens Gedichten', in Kaiser, *Landschaft als literarischer Text*, pp. 137-53.

[14] Svetlana Boym, *The Future of Nostalgia*, New York: Basic Books, 2001, p. xvi.

[15] Ibid.

[16] Ibid., p. xvii.

Heinz-Peter Preußer

Institutionen hatten 'sich in der Landschaft festgesetzt wie ägyptische Pyramiden':[1] Volker Brauns Lebens/Werk und sein *Hinze-Kunze-Roman* in der Dialektik von Stagnation und Radikalkritik[2]

The GDR was and is – even two decades after its demise – the fixed point in Volker Braun's life's work. Indeed, his life and work can neither be separated from each other, nor from the East German state. The three reflect each other in Braun's texts as a 'Life/Work/GDR', in a range of dissolves between fiction and reality, including autofiction. His writing is, however, less a fictional embellishment of biographical experience than an imaginative experimentation with different positions in society. In *Hinze-Kunze-Roman*, Braun represents the key dilemma of institutional stagnation, presenting it as something which can be overcome by force of will, in the form of a universalised Eros. In contrast, Braun's texts after the *Wende* seek to come to terms with the loss of this projection, which implies both self-denial and a reduced form of life.

Das Versagte und das Gewollte

In Volker Brauns Theaterstück *Limes. Mark Aurel* wird der historische stoische Kaiser, der nicht allein als Herrscher des Römischen Reiches, sondern auch durch sein philosophisches Werk *Ad se ipsum* der Nachwelt präsent geblieben ist,[3] zur Karikatur verzerrt. Sein Vertrauen in die Weltvernunft und die eigene Blindheit, so zeigt ihn das Stück, bedingen einander.[4] Wie sein Arzt richtig bemerkt, wehrt der Denker mit Vorliebe das ab, was offensichtlich ist und entwertet, was Vergnügen, gar Lust bereiten könnte (LMA, 58). Die Bändigung der Leidenschaften durch Vernunft, die Zügelung der Emotionen im Kalkül werden in den Machtkonstellationen Roms zur komischen Nummer travestiert.

Überall muss der Philosoph auf dem Kaiserthron Grenzen ziehen: zur eigenen Machtsicherung im Innern (LMA, 59-60), gegen die fleischlichen Verlockungen (LMA, 68), gegen den Leib, die Lebenslust und die Infamie seiner Frau (LMA, 62-3), gegen das Aufwallen der Emotionen wie der Gewalt (LMA, 61); und nach außen setzt er den titelgebenden Limes: gegen die Barbaren (LMA, 64).[5] Die Fronten verlaufen innen wie außen; der Prozess der Zivilisation bedeutet überall Kampf. Auch 'das Denken' sei, so der Imperator, 'eine Festung, um unbezwinglich zu sein' (LMA, 67). Als Fulvia, seine Frau, durch die Pest zu Tode kommt, bleibt Mark Aurel, wie kaum anders zu erwarten, gefasst (LMA, 64). 'Sterben ist ja eine von den Aufgaben unseres Lebens', sagt er. 'Das ist der vollkommenste Mensch, der von uns scheidet, um der Schlechtigkeit zu entgehen.' (LMA, 67)

'Nur wer die Welt aushält, kann handeln' (LMA, 58), sagte sein Ziehvater Antoninus Pius einst zum noch jungen Marcus Aurelius. Gegen Ende des Stücks dekliniert der Philosophenkaiser den Satz durch und kommt zu einem ganz anderen Resultat: 'Man muss es aushalten, um es zu kennen. Man muss es kennen, um zu handeln. Handeln heißt, es nicht mehr auszuhalten.' (LMA, 66) Trotz allen Spotts für den Kaiser und seine vielfältigen, grotesken Untergänge scheint dieses Dilemma, dieser Zirkel, auch eine Summe der *Selbstbetrachtungen* ihres Autors Volker Braun zu sein.

Selbstbeschreibungen im Gewand der Fiktion sind nicht neu. Sie mögen vielleicht einer der Hauptgründe für die Erfindung fiktionaler Figuren sein, um die eigene Person zu schonen.[6] Zwischen der fiktionalen und der faktualen Welt – diesen beiden kategorischen Trennungslinien innerhalb der erzählerischen und der darstellenden Universen[7] – gibt es freilich unzählige Überschneidungspunkte und Überblendungen: bis hin zur Autofiktion,[8] der nur camouflierten Autobiografie im Gewand der narrativen Fiktion. Gerade in letzter Zeit hat man den fiktionalen Anteil an den faktualen Geschichten, am sogenannten Dokumentarischen und an den großen Geschichtskonstruktionen hervorgehoben.[9]

Hier geht es aber nicht, wie etwa bei Wolfgang Hilbig, um die fiktionale Auskleidung biografischer Einzelheiten, die den (Ich-)Erzähler und die Person des Autors scheinbar amalgamieren. Zu viele Details des Lebenswegs finden sich dort in der Fiktion wieder, sodass immerfort eine Referenz auf reale Lebensläufe unterstellt wird. Das Selbst hat sich erst, indem es schreibt. Es vergewissert sich seiner Existenz und erlangt sie gleichsam erst im Vollzug des Schreibens.[10] Bei Volker Braun, wie bei kaum einem anderen Schriftsteller, gerät dieser Verarbeitungsprozess des eigenen Lebens aber nicht zur Selbstkonstruktion einer Biografie im Schreibakt, sondern, statt dessen, zur politischen Allegorie:[11] vermutlich deshalb, weil bei ihm die Identifikation mit dem untergegangenen Staat DDR so umfassend war wie bei fast keinem anderen Dichter. Braun entfaltet sich in die möglichen Spielarten seines Selbst, um in der Fiktion die Bindung an den Staat zu reflektieren und durchzuspielen. Viel von dem Interesse des Autors an 'seinem Staat', diesem 'kleinen Land' (T, IX, 52), fließt deshalb direkt in die fiktionalen Figuren ein. Zuweilen aber schaltet sich der eigentlich heterodiegetische, also am Geschehen unbeteiligte Er-Erzähler sogar direkt in die Fiktion ein und wandelt sich dann zum Ich-Erzähler, der, noch dazu, mit einiger Absicht intendiert, als sein eigener 'Autor' identifiziert zu werden.[12] Dergestalt wird die Grenze zum homodiegetischen Erzählen verwischt. Der 'Autor' ist in diesen Momenten neben seine Figuren gestellt, ja er mischt sich gelegentlich unter sie. Braun schreibt sich also vielfach ein, macht sich auch selbst zum Bestandteil der allegorischen Bilder seiner Prosa.

So ist die Melancholie nach der 'Wende' nur zu verständlich, die er auf die Geschichte projiziert – und damit eben zugleich sich selbst beschreibt.[13] Dieser Selbstbezug erscheint nur vordergründig weniger evident. Seit zwei Jahrzehnten verarbeitet Volker Braun einen Verlust, der einer Fata Morgana gleicht: Das 'Möglichwerden'[14] ist dem Denken und Dichten abhanden gekommen. Geschichte und Subjekt, Weltveränderung wie Deutung sind gleichermaßen gescheitert. Dennoch, oder gerade deshalb, führt die Selbstbetrachtung nicht zu einem Gefühl der Scham (den Opfern gegenüber), sondern in einen merkwürdigen Spagat von Vitalismus, Willensmetaphysik und Kulturkritik, den der Autor postmodernistisch inszeniert. So entsteht eine Hybridform nachsozialistischer Identität, die gleichwohl signifikant ist. Das lyrische Ich wie die Protagonisten der schmalen Erzählungen oder Theaterstücke hadern mit ihrem Selbst, das sie entleert, am Ende eines Weges glauben, der zutiefst vergeblich, unnütz erscheint. Der gewesene reale Sozialismus gerinnt dabei zu einer Chiffre des besseren, des sinnvollen Lebens, das freilich nicht gelebt, ja nicht einmal wirklich gewollt worden ist. Daraus erklärt sich die Tragik, zugleich aber auch die Borniertheit des Autors, der meint, allein mit dezisionistischer Entschiedenheit hätten das andere Leben und eine sinnvolle Arbeit herbeigeführt werden können.

Der Wille wird verklärt zur Instanz des Anderen, rein tautologisch: Wäre der Wille gewollt worden, hätte das nichtgelebte Leben lebbar sein können.[15] Gestraft werden die fiktiven Figuren wie ihr Autor selbst durch die tatsächliche Wende der Verhältnisse, die nicht die herbeigesehnte gewesen ist, und die in den politischen Kategorien

Brauns nur als Reaktion und Restauration alter Besitzverhältnisse von
arm und reich erscheint.[16] Bei all der eingestreuten Kulturkritik, bei
allem romantischen Antikapitalismus, der hier wieder auferstehen
darf, fällt die Schwundform von Utopie, an der Braun allem Anschein
nach immer noch festhält, sehr bescheiden aus. In den letzten Jahren
mehren sich die dunklen Töne der Melancholie mit einem resignativen
Blick auf das eigene Altern und die Vergeblichkeit der Lebensan-
strengung an sich,[17] gerade weil sie geschichtlich nicht entlohnt worden ist. So changiert das Wirklichgewollte in nur noch kryptischen
Erzählfragmenten zu Fantasien über den eigenen Tod, der gewaltvoll
hereinbricht, und der anzeigt, 'was [zuletzt] kommt':[18] die Transformation in einen anderen, elementaren Aggregatszustand. Das Selbst
kehrt zurück zum gärenden Leben, und das historische Subjekt löst
sich auf in Lebensphilosophie.

Utopie zwischen Herr und Knecht

Im letzten Jahrzehnt der DDR war das noch anders. Mit dem *Hinze-
Kunze-Roman* schrieb Braun die Hoffnungsphilosophie Ernst Blochs
in die Herr-Knecht-Dialektik ein. Der Autor befand sich, wie Verena
Kirchner geschrieben hat, noch auf der Suche nach einem neuen,
einem anderen revolutionären Subjekt, das den realpolitischen Sinn-
verlust kompensieren sollte.[19] Obgleich der Text in seiner Dimension
als konkrete Utopie nicht verstanden wurde, ist er einer der letzten
großen Legitimationsdiskurse für den real existierenden Sozialismus
vor dessen Ende gewesen. Das mag verwundern, prägt die Rezeption
der essayistisch thesenhaften Narration doch vor allem die Zensur-
geschichte, die für vier Jahre das Erscheinen verzögerte. York-Gothart
Mix hat dies in seinem immer wieder zitierten Materialienband ausführlich dokumentiert.[20] Die Autorengespräche, Aktenvermerke, die
Gutachten, gerade die ausführlichen von Dieter Schlenstedt und Hans
Kaufmann, die Korrespondenz mit dem Ministerium für Kultur der
DDR, Hauptverwaltung Verlage und Buchhandel, die 'schöngeistige
Lesehilfe' für die Ausgabe des Mitteldeutschen Verlages 1985 im Anhang des Romans, wiederum von Dieter Schlenstedt, die Verrisse von
Hans Koch und Anneliese Löffler, die in der Rezension agierte, als
wolle sie belegen, mit der fiktionalen Figur der 'Frau Professor Mes-
serle' identisch zu sein, der nachträgliche Stopp der Erstauflage,
schließlich die Verhinderung der zweiten Auflage: All das ließ doch

offenkundig nur zu, in Volker Brauns Roman allein Chiffren der Subversivität suchen zu müssen, wie Jaak de Vos schreibt.[21] Dabei hat man in der Regel den Funktionär Kunze als Machtmenschen begreifen wollen, ein Zerrbild der politischen Elite des Landes, der dadurch der Spiegel vorgehalten werde. Konrad Naumann, der 1. Sekretär der Bezirksleitung der SED in Berlin, soll sich durch die Figur angesprochen gefühlt haben.[22] Aber der Text ist kein Schlüsselroman. Intertextuell folgt er deutlich einer Vorgabe Fühmanns, wie mehrfach, und ausführlich bei Kai Köhler, bemerkt wurde.[23] Unterschlagen wird in solchen Betrachtungen das utopische Potenzial gerade dieser Figur, ihr 'visionäres Denken'.[24] Kritisiert wird bei Braun vielmehr der Fahrer Hinze, der Abhängige, der Knecht, der sich nicht weit vom Fatalismus seines literarischen Vorbildes Jacques bei Diderot entfernt[25] und die Trägheit des Herrn in der französischen Vorlage auch noch für sich reklamiert.[26]

Naturgemäß hat Braun in der weiblichen Hauptfigur Lisa mehr 'Entwicklungspotenzial' ausgemacht. Wo Möglichkeit sein soll, setzt der Autor stets Frauen ein. Das gilt seit den Frauenfiguren im vierten Teil des *Kast*, *Die Tribüne*, der 1974 geschrieben wurde und 1979 erschien (vgl. T, V, 7-55, 313). Sie tragen den Ballast der utopischen Projektionen, ohne hinlängliches erzählerisches Eigengewicht zu erhalten. Kunze ist dagegen durch seine Ambivalenzen komplexer, interessanter. Er ist es, der Lisa fördert; sie soll und wird sich qualifizieren. Andererseits nutzt er ihr gegenüber die Macht aus, für die er steht, und macht sie zum Objekt seiner Begierde. Wie Marlies aus dem *Hinze-und-Kunze*-Stück bleibt deshalb auch Lisa eigentümlich blass. Kunze dagegen ist ein Kraftmensch fast aus dem *Sturm und Drang*, ein Ausbund an Vitalität. Seine Sinnlichkeit macht ihn zum 'Schwein', wie es mehrmals wörtlich heißt (T, VII, 87, 108, 111, 122), aber auch zum Vorschein einer befreiten Sensualität, so widersinnig das zunächst klingen mag.

Damit ist er die Gegenfigur des resignierenden, sich versagenden Mark Aurel, den Braun zum zentralen Protagonisten nach der Wende erhebt. Kunze folgt mehr seinen Trieben als dem Logos; ihn regiert sein Geschlecht, nicht umgekehrt. Triebaufschub im Sinne des Zivilisationsprozesses (Norbert Elias) lässt er nur gelten, solange dies zur Erreichung seiner sexuellen Ziele nötig ist. Der Funktionär ist ein sozialistischer Don Juan oder Don Giovanni, wie Bloch ihn verstehen würde: als 'Leitfigur[..] der Grenzüberschreitung'.[27] Seine Absolutheit

im Begehren macht ihn einerseits zur komischen Figur im satirischen
Geschehen, andererseits zum projektiven Ideal einer befreiten
Menschheit.[28] In ihm arbeitet etwas, das mehr ist, als er weiß. Er ist
die Verkörperung des 'Noch-Nicht-Bewußten oder der Dämmerung
nach Vorwärts'.[29]

Das Macht-Wollen

Kunzes Problem ist nicht, dass er will. Er soll wollen. Nur will er mit
den falschen Mitteln. Hinze dagegen gehört zu jenen, von denen sein
Autor später sagen wird, sie hätten 'es nicht gewollt'.[30] Sein Chef aber
will: im Sinne von Schopenhauers dunklem Lebenstrieb, der alle Er-
scheinungen der Welt durchdringt;[31] und er will den Sozialismus. Der
liegt im 'gesellschaftlichen Interesse' (T, VII, 49, 212, *passim*). Und
seine sexuellen Interessen am anderen Geschlecht sollen mit diesen
politischen Interessen zusammenfallen. Das ist das utopische Programm des real existierenden Anarchisten Volker Braun. Es geht darum, die Trennungen aufzuheben: die zwischen Mann und Frau, die in
den Arbeitsprozessen.[32] Das Problem des '*Führenden*', Kunze, liegt
darin, dieses Wollen mit Machtmitteln gegen die '*Geführten*' durchzu-
setzen (T, VII, 237). Er nutzt seine Position aus, um sich die Frauen
gefügig zu machen, die er begehrt. Damit verrät er die entgrenzende
Funktion des Eros,[33] die ihn selbst verwandeln würde. Kunze soll auch
genießen dürfen, meint der Roman. Die ihm das neiden, sind Spießer,
behauptet der Text. Aber Kunze gibt nicht zurück, was er empfängt.
Er will nur haben, könnte Erich Fromm sagen, statt zu sein.[34] In
anderen Begriffen: Er verrät den Eros an den Sexus.[35] Nach 'sieben
Jahren in seinem Ehebett', heißt es in den *Berichten von Hinze und
Kunze*, 'tastete [...] [s]ein Rüssel nach dem Besitz. Sie floh kalkweiß
an die Wand.' (T, VII, 33) 'Die Liebe ist ein Kind der Freiheit', ist der
Passus überschrieben; und frei zur Liebe ist eben Kunze nicht oder
nicht mehr.
    Spontaneität, als Austritt aus dem Zwangsverhältnis von Herrschaft
und Knechtschaft, wie Fromm es sieht, erlaubt der Funktionär sich nur
im sexuellen Übergriff. Damit überführt er das Handeln aus freien
Stücken – aus eigenem Willen oder Antrieb (*sponte*) –[36] aber wieder
in den Zwang, den er selbst den anderen aufnötigt. Er bestätigt sein
Selbst und damit zugleich die Herrschaft über andere. Er ist Subjekt
im Sinne von Adorno und Horkheimers *Dialektik der Aufklärung*

(1947) nur, weil er andere zu Objekten macht. Und Objekt wird auch die äußerliche wie die eigene Natur. Sein Triebleben wird ihm ein Instrument der Selbstbestätigung. Das gilt selbst für Hinze, der 'seine Lisa' nur routiniert, wie einen Besitz begehrt, sie nicht mehr achtet (T, VII, 56, 72-3). Lisa wird ihm deshalb vom Vorgesetzten entwendet (T, VII, 61), der letztlich doch nicht anders mit ihr verfährt. Kunze, Hinze und selbst der abrupt in die Ichform wechselnde Erzähler[37] lösen einander im erzählend personalen Modus der erlebten Rede und im dramatischen Modus der nicht markierten direkten Figurenrede ab, um die Schöne zu beschreiben.[38] '[W]as bleibt noch? Die Körperteile, die beide unberührt ließen: Schultern, Hände und Knie, ihre ausdrucks-vollsten Partien, die rührendsten' (T, VII, 63). Allein die Kunst, hier personifiziert durch den Erzähler, verklärt den Trieb zur Schönheit – womit wir wieder, indirekt, bei Schopenhauer wären.[39]

Was den Eros dem Ideal des Kommunismus annähert, ist seine ichauflösende Funktion. Das Selbst sollte sich verlieren an den An-deren, so die romantische Sehnsucht, die im Interesse des Erzählers liegt. Im Eros verschenkt sich der Körper als Natur an die Natur. Eben das wäre, in der romantischen Konstruktion, schön.[40] Kunze hingegen geht auf Beutefang aus. Das ist Sexus im strikten Sinne, so wie Klages die Dichotomie entfaltet.[41] Nicht zufällig gerät der sozialistische Funktionär deshalb in Hamburg auf die Reeperbahn (T, VII, 119). Hier erkennt er die seinem Verhalten adäquate, wenngleich geldförmige Variante des Geschlechtslebens. Der Fortschritt des Kapitalismus auf diesem Sektor hat seine verlockenden Seiten, erfährt Kunze (T, VII, 123), auch wenn man dafür zahlen muss – und mehr zu zahlen hat, als man zunächst denkt (T, VII, 122). Das ist, unter der Hand, eine subtile Kritik aller Fortschrittsideologie, die Braun zunehmend auch am eigenen Lager betreibt.

Es gehört zu den Kunstgriffen dieser besonderen Verschränkung von *Triebstruktur und Gesellschaft* (Marcuse), dass der sexualisierte Diskurs des Romans ja an kaum einer Stelle handfest zu greifen ist. Anzügliche Formulierungen verwandelt der Text erst durch die Kon-texte in eine vulgäre, leicht klebrige Sprache. Hier zeigt sich ein genuin strukturalistisches Verfahren des Autors, ein paradigmatisch operierendes Gegenstück zu Elfriede Jelineks syntagmatischem Stak-kato. Während die Autorin allein in der Verkettung der Signifikanten die Bloßstellung der sexualisierten Umwelt betreibt, die maskierenden und demaskierenden Wortwendungen sich unmittelbar aufeinander

folgend ablösen und enttarnen, etwa im Roman *Lust* (1989), braucht
man bei Braun immer zusätzlich die Rückversicherung im Paradigma.
Nie ist dann die eigentliche Rede das Gemeinte. Immer gibt sich das
wirkliche Interesse in der Transformation des billigen Herrenwitzes
oder der jugendlichen Kraftmeierei zu erkennen. Eine *Sprache der
Liebe* (Barthes) existiert nur als grobianische Verballhornung. Keiner
könnte diese Anspielungen in ihrer Eindeutigkeit übersehen. Und
doch sind es nur Allusionen. Sie zeigen auf, wie sehr die Sphäre der
Macht auf die Bereiche des Sinnlichen sich abbilden lässt.

Die Denktradition seit der Studentenrevolte aber will, dass dieses
sehr private Interesse das allgemeine sein sollte.[42] Braun intendiert
eine Aufhebung der Trennung von Arbeit und Lust, von öffentlich und
privat, von gesellschaftlichen und Einzel-Bestrebungen. Und das
avantgardistische Postulat, Kunst und Leben sollten eins sein,[43]
schließt sich dem an. 'Lisa wollte leben' (T, VII, 89); das wirbelt die
Gesellschaft mit ihren Hierarchien durcheinander. In lichten Momenten erkennt es auch Kunze:

> Vor diesem Luder zähl ich nicht, nicht mehr als mein Fahrer [...] Wir sind gleich.
> Sie ist eine fantastische Frau, eine utopische Körperschaft, wer ihr nahe kommt
> wird ausgezogen, seiner *Würde* entkleidet, fliegt glatt aus dem Amt, der findet
> sich in der Masse wieder und kann anstehn vor dem Fleischladen Platzkarten-
> schalter Wohnungsamt, mit der laufenden Nummer! (T, VII, 88)

Dynamik und Stagnation

Kunze ist es darum, der die Dynamik der Gesellschaft in Gang setzt.
Hinze steht für die Stagnation. So gesehen, 'operiert der Funktionär
Kunze als verborgener Utopist' (T, VII, 229). 'Kunze ist [...], in seinen
innersten Regungen, [...] ein Mensch von morgen' (T, VII, 228), erläu-
tert der Autor selbst in seinen Notizen. Damit signalisiert Braun ein,
wenngleich befremdliches, Bündnis mit den Herrschenden, das von
den Zensurinstanzen allerdings nicht begriffen wurde.[44] Die ägypti-
schen Pyramiden sind die festgefahrenen Verhältnisse: Institutionen,
die das vitale Durcheinander unter sich ersticken wollen, die nur durch
die Kunstgriffe des Eros aufgelöst und in Bewegung gehalten werden.
Die Bewegtheit im Auto, in den Strukturen hingegen ist nur schein-
haft. Sie zementiert die Positionen. Auffällig wenig ereignet sich im
Plot des Romans. Man fährt gemeinsam durch Straßen in Berlin oder
über Land, besucht Versammlungen und Betriebe, reist ins Ausland

oder tauscht die Frauen. Der letzte Dialog offenbart den Stillstand: 'Fahr zu', befiehlt Kunze. 'Wohin?', fragt der Knecht. 'Na vorwärts… Weiter halt', gibt der Herr zur Antwort. Es ist nur eine Frage der Intonation, ob es nach diesem Satz weiter gehen kann: Weiter halt oder Weiter, halt! 'Sie fuhren weiter', beruhigt der Erzähler, 'aber ich kann nicht so fortfahren in diesem Text' (T, vii, 211). Wie sehr Erzähler und Autor hier wieder als eine Instanz zu denken sein sollen, macht die Notiz vom 6. 9. 1985 deutlich:

> der *Hinze-Kunze-Roman* eine zustandsbeschreibung, der unsere festgefahrenheit in der selbstverschuldeten divergenz zeigt; er hat nichts transitorisches, er sprengt seine welt nicht auf. Auch lisa, die kolportierte positive heldin, hat nicht die verwandelnde kraft, sie wird nur qualifiziert, als eine sozialistische emanze, mit konventionellem gemüt. (T, vii, 223)

Den letzten Satz hat der Autor offenbar bereut. Er fehlt in dem umfänglichen Arbeitsjournal *Werktage 1* von 2009, das die Passage sonst unverändert wiedergibt.[45] Volker Brauns proletarischer *Hans Faust* (überarbeitet erschien das Stück unter dem Titel *Hinze und Kunze*) verband noch ein pathetisches Ja zur sozialistischen Gesellschaft mit der Vision einer möglichen 'anderen Arbeit' und der 'Gretchenfrage' nach 'sozialistischer Demokratie'. Der gesellschaftliche Pakt zwischen dem Funktionär Kunze und dem Arbeiter Hinze führt zu einer mustergültigen sozialistischen Karriere des Arbeiters, ändert aber nichts an den politischen Hierarchien. Die Voraussetzungen für strukturelle Veränderungen schafft stattdessen Hinzes Frau Marlies. Die Ingenieurin entwickelt nicht nur ein neues technisches Verfahren, sie überzeugt auch die Arbeiter vom individuellen wie gesellschaftlichen Nutzen der damit verbundenen Fortbildungsmaßnahmen (T, ii, 159-227): 'Sie wollte nicht das Opfer sein und kein Objekt der Pläne, sondern ihr Leben packen und entscheiden, und sei es falsch!' (T, ii, 220) Mit der Entscheidung für die Arbeit wird aber zugleich das Leben negiert, was den Text in eine grundsätzliche Ambivalenz manövriert. Marlies treibt ein eigentlich gewolltes Kind ab:

> Ich reiße mich selber aus mir. Mein Blut aus meinem Bauch in den Boden, auf dem wir bauen. Jetzt bin ich wer: Wer bin ich. Das Leben tot, mir aus dem Gesicht geschnitten. Eine Mörderin. Eine unserer Besten. (T, ii, 220)[46]

Die Berichte von Hinze und Kunze, Miniaturen im Stil von Brechts *Flüchtlingsgesprächen*,[47] kommen, seltsamerweise, ohne die weibliche Nebenfigur aus, die in den beiden anderen Fassungen doch so offenbar eine bedeutsame Rolle spielt. Zumeist in Form kurzer, lakonischer Dialoge zeigt Braun Missstände wie die Diskrepanz zwischen offizieller Schönfärberei und politischer Realität, allgemeine Stagnation, Privilegien, die Unterdrückung von Kritik und, zentral, das gesellschaftliche Machtgefälle. In den *Berichten von Hinze und Kunze* aber ist das Verhältnis der beiden Antagonisten zueinander gerade anders herum gestrickt als im Roman. Hier klagt der Knecht ein, was ihm nicht behagt, was an Ungleichheit geblieben ist in der Gesellschaft. Der Hinze des Romans findet sich mit allem ab, derjenige der Berichte zeiht hingegen den Kunze des Defätismus, weil der in den Strukturen verharren will (T, VII, 16). Es komme hingegen darauf an, 'das Ändern zu ändern', damit die Welt bestehen bleibt (T, VII, 20).

Im Roman, der 'kein belletristischer' sein darf (T, VII, 224) und tatsächlich als Essay in Rollen spricht, ist es der Funktionär, der nach den Möglichkeiten sucht: 'was sucht er bei den Frauen? Es ist eine Sucht, eine Sehnsucht, eine Gier ... die der Dienst nicht stillt. Und doch ist es das beste Gefühl' (T, VII, 225). Suche und Sucht, Sehnsucht und Gier verhalten sich wie Freiheit zu Notwendigkeit, wie Eros zu Sexus, wie gesund zu krank (vgl. T, VII, 66). 'Was Liebe will', sagt eine Schwarzgelockte am Rednerpult, 'das will sie bald'. Kunze, begeistert und gefangen, erleidet einen Anfall (T, VII, 67). Der Funktionär, 'ein Faun in Funktion' (T, VII, 218), den der Trieb leitet und nicht die Partei, schafft es nicht, sich auszuliefern an die Anderen. Also hört man ihn 'wüste, zynische, brutale Dinge' rufen 'gegen die *Weiber*' (T, VII, 220). Er verleugnet, was er nicht besitzen kann. Und den Besitz will er nicht lassen. Das ist das Drama des Kunze.

Hinze hingegen kommt nicht zu sich und auch nicht recht zu den Frauen. Für diese Fehlleistung hat er sich eigens eine geschlechtertypologische Theorie gebastelt, die ihm das 'Weib', weitestgehend, auf Distanz hält (T, VII, 110). Gegen Hinze spricht deshalb weniger, dass er die eigene Frau dem Vorgesetzten überlässt. Auch kritisiert der Roman nicht die Umkehrung dieses Prozesses. Hinze darf mit dem Zuspruch der Narration die abgelegten Verhältnisse Kunzes übernehmen (T, VII, 135, 138-9). Nein: Kritisiert wird Hinze dafür, dass er Lisa nicht will, sie nicht erkennt in ihrem Selbstsein – und den Verlust nicht einmal empfindet: 'Kunze lebte für alle, auch für Hinze, er nahm ihm ein Stückchen Leben ab. Hinze merkte nicht, daß ihm etwas fehlte' (T, VII, 143).

Wo der Dialog zwischen Funktionär und Werktätigem in den *Berichten* als probates Mittel erscheint, um gesellschaftliche Widersprüche produktiv zu machen, 'bremsen' im *Roman* der Funktionär Kunze und sein Fahrer Hinze, ehemaliger 'Dreher [und] Bestarbeiter' (T, VII, 117; vgl. 155), sich selbst und einander. Bei Kunze ist Freiheits- und Gemeinschafts-Streben mit Herrschaftsbedürfnis gepaart, Hinze dagegen lähmt, bei aller Kritik an der Gesellschaftspyramide, eine innere Verbundenheit mit den Herrschenden: Er ballt die Faust nur hinter dem Rücken – oder 'um die Lohntüte' (T, VII, 118). Innerhalb der autoritären Konstellation, die Funktionär und Fahrer bilden, ist keine grundsätzliche, qualitative Änderung möglich. Die komplexen Beziehungen zwischen Geschichts- und Kulturphilosophie, von Bewusstsein und Triebstruktur, Ökonomie und Sprache projiziert Brauns Roman demnach nur auf das eine Modell von Herr und Knecht (vgl. T, VII, 227).[48]

Entgrenzung und Kommunion

Utopisch weitreichende Impulse sieht der Roman, wo überhaupt, außerhalb dieses Zirkels der Stagnation, in 'weiblichen' Vorstellungs- und Verhaltensmustern, bei Künstlern, in der Kunst. Weil Kritik im pyramidalen Diskurs unmöglich wird, muss sie *radikal* werden, an die Wurzeln gehen, anders sein als das von ihr Kritisierte, glaubt der Text. Männlich instrumentellem Denken, dem Besitzenwollen, setzt der Autor die subversive Wirkung von Vielfalt, Solidarität, Kreativität, Lust und Liebe entgegen. Die Entgrenzung der Kunst, meint Braun, ist eine erotische, zu der sich die Männer Hinze und Kunze nicht befreien können, die dem Sexus verhaftet bleiben. Sie ist weiblich konnotiert gemäß dem Rollenklischee, aber nicht weiblich besetzt, wie vor allem an Lisa zu sehen war. Es ist, abermals, der 'Autor' als Ich-Erzähler, der deshalb diese Fantasie entwickelt – zunächst als Intermedium der '*schönste[n]* Liebesgeschichte' (T, VII I, 157) – und sie dann verbindet mit der 'Großen Kommunion', wie Horst Domdey, bezogen auf Brauns Gedicht *Das Eigentum*, sagt (T, X, 52).[49] Der Ich-Erzähler berichtet von einer Lesung in Dresden,

unter dem Himmel der Heimat im Großen Garten vor dem Halbrund des Theaters. Es dunkelte. Ich las die gefährlichsten Texte: Liebesgedichte; die laue Nacht, die abenteuerlich stummen Zuhörer verleiteten mich zu dem subversiven Thema. Aus den Wiesen, aus den breiten Wegen wehte ein betäubender Duft. Die riesigen Bäume standen, das blühende Leben, da, mit herausgestreckten Organen. [...] Ich hörte mir kaum zu, ich hörte auf das Knistern in der Luft. Ich sah die dunkle Gemeinde nicht, mit der ich mich verbrüdern wollte. (Konnte es sein? Wir miteinander? Sie, auf denen morgen wieder die Arbeit lastete – und mir ist sie eine Lust. Mir ist sie ein *Vergnügen* [...]. Konnten wir uns lieben?) [...] Ich las mit murmelnder, eintöniger Stimme, ich redete wie gewöhnlich, um mein Leben. (T, VII I, 212)

Im Schlussbild des Romans ist der Ich-Erzähler ganz nahe bei der Figur Kunze, als würde er, 'aus dem Fenster starrend einem Rock hinterher' blicken. Der kleine Flirt nach der Lesung bringt den Autor aus dem Konzept. 'Ich schnappte nach Luft, ich redete dummes Zeug. Der Schweiß brach mir aus der Maske'. Aber dann greift die Metamorphose. Der Ich-Erzähler bemerkt,

wie in der Bewegung ein anderer Kopf aus meinem Rumpf schnellte mit mühelos fröhlichem Gesicht. [...] Der fröhliche Kerl stieg in meinen ganzen Körper schaukelte sich darin daß die Äste flogen. [...]; ich runzelte nur die Stirn wie ein überfahrener Chef. Und doch hätte ich mich umarmen mögen, den unvorsichtigen Fahrer, die gesengte Sau. Die Frau betrachtete meine Verwandlung, ohne zu erschrecken. Sie schien alles zu begreifen, was ich nicht begriff... was ich beschreibe. (T, VII, 213-14)

Ich ist nun Kunze und Hinze zugleich und vielleicht immer nur eine Auffächerung dieser beiden falschen Alternativen gewesen: sein eigener Fahrer, 'der sich anweist und selber denkt' und den Knoten nicht zerschlagen kann. So überkommt ihn das Fieber. 'Ich wußte es, ich bin krank, ich kann jetzt nicht weiter. Ich schäme mich, Kameraden. Es ist bei mir weit hinein böse. Ich begreife mich nicht...' (T, VII, 214)

Bei aller Kritik und Selbstkritik, wie sie hier paradigmatisch für das Werk des Autors geäußert wird, blieb es für Braun stets gewiss, im besseren der beiden Deutschland zu leben. Auch wenn sich die Institutionen 'in der Landschaft festgesetzt hatten wie ägyptische Pyramiden', wie es im *Hinze-Kunze-Roman* heißt, hat der Besitz der Produktionsmittel doch eine grundlegende Korrektur herbeigeführt. Hinze 'gehörten die Maschinen, jedenfalls nicht Krupp Flick Thyssen', behauptet die Narration über einen auktorialen Er-Erzähler (T, VII, 117), nicht allein die Figur. So zeigt die Verweigerung der Funktionalisierung, die Flucht vor Verwertungsansprüchen, am Ende des Romans noch Auswege aus den Schädigungen, welche die Moderne in den planwirtschaftlichen Subjekten hinterlässt. Es sind Motive, dem Altvertrauten und Kritisierten doch verbunden zu bleiben: einem Sozialismus, der nur nie zu sich selbst kommen konnte. Seine deformierte reale Existenz trage noch den wahren Kern und den Keim seiner Realisation in sich. Er stecke, mit dem gern verwendeten Bild, im *Larvenstadium*: unansehnlich, scheintot gar als Puppe, 'bis man sie nur für eine Mumie ansehen kann: dies werdende Flügelwesen' – doch mit der eingebauten Sprengkraft ausgestattet, sich zum Schmetterling zu entfalten. Kunze immerhin hat erkannt, wie 'wahr und wichtig' das Unbehagen sei am neuen Raum, der 'eng und dunkel dünkt wie eine Hülse, und unser Druck, der sie sprengen wird' (T, VII, 43).

Im 'historische[n] Moment' 1989, als 'die Larve den Panzer zerbrach', entpuppte sich für Volker Braun aber das Gegenteil dessen, was er erhofft hatte: 'Ein Schmetterling – der Name hätte mich warnen können, jetzt war mein Besitz zerschmettert.'[50] Der Rest ist Melancholie: eine immer noch ideologische Trauer um das *Nichtgelebte* und das *Wirklichgewollte*. 'Warum hat er sie nicht gefreit. Warum hat er sich nicht befreit?', fragt sich, zunächst vermittelt über die dritte Person, Georg, als wäre er mehr der Erzähler als eine erzählte Figur im *Hinze-Kunze-Roman*, um dann, in direkter, unmarkierter Gedankenrede zu konstatieren: 'Es geschieht uns recht. Nun müssen wir damit leben, in diesem Universum des Nichterlebten.'[51] Und als wollte er diesem und Georg zugleich antworten, horcht die Figur Borges aus *Das Wirklichgewollte* in sich hinein – und sinniert, hier in erlebter Rede, wie einst Marc Aurel: 'Was ging ihn der Lärm der Welt an? [...], denn nun lag es nicht mehr an ihm, was kommt'.[52]

Anmerkungen

1 Volker Braun, *Hinze-Kunze-Roman*, in: *Texte in zeitlicher Folge*. Halle/Saale: Mitteldeutscher Verlag, 1991, I, S. 47-229 (hier: S. 117). Im Folgenden werden Texte Brauns aus dieser Ausgabe nach der Sigle T mit Bandzahl und Paginierung zitiert.

2 Zuerst in kürzerer Form als Vortrag im Rahmen der Tagung 'Volker Braun. Journée d'étude (dans le cadre de la préparation aux concours du CAPES et de l'Agrégation d'Allemand)'. Coopération CR₂A, Université de Rouen, avec la Maison Heinrich Heine. Paris, 19. Januar 2008.

3 Marcus Aurelius Antoninus, *Selbstbetrachtungen [Ad se ipsum]: Gr.-Dt.*, hg. und übers. von Rainer Nickel, 2. Aufl. Mannheim: Artemis & Winkler, 2010.

[4]   Siehe Volker Braun, 'Limes. Mark Aurel', *Theater der Zeit*, 57:3 (2002), 58-70. Im Folgenden als Sigle LMA.

[5]   Im Gedicht 'DIE SEELENRUHE oder LIMES. MARK AUREL' sind es ganz plakativ 'Tellerminen', welche die Grenze – vom 'Tellerrand' aus – befestigen sollen. Vgl. Volker Braun, *Auf die schönen Possen. Gedichte*, Frankfurt/Main: Suhrkamp, 2005, S. 25. In *Limes. Mark Aurel* ist, ganz ähnlich, die Rede vom 'Hunger der Welt auf dem Tellerrand Roms' (LMA, 58).

[6]   Zu deren ontologischer Differenz vgl. ausführlich Fotis Jannidis, *Figur und Person. Beitrag zu einer historischen Narratologie*, Berlin und New York: De Gruyter, 2004, *passim* und S. 172-84 insb.; vgl. S. 30-1, 244, 252.

[7]   Für die Begriffsdefinitionen einschlägig Frank Zipfel, *Fiktion, Fiktivität, Fiktionalität. Analysen zur Fiktion in der Literatur und zum Fiktionsbegriff in der Literaturwissenschaft*, Berlin: Erich Schmidt, 2001, hier insb. S. 115-16, 119, 133-4, 135-6, 179-81 und *passim*.

[8]   Zum Begriff, den man gemeinhin auf Serge Doubrovsky zurückführt, vgl. etwa Frank Zipfel, 'Autofiktion. Zwischen den Grenzen von Faktualität, Fiktionalität und Literarität?', in: Simone Winko, Fotis Jannidis und Gerhard Lauer, Hg., *Grenzen der Literatur. Zu Begriff und Phänomen des Literarischen*, Berlin und New York: De Gruyter, 2009, S. 285-314. Siehe auch Martina Wagner-Egelhaaf, 'Autofiktion oder: Autobiographie nach der Autobiographie. Goethe – Barthes – Özdamar', in: Ulrich Breuer und Beatrice Sandberg, Hg., *Grenzen der Identität und der Fiktionalität. Autobiographisches Schreiben in der deutschsprachigen Gegenwartsliteratur*, Bd. 1, München: Iudicum, 2006, S. 353-68.

[9]   Vgl. Heinz-Peter Preußer und Helmut Schmitz, 'Autobiografik zwischen Literaturwissenschaft und Geschichtsschreibung. Eine Einleitung', in Preußer und Schmitz, Hg., *Autobiografie und historische Krisenerfahrung*, Heidelberg: Winter, 2010, S. 7-20 (hier: S. 10-15).

[10] Vgl. André Steiner, '"Ich" und das Leben im "Provisorium". Die kaum versteckte Autobiografie des Wolfgang Hilbig', in: Preußer und Schmitz, Hg., *Autobiografie und historische Krisenerfahrung*, S. 127-38 (insb. S. 134-5). Ausführlicher ebenfalls André Steiner, *Das narrative Selbst – Studien zum Erzählwerk Wolfgang Hilbigs. Erzählungen 1979-1991. Romane 1989-2000*, Frankfurt/Main u. a.: Lang, 2008, S. 50-71 und *passim*.

[11] Sein Werk, bemerkt Christa Wolf, habe 'sich der Zeit ausgesetzt [...] wie kaum eines'. Zitiert nach Martin Straub, 'Geleitwort', in: Ingrid Pergande und Ulrich Kaufmann, Hg., *'Gegen das GROSSE UMSONST'. Vierzig Jahre mit dem Dichter Volker Braun*, S. 5-6 (hier: S. 5).

12 Vgl. Frank Zipfel: *Fiktion, Fiktivität, Fiktionalität*, S. 150-1. Siehe auch Matias Martinez und Michael Scheffel, *Einführung in die Erzähltheorie*, München: Beck, 2007, S. 82. Das gilt bei Braun z. B. für den nachfolgend besprochenen *Hinze-Kunze-Roman*. Dazu etwa Hans Kaufmann, 'Arbeitsgutachten zu Brauns "Hinze-Kunze-Roman"', in: Pergande u. a., Hg., *'Gegen das GROSSE UMSONST'*, S. 67-76 (hier: S. 71).

13 Vgl. Wolfgang Emmerich, 'Status melancholicus. Zur Transformation der Utopie in der DDR-Literatur', in: Heinz Ludwig Arnold und Frauke Meyer-Gosau, Hg., *Literatur in der DDR. Rückblicke*, München: Text + Kritik, 1991, S. 232-45, insb. S. 234 mit der Charakterisierung Brauns als 'trotzige[m], nicht [...] weinerliche[m] Melancholiker'.

14 Volker Braun, 'Gespräch mit Rolf Jucker', in: *Wir befinden uns soweit wohl. Wir sind erst einmal am Ende. Äußerungen*, Frankfurt/Main: Suhrkamp, 1998, S. 99-109, (hier: S. 100).

15 Volker Braun, *Das Nichtgelebte. Eine Erzählung*, Leipzig: Faber und Faber, 1995; und *Das Wirklichgewollte*, Frankfurt/Main: Suhrkamp, 2000.

16 Dazu etwa Volker Braun, 'Die Lemminge', 'Wüstensturm', oder 'Mein Terrorotorium' (X, 26-7, 53, 57).

17 Vgl. Volker Braun, 'Die Verhältnisse zerbrechen. Was werden wir die Freiheit nennen? Rede zur Verleihung des Büchner-Preises vor der Deutschen Akademie für Sprache und Dichtung', *Frankfurter Allgemeine Zeitung*, 30. Oktober 2000, 56.

18 Braun, *Das Wirklichgewollte*, S. 53-4. Vgl. Volker Braun, 'Der Totenhügel', in: *Tumulus*, Frankfurt/Main, Suhrkamp, 1999, S. 16.

19 Vgl. Verena Kirchner, *Im Bann der Utopie. Ernst Blochs Hoffnungsphilosophie in der DDR-Literatur*, Heidelberg: Winter, 2002, S. 126-70 (hier: S. 158, 160-1, 168).

20 Vgl. York-Gothart Mix, Hg., *Ein 'Oberkunze darf nicht vorkommen'. Materialien zur Publikationsgeschichte und Zensur des 'Hinze-Kunze-Romans' von Volker Braun*, Wiesbaden: Harrassowitz, 1993.

21 Jaak de Vos, '"Im gesellschaftlichen Interesse". Chiffren der Subversivität in Volker Brauns "Hinze-Kunze-Roman"', in: Elrud Ibsch und Ferdinand van Ingen, Hg., *Literatur und Politische Aktualität*, Amsterdam und Atlanta: Rodopi, 1993, S. 155-78.

22 Vgl. Mix, Hg., *' Ein Oberkunze darf nicht vorkommen'*, S. 230.

23   Kai Köhler, *Volker Brauns Hinze-Kunze-Texte. Von der Produktivität der Widersprüche*, Würzburg: Königshausen & Neumann, 1996, S. 130.

24   Mix, Hg., *Ein 'Oberkunze darf nicht vorkommen'*, S. 230.

25   Dazu auch Hans Kaufmann, 'Der Gestus der Unehrerbietigkeit in Brauns "Hinze-Kunze-Roman"', in: Pergande u. a. Hg., *'Gegen das GROSSE UMSONST'*, S. 105-8 (hier S. 107).

26   Köhler, *Brauns Hinze-Kunze-Texte*, S. 129. Vgl. dazu Claudia Albert, 'Diderots "Jacques le fataliste et son maître" als Modell für Volker Brauns "Hinze-Kunze-Roman"', *Jahrbuch der Deutschen Schillergesellschaft*, 33 (1989), 384-96. Außerdem ausführlich Isabella von Treskow, *Französische Aufklärung und sozialistische Wirklichkeit. Denis Diderots 'Jacques le fataliste' als Modell für Volker Brauns 'Hinze-Kunze-Roman'*, Würzburg: Königshausen & Neumann, 1996, S. 214-8.

27   Ernst Bloch, *Das Prinzip Hoffnung*, in: *Gesamtausgabe*, Frankfurt/Main: Suhrkamp, 1979, II, S. 180-8. Vgl. Kirchner, *Im Bann der Utopie*, S. 41-3.

28   Vgl. Kaufmann, 'Gestus der Unehrerbietigkeit', S. 108.

29   Bloch, *Das Prinzip Hoffnung*, I, S. 129-203. Vgl. Kirchner, *Im Bann der Utopie*, S. 36-7.

30   Braun, *Das Nichtgelebte*, S. 36.

31   Arthur Schopenhauer, *Die Welt als Wille und Vorstellung*, in: *Sämtliche Werke*, hg. von Wolfgang Frhr. v. Löhneysen, Darmstadt: Wissenschaftliche Buchgesellschaft, 2004, I, S. 157-8, 164, 180 und *passim*.

32   Zur Kritik der Arbeitsteilung und Entfremdung in romantischer und marxistischer Tradition vgl. Heinz-Peter Preußer, *Mythos als Sinnkonstruktion. Die Antikenprojekte von Christa Wolf, Heiner Müller, Stefan Schütz und Volker Braun*. Köln, Weimar und Wien: Böhlau, 2000, S. 33-46.

33   Dazu Georges Bataille, *Die Erotik*, übers. Gerd Bergfleth, München: Matthes & Seitz 1994, S. 63-70, 91-105 und *passim*.

34   Vgl. Erich Fromm, *Haben oder Sein. Die seelischen Grundlagen einer neuen Gesellschaft*, übers. Brigitte Stein, Stuttgart: Deutsche Verlagsanstalt, 1977.

35   Ludwig Klages, *Vom kosmogonischen Eros*, in: *Sämtliche Werke*, hg. von Hans Eggert Schröder, Bonn: Bouvier, 1974, III, S. 353-497 (hier: S. 356, 483, 490).

[36] Erich Fromm, *Die Furcht vor der Freiheit*, übers. Liselotte und Ernst Mickel, München: DTV, 1995, S. 186-89. Vgl. Kirchner, *Im Bann der Utopie*, S. 164.

[37] 'Jetzt bekomme auch ich Lust, Lisa zu beschreiben, als dritter Mann' (T, VII, 63).

[38] Vgl. Martinez und Scheffel, *Einführung in die Erzähltheorie*, S. 51, 59, 62.

[39] Schopenhauer, *Die Welt als Wille und Vorstellung*, I, S. 257, 372.

[40] Vgl. etwa die paradigmatischen *Hymnen an die Nacht*, in: Novalis, *Schriften*, hg. von Hans-Joachim Mähl und Richard Samuel, Darmstadt: Wissenschaftliche Buchgesellschaft, 1999, I, S. 172-3.

[41] Klages, *Vom kosmogonischen Eros*, passim und erneut die oben genannten Belegstellen.

[42] Vgl. etwa Belinda Joy Davis, 'Das Private ist politisch. Geschlecht, Politik und Protest in der neuen deutschen Geschichte', In: Karen Hagemann und Jean H. Quataert, Hg., *Geschichte und Geschlechter. Revisionen der neueren deutschen Geschichte*, Frankfurt/Main: Campus, 2008, S. 155-80.

[43] Vgl. Peter Bürger, *Theorie der Avantgarde*, Frankfurt/Main: Suhrkamp, 1984, S. 67, 72-3.

[44] Vgl. dagegen Kaufmann, 'Arbeitsgutachten', S. 68-9, 73, 76.

[45] Vgl. Volker Braun, *Werktage 1. Arbeitsbuch 1977-1989*, Frankfurt/Main: Suhrkamp, 2009, S. 706. Siehe zu diesem Komplex in *Werktage 1* auch S. 707-10, 712-14, 716-17, 720-1, 723, 728. Braun setzt den Romantitel in Versalien. Diese Hervorhebung wurde hier durch Kursivierung ersetzt.

[46] Vgl. dazu Katrin Bothe, *Die imaginierte Natur des Sozialismus. Eine Biographie des Schreibens und der Texte Volker Brauns 1959-1974*, Würzburg: Königshausen & Neumann, 1997, S. 272-316 (hier: S. 280-97).

[47] Bertolt Brecht, *Flüchtlingsgespräche*, in: *Prosa*, hg. von Wolfgang Jeske, Frankfurt/Main und Wien: Büchergilde Gutenberg, 1991, II, S. 411-535. Den Bezug sieht bereits von Treskow, *Französische Aufklärung und sozialistische Wirklichkeit*, S. 305-8.

[48] Ausführlich dazu Kirchner, *Im Bann der Utopie*, S. 126-74 (hier vor allem: S. 126-7. 129-34, 140, 146-7). Vgl. auch Köhler, *Brauns Hinze-Kunze-Texte*, S. 112, 114, 117 und die Kritik an dessen sporadischer Befassung bei Kirchner, *Im Bann der Utopie*, S. 127.

[49]   Vgl. Horst Domdey, 'Volker Braun und die Sehnsucht nach der Großen Kommunion. Zum Demokratiekonzept der Reformsozialisten in der DDR', *Deutschlandarchiv*, 23:11 (1990), 1771-4.

[50]   So Volker Braun in *Der Wendehals. Eine Unterhaltung*, Frankfurt/Main: Suhrkamp, 1995, S. 113.

[51]   Braun, *Das Nichtgelebte*, S. 36-9.

[52]   Braun, *Das Wirklichgewollte*, S. 55.

Part Three:

Shifting Perspectives after 1989

Owen Evans

'Ein Botschafter des Vergessenen': Günter de Bruyn, the Chronicler

Günter de Bruyn reflected aspects of his own situation as a writer in the GDR in works depicting Jean Paul and Theodor Fontane: his biography of Jean Paul is shown to be a proto-autobiography, and his novel *Märkische Forschungen* contained auto-biographical elements. The main focus of this essay is however the post-*Wende* auto-biographical work, *Unzeitgemäßes* (2001).

Towards the conclusion of his *laudatio* for Günter de Bruyn at the bestowing of the 'Ernst-Robert-Curtius-Preis für Essayistik' in 2000, Joachim Gauck made an intriguing attempt to isolate the author's unique qualities as a purveyor of the literary form in question:

> Obwohl weder Jubelschreie noch Trauergesänge seine Essayistik bezeichnen, begegnet uns eine Entschiedenheit des Gefühls, der Freude und bei aller sprachlichen Mäßigung eine Sicherheit des Urteils, die beide als unzeitgemäß erscheinen.[1]

To refer to one's respected subject on an occasion such as this as 'unzeitgemäß' might, perhaps, appear to be damning with the faintest praise, were it not for the fact that de Bruyn has, throughout his career, been someone engaged with exploring and mapping the highways and byways of the literary and cultural past of Germany. Nevertheless, whilst he is obviously at home in this past, what has characterised his oeuvre, both fiction and fact, has been his keen eye for the connections, continuities and discontinuities between past and present. His sensitive and insightful biography of Jean Paul represents the finest example of this dialogue between these temporal realms, deploying his portrait of the life and times of the iconoclastic writer from the late eighteenth and early nineteenth century as a delightfully subtle critique of the GDR of the 1970s, as well as to all intents and purposes using the project as proto-autobiography. Gauck highlights in particular de Bruyn's handling of the issue of censorship as the prime example of this critical approach in the biography. There are many other instances in the Jean Paul biography of de Bruyn's wry commentary on the East German cultural sphere, but the passages pertaining to censorship do stand out, seeming uncannily prescient with the benefit of hindsight: the year after the book's publication saw the expatriation of Wolf Biermann, in November 1976, heralding a clampdown that would see many other intellectuals leave the GDR in the ensuing years.

In spite of his celebration of the literary past, and his deep love of authors such as Jean Paul, and most especially Theodor Fontane, de Bruyn has always been very much a man of the present, a chronicler of German life in all its forms, in both the divided and now reunified Germany. Belated recognition of this role came in the form of the prize of the *Konrad-Adenauer-Stiftung* in 1996, when leading CDU politician Wolfgang Schäuble labelled him the 'Schriftsteller der deutschen Einheit'.[2] For a writer long overshadowed by his more illustrious colleagues such as Christa Wolf, Stefan Heym and Heiner Müller in the East and Günter Grass and Heinrich Böll in the West, such an accolade was well deserved, in view of his quietly critical endeavour during the GDR and thoughtful observations on the events surrounding the *Wende* and the reunification of Germany: in particular, he was, and remains, a strong advocate of cultural unity, a belief that underpins his essay work. Nevertheless, for a man who always preferred to avoid the limelight as much as possible, this higher profile as something akin to being a 'conscience of the nation', a label bestowed on the likes of Böll and Grass before him, must have inspired mixed feelings in him.

The title of de Bruyn's 2005 book *Abseits: Liebeserklärung an eine Landschaft* thus seems very telling, for here was a writer who very happily found sanctuary, an inner emigration, from the worst pressures of GDR cultural life in the countryside. As he puts it in *Vierzig Jahre* (1996), his autobiographical account of GDR life, his flight into the remote Brandenburg countryside was designed to help him creatively: 'Dem Staat war ich auf seinem eignen Territorium entflohen. Hier würde es mir besser als vorher gelingen, die Zensur beim Schreiben aus meinem Bewußtsein zu tilgen'.[3] The reality, of course, was that it was very hard to achieve this freedom, but de Bruyn increasingly refused to pull his punches. His fiction became more caustic in tone, culminating in his pointed satire *Neue Herrlichkeit* (1985), which exposed the uncomfortable Prussian legacy underpinning the GDR, and was duly banned briefly. Even from this remote position, then, he remained dedicated to commenting upon the present.

Günter de Bruyn's eye for the presence of the past in the present is at the heart of *Unzeitgemäßes: Betrachtungen über Vergangenheit und Gegenwart* (2001), which is in essence an expanded version of his acceptance speech for the 'Ernst-Robert-Curtius-Preis'. The essay represents a perfect distillation of the features, and qualities, that have always characterised the author's work, but also marks a shift in tone, as befits a man who had become, despite himself, an elder statesman of the German nation. The measured tones so typical of his narratives, in essay, novel and autobiography, are complemented at times with some more outspoken observations on developments since reunification, not all of them welcome in the author's opinion.

The title itself betrays something of de Bruyn's naturally self-deprecating style, and in fact draws on an experience he relates in the lead essay in *Deutsche Zustände* (1999), when he recounts his delight in hearing an announcement at the Alexanderplatz underground station that the destination of the next train was to be Ruhleben, signalling the re-establishment of a line ruptured in 1961:

> Als wollte man mir das Unzeitgemäße des Freudengefühls ins Bewußtsein rufen, begannen im gleichen Moment mehrere Fahrgäste darüber zu schimpfen, daß die Verbindung, die Leuten meines Alters Wiederherstellung, den Jüngeren aber Neuerung bedeutete, ihnen andere Fahrtrouten aufnötige und das Zurechtfinden erschwere.[4]

One senses de Bruyn's amusement, surprise even, at these grumbles from the early 1990s. By the time he writes *Unzeitgemäßes*, however, he seems a little more exasperated, if not exactly irritated, by some of the things he sees around him at the turn of the millennium in Germany. Where once being 'unzeitgemäß' might have been used ironically, de Bruyn now advances it much more insistently as a virtue in a society that seems to be losing a sense of its identity:

> Wer aber versucht hat, sich selbst die Treue zu halten, möchte nicht gern zu jenen Alten gehören, die sich mit Baseballmützen, die sie auch in der Kirche nicht abnehmen, wie Junge gebärden, Schönes als cool bezeichnen, sich den Unterschied zwischen Kunst und Vergnügungsbetrieb ausreden lassen, Höflichkeit für veraltet halten und in jedem Tabubruch einen Segen für die Menschheit sehen.[5]

For a man who has been so long immersed in German cultural life, delighting in its delights and idiosyncrasies, its darkness and light, it is easy to understand de Bruyn's dismay at these developments, and why he should treasure any suggestion that he himself is out of step with the times. The essay thus stands as an attempt 'den Kummer und die Sorgen von der Seele [zu] schreiben, in der wahnwitzigen Hoffnung, daß das außer dem Schreiber auch noch einigen Lesern ein wenig nützt' (U, 9), and at a stroke the irony returns. Nevertheless, the text as a whole makes for an at times wry, humorous, searching and provocative assessment of the state of the German nation.

Picking up on his delight at the train to Ruhleben, de Bruyn reiterates his delight in German reunification, confessing that since World War Two no historical event had moved him as much as events in 1990 and 'daß diese angenehmen Empfindungen, die sich anfangs als Jubel äußerten, in schwächerer Form andauern, allen Dummheiten, Fehlern, Ärgernissen und Widrigkeiten zum Trotz' (U, 10). In his autobiography he had admitted to mixed feelings in November 1989, a delight tinged with sadness that perhaps this had all come too late for him. By 2001, that sorrow seems to have faded as he reflects on what the *Wende* has made possible:

> Das Glücksgefühl, das der Abriß der Mauer brachte, ist bei mir fast noch gegenwärtig, und ein Einkaufsbummel, bei dem nicht mehr Mangel, sondern die Überfülle Qualen bereitet, ein Blick auf heimatliche Dörfer und Städte, wo häßliche Lücken gefüllt wurden und alte Bauten in Schönheit wiedererstanden, die tägliche, manchmal zwar ärgerliche, aber doch nicht mehr langweilige Zeitungslektüre oder eine Fahrt über die ehemalige, heute kaum noch erkennbare Grenze beschwören immer wieder die wunderbare Wende unseres Lebens herauf. (U, 10)

As a realist, de Bruyn has always sought to navigate a path between extremes, between the 'Jubelschreie und Trauergesänge', and thus is careful to acknowledge the problems that the fall of the Wall has brought with it for other people. Nevertheless, a man who experienced both totalitarian systems on German soil is entitled to enjoy, and celebrate, reunification, not least because it validated his belief in an enduring German cultural unity. Indeed, for many he has become the personification of that union, as Schäuble's definition of him attests.

In view of his advocacy of the enduring cultural ties between the two Germanys throughout the Cold War period, as well as his own extensive work on the past, it is no surprise that the notion of Germany somehow creating a post-national identity for itself, by dispensing with 'das Deutsche', should trouble de Bruyn. He questions the presumption that the culture that had shaped society could simply be laid aside, and with it the nation's guilt during the Third Reich, issuing a stark warning about the possible ramifications of such an endeavour:

> Mit dem Identitätsmangel würde eine Gleichgültigkeit gegenüber der deutschen Geschichte einsetzen, Vergangenes würde Verpflichtendes ganz verlieren, die bedrückende Last würde abgewälzt werden. Denn die Verantwortung für die von Deutschen begangenen Verbrechen kann nur jemand, der sich als Deutscher versteht, empfinden. Das Vergessen des in den Hitlerjahren Geschehenen, vor dem zu warnen wir nicht müde werden, träte, wenn wir uns des Nationalen entledigten, mit Sicherheit ein. (U, 20)

Such concerns reveal a very deep-rooted personal anguish for the author, whose first novel, *Der Hohlweg* (1963), which he disowned a decade after publication because of its formulaic socialist realist nature, had been an attempt to come to terms with his own horrific experience of the Hitler years. For all its failings, *Der Hohlweg* offered glimpses of de Bruyn's wish to weave his subjectivity into his fiction, as well as of his commitment to engage with reality and the past. His warning in *Unzeitgemäßes* about the potential onset of indifference about the past reflects the extent to which his commitment to chronicling of past and present, as both a personal and public preoccupation, has endured. One might even argue that it bespeaks the strength of his credentials to be considered a conscience of the nation.

Joachim Gauck's definition of de Bruyn as a 'Botschafter des Vergessenen' is especially apposite.[6] Many of the author's essays have indeed been devoted to bringing people, places and traditions to light that have been overlooked, or forgotten, as the master historical narrative is written. That is not to say that de Bruyn does not have an eye for the bigger picture, as his comments about the potential loss of 'das Deutsche' reveal in *Unzeitgemäßes*. Nevertheless, he has worked assiduously to fill out that picture, adding the finer details and accentuating the tones and textures, which mean that a more comprehensive, nuanced picture of history might emerge, a history from below. As he made explicit in an essay on F.A.L. Marwitz, 'Geschichte ist immer das Ganze, nicht nur das Angenehme'.[7] His concern for 'Vergessenes' is thus not an obsession with the trivial or irrelevant. On the contrary, his work on the cultural past has been characterised by an insistence that cultural memory needs to eschew 'ein Weglassen- und Wegsehenkönnen, ein bißchen Fiktion und ein bißchen Leichtfertigkeit' and instead 'der Wahrheit ins Auge zu sehen'.[8]

This dedication to a truthful exploration of the past underpins his work on his beloved Jean Paul and Fontane. Irrespective of his passion for these authors, his assessments of their respective oeuvres never seek to present them as paragons of virtue by ignoring their faults or embellishing their strengths. De Bruyn's Jean Paul biography has often been seen as a direct response to a rival study of the forgotten author. Wolfgang Harich's *Jean Pauls Revolutionsdichtung* had appeared the year before, and sought to celebrate the author as a proto-socialist poet, absolving him from Georg Lukács's indictment of him as a 'kleinbürgerlicher Versöhner'.[9] While de Bruyn did not object to this motivation, one indeed he shared for the most part, and while he admitted to being impressed by Harich's study in other respects, he nevertheless had reservations, 'weil hier Jean Paul zwar sozusagen rehabilitiert wird, aber mit den Methoden dessen, der ihn vorher verdammte':

> Keine Lösung von Lukács liegt hier vor, sondern seine Berichtigung in diesem einen Punkt. Mit Recht wird hier das bürgerlich-biedermeierliche Bild Jean Pauls [...] entscheidend revidiert. Statt aber die schon zu lange einseitig belastete Waage des Urteils ins Gleichgewicht zu bringen, wird sie auf der anderen Seite überlastet.[10]

His own book, by contrast, sought to celebrate the iconoclastic author's colourful life and work, the ebbs and flows of which, he believed, could *not* be brought together in conveniently coherent order:

> Wie jedes bewegte Leben wird auch das seine voll von Widersprüchen sein; voll von Widersprüchen auch sein Werk: darin liegt dessen Größe, dessen Grenze, dessen Schönheit und Faszination. Jede Interpretation bewegt sich hier auf doppeltem Boden; schnell ist sie eingebrochen. Nur wer wenig weiß oder absichtlich viel übersieht, kann mit der Geste der Gewißheit auftreten.[11]

The same impartial approach characterises his work in various essays on Fontane, whom he described as a 'Fixstern'[12] and whose love of the Mark Brandenburg inspired, and inflected, de Bruyn's own. While happy to celebrate Fontane's extensive literary work, not least in compiling the famous multi-volume *Wanderungen durch die*

Mark Brandenburg, de Bruyn deconstructs his illustrious predecessor's perception of the region, and discovers some disappointing truths. By effectively retracing Fontane's footsteps, de Bruyn is forced to concede that his forebear's fascination with the area was often predicated on its 'Geschichtsträchtigkeit'.[13] For Fontane, a Prussian with an almost devout reverence for the traditions of the 'Utopie Alt-Preußen'[14] and who harked back to a nostalgic conception of *Preußen-tum*, historical interest and value were synonymous with the nobility, but most especially with militarism and conflict. As a consequence, the area around Beeskow, the subject of de Bruyn's 'Liebeserklärung' in *Abseits*, is 'geschichtslos für [Fontane]; und da ein Reisender nur sieht, was er weiß, sieht dieser [...] hier nur das Elend'.[15] In view of de Bruyn's abhorrence of war, derived from his own traumatic experience of the Second World War, it is evident how Fontane's bellicosity might be a source of regret. As de Bruyn then wryly observes, World War Two was to rectify the lack of history that Fontane associated with the area:

> [...] Denn hier an der Dahme, zwischen Königs Wusterhausen, Halbe and Teupitz, fand mit der Einkesselung der deutschen 9. Armee durch die Russen die letzte Vernichtungsschlacht des Zweiten Weltkrieges statt. 40 000 Soldaten mußten hier kurz vor Kriegsende noch sterben.[16]

Just as with Jean Paul, in order to understand Fontane, to appreciate his work, one has to be fully aware of all facets of the man and embrace the contradictions.

Some critics have suggested that de Bruyn's work on Brandenburg's cultural history, in collections such as *Mein Brandenburg* and *Deutsche Zustände*, should be seen as an attempt to challenge, even correct, Fontane. However, de Bruyn's essayistic and scholarly texts should be more accurately seen as working in conjunction with his illustrious forebear's oeuvre, supplementing and expanding where appropriate, providing 'das Ganze, nicht nur das Angenehme'. They not only freshen the historical and geographical detail, but also plug the lacunae left as Fontane, 'der fahrende Wanderer',[17] raced through the countryside in coaches, from one *Herrensitz* to another, not really taking note of the world outside. De Bruyn thus subtly deconstructs Fontane's preconceived notions, watching the latter watching, or rather ignoring, what was passing by the window, and in so doing, brings to light his predecessor's prejudices and partiality.

In his own work on Brandenburg and its history, de Bruyn reveals great sympathy for the minutiae that Fontane had little time for, and in particular places great importance on communal life, whilst not ignoring the figures who would have drawn Fontane's interest and admiration. It allows de Bruyn to celebrate hapless, long forgotten literary figures such as Schmidt von Werneuchen, whose work he is not averse to criticising for its deeply parochial nature, but whose integrity and sincerity he prizes as those of a poet inspired by 'das Gewöhnliche und Alltägliche'.[18] At the same time, de Bruyn has also produced sympathetic and engaging portraits of Prussian nobility with his studies such as *Die Finckensteins: Eine Familie im Dienste Preußens* (1999) and *Preußens Luise: Vom Entstehen und Vergehen einer Legende* (2001).

Just as it was for Fontane, then, Prussia has been a preoccupation of de Bruyn, a native Berliner, throughout his career; it is an interest that has permeated his essayistic and scholarly publications, but also his fiction. As well as thematising his own clash of methodologies with Harich in their respective Jean Paul projects, de Bruyn's *Märkische Forschungen* tells the tale of fictitious writer Max Schwedenow and attempts to incorporate this awkward Prussian into the cultural pantheon of the GDR. *Neue Herrlichkeit* is much less subtle in its juxtaposition of the ruling SED caste and their attitudes with those that characterised Prussian nobility, illuminating the troubling continuity between the old and new orders that pertains. Moreover, the majority of characters in the novel, indeed many of de Bruyn's protagonists as a whole, betray subservient and dutiful traits, inured to a feudal structure that affords them no freedom; it is a mindset, de Bruyn has argued, which might explain why the GDR survived as long as it did:

> In der DDR-Geschichte spielen [diese sogenannten preußischen Tugenden] eine große Rolle. Die Leute, die ich in der Mark Brandenburg kenne, sind ausgesprochen preußischer Prägung, mit allen Vor- und Nachteilen: sehr verläßlich, arbeitsam, leicht zu lenken, immer nach Obrigkeit Ausschau haltend. Diese treue Nüchternheit in kleinen Verhältnissen hat etwas historisch-Geprägtes.[19]

It is without doubt these innate qualities that contributed to de Bruyn's own decision to stay in the GDR, as he himself has mentioned.

It is no surprise that de Bruyn should touch upon Prussia in *Unzeitgemäßes*, given it was published 'im Jahr des Preußen-

Gedenkens' (U, 32), and that he should stress yet again the need to look at the whole picture, rather than instrumentalising only those aspects that fit the designs of the present: 'Man will nicht wissen, wie es war damals in Preußen, sondern man will im Damals Bestätigungen für heutige Haltungen und Absichten finden' (U, 33). Thus it is, for example, that features such as Prussian militarism, upheld as a virtue in the past, have been replaced by talk of the old state's alleged exemplary qualities as a land that embraced immigrants and practised religious tolerance; in effect, Prussia has been heralded as a model of multicultural social harmony for contemporary German society. But just as de Bruyn lamented the 'einseitiges Bild' that Harich presented of Jean Paul,[20] he is careful to put the positive representation of Prussia in contemporary Germany into context. It is the consistency with which he has enunciated his ethos, the advocacy of honesty and objectivity, throughout his career that has elevated him to the respected position he now holds. For example, his rigorously self-critical engagement with his experience with the Stasi, contacts which were, in truth, tenuous, fleeting and, by and large, embellished in his file by the officers responsible, is arguably the most striking example of his honesty, earning him what Dennis Tate has called a 'fully deserved moral bonus'.[21] But there are numerous other examples of his self-critical candour, ranging from his own searing indictment of his debut novel to the passages in *Vierzig Jahre* that deal with the role of intellectuals in the GDR and the compromises demanded of them. Terms such as 'Angst', 'Scham' and 'Verzweiflung' recur frequently in his autobiographical accounts.

With *Unzeitgemäßes*, though, it is hard to ignore the different tone to his writing which begins to resonate, a growing sense that de Bruyn has become increasingly world-weary, perhaps, disenchanted with the

neuen Formen der kulturellen Einebnung oder auch Gleichschaltung, die im Zuge der sogenannten Globalisierung auftreten und von manchem ohne Beurteilung hingenommen werden, als sei Existenz auch schon Ausweis für Qualität. (U, 20-21)

The choice of the term 'Gleichschaltung', with its associations with the Third Reich, seems most telling in this context, bespeaking a deep dismay. In particular, for a man so long immersed in literature, it is the dilution of the German language by increasingly ubiquitous Anglicisms that attracts his ire. 'Das flotte Nachplappern überflüssiger

Anglizismen' is evidence of little more than 'ein[e] partiell[e] Beschränktheit, die von Schönheit und Prägnanz einer Sprache nichts weiß' (U, 31).

He is equally perturbed by the plans for the Holocaust memorial, which have since come to fruition. Some of his reservations chime with those widely expressed at the time, about whom the memorial should be commemorating, lamenting that 'Millionen von Toten' might be excluded from memory, thereby creating 'eine Rangfolge des Gedenkens' (U, 23). But his objection is also based on architectural and aesthetic grounds. For the writer who provided a fascinating history of Unter den Linden, recreating in words the architectural splendours that once characterised this boulevard and the areas around it, the 'riesige Betonfeld' of the eventual memorial represents little more than evidence of 'eine Gigantomanie [...], der Berlin ein halbes Jahrhundert zuvor gerade noch so entgangen war' (U, 24). Instead of the 'beziehungslose Ödnis am Rande des Tiergartens' (U, 25), de Bruyn's own proposal for the site of a memorial is the Große Hamburger Straße, the heart of the old Jewish quarter in Mitte, but also home to significant churches of other faiths; it was also the location where the Jewish community in Berlin were mustered to be sent to their deaths in the extermination camps from 1942 onwards.

For de Bruyn, there is an additional, very personal, reason for favouring such a site; namely that it was here, as a young boy, that he first encountered people wearing yellow stars on their clothing, only grasping the significance many years later when he lived in the area. The street was to become the subject of his very first essay dealing explicitly with the historical past of Berlin, an important precursor to the work that has become his main focus since publishing *Vierzig Jahre*, although the autobiographical motivation for the piece would only become truly apparent in *Zwischenbilanz* in the chapter 'Abschied von der Kindheit'.[22] This personal connection with the area might help to explain the author's unusually bitter-sounding dismissal of the Holocaust memorial that would eventually be erected:

> Daß die Große Hamburger Straße als zentrale Gedenkstätte nicht in Erwägung gezogen oder verworfen wurde, kann nur damit erklärt werden, daß man nichts Anschauliches und Anrührendes, sondern etwas Auffallendes wollte. Nicht ums Trauern scheint es hier zu gehen, sondern um Trauerdemonstration. (U, 25)

The original essay from 1969 concluded with a poignant plea for the Holocaust never to be forgotten, but as de Bruyn's reaction to the eventual memorial demonstrates, there are very different ways and means of achieving that commemoration. His dismay is clear.

As Dennis Tate has suggested, the essays that de Bruyn was writing around the turn of the millennium reveal 'a conservative distaste for the architectural changes that have in his eyes disfigured the capital both in the GDR era and since reunification'.[23] This distaste arguably finds its most strident expression in *Unzeitgemäßes*, and it is perhaps unsurprising that de Bruyn's subsequent work, *Abseits*, should be a celebration of the landscape of his home in the remote corner of the Mark Brandenburg, therefore a definitive retreat from the city of his birth. In many ways, *Unzeitgemäßes* can now be seen to herald the irrevocable nature of this move. Tate notes the mournful quality that abides in *Abseits*, 'an elegiac commitment to recording a communal awareness of human transience', which has replaced the author's 'earlier insistence on the truth of individual experience as found exclusively in autobiographical writing'.[24] But de Bruyn's work on the literary and cultural past has always possessed a mournful register, commenting on the passage of time and what might potentially be lost, in terms of architecture, culture and tradition. His own wandering through the Mark Brandenburg, recorded in myriad essays since the late 1960s, might be seen as his private attempt to preserve the heritage, and with it to secure the 'Erhaltung von Menschlichkeit'.[25] That this might be seen in some quarters as an old-fashioned endeavour, 'unzeitgemäß' even, would trouble de Bruyn very little. He is merely fulfilling his self-imposed 'Chronistenpflicht des Autors',[26] a duty he has never shirked in fact or fiction, and we should be grateful to him for that work, for what he has recovered and what he has preserved.

Notes

[1]   Joachim Gauck, 'Laudatio auf Günter de Bruyn', in: Anon., ed., *Ernst-Robert-Curtius-Preis für Essayistik 2000: Dokumente und Ansprachen*, Bonn: Bouvier, 2000, pp. 37-47 (here: p. 46).

[2]   Wolfgang Schäuble, 'Laudatio auf Günter de Bruyn', in: Günther Rüther, ed., *Verleihung des Literaturpreises der Konrad-Adenauer-Stiftung e.V. an Günter de*

Bruyn: Weimar, 15. Mai 1996, Wesseling: Konrad-Adenauer-Stiftung, 1996, pp. 7-17 (here: p. 17).

[3] Günter de Bruyn, *Vierzig Jahre: Ein Lebensbericht*, Frankfurt/Main: Fischer, 1996, p. 158.

[4] Günter de Bruyn, *Deutsche Zustände: Über Erinnerungen und Tatsachen, Heimat und Literatur*, Frankfurt/Main: Fischer, 1999, p. 7.

[5] Günter de Bruyn, *Unzeitgemäßes: Betrachtungen über Vergangenheit und Gegenwart*, Frankfurt/Main: Fischer, 2001, p. 7. Subsequent references are given by U followed by page number in parenthesis in the text.

[6] Gauck, 'Laudatio auf Günter de Bruyn', p. 42.

[7] Günter de Bruyn, 'Opposition und Gehorsam', in: Uwe Wittstock, ed., *Günter de Bruyn: Materialien zu Leben und Werk*, Frankfurt/Main: Fischer, 2011, pp. 22-49 (here: p. 49).

[8] Günter de Bruyn, *Mein Brandenburg*, Frankfurt/Main: Fischer, 1999, p. 13.

[9] Günter de Bruyn, 'Jean Paul und die neuere DDR-Literatur', *Jahrbuch der Jean-Paul-Gesellschaft*, 10 (1975), 205-11 (here: 205).

[10] De Bruyn, 'Jean Paul und die neuere DDR-Literatur', 206-7.

[11] Günter de Bruyn, *Das Leben des Jean Paul Friedrich Richter*, Halle: Mitteldeutscher Verlag, 1975, p. 113.

[12] Günter de Bruyn, *Frauendienst*, Halle: Mitteldeutscher Verlag, 1986, p. 314.

[13] De Bruyn, *Mein Brandenburg*, p. 51.

[14] De Bruyn, 'Opposition und Gehorsam', p. 139.

[15] Günter de Bruyn, *Jubelschreie, Trauergesänge: Deutsche Befindlichkeiten*, Frankfurt/ Main: Fischer, 1991, p. 87.

[16] De Bruyn, *Mein Brandenburg*, p. 51.

[17] De Bruyn, *Jubelschreie, Trauergesänge*, p. 87.

[18] Günter de Bruyn, *Lesefreuden: Über Bücher und Menschen*, Frankfurt/Main: Fischer, 1986, p. 60.

[19] Helmtrud Mauser, 'Blick zurück', in Wittstock, ed., *Günter de Bruyn*, pp. 102-20 (here: p. 111).

[20] De Bruyn, *Das Leben des Jean Paul Friedrich Richter*, p. 377.

[21] Dennis Tate, 'Changing Perspectives on Günter de Bruyn: An Introduction', in: Tate, ed., *Günter de Bruyn in Perspective*, Amsterdam: Rodopi, 1999, pp. 1-8 (here: p. 1).

[22] Günter de Bruyn, 'Berlin, Große Hamburger', in: Elli Schmidt, ed., *Städte und Stationen*, Rostock: Hinstorff, 1969, pp. 7-11.

[23] Dennis Tate, *Shifting Perspectives: East German Autobiographical Narratives Before and After the End of the GDR*, Rochester, NY: Camden House, 2007, p. 187.

[24] Ibid., p. 188.

[25] De Bruyn, *Deutsche Zustände*, p. 116.

[26] Sigrid Töpelmann, 'Interview mit Günter de Bruyn', *Weimarer Beiträge*, 14 (1968), 1171-83 (here: p. 1177).

Peter Barker

Re-writing My Life and Work:
Jurij Brězan's Autobiographical Writings

Jurij Brězan was the major Sorbian writer of the 20th Century, who was known above all for his novels, a genre which before 1945 hardly existed in Sorbian literature. Despite his view that his most important task was the protection of the Sorbian language and identity, he was a significant literary figure at national level in the GDR. His two major autobiographical works, *Mein Stück Zeit* (1989) and *Ohne Pass und Zoll* (1999), illustrate the dilemmas of a socialist writer caught between politics and writing in the GDR who in the end gave up his belief in the power of literature to have a direct influence on politics.

The Sorbian prose writer, Jurij Brězan, born in 1916, had a writing career which spanned the whole of the life of the GDR, and continued beyond unification until his death in March 2006 at the age of 89. He started to write his autobiography, *Mein Stück Zeit*,[1] in the mid-1980s, completing it in February 1989. Its unfortunate publishing date was 9 November 1989, which meant that it was largely ignored at the time. This first attempt to assess his political and literary role was mostly concerned with his early life in the Third Reich. Significant experiences were his underground activities in Poland and Germany for a Sorbian/Polish organisation in the late 1930s, which led to his arrest in Dresden in 1938; his forced removal from Lusatia to North Germany, where he worked as an agricultural labourer; his experiences in the army and as a prisoner of war (1942-6); his return to Bautzen in 1946 and his alignment with the new political forces in the Soviet Zone and the beginnings of his literary career. The first volume of his autobiography did not extend far beyond the 1950s, but did include the problems caused by his participation in youth brigades in Yugoslavia in the late 1940s and his confrontations with the new Stalinist leadership of the Sorbian cultural organisation, the Domowina, which led to observation and interrogation by officers from the Ministry for State Security (MfS) in 1956. After the collapse of his original GDR publishers, Verlag Neues Leben, it reappeared in 1998 with a new publishing house, Gustav Kiepenheuer, almost unchanged, the only additions being a foreword and an epilogue. In the foreword he described how, when he started work on the autobiography in 1986,

he was denied access to certain papers.[2] In the absence of documents
he set up a framework to the book in which a traveller tries to buy a
ticket to an imaginary town, which he is then told does not exist. This
provided the impetus to his autobiographical journey in which he tries
to show how his original ideals become illusionary.[3] In 1999 he published the second volume of his autobiography, *Ohne Pass und Zoll*,[4]
which concentrated on his life in the GDR, his literary work, in particular the Felix Hanusch Trilogy and the novel *Krabat oder die Verwandlung der Welt* (1976), and his role in the Writers' Union, of
which he was a vice-president from 1969 to 1989.

Brězan was the first Sorbian writer to publish his works bilingual-
ly. Usually he wrote the Sorbian version first, and soon after a German
version. He continued this practice for all his major works, with the
exception of his two autobiographical works, both of which have only
appeared in German. This divergence from his normal practice probably had much to do with his own particular problems with the political group which had taken over the running of the Domowina in the
early 1950s, and his escape into the wider cultural landscape of the
GDR in the mid-1950s. He wrote about his intentions with *Mein Stück
Zeit* in the second volume, stating that he was arguing for 'ein natür-
liches Miteinander mit den Deutschen'.[5] He then went on to explain
why he had written it only in German:

> Bewußt mich ausschließlich an den nichtsorbischen Leser wendend, schrieb ich
> zum erstenmal ein Buch nur in Deutsch. Das hatte eine für enges Denken typische
> Reaktion zur Folge, indem es – außer in einem törichten Pamphlet eines Student-
> leins – in der sorbischen Öffentlichkeit nicht registriert wurde.[6]

The second edition was thought necessary because the publication
of the first edition had coincided with the fall of the Wall and was lost
in the subsequent political turmoil. The second volume was a response
to reviews of the 2nd edition of *Mein Stück Zeit*, which pointed to the
fact that it contained little about his literary work and excluded the
1970s and 1980s. Brězan contended that this was not true, but admitted that the last two decades of the GDR were only present in a
'Geheimsprache', otherwise it would not have been allowed to appear.[7] The title of the second volume refers to Brězan's desire to see
his works appear in both Sorbian and German: 'Die Alternative, zwischen meinen beiden Sprachen wählen zu müssen, löste sich auf und
bildete sich neu als Möglichkeit einer Brücke, passierbar ohne Paß

und Zoll.' He saw this second volume as a kind of bridge between the two cultures.[8]

Brězan started his literary career by publishing his works only in Sorbian: his first collection of poems, *Do noweho časa* (Towards a New Era), came out in 1950 and his first collection of prose works, *Prěnja brózda* (First Furrow), in 1951. But in 1951 he made a significant move by publishing a collection of poems and stories in German, *Auf dem Rain wächst Korn*. Brězan was therefore the first post-war Sorbian writer to publish his own German version of stories and poems which had only recently appeared in Sorbian. He went on to relate this event to the changed attitude of the GDR government to the Sorbs, compared with all earlier German states: for the first time a German state was in his view not intent on forcing assimilation; '…so ist die Deutsche Demokratische Republik heute zur Heimat, zum wirklichen Vaterland für die Sorben geworden'.[9] The pathos of this declaration was accentuated by the fact that the first poem in this collection was a translation of Brězan's own statement of identification with the GDR, 'Kak wótčinu namakach' (How I discovered my Fatherland). Shortly afterwards the cultural journal *Aufbau* announced the award of the National Prize to a group of Sorbian artists and writers, including Brězan, for their work in providing the impetus for a new period of Sorbian cultural activity. The journal went on to provide Sorbian writers with the major platform for the publication of their works in German in the early 1950s. This role was taken over by the journal of the GDR Writers' Union, *neue deutsche literatur*, in 1954 when it published a number of poems from the next collection in German, edited and translated from the Sorbian versions by Brězan, *Sorbische Lyrik*.[10] One longer prose piece by Brězan, 'Wie die alte Janschowa mit der Obrigkeit kämpfte' – the German version was published in *Auf dem Rain wächst Korn* – came to be regarded as a classic portrayal of Sorbian resistance to German oppression before 1945.

The price which Sorbian literature and culture had to pay for these increased opportunities to publish and perform was submission to the ideological pressures exerted by the cultural policy of the GDR, which in the 1950s was dominated by the Soviet doctrine of socialist realism. The state had largely taken away one of the functions of a minority literature, its educational role as protector and promoter of the language, by creating a bilingual educational system. This function did not disappear entirely, and still remains more important than for a majority literature; but the task of overcoming the linguistic and cultural repression of the Nazi period now fell primarily to the state. In return for this support the state required greater integration of Sorbian cultural activities into the mainstream of GDR society. While the state provided the opportunity of greater expression in the Sorbian language through education, it demanded a greater social role for writers and literature, a demand which applied to both German and Sorbian writers. Some Sorbian writers rejected this social role. They felt that the national interests of the Sorbs were being jeopardized by the subjugation of Sorbian culture to the political demands of the SED. But through the lifetime of the GDR a new generation of writers emerged, such as Brězan, Kito Lorenc and Jurij Koch, who were prepared to be regarded as GDR, as well as Sorbian, writers. Perhaps the fact that the GDR was a much smaller entity than the German Reich, with a total population of only around seventeen million, made it appear less threatening, despite the obvious ideological pressures. Those writers who did accept this social role, alongside their national one as Sorbian writers, found that the state encouraged and supported their work in ways which had been inconceivable in previous German states.

In the 1950s this social role involved support for the GDR's programme of socialist reconstruction, which in Lusatia meant presenting a positive picture of the processes of industrialization and collectivization of agriculture. In 1955 Brězan demonstrated his loyalty to socialism by writing a number of works which reflected uncritically the changes taking place in the Sorbian villages as a result of the industrialization of Lusatia. He wrote a poem on 'Schwarze Pumpe' for the Fourth Writers' Union Congress in January 1956 in praise of the new power station. He also announced at the Congress that he was planning to write a novel about the power station, but it never came to fruition, reflecting his worries about the negative effect of the plant on the Sorbian way of life.[11] By the mid-1950s disillusionment at the destructive nature of the GDR's energy and industrial policy had set in amongst those Sorbian writers and artists who supported socialism, including Brězan, and this was expressed most strongly in an article published in the Upper Sorbian newspaper, *Nowa doba,* in October 1956, 'Tysac dobrych skutkow' (A thousand good deeds), by the Circle of Young Sorbian Writers, in which Brězan was heavily involved. This article was criticized as an example of 'national pessimism'

by the Politbüro member responsible for Sorbian affairs, Fred
Oelßner, at the Fourth Federal Congress of the Domowina in March
1957. The Circle was dissolved shortly afterwards.

Brězan's prose works dominated Sorbian literature in the 1950s
and 1960s, but the fact that he seemed to be more active in the German cultural sphere was criticized by some other writers and functionaries. Brězan's escape into the German cultural landscape represented
a variation on the escape from the island mentality, since it seemed to
derive more from his own political problems in Lusatia and from a
desire to enter the mainstream of GDR cultural life than from a wish
to explore the potential of a bicultural approach. He was subject to
constant harassment in the mid-1950s from SED party bodies as a
result of accusations of 'nationalism' directed against him by, in particular, the leadership of the Domowina. In a series of meetings of the
SED group in the Domowina in 1955 Brězan was accused of having
strong nationalist tendencies. During one meeting, on 29 January,
Brězan announced his intention of leaving Lusatia.[12] Brězan's own
account of these confrontations with the leadership of the Domowina
and the SED are recounted in detail in both volumes of his autobiography.[13]

Brězan's move into the centre of GDR cultural life was underlined
by the direction of his work in the latter part of the 1950s, especially
in his prose works. The attempt to turn his Felix Hanusch trilogy (*Der
Gymnasiast*, 1958; *Semester der verlorenen Zeit*, 1960; *Mannesjahre*,
1964) from a Sorbian 'Entwicklungsroman' into a GDR social novel
seemed to owe much to the pressure of GDR cultural politics. The
novels bear a close resemblance to Brězan's own life, following the
development of the central character from the end of the First World
War to the social and political changes of the 1950s, and it is difficult
to avoid the conclusion that the writing of the third part in particular,
which is set in the GDR, was influenced by the demands of GDR
cultural policy which culminated in the 1950s in the 'Bitterfelder
Weg'. Whatever Brězan's motivation at the time, it is significant that
it was the German versions of these works, particularly *Mannesjahre*,
which received most attention from critics in the GDR. They were
discussed in the same breath as Erwin Strittmatter's *Ole Bienkopp*
(1963) and Christa Wolf's *Der geteilte Himmel* (1963), as works
within the socialist realist tradition which had been stimulated by the
'Bitterfelder Weg'.

The imposition of these precepts from outside, which placed social questions before national ones, was not wholeheartedly endorsed by all Sorbian writers and artists. Sorbian functionaries had already criticized various aspects of cultural activity at the conference on culture of the Domowina in February 1958, and afterwards writers such as Brězan had criticized their colleagues for having ignored the new social reality of Lusatia in their works. Brězan's own *Mannesjahre* reflected the social and political changes in the villages of Lusatia. But there were other voices from the Sorbian cultural intelligentsia which were critical of the imposition of a political perspective on Sorbian culture. Nevertheless, despite the specific political difficulties that Brězan had had with the SED leadership of the Domowina, he demonstrated through his works of the 1950s into the 1960s a clear commitment to the overall socialist reconstruction of the GDR.

Brězan's development in the 1970s and 1980s saw him return more explicitly to his Sorbian roots for his central themes. *Krabat* and *Bild des Vaters* (1982) aroused critical controversy as a result of their treatment of particular general themes: in *Krabat* it was the question of genetic engineering and in *Bild des Vaters* Brězan's portrayal of the subject of death. But more importantly from the point of view of his role as a Sorbian writer, both works saw him returning to his childhood as a source of imagination. In 1981 Brězan described in an autobiographical essay the way in which he had had to turn his back on what he now saw as a betrayal of his own imagination in his works of the 1950s and 1960s and discover a new formula for his writing.[14] *Krabat* was widely reviewed in the GDR, and although much of the discussion focussed on the central ethical question, a number of critics recognized in the novel Brězan's attempt to write the great epic of the Sorbian people. Brězan had clearly signalled when he started to write the novel that his return to the Krabat myth was part of his search to express that which is specifically Sorbian. *Bild des Vaters* represented a different route back to his Sorbian roots. In an interview in 1983 he indicated that he had considered writing a book based on his father ten years earlier, but that he had found this impossible to do while his father was still alive.[15] The novel represented an attempt not only to pay homage to the memory of his father, but also through him he seemed to be trying to return to some of the main elements of his roots, such as the importance of religion in Sorbian life. Brězan's commitment to socialism had led him away from recognizing such elements as an essential part of a continuing Sorbian identity. It is true that in the novel there is a clear distance between the son and the father in this respect, but there is a recognition of the importance of the relationship between the homeland and religion. Nevertheless, Brězan made it clear in the same interview that despite this greater emphasis on certain aspects of his Sorbian roots, which had been submerged in his earlier works, he still saw Sorbian literature in the context of GDR literature, as an enrichment of the literature of the GDR. The thematic concerns of the two literatures had similar roots: both *Krabat* and *Bild des Vaters* were primarily concerned with themes which were in the mainstream of GDR literature, but the form and the language gave the works elements which Brězan regarded as being specifically Sorbian.

The autobiographical works also reflect this dual focus. Firstly he was concerned with justifying his role as a writer who remained a loyal, if critical, member of the SED until 1989; secondly he used his autobiographies to demonstrate his continuing commitment to defending Sorbian culture and identity, while at the same time settling scores with his adversaries within the Sorbian community. Much of what he experienced was common to both Sorbs and Germans: life in the Third Reich; experience of war as a soldier and as a prisoner of war; coming-to terms with post-war reality, which ultimately led to the question of how far to commit oneself to the new political order. But at the same time there was nearly always a specific Sorbian layer. In the Third Reich he became involved in underground activities in Poland after the suppression of Sorbian institutions in 1937. In the GDR there were particular points of tension when SED policy seemed to be undermining Sorbian national interests. The high point in this tension came in 1964 when the bilingual school system was cut back. Brězan felt moved to withdraw his 'Vaterland' poem of 1951 and write a second poem, 'Wie ich mein Vaterland verlor', which he read out to Kurt Hager, who was responsible for culture in the Politbüro.

This apparent closeness of Brězan to key figures in the SED hierarchy and his role as a functionary in the Writers' Union caused others to question his genuineness as a 'critical' writer. He himself described his role in the presidium as that of somebody who was on the 'Ersatzbank'.[16] There is a sense, particularly in the second volume, that he was constantly trying to defend himself against the charge, which was levelled against him by the writer, Erich Loest, at the last

Writers' Union congress, that he had also been a 'Mitspieler'.[17] It is
true that right to the end he was using his influence with the leadership
of the SED. In March 1989 he went to see Honecker to persuade him
to allow the Domowina to remove the term 'sozialistische Organisation' from its statute. Honecker had in practice already done this by
replacing this term with 'nationale Organisation' when a delegation
from the Domowina visited the Staatsrat in October 1987 on the 75th
anniversary of the Domowina's foundation.[18] But it had somehow
crept in again in his draft 'Grußadresse' to the Sorbian Festival of
Culture, scheduled for June 1989, probably as a result of pressure
from Sorbian SED functionaries. When Brězan managed to see Honecker in March 1989, he readily agreed to drop the term 'sozialistisch'
again.[19] But when the 'Grußadresse' was actually sent, the term
'sozialistisch' had been reinstated. Brězan then wrote on 22 May 1989
about this matter to Honecker and the latter replied on 31 May, agree-
ing to reinstate the originally agreed term, 'allumfassende, nationale
Organisation'.[20]

This closeness to power in the GDR was held against Brězan by
some in the Sorbian community. On the one hand there were middle-
ranking SED functionaries who resented his ability to go over their
heads and get decisions they had made reversed. On the other hand he
was accused, particularly by the Churches, of being a 'Kumpan von
Honecker'.[21] Others accused him of having insulted the people of
Yugoslavia when in 1952 he had handed back the medal given to him
by Tito for his service with the youth brigades in the late 1940s.[22] He
was also attacked for having received favours from the state, such as
the tenancy of a house in Bautzen. But there was never any suggestion
that he had cooperated with the Ministry of State Security[23] and on his
own account he was still under surveillance by the MfS in 1988. In his
last meeting with Hager in March 1989, Hager told him that he had
been given the manuscript of *Mein Stück Zeit* to approve. He picked
out one sentence at the end in which Brězan seems to be accusing the
SED of bringing about its own downfall.[24] The relevant sentence
actually implies that Brězan realized he had not given his full commitment to GDR socialism:

> Zu Olims Zeiten, denkt der Mann ohne Anteilnahme, während er im Spiegel sich
> näher treten sieht, nicht verwundert, daß er ich ist. Dunkelfleckiges, rissiges
> Spiegelglas zwischen uns, ich sehe, daß meine rechte Schulter ein wenig hängt,
> ich habe immer nur auf einer getragen. Meinen Anteil für das Große Experiment

am Ende unseres Jahrtausends. Wenn es mißlingt – wenn wir es mißlingen machen –, zählt sich unsere Welt selbst aus dem Ring.[25]

Brězan agreed with the accusation made against him in the 1930s and the 1950s that he was 'politisch unzuverlässig' and speculated that he was probably seen in the same light by the political authorities in Saxony after 1990, as somebody who is suspicious of political power, while at the same time being in favour of change.[26] Ultimately Brězan was trying to answer through his autobiographical writing the questions that he posed at the beginning of *Mein Stück Zeit*:

> Sind meine Ideale Illusionen geworden? Oder war das Zeitlimit, das die Träume der Wirklichkeitswerdung der Ideale setzten, illusionär? Wann ist die Desillusionierung eingetreten? Und wodurch vor allem, durch welche Erfahrungen? Ist unter den Erfahrungen vielleicht die dafür gewichtigste die, daß ungerechte Gewalt sich zum Ungeheuer ausgewachsen hat und alles frißt, was menschlich ist, auch Ideale? Wenn das die gewichtigste Erfahrung wäre, warum resigniere ich dann nicht, entwaffne mich und hebe die Hände?[27]

In the end Brězan admitted in the second volume of his autobiography that his experiences in the 1950s led him to give up his belief in the power of literature to have a direct political impact, and he even questioned whether it was desirable for it to have this power. But he did not feel able to say so directly until after the political changes of 1989/90.

> Diese Umstände bewirkten, daß ich begann, mich von der Vorstellung zu lösen, Literatur könne – oder solle – unmittelbar Einfluß auf politisches Geschehen haben. Das schreibt sich so heute hin, in Wirklichkeit war es ein langer, widersprüchlicher Prozeß.[28]

But this realization did not detract from his belief in socialism. Although he had become disillusioned with certain aspects of GDR socialism, he remained a member of the SED until 1989.

Notes

[1]   Jurij Brězan, *Mein Stück Zeit*, 1st edn, Berlin: Verlag Neues Leben, 1989; 2nd edn, Leipzig: Gustav Kiepenheuer, 1998. All references will be to the first edition, unless otherwise stated.

[2]   Brězan, *Mein Stück Zeit*, 2nd edn, p. 7.

3   Brězan, *Mein Stück Zeit*, p. 15.

4   Jurij Brězan, *Ohne Paß und Zoll*, Leipzig: Gustav Kiepenheuer, 1999.

5   Ibid, p. 213.

6   Ibid.

7   Ibid.

8   Ibid., p. 28.

9   Jurij Brězan, *Auf dem Rain wächst Korn*, Berlin: Verlag Volk und Welt, 1951, pp. 7-8.

10   See *neue deutsche literatur*, 2 (1954), which contains a selection of poems from *Sorbische Lyrik*, ed. J. Brězan, Berlin: Verlag Volk und Welt, 1954.

11   After the early phase of the building of the 'Schwarze Pumpe' power station, Sorbian writers and artists tended to avoid it as a theme, and it was German writers, such as Heiner Müller and Brigitte Reimann, who placed it at the centre of their works.

12   'Information über Parteigruppenversammlung der Domowina', 21 February 1955, SAPMO-BArch, DY30 IV 2/13/380.

13   Brězan, *Mein Stück Zeit*, pp. 342-7; *Ohne Pass und Zoll*, pp. 130-3.

14   Jurij Brězan, 'Sophokles und Spellerhütte', *Sinn und Form,* 33:3 (1981), 524.

15   Jurij Brězan, 'Geschichten sind die Brille, die man weitergeben kann', *Sonntag,* 19 May 1983.

16   Brězan, *Ohne Paß und Zoll*, p. 169.

17   Ibid., p. 169.

18   See the autobiography of the last head of the Domowina, Jurij Grós, *Staatsange-hörigkeit: Deutsch. Nationalitat: Sorbe*, GNN Verlag: Schkeuditz, 2004, pp. 145-6.

19   Brězan, *Ohne Paß und Zoll*, pp. 187-8.

20   Ibid., pp. 188-9. See also SAPMO-BArch, DY30 IV 2/2.039/224, Büro Egon Krenz, Beziehungen Domowina mit ZK, 1987-1988, pp. 43-4.

21   Brězan, *Ohne Paß und Zoll*, p.232.

[22] Ibid.

[23] According to Joachim Walther, Brězan seems to have been the one vice-president of the Writers' Union who had not been recruited by the MfS and was 'negativ erfasst' as a result of their surveillance operations. See Joachim Walther, *Sicherheits-bereich Literatur*, Berlin: Ullstein, 1999, p. 872.

[24] Brězan, *Ohne Paß und Zoll*, p. 184.

[25] Brězan, *Mein Stück Zeit*, p. 357.

[26] Brězan, *Ohne Paß und Zoll*, pp. 189-90.

[27] Brězan, *Mein Stück Zeit*, p. 12.

[28] Brězan, *Ohne Paß und Zoll*, p. 226.

Christine Cosentino

'Idylle mit Gewehr': Volker Brauns Versuche einer Annäherung an den Vater in *Das Mittagsmahl*

Volker Braun's slim volume *Das Mittagsmahl* (2007) may be viewed as an autobiography – or rather a fictionalized autobiography; one could also call it a chronicle or a memory book. The volume attempts to reconstruct the contradictory character of Erich Braun, Volker Braun's father, who died a 'hero's death' in WWII, when the son was barely six years old. Written in the first person singular, Braun's text narrates his memories from two levels: from the perspective of a young child, as well as from the perspective of the mature author who spent his formative years in the GDR and had to make adjustments to find his place in the FRG. Working to unearth the truth about those wartime years and about his father's thinking, Braun probes deeply into memory – his own, his mother's, his relatives' – and the way it roots him in the past, in the present, and in the future. Analysing the father-figure, Braun questions himself, his own historical and political consciousness. Less interested in blaming than in understanding the generation of his father, Braun poses hard questions about responsibility, about trauma – national, social, familial, and personal – and about the long pall it casts over both space and time.

Die Auseinandersetzungen der im Umfeld des Nationalsozialismus Geborenen mit der Vätergeneration füllen Regale und scheinen nicht enden zu wollen. Im Jahr 2007 meldete sich nun auch Volker Braun (Jahrgang 1939) mit einem solchen Reflexionsbuch, betitelt *Das Mittagsmahl*,[1] einem schmalen Bändchen mit acht Kupferstichen des Leipziger Künstlers Baldwin Zettl. Damit reiht sich eine neue Perspektive in die Vielfalt der Rekonstruktionsversuche ein. Ging es Peter Weiß um einen *Abschied von den Eltern*, so handelt es sich bei Braun wohl eher um den Versuch, den 'Elenden zu umarmen' (M, 55) und zu verstehen. Der Marxist Braun schrieb dieses Büchlein von der Perspektive eines in der DDR sozialisierten Deutschen, der illusionslos und pragmatisch denkend, weiß, daß der Westen die Zukunft des Ostens voll im Griff hat. Dem Buch war bereits im Jahre 2004 ein Privatdruck des Leipziger Bibliophilen-Abends vorausgegangen. Grübelndes, sezierendes Nachsinnen über das 'glückliche furchtbare Leben' (M, 53) von Vater und Mutter in den Jahren 1933 bis 1945, den Jahren von Hochzeit und Tod, ist nichts Neues in Brauns Gesamtwerk; schon in früheren Jahren hatte der Dichter die Eltern zu verstehen versucht, hatte einschneidende Lebensstationen der beiden in

seiner Lyrik und Essayistik nachgezeichnet. Nach wie vor bleibt es jedoch auch in diesem neuen Werk bei einem Rekonstruktionsversuch,
einer 'autobiographischen' d.h. wahrheitsgetreu erfindenden 'Annäherung an den verlorenen Vater',[2] bei Fragestellungen ohne Antworten:
'Ich geh ihm nach' (M, 7).

In der ihm eigenen Manier lapidarer Widerspruchserhellung
schreibt Braun von Tod und Leben, vom 'Schönsten und vom
Schrecklichsten' (M, 12) einer Liebe, die in der Nazizeit begann und
in ihr endete: der Vater stirbt kurz vor Ende des Krieges den sinnlosen
'Helden-Tod'; konträr dazu demonstriert die verwitwete Mutter mit
ihren selbstquälerischen Erinnerungen an den Geliebten ein zwar
widersprüchliches und aufreibendes, aber doch erfülltes 'Helden-
Leben' und Überleben in deutscher Not- und Nachkriegszeit. In dem
dem Band beigefügten Gedicht '6.5.1995' über den Tod der Mutter
erinnert Braun sie als eine handelnde, mutige Frau, die im Kranken-
haus einen Moment den Mut verlor, müde wurde, nicht mehr kämpfen
wollte und folglich medizinisch 'RUHIGGESTELLT' (M, 65) wurde.
In der Gestalt der Mutter wiederholt Braun assoziativ jenen Gedanken,
dem er bereits ein paar Jahre früher im Bild der großen steinernen
Frauenfigur in dem Essay 'Dresdens Andenken'[3] Ausdruck gegeben
hatte. Die Hand der beschriebenen weiblichen Skulptur weist wie
mahnend auf die unabsehbare, grauenhafte Trümmerfläche:

> Sie serviert uns das Unsere, das Menschenwerk. Der entsetztliche Widerspruch
> von Grauen und Schönheit, die Wirkung von Tod und Kunst, rückte mir die
> Geschichte in ein scharfes Licht, als etwas Gewaltsames und Offenes, das
> Anteilnahme und Widerspruch fordert. (DA, 113)

Politische Anteilnahme und Widerspruch sind auf dem Boden der
DDR entstandene Bewußtseinshaltungen, die Braun in den pragmatischen Prozeß einer versuchten Neukonstituierung des Ich im verein-
igten Deutschland neu einsetzt.

Das Mittagsmahl ist eine Collage von zehn Prosaminiaturen, acht
die Episoden untermalenden oder verfremdenden Kupferstichen, zwei
Gedichten älteren Datums: 'Der Teutoburger Wald' (aus *Training des
aufrechten Gang*s, 1979) und '6.5.1996' (aus *Tumulus*, 1999) sowie
Versatzstücken aus Brauns Essayistik. Dieses Eingebettetsein der
Braunschen Reflexionen zwischen kategorisierenden Genres führt auf
ein ästhetisches Territorium, das das Vermischen authentischer
Fiktion mit eigenem Erleben erlaubt. Dennis Tate – auf der Folie von

Christa Wolfs Essay 'Lesen und Schreiben' – hat diesen zwielichtig-autobiographischen Bereich in seinem Buch *Shifting Perspectives: East German Autobiographical Narratives Before and After the End of the GDR* (2007) eingehend untersucht und kritisch durchleuchtet. Es handelt sich in Brauns *Das Mittagsmahl* um Reminiszenzen. Der Text gehört somit also in der Tat ins fragwürdige Genre des Autobiographischen, in jenen subjektiven Bereich des lückenhaften Sprechens, des Präsentierens von Teilwahrheiten, des Selektierens, des Verschönerns, des Verdichtens. Der Ich-Sprecher ist auf den ersten Blick der 1939 geborene Fünfjährige oder Sechsjährige, der – so meint Frauke Meyer-Gosau – 'die Eltern aus Kinderaugen [sieht]',[4] aus einer Perspektive also, die Fragen nach moralischer, sozialer oder historischer Schuld sinnvoll nicht zuläßt. Ein sehr fragwürdiger Zeitzeuge präsentiert sich folglich in diesem Annäherungsversuch, dessen Erinnerungen sich wohl vorrangig auf die der anderen Familienmitglieder und auf die eigene Vorstellungskraft stützen.

Zu diesem sprechenden Zeitzeugen gesellt sich von Anfang an der spätere, nachdenkende Erzähler. Braun 'sieht' die Eltern; er montiert ideologisch gestanzten Wortmüll, abgedroschene idiomatische Redewendungen und Politjargon in den Text, evoziert Bilder, Gesten, Sprachfetzen, die er verdichtend weiterzugeben versucht. Sieht man das Buch also als Ganzes, so geht es hier um eine Erzählhaltung der gebrochenen Perspektive, ein duales Erzählen, d.h. die Episoden um Vater und Mutter werden in einer Gleichzeitigkeit von Innen- und Außenwahrnehmung geschildert: gesehen mit den Augen des Kindes und aus der Position des distanzierten, reflektierenden Erzählers. Dieses Ineinander der Perspektiven schafft einen offenen Assoziationsbereich. 'Shifting perspectives' erlauben – so könnte man Dennis Tate zitieren – das Experimentieren mit verschiedenen Bewußtseinslagen: 'to experiment with the multiple opportunities for self-reconstruction'.[5] Zweck ist die Erforschung des Vaters und die Selbsterforschung: 'Er/Ich' (M, 8). Das korrespondiert mit Roy Pascals Maxime: 'Die eigentliche Autobiographie [...] ist die Gestaltung einer Persönlichkeit,'[6] bzw., so der amerikanische Theoretiker Timothy Dow Adams: 'Autobiography is the story of an attempt to reconcile one's life with one's self and is not, therefore, meant to be taken as historically accurate but as metaphorically authentic'.[7]

Der 'unschuldige Kinderblick', die doppelte Perspektive in der Nazizeit geborener Erzähler ließ sich in letzter Zeit – primär im

Umfeld des 60. Jahrestages der Zerstörung Dresdens oder anderer
Großstädte – in einer Reihe von literarischen Werken beobachten,
Werken etwa von Helga Schütz, Kurt Bartsch, Dieter Forte, Uwe
Timm.[8] So fungiert der fünfjährige Volker Braun in dem neuen
Prosabändchen als Bildarchiv von Privatem und Historischem, von
kindlichen Ängsten und daraus resultierender politischer Verantwortung des Erwachsenen, oder – so könnte man sagen – das Kind fungiert
als ein Dokumentationszentrum, mit dem sich der Erzähler verstän-
digt, das er befragt, hinterfragt, mit dem er sich aber nicht identifiziert.
Christoph Hein, der Dichterkollege, spricht vom 'unvermuteten Auf-
reißen einer alltäglichen Beobachtung in einen größeren, in einen
weltumspannenden, philosophischen Zusammenhang'.[9] Brauns sehr
private Reflexionen über die Eltern in diesem Familienbericht sind
lebendige Momentaufnahmen mit historischer Tiefenschärfe, mit ak-
tuellem Bezug und Ausblick auf die Zukunft. Aus dem Einzelfall des
Landsers Erich Braun entsteht somit, was Günter de Bruyn einmal als
'eine Geschichtsschreibung von unten'[10] bezeichnete. Letztlich dienen
die grübelnden Annäherungsversuche an den Vater jedoch der Selbst-
auseinandersetzung, der Selbsterforschung und Selbsterklärung. Sie
entspringen der Notwendigkeit, über die Voraussetzungen der eigenen
Biographie Klarheit zu gewinnen. Braun läßt keinen Zweifel: 'Ich geh
ihm nach […] Er/ich ist die Person, nach der ich fahnde' (M, 8).
      Braun glorifiziert den Vater nicht; er verurteilt ihn nicht; er stellt
ihn einfach dar und zwar in seiner Widersprüchlichkeit. Vieles ist
dabei Mutmaßung, anderes beruht auf erinnerten Tatsachen, auf
familiär und weltanschaulich Prägendes, das sich permanent ins
Gedächtnis eingebrannt hat. Wie ein roter Faden windet sich durch
das Braunsche Gesamtwerk eine Episode, die der Dichter splitterhaft
durch die Jahre hinweg in variierter Form immer wieder neu ein-
blendet, u.a. in dem Essay 'Dresdens Andenken': 'Erinnerung an den
Vater: wie uns fünf Söhnen der *beste* Mensch, auf der Veranda
sitzend, das *schrecklichste* Ding erklärt, sein Gewehr' (DA, 112,
meine Kursivierung). Auch in der Prosaminiatur 'Waffengang' in *Das
Mittagsmahl* erinnert sich der Fünfjährige – oder ist es der spätere
Erzähler? – mit Schrecken daran, wie er die Waffe berührte: 'Er ließ
es zu; er spürte nicht mein Schaudern' (M, 31). Brauns Text lebt von
diesen Polaritäten, dem Unverständlichen, Unversöhnlichen.
      Die allererste Episode, 'ER ICH', setzt den Ton für die dann
folgenden Prosaminiaturen. Sie liefert die Vorlage für die im Band

vorherrschende narrative Struktur kontrastierender Gegeneinanderstellung. Diese Kontrasttechnik zeigt den Charakter des Vaters, die Liebe der Eltern, das Schicksal des Einzelnen während des Hitlerregimes in schillernder Komplexität, Vielschichtigkeit und Widersprüchlichkeit: 'Erich: Er/ich', 'rasend schön und unverschämt', 'sei halb vier am Bus, und brav', 'die warme Kammer, [der] Panzergraben', 'Er: der mich zeugte, er, der in den Krieg zog' (M, 7). Der Text ist getragen vom Gestus des Scheiterns, dem Gefühl des Autors, nicht zum Kern der Sache zu kommen, ohne sagen zu können, was dieser Kern wäre. Wer war dieser Vater mit dem 'nicht mehr gebräuchlichen Namen *Erich*', den er kühn kürzte zu: "*Ich*"' (M, 7). War er ein leidenschaftlich und selbstlos Liebender oder ein Egoman? War er ein unsteter, zum Leichtsinn neigender Kunstfreund, der heimlich Bücher, Noten und Schallplatten kaufte, oder war er ein verantwortungsvoller Familienmensch? War dieser Volkssturmsoldat, dem es im entscheidenden Augenblick nicht ums reine Überleben ging, ein Blinder, ein Bedauernswerter? Oder war er eher ein Unbesonnener, tollkühner Draufgänger, hatte er sich doch freiwillig gemeldet, einen feindlichen 'Tank unschädlich zum machen […] ohne an Weib und Kinder zu denken' (M, 41), eine 'Heldentat' in den letzten Stunden des Krieges, die ihm das Leben kostete. Der Vater, Erich Braun, war das eine und das andere, ein komplexes Bündel von Widersprüchen. Der Sohn, Volker Braun, 'Er/Ich', reflektiert über diese Widersprüche, wagt es aber nicht, ein Urteil zu fällen: 'Ich bin es, der sein Leben wagt, der scheiternd schreibt' (M, 8).

Auch die Mutter sinniert im nachhinein über die furchtbare und glückliche Ehe mit Erich Braun, die vielversprechend begann: 'Der Bund fürs Leben wurde im Jahr der Machtergreifung geschlossen und aufgelöst im Jahr der Kapitulation' (M, 13). Der Mann sah nur das Schönste in ihrer Beziehung: 'Ja, sieh nur zu, an Liebe sollst du mich nicht übertreffen' (M, 13), ein Versprechen, das er trotz Leichtsinn und Eigensinn, trotz der anhaltenden zermürbenden Notlage der Familie einhielt. Die Braut war im siebten Monat schwanger, als sie heirateten. Einen Tag nach der Hochzeit stand der Gerichtsvollzieher vor der Tür. Es war eine höllische, im Zeichen der Nazis stehende 'wunderbare' Idylle: 'FAMILIEFASCHISMUS' (M 53). Braun setzt diese Widersprüchlichkeit zeichenhaft in scharfes Licht, indem er – laut Text – ein Bild des Vaters einfügt, der in Uniform vor einer Vogelscheuche im Feld salutiert. Das Bild ist ein Kupferstich.

Baldwin Zettls komplementierende Kunstwerke über die in Reih und
Glied stehenden oder die Befehle folgenden deutschen Soldaten
vertieft das Abgründige und Grauenvolle dieser Periode. Tief eingebrannt ins Gedächtnis des Kindes/des Mannes hat sich das Ende dieser
'glücklichen und furchtbaren' Liebe: der Abschied des Vaters, als er
in den Krieg zog und die Mutter verzweifelt und stumm mit ihm
kämpfte, um ihn festzuhalten, bis sie ihn resignierend zur Tür hinaus-
schob. Ihm eingebrannt hat sich ebenfalls die Szene, die dem Bändchen den Titel gab, *Das Mittagsmahl*, der spezifische Moment, als die
Postbotin den Brief über den 'Heldentod' des Vaters im Teutoburger
Wald brachte. Die Familie klammert sich aneinander: 'Und sie [die
Mutter] umfaßte uns, und wir sie mit allen Armen […] als wollte sie
uns zusammenschließen, zusammenschwören zu einer Gemeinschaft'
(M, 47). Der reflektierende Dichter summierte diese prägenden Momente in einem Satz, der auf das weltanschauliche Fundament seines
Pazifismus und seines Geschichtsbilds weist: 'Ich kam zur Schule,
und lernte Gewißheit' (M, 47).

Braun zitiert einen Satz seiner Mutter, den er nicht vergessen kann.
Er hörte sie einmal sagen: 'Wer weiß wofür es gut war, daß er nicht
wiederkam' (M, 11). Der Dichter interpretiert diese Äußerung als
Ausdruck größter Liebe, einer Liebe, die nicht mehr bedroht werden
konnte von Verrat, Ehebruch, Kleinlichkeiten oder dem Verschleiß
eines zerreibenden Alltags. Könnten sich in diesem 'ungeheuren Satz'
(M, 11) jedoch nicht auch noch tiefere Bedeutungschichten ver-
bergen? Etwa die utopische Hoffnung, der dringliche Wunsch, daß
sich aus dem sinnlosen Tod des Geliebten historisch Sinnvolles, die
Verhinderung von Kriegen lernen ließe? Das greift in das im Band
eingegliederte Gedicht 'Der Teutoburger Wald' aus dem Jahre 1975,
in dem der spezifische Tod des Soldaten Erich Braun im Zweiten
Weltkrieg, also der Heldenmythos, simultantechnisch verzahnt ist mit
der Reflexion der Menschheitsgeschichte des Blutvergießens, die in
germanische Fernen zu einem anderen 'Helden', zu Hermann, dem
Cherusker, führt.

Braun wartet in der letzten Prosaminiatur, 'Verächtlicher Gedanke', mit einer Vision des erwachsenen Autors auf. In der Stadt Wien
findet er ein Konfektionsgeschäft mit dem Namen des Inhabers an der
Tür: 'Erich Braun' (M, 55). Einen Moment lang hegt er den Gedanken, es könnte der Vater sein, der überlebt hat, aber seine Familie
verlassen hat. Christoph Hein kritisiert in seinem Essay 'Das Sterben

im Krieg' das abwertende Adjektiv 'verächtlich', denn in der Heraufbeschwörung des 'Vaterphantoms' handele es sich um eine 'kindliche Verlusterfahrung, die Sehnsucht nach dem früh verlorenen Vater'.[11] Man könnte den Akzent auch anders setzen: die Liebe des Vaters zur Mutter ließ keinen Verrat zu. Ein verächtlicher Gedanke also. Aber der Inhaber des Geschäftes wird in der Vision des Sohns trotzdem momenthaft zur Vaterfigur. Der Sohn ist versucht, den 'Elenden zu umarmen' (M, 55). Das imaginierte Umarmen des Bedauernswerten, früh Gefallenen – eine versöhnliche, liebevolle Geste – setzt den Gedanken der Abwertung außer Kraft.

'Offnen Augs blind' (M, 59) gingen die Soldaten durch die Jahrhunderte der Menschheitsgeschichte auf den Schlachtfeldern in den Tod. Brauns Gesamtwerk umkreist diesen Gedanken. In *Das Mittagsmahl* präsentiert der Dichter den konkreten Fall am Beispiel des eigenen Vaters, ein Vorgang, der schmerzhaft ist. In einem Interview mit Rolf Jucker äußerte der Autor einmal, die Literatur nähme

Position, indem sie die Sache selbst zum Sprechen bringt. Wenn die Kreatur, wenn Woyzeck redet, was ist daran das Gefährliche und sozial Interessante? Daß es in *seiner* Weise geschieht, in einer seine eigenen Verhältnisse fassenden Ungeheuerlichkeit, das ist das Politikum.[12]

Brauns Text *Das Mittagsmahl* demonstriert diese *eigene* Kommunikationsweise, das 'sozial Interessante' der am Weltkrieg Teilnehmenden. Der Autor wertet selten, und wenn er historisch wertet, also vom Erinnerten abweicht – zu erwähnen wäre z.B. die strapazierte Einblendung des Statements 'Die anglo-amerikanischen Luftangriffe gehen in Bagdad weiter' (M, 29) – verliert das Gesagte an Überzeugungskraft. Generell bleibt es jedoch bei der Darstellung, beim Aufzeigen: vorgeführt werden die Sprache der Eltern, ihre Gesten, *ihre* Art der Verständigung und der im spezifischen geschichtlichen Kontext grassierende Nazi-Politjargon. Brauns von Widersprüchen, Kontrasten und Brüchen durchdrungener Text reflektiert auf subtile Weise den Protest und das Aufbegehren des Dichters, sein Anliegen. Geschichte, um noch einmal den Essay 'Dresdens Andenken' zu erwähnen, präsentiert sich als etwas 'Gewaltsames und Offenes, das Anteilnahme und Widerspruch fordert' (DA, 113). Brauns Text ist ein Dokument des Widerspruchs.

Volker Braun erhielt für sein Werk *Das Mittagsmahl* im Jahre 2007 den ver.di-Literaturpreis von Berlin-Brandenburg. Die Sprecher-in der Jury, Carmen Winter, erklärte die Wahl: 'Volker Braun erzählt in dem schmalen Bändchen sprachlich geschliffen, nur scheinbar Privates, denn in den tieferen Schichten der Erzählung wird ein Kapitel deutscher Geschichte abgehandelt'.[13] Die Lebensgeschichte des Vaters ist eine private Familiengeschichte, sie ist eine Chronik der Nazizeit; sie ist ebenfalls das fiktiv-autobiographische Erinnerungsbuch eines in der DDR sozialisierten Menschen, der die Konsequenzen aus der Nazizeit gezogen hat. Christoph Hein hielt die Laudatio bei der Verleihung des Preises am 23. April 2008. Er nannte seinen Kollegen einen 'verläßlichen Chronisten der stattfindenden Geschichte [...] Er war und ist wohl der politischste aller deutschen Autoren der letzten Jahrzehnte'.[14] Brauns unversöhnliche 'dresdner Haltung' (DA, 114) in dem Bändchen *Das Mittagsmahl* ist am Beispiel des Vaters ein beharrliches 'An-Denken gegen die Vernichtung' (DA, 114).

Anmerkungen

[1]   Volker Braun, *Das Mittagsmahl*, Frankfurt/Main und Leipzig: Insel, 2007. Zitate im Text abgekürzt mit der Sigle M.

[2]   Jörg Magenau, 'Annäherung an den verlorenen Vater', *Deutschlandradio-Kultur-Kritik* 2008. www.dradio.de/dkultur/sendungen/kritik/624106/ (abgerufen am 10. Mai 2011).

[3]   Volker Braun, 'Dresdens Andenken', in: Braun, *Wir befinden uns soweit wohl. Wir sind erst einmal am Ende*, Frankfurt/Main: Suhrkamp, 1998. Zitate im Text abgekürzt mit der Sigle DA.

[4]   Frauke Meyer-Gosau, 'Kurz und bündig: Volker Braun, Das Mittagsmahl', *Literaturen,* 5 (2007), S. 84.

[5]   Dennis Tate, *Shifting Perspectives. East German Autobiographical Narratives Before and After the End of the GDR*, Rochester, NY: Camden House, S. 61.

[6]   Roy Pascal, 'Die Autobiographie als Kunstform,' in: Günter Niggel, Hg., *Die Autobiographie. Zur Form und Geschichte einer literarischen Gattung*, Darmstadt: Wissenschaftliche Buchhandlung, 1989, S. 148-58 (hier: S. 148).

[7]   Timothy Dow Evans, *Telling Lies in Modern American Autobiography*, Chapel Hill, NC: University of North Carolina Press, 1990, S. ix.

[8] Siehe hierzu meinen Artikel: Christine Cosentino, '"Der Krieg, ein Kinderspiel": Romane mit Kinderperspektive im Kontext der Luftkriegsdebatte', *Neophilologus*, 91 (2007), S. 687-99.

[9] Christoph Hein, 'Das Sterben im Krieg. VATERPHANTOM: Kleine Lobrede auf den Schriftsteller, Begleiter und Chronisten Volker Braun', *Freitag* 25. Juni 2008. Siehe http://www.lyrikwelt.de/hintergrund/braunvolker-bericht-h.htm (abgerufen am 10. Mai 2011).

[10] Günter de Bruyn, *Das erzählte Ich. Über Wahrheit und Dichtung in der Autobiographie*, Frankfurt/Main: Fischer, 1995, S. 20.

[11] Hein, 'Das Sterben im Krieg'.

[12] Rolf Jucker, 'Ich bin zu Ende mit allen Träumen / Was soll ich unter den Schläfern säumen: Volker Braun im Gespräch mit Rolf Jucker Berlin, 10. August 2002 und 10. Juni 2003', in: Jucker, Hg., *'Was werden wir die Freiheit nennen?' Volker Brauns Texte als Zeitkritik*, Würzburg: Königshausen & Neumann, 2004, S. 97-106 (hier: S. 104).

[13] 'Ver.di-Literaturpreis 2007 an Volker Braun. Presseinformation vom 12. Februar 2008', http://vs.verdi.de/aktuelles/leute/volker_braun (Letzter Zugriff am 20. Juli 2008).

[14] Hein, 'Das Sterben im Krieg'.

Ute Hirsekorn

Vom verblendeten Selbst zum gewendeten Selbst: Der Wandel in der narrativen Identität in den Selbstreflexionen Günter Schabowskis nach 1989

Günter Schabowski, a younger but long-serving member of the SED party elite, was a staunch defender of communist ideology throughout GDR times. Despite this, he became a reformer during the political upheavals of 1989. Initially he simply denied the institutional failings of the GDR system, but within a few years had entirely renounced the old ideologies, from the early 1990s embracing the democratic values of a unified Germany. This contribution explores Schabowski's self-reflections in a sequence of texts, with the aim of investigating the dramatic shifts in his perspective on his GDR past, and how he processes autobiographical memory in order to construct a narrative identity that subsequently allows him to integrate into post-unification German society with a new social role.

Der komplexe Zusammenhang von dem Geschichtssinn und dem Sich-Verstehen, den bereits Wilhelm Dilthey 1883 in seiner *Einführung in die Geisteswissenschaften* beleuchtet hat, wurde in der Autobiographieforschung im Laufe der Zeit mit den verschiedensten Zugängen aus unterschiedlichen Disziplinen mehr und mehr ausdifferenziert. Dennis Tate zeigt in *Shifting Perspectives* die Vielschichtigkeit des Prozesses der Selbstdefinition und Selbst-Verständigung bei einschlägigen DDR-Schriftstellern auf, z.B. wie die Autoren in verschiedenen Werken im Laufe individueller Schaffensperioden durch politische und historische Umbrüche hindurch ihre Identität immer wieder neu ergründet haben, besonders auch unter den neuen Bedingungen des vereinten Deutschlands. Im Gegenzug sollen hier Selbstreflexionen entschlüsselt werden, deren methodische und methodologische Strategien, mit denen Vergangenheit und Gegenwart komplex verkoppelt werden, Licht auf Perspektivumbrüche in der narrativen Identität bei einem Vertreter einer anderen DDR-Elite werfen, der den historischen Einschnitt von 1989 ebenfalls unter dem streng prüfenden Blick der Öffentlichkeit erlebt hat. Günter Schabowski, zu DDR-Zeiten Politbüromitglied und 1. SED-Sekretär von Berlin, ist in diesem Zusammenhang besonders interessant, weil er sich zu unterschiedlichen Zeitpunkten öffentlich mit seiner DDR-Vergangenheit auseinandergesetzt hat und über seine verschiedenen Texte eine neue Sichtweise entwickelt und verfeinert hat.

Seit dem klassischen Werk *Geschichte der Autobiographie* von 1907, in dem Georg Misch die Autobiographie zu einer literarischen Gattung erhob, haben gattungstheoretische Diskussionen versucht, Autobiographien konkret zu definieren, ohne wirklich einen übergreifenden Konsens zu finden. Selbst Philippe Lejeune, der mittels seines 'autobiographischen Pakts' zwischen Autor und Leser zunächst um Abgrenzung verschiedener Gattungstypen bemüht war, rückte 1975 den disziplinübergreifenden anthropologischen Wert der Autobiographie in den Vordergrund[1] und vollzog nach eigenen Angaben 1977 'eine große Wende', in der er seine Ansichten zur literarischen Autobiographie 'demokratisiert' habe und diese fortan als einen 'Sonderfall eines umfassenden Phänomens' eingestuft hat. Denn jeder Mensch trage 'eine ständig überarbeitete Rohfassung seiner Lebensgeschichte' in sich, die sich auch über andere Textformen wie Interviews herausholen ließe.[2] Hans Joachim Schröder sieht in dem Interview einen Untersuchungsgegenstand, der 'auf empirischer Grundlage zwischen Literaturwissenschaft, Soziologie, Sozialgeschichte und verschiedenen weiteren Disziplinen einen Knoten zu schürzen gestattet'.[3] In diesem Sinne sollen in diesem Beitrag unterschiedliche autobiographische Textformen von Autobiographie über Interviews bis hin zu Essays berücksichtigt werden,[4] denn die Vertreter der politischen Elite der DDR haben besonders nach der Wende im Rahmen der öffentlichen und gerichtlichen Anschuldigungen gegen sie Material der eigenen Lebensgeschichte in sehr unterschiedlichen Texten verarbeitet.

Ausgangspunkt der Betrachtungen sind Lebensgeschichten vor allem als (psycho)soziale Konstrukte, die im Ergebnis von Entwicklungsphasen und kulturellen Anforderungen an ein Individuum in einer konkreten gesellschaftlichen Epoche entstehen.[5] Entsprechend bemerken die Gedächtnispsychologen Jessica Cameron, Anne Wilson und Michael Ross: 'People reconstruct and interpret episodes from their pasts by using the bits and pieces they retrieve from memory together with their current knowledge and understanding of themselves and their social world'.[6] Nach historischen Umbrüchen wie dem von 1989/90 sehen sich daher viele Miterlebende zu 'biographischen Umdeutungen' gezwungen.[7] Hier soll Günter Schabowskis Aufarbeitung seiner Vergangenheit untersucht werden und wie er der

(narrativen) Identität seiner Lebensgeschichte Stabilität und Kohärenz
verleiht. Identität ist laut Jefferson Singer und Pavel Blagov ein
System der Persönlichkeit, das dafür verantwortlich ist, eine über-
greifende Kohärenz der individuellen Lebenserfahrungen zu erzeugen
und dem Leben Sinn zu geben. '[I]dentity is synonymous with the
autobiographical narrative individuals construct to weave together
their past, present, and anticipated future into a unified whole'.[8] Das
heißt, Fakten werden in eine Geschichte 'replete with plot twists,
suspense, key characters and an underlying moral or theme' gewo-
ben.[9] Dan McAdams zeigt dazu, wie sich in der persönlichen Identität
Aspekte der erinnerten Vergangenheit mit der erfahrenen Gegenwart
und der antizipierten Zukunft verbinden: '[Identity] brings together
skills, values, goals and roles into a coherent whole. It brings together
what the person can and wants to do with what opportunities and
constraints for action exist in the social environment'.[10]

Diese Überlegung gewinnt im Rahmen der Untersuchungen zu
Schabowskis Texten um so mehr Bedeutung, da sie konkrete Parameter bei der Identitätsbestimmung bietet. Mit dem politischen Umbruch
musste für den Parteifunktionär ein individueller Lebenseinbruch folgen, denn die bis dahin vorhandenen persönlichen (individuellen) wie
auch gesellschaftlichen (kollektiven) Definitionen dieser Identitäts-
parameter wurden ganz plötzlich von der Gesellschaft in Frage gestellt
bzw. nicht zuletzt durch die deutsche Einheit ungültig (Relevanz-
verlust von Führungspotenzial und -fähigkeiten, Gültigkeitsverlust
von bisherigen Werten und Zielen, Macht- und Funktionsverlust). Mit
diesem Verlust sind einzelne in der DDR-Führung unterschiedlich
umgegangen. SED-Generalsekretär Erich Honecker und z.T. auch sein
Nachfolger Egon Krenz haben zum Beispiel versucht, diese Selbst-
Definitionen, die durch die Parameter gesetzt waren, aufrechtzuerhal-
ten, was sie zu gesellschaftlichen Outcasts gemacht hat. Schabowski
dagegen hat eine potenzielle Identitätskrise abgewehrt, indem er das
Verlustmoment akzeptiert und sich konsequent umorientiert hat, um
trotz öffentlicher Anschuldigungen nicht im gesellschaftlichen Abseits
zu landen.[11] Das heißt, er musste die Parameter für sich völlig neu
bestimmen. Über einen kürzeren oder längeren Zeitraum hat er diese
weiter austariert und damit eine für sich selbst plausibel erscheinende
neue Identität etabliert. Singer und Blagov stellen fest: 'Our capacity
to translate information [...] into "storied thought" is our means of
linking specific past experiences to the enduring concerns of the over-

all personality system, as expressed through a sense of coherent and ongoing narrative identity'.[12]

Im Fokus der nachfolgenden Diskussion steht daher die Auslotung der Neuorientierung und Identitäts(um)bildung bei Schabowski, der nach dem Zusammenbruch der DDR sein Selbstbild behaupten bzw. anpassen musste, um in der neuen Gesellschaft des vereinten Deutschlands zu bestehen. Die über verschiedene zeitliche Etappen veröffentlichten autobiographischen Texte Schabowskis bieten ein interessantes Zeugnis über Dynamiken des autobiographischen Gedächtnisses[13] und damit über seine Neuinterpretation der DDR-Vergangenheit und die so möglich werdende Überwindung von Identitätsbrüchen. Dabei zeigt sich, *wie* Schabowski seine (narrative) Identität trotz des massiven Lebenseinbruchs durch den Untergang der DDR und trotz seiner ideologischen Kehrtwendung aufrechterhält oder umkonstruiert. Schabowskis 'gewendete' Ansichten zum DDR-System werden als eine spezifische Nachwende-Verarbeitungsweise der Vergangenheit analysiert, in der er aktiv Diskontinuitäten zu überwinden sucht, eine kohärente Lebensgeschichte konstruiert und sich gleichzeitig in die neuen gesellschaftlichen Gegebenheiten einfügen will, indem er einem neuen DDR-Bild Rechnung zu tragen sucht.

Noch Anfang der achtziger Jahre nahm sich die medienstrategische Haltung des damaligen Chefs des *Neuen Deutschland* Günter Schabowski nach eigenen Aussagen wie folgt aus:

> Die wirkungsvollste Kritik, die wir gegenwärtig betreiben und fortführen werden, ist die Kritik am Alten […] am Uneffektiven, am Kostenaufwendigen […]. Wir sind Anwälte des Sozialismus. Deshalb ist die Hauptform der Kritik […] die Kritik am Bestehenden in dem Sinne, das Gute von heute in das Bessere von morgen umzuformen.[14]

In einem Gespräch mit dem amerikanischen Politwissenschafter A. James McAdams nur einen Monat vor dem Fall der Mauer habe Schabowski noch immer wie ein 'Apparatschik' geklungen und auf der Basis argumentiert, dass sich die DDR erneut aus Ruinen erheben würde.[15] Laut dem Historiker Christian Jung hat sich Schabowski bis 1989 selbst als Mitglied einer durch die gesamte DDR-Gesellschaft legitimierten Parteiführung gesehen.[16] Frank Sieren, der mit Schabowski als erster Journalist Interviews 1990 und erneut 2009 geführt und veröffentlicht hat, gibt in ähnlicher Weise zu bedenken, 'dass

Schabowski mit hoher Wahrscheinlichkeit noch Jahrzehnte im Politbüro gesessen hätte, wäre die DDR nicht zusammengebrochen'.[17] Als
'Musterbeispiel an Unentschlossenheit und Opportunismus' hat Volker Klemm, Stellvertreter des Untersuchungsausschusses der Volks-
kammer zu Korruption und Amtsmissbrauch von 1990, Schabowski
vor dem Ausschuss erlebt.[18] Nach einer steilen Parteikarriere in der
DDR sprang Günter Schabowski in der spannungsgeladenen Wende-
periode öffentlich auf die kritische Schiene und vermittelte nach dem
Mauerfall seine neue Sichtweise zur Führungsproblematik sehr
schnell in schriftlicher Form.[19] So z.B. 1990 in publizierten Interview-
projekten wie *Der Honecker muss weg* oder *Das Politbüro. Ende
eines Mythos*, wo er um eine Erklärung seiner Person und seiner persönlichen Rolle in der DDR-Führung bemüht ist.

Nahtlos schloss sich 1991 ein weiterer Erklärungsversuch in seiner
offiziellen Autobiographie *Der Absturz* an. Als jüngerer Vertreter der
SED-Spitzenfunktionäre war Schabowski (geb. 1929) zur Zeit des
Zusammenbruchs der DDR in den mittleren Lebensjahren und entsprechend wird seine Analyse vor allem von dem Bedarf getragen,
eine neue Lebensorientierung zu finden, die ihm eine Perspektive in
der Nachwendegesellschaft eröffnen kann. Für Schröder wird es dabei
zur Überlebensfrage, dass ein Funktionär sich in ein vorteilhaftes
Licht rücken kann.[20] In einem polemischen Essay unter dem Titel
'Selbstblendung. Über den Realitätsverlust der Funktionäre' von 1993
sagt sich Schabowski dann auch von der kommunistischen Ideologie
völlig los und formuliert seine These von der 'Selbstblendung', die
zur Selbstzerstörung geführt habe.[21] 1994 versucht sich Schabowski
erneut in Aufklärerräson zum Untergang und zum persönlichen
Scheitern in einem Aufsatz zu äußern: *Abschied von der Utopie* richtet
sich direkt an DDR-Forscher. Pünktlich zum zwanzigsten Jahrestag
des Mauerfalls erscheint der bereits erwähnte jüngste Interviewband
Wir haben fast alles falsch gemacht, der Identität nicht mehr wirklich
neu verortet, sondern bisherige autobiographische Rückblicke und
Neuüberlegungen zu einem Ganzen zusammenfügt. Dieser Text erfüllt
also eine integrative Funktion, die Dan McAdams so kategorisiert:

> Identity needs to integrate these kind of contrasts ['I was a born-again Christian,
> but these days I feel I am an agnostic'] so that while self-elements are separated in
> time (and in content quality) they can be brought meaningfully together in a tem-
> porally organized whole.[22]

Wenn auch nicht immer gleich offensichtlich, stützt sich Schabowski auf frühere Nachwendepublikationen, um eine Art Fazit zu ziehen und die erreichte Identität zu festigen. Aussagen aus früheren Texten werden 2009 oft wortgetreu teils mit und teils ohne expliziten Bezug auf die Textquelle wieder aufgenommen, wie das folgende Beispiel verdeutlicht. Über sein Umdenken und seinen Einstellungswandel sagt er 1993:

> Am Anfang meines geistigen Wandels standen Gespräche, erstaunlicherweise Gespräche mit Journalisten der Bundesrepublik. Von den jähen und sich überschlagenden Veränderungen in der DDR des Jahres 1989 fasziniert, haben etliche stunden-, ja tagelang mit mir diskutiert, um hinter alle Gründe für diesen rapiden gesellschaftlichen Verfall zu kommen. Sie stellten mir Fragen, die ich mir damals noch nicht hätte stellen können. Damit erst wurden bestimmte Schleusen geöffnet. Ein zweites Stimulans war [...], mich mit einem Buch über das Ende der DDR zu äußern. Es war eine Chance und ein heilsamer Zwang zu kritischer Introspektion (Sb, 213).

2009 liest man bei Schabowski beinahe identisch:

> Am Anfang meines geistigen Wandels standen Gespräche, erstaunlicherweise Gespräche mit Journalisten der Bundesrepublik. Von den jähen und sich überschlagenden Veränderungen in der DDR des Jahres 1989 fasziniert, haben etliche von ihnen tagelang mit mir diskutiert, um diesen rapiden gesellschaftlichen Verfall besser verstehen zu können. Sie, Herr Sieren, gehörten dazu. Diese Gespräche öffneten bestimmte Schleusen. Ein zweites Stimulans war meine bereits mehrfach erwähnte Publikation über das Ende der DDR. [...] [D]enn das Schreiben war ein heilsamer Zwang, mich und mein Tun kritisch zu hinterfragen. (Wh, 71)

In beiden Fällen versucht Schabowski einen linearen Bewusstseinswandel zu konstruieren, der von seiner Beteiligung in den Verschwörungsaktionen gegen Honecker über Reformbemühungen nach dem Absetzen Honeckers, wodurch er öffentlich zum 'Wendehals' abgestempelt wurde,[23] bis hin zu seiner Absage an den Kommunismus reicht. 1991 erklärte Schabowski in *Der Absturz*:

> Ich will keinen Abstrich davon erfeilschen, daß ich zu lange und exponiert eine falsche Politik vertreten habe. Die Marxschen Ideen der Gesellschaftsentwicklung und Veränderung wurden zu Mittelmaß und Dogma verballhornt. Nicht zu entschuldigen ist, daß wir Unrecht an Menschen begingen, um recht zu behalten. (Ab, 102-3)

In der Schrift *Abschied von der Utopie* von 1994 und auch 2009 in dem erneuten Interview mit Sieren will Schabowski seine Mitschuld an der Verballhornung der Marxschen Ideen berichtigen: 'Heute würde ich nicht mehr sagen, dass wir Marx so sträflich entstellt haben. Ich glaube vielmehr, dass wir ihn so ernst genommen haben wie er es vielleicht wollte. Das spricht uns nicht frei und ihn postum nicht schuldig.' (Wh, 99)[24]

Solche Bezugnahmen auf frühere Textstellen können vor allem als Bestätigung einer neuen Sinngebung der Vergangenheit gewertet werden, in der das Leben in der DDR nunmehr als ein Entwicklungsstadium in der Biographie Schabowskis beschrieben wird, aus dem er in seiner Nachwendeentwicklung als eine durch Erfahrungswerte geläuterte und gefestigte Persönlichkeit mit korrigierter Weltanschauung hervorgegangen ist. Mit neuen Werten ausgestattet, fühlt er sich in der Gesellschaft des vereinten Deutschlands angekommen und hat sich eine kohärente Lebensgeschichte erschaffen. Den Kommunismus wegen seines permanenten Widerspruchs zwischen Machttrieb und Wirklichkeit als Utopie verwerfend (Wh, 87), hat er sich nun der Demokratie zugewandt:

> Der große Vorzug der Demokratie liegt darin, die widerstrebenden Interessen und Bedürfnisse der Menschen auszutarieren. […] In einer Demokratie können die relativen Machthaber dazu gebracht werden, abzutreten oder ihre Politik zu verändern. (Wh, 55)

Doch wie konkret gelang Schabowski eine solche ideologische Kehrtwendung? Wie versucht er in seinen Texten über einen zwanzigjährigen Zeitraum eine narrative Identität zu entwickeln, die seine Vergangenheit und Gegenwart so verwebt, dass daraus am Ende ein gefestigtes Persönlichkeitsschema hervorgeht? Dazu sollen einige Selbst-Erklärungsstrategien, derer sich Schabowski – ob bewusst oder unbewusst – in seinen Texten bedient, beleuchtet werden. Anfänglich war seine Suche nach Erklärungen zu seiner Vergangenheit und dem Denkumschwung von 1989 von Unsicherheiten geprägt. Zunächst wirkte vor allem die 'situationsbedingte Atmosphäre' der massiven öffentlichen Kritik auf Schabowski, wie die Sozialwissenschaftler des Zentralinstituts für sozialwissenschaftliche Forschung an der Freien Universität Berlin Hans-Hermann Hertle, Theo Pirker und Rainer Weinert in ihrem Interviewprotokoll *Der Honecker muß weg*, einem vierstündigen Gespräch mit Schabowski im Frühjahr 1990, reflektieren. Singer und Blagov heben hervor, dass Erinnerungsnarrative immer auch dialogisch seien, d.h. sie rufen eine Reaktion beim Selbst und Zuhörern oder Lesern hervor.[25] In seinem Nachwort zu dem Gesprächsprotokoll analysiert Pirker:

> Schabowski [nutzte] die Gelegenheit, [...] Anklagen zu entkräften, sich selber im Gespräch [...] über die eigene Position von gestern und heute klarzuwerden und das Muster der eigenen Legende zu stricken. [...] In dem Legendenmuster, das er uns vorgelegt hat, gibt es jedoch Strickfehler.[26]

Was Pirker an Schabowskis Darstellung vor allem zweifelhaft erscheint, ist, dass er sich wiederholt als 'Seiteneinsteiger' beschreibt und vehement ablehnt, seine politische Karriere der Zugehörigkeit zu einer SED-'Seilschaft' zu verdanken (DH, 74). Schabowski beginnt gleich 1990 sich als untypischen SED-Kader zu porträtieren, der seine Karriere 'sozialistischen Unglücken' zu verdanken habe (DP, 9).[27] Dabei legt er großen Wert darauf, dass er *nicht* aus einer Familie komme, wo der Vater im KZ gesessen hätte oder Antifaschist gewesen sei, sondern dass er seine berufliche und politische Laufbahn dem Umstand zu verdanken gehabt habe, dass die Partei pauschal Nachwuchs suchte und er sich als entwicklungsfähig und förderungswürdig bewährte (DH, 4).

> [I]ch bin also nicht auf besondere Empfehlung von Mielke auf diesen Platz [1. Sekretär von Berlin, Politbüro, UH] gerückt. Ich habe mich selbst immer als Seiteneinsteiger empfunden und bin auch immer so betrachtet worden. (DH, 11; vgl. auch DH, 7 und 29)

An die 'Seiteneinsteiger'-Darstellung der Interviewtexte anschliessend, beschreibt Schabowski 1991 in der Autobiographie *Der Absturz*, wie er in den Kommunismus hinein- und von dort durch die Wendezeit wieder hinausfindet. Seine Erläuterungen in *Der Absturz* setzen entsprechend bei seiner Gesinnungsentwicklung an. Dort wählt er Kapitelüberschriften, die seine selbstkritische Einstellung vermitteln sollen. Die, die sich mit seinem frühen Werdegang beschäftigen, tragen dann auch die Titel 'Ohne roten Taufschein' und 'Die politische Tätowierung'. Daraus lässt sich entnehmen, dass Schabowski erstens biographisches Augenmerk darauf legen will, dass er nicht wie viele andere Funktionäre bereits 'als Kommunist geboren' worden war, sondern in die kommunistische Ideologie hineinwuchs. Zweitens impliziert die Formulierung, dass seine Entwicklung hauptsächlich durch äußere Einflüsse bestimmt wurde. Damit suggeriert er, dass seine Persönlichkeit formbar gewesen war und mehr von außen her geformt wurde als dass sie sich von innen entwickelt hat. Die Ideologie hat sich Schabowski also *angeeignet*.

Die Eltern beschreibt Schabowski als unpolitisch und wenig einflussreich auf seine Entwicklung. In der Familie habe man die Gräueltaten der Nationalsozialisten und den Krieg verdrängt und sich stattdessen 'auf den Familienteppich' zurückgezogen (Ab, 56). Diese Verdrängungsakte werden in der unpersönlichen *man*-Form oder im Passiv beschrieben, so als ob ihnen dies Allgemeingültigkeit verleihen soll. 'Man verschloß die Augen vor den blutigen Rinnsalen, die aus den Ritzen der Gestapo-Keller quollen. Die Kristallnacht wurde wie ein böser Spuk verdrängt.' (Ab, 56) Solche unpersönlichen Formulierungen aus der journalistisch geschulten Feder Schabowskis untermauern zum einen, dass er eben keine kommunistischen Wurzeln hat, zum anderen gelingt es ihm auf diese Weise seine Herkunft einer nicht nur unpolitischen sondern für die Hitlerzeit typischen Mitläuferfamilie zuzuordnen.

Damit schafft er sich zugleich eine Darstellungsplattform für die Zeit nach dem Hitlerfaschismus und für die Zeit der Verdammung der Naziideologie, von der aus er seine Öffnung zum Neuen erklären kann. Die Tatsache, dass er das Neue in der kommunistischen Ideologie findet, erscheint bereits in *Das Politbüro* beinahe als Zufallsakt oder aus Mangel an alternativen Einflüssen: 'Der denkende Mensch sucht immer nach Antworten. […] Die kann er nur dem Trog entnehmen, den ihm die Gesellschaft in seinem Umfeld hinhält.' (DP, 170) Dementsprechend zeichnet er seine Nachkriegsentwicklung als stark politisch gefärbt: 'Die Theorie stand nicht am Anfang. Es waren zunächst einfach sympathische Menschen da, die uns beeindruckten, weil sie mit ihrem Leben für Ideale eingestanden hatten.' (DP, 172) Zu dem Ergebnis, dass das Konzept des Antifaschismus in Funktionärsautobiographien nicht unbedingt allein als Handlungsmotiv in der Nachkriegszeit herangezogen wird, gelangen auch Annette Leo und Jeannette van Laak.[28] Nach 'dauerhaften Wahrheiten' (Ab, 60) auf der Suche fühlte sich Schabowski, laut Angaben in *Der Absturz*, von den neuen politischen Einsichten 'elektrisiert' (Ab, 78).

Kommunismus ist einfach vernünftig [...] Wie ein trockener Schwamm saugten wir ihre einfachen und schlüssigen Wahrheiten [d.i. die der altkommunistischen Antifaschisten, UH] auf. [...] Ja, das [die Wahrheiten] beantwortete mehr Fragen, als wir zu formulieren imstande waren. (Ab, 79)

Vergleicht man Schabowskis Darstellungen zur Gesinnungsentwicklung mit denen anderer Vertreter der jüngeren DDR-Führungselite, wie zum Beispiel Egon Krenz oder Alexander Schalck-Golodkowski, offenbart sich ein Beschreibungsmuster, in dem es einen Ort der Aneignung (eine Institution oder Organisation) gibt und charismatische Personen, die zumeist aus der alten Garde der Widerstandkämpfer stammen. Letztere verstehen, den Enthusiasmus der jungen Generation für den gesellschaftlichen Aufbau zu wecken, und lenken sie zunächst mehr durch Charisma als durch offenen ideologischen Dogmatismus, so dass die Mitgliedschaft in der SED als 'vernünftig', d.h. wie ein selbstverständlicher Schritt erscheint. Hier tritt der Staat also als ideologische Erziehungsdiktatur in Erscheinung.[29] Ähnlich räsoniert Bernd Wittich über die politische Kultur der DDR, die mit einer 'Der-Zweck-heiligt-die-Mittel-Dialektik' operiert habe, in der der Kampf um Leben und Tod aus der faschistischen Epoche *ererbt* und in der politischen Mentalität der politischen Führer verinnerlicht worden sei.[30] Zweifel an der kommunistischen Idee seien Schabowski damals nicht gekommen. 'Wer sucht, ist für Zweifel nicht sonderlich empfänglich, sondern reagiert mit Dankbarkeit auf Plausibilitäten.' (DP, 172)

Dass das kommunistische Ideal und die DDR-Realität auseinanderklafften, legte Schabowski in der Anfangsphase seiner Nachwende-Reflexionen zunächst vor allem der Handlungsweise einzelner zur Last. In den Texten *Das Politbüro* und *Der Absturz* wird dabei besonders Honecker zum Sündenbock, der für Schabowski eine Art 'Leihkommunismus' ausübte und die Politbüromitglieder in ein 'korrumpierendes Netz von Abhängigkeiten' verspann (Ab, 104 und 106).

Jeder verdankte im Grunde [...] seinen Platz im Politbüro einem Mann, dem Generalsekretär. [...] Der Generalsekretär hat's gegeben; er wird es nehmen, wenn du die Parteiraison, die Disziplin, die Spielregeln verletzt, die er bestimmt. (Ab, 104-6)

Auch der Wirtschaftssekretär Günter Mittag, der 'Mephisto des Politbüros' (DP, 37), sowie der für Medien zuständige Sekretär im Politbüro Joachim Herrmann und Minister für Staatssicherheit Erich Mielke kamen in Schabowskis Betrachtungen nicht gut weg. Doch Schabowski bewegt sich in seinen Einsichten von 1990 bereits über die personelle Ebene hinaus und meint, dass es nicht einfach eine Frage der Person, sondern des Systems sei (DH, 19). Im Vergleich beider Texte von 1990 *Der Honecker muss weg* und *Das Politbüro* tun sich bei Schabowski Analyseunsicherheiten bzw. Widersprüche in seiner Sichtweise auf. In dem Interview *Der Honecker muss weg* zieht er dahingehend Fazit, dass der Zerfall der DDR mit der *Substanz* zusammenhängt, 'mit den unerfüllten Erwartungen, mit Vorstellungen, die so nicht mehr realisierbar waren. […] [Die Apparate] waren in gewisser weise Willens, sich anzupassen, aber die Anpassung ist natürlich kein Motiv für eine Umwälzung.' (DH, 42)

Wie der Titel dieses veröffentlichten Interviewprotokolls bereits suggeriert, vermittelt Schabowski hier, dass er das DDR-System bis zu einem Zeitpunkt, der mehr oder weniger mit Gorbatschows Reformansätzen in der Sowjetunion zusammenfällt, für reformierbar hielt. Wäre die Krise in der DDR rechtzeitig erkannt worden, hätte, so Schabowski, 'die Chance, die Sache noch ökonomisch in den Griff zu kriegen, […] vielleicht gerade noch 1986 genutzt werden können'. (DH, 17) Dagegen kommt er in *Das Politbüro* zu dem Schluss, dass seine Arbeit dazu beigetragen habe, 'die prinzipiell untauglichen Seiten des Systems […] zu verdecken' und sich selbst 'die *Illusion* zu vermitteln, daß dieses System reformierbar sei' (DP, 173, Hervorhebung UH). Als Handlungsträger eines repressiven Systems bekennt er:

> *Wir* waren nicht demokratiefähig, sondern haben versucht mangels besserer Argumente *uns* der anderen Meinung mittels direkter Gewalt zu entledigen. Ich meine hier das *System. Ich selbst* habe und hätte es im individuellen Fall nie dazu kommen lassen. (DP, 175, Hervorhebung U.H.)

In seiner Wortwahl lässt sich noch ein anderes Dilemma bei Schabowski bloßlegen. Ausdrücklich bemüht, seine *persönliche* Verantwortung zu analysieren, verfällt er doch wieder ins *Wir*, was er in diesem Fall nicht einmal nur als kollektives *Wir* schlechthin gebraucht, sondern das ein Abstraktum bezeichnet, *das System*. Er sieht sich lediglich als 'Repräsentant' des Systems und umgeht damit konkrete persönliche Verantwortung, verliert sich also letztendlich in *Mit*schuld. Gleichzeitig beurteilt er seine persönliche Macht in der DDR im Prinzip dahingehend positiv, dass er seine Spielräume für andere nutzen und 'Schlupflöcher des bürokratischen Systems' (DP, 158) für andere erschließen konnte. Die Ambition zur kritischen Selbstbetrachtung einerseits und die Grenzen seiner Analysefähigkeit andererseits werden bei Schabowski vor allem von den Bemühungen getragen, die Kohärenz der Persönlichkeit und des Selbstbildes zu bewahren und davon, dass seine Unsicherheiten sich nicht in einer tiefen Identitätskrise manifestieren sollen.

Seine DDR-funktionärstypische Denk- und Handlungsweise schrieb Schabowski in seiner Autobiographie *Der Absturz* einem 'Mechanismus der Selbsttäuschung' zu (Ab, 130). Rückblickend urteilt Schabowski, dass er 'jenseits der Parteidisziplin und der permanent eingeforderten "Treue zur Sache des Sozialismus" keinen moralischen Überlebensraum sah' (Ab, 98). Dem System in der DDR erteilt er seine Absage:

> Selbst wer kritisch und weniger dogmatisch gesinnt war, konnte und wollte nur gelten lassen, daß Bestandteile [des Systems] veränderungs- oder verbesserungsbedürftig waren, nicht aber das System. […] Unser System war die Projektion der Vollkommenheit, ein Ideal; aber Idealen– so beruhigten wir uns selbst – nähert man sich nur via Unzulänglichkeiten. (Ab, 130-1)

Während der Historiker Jung urteilt, dass es Funktionären wie Schabowski nicht gelingt, das Zusammenspiel von Fremdbestimmung und Fügsamkeit zu entschlüsseln,[31] bieten Jessica Cameron, Anne Wilson und Michael Ross in ihren gedächtnispsychologischen Betrachtungen zur Selbsteinschätzung einen Einblick, warum dies von jemanden in Schabowskis Position nicht erkannt wird: 'When people feel distant from a past self, they can dissociate themselves from its experiences and outcomes, regardless of actual temporal distance.'[32] Psychologische Studien hätten den Trend belegt, dass die Menschen ihre früheren 'Selbste' abwerten, um das gegenwärtige Selbstwertgefühl zu erhöhen.[33]

In seinen Essays 'Selbstblendung. Über den Realitätsverlust der Funktionärselite' von 1993 und *Abschied von der Utopie* (1994) verurteilt Schabowski dann nicht nur mehr das System, sondern entsagt sich dem ihm unterliegenden ideologischen Ideal. In 'Selbstblendung' bewertet er den Marxismus sogar als 'Utopiesyndrom', als eine 'ver-

führerische Hypothese, eine unbewiesene Spekulation, ein[en] Mythos'. Zynisch kommentiert er:

> Die Mängel, die Niederlagen, die Verirrungen und Perversionen, die den endlosen
> Weg zur Utopie säumen, sind nur die Schuld derjenigen, die sich der Wahrheit
> dumpf verschließen oder sich ihr feindselig in den Weg stellen. Wenn die auf der
> einzigen Wahrheit beruhenden politischen Strategien versagen, liegt das nicht an
> der Prämisse, sondern an der Widrigkeit äußerer Faktoren oder der individuellen
> Unzulänglichkeit der betreffenden 'Missionare'. Die Prämisse selbst bleibt unan-
> getastet und ungeprüft. (Sb, 115)

Die Situation des Kalten Krieges habe derartige Einstellungen bestärkt
und laut Schabowski zur *Realitätsverdrängung* und Selbstverwei-
gerung gegenüber der Wahrheit geführt. In seinen nun ausgereifteren
Erklärungen stützt sich Schabowski fortan auf ein Werk über psy-
chologische Handels- und Wandelstheorien von Paul Watzlawick,
John Weakland und Richard Fisch. In ihrem Band *Lösungen – Zu
Theorie und Praxis menschlichen Wandels* haben sie das so genannte
Utopie-Syndrom als ein krankhaftes Symptom bzw. Problem mensch-
lichen Handelns identifiziert. Schabowskis Herleitungen zum Utopie-
Syndrom der DDR-Funktionäre reflektierten eine Form des Utopie-
Syndroms, die Watzlawick u.a. als *projektiv* bezeichnen und von
ihnen so skizziert wird:

> Der von ihr [d.i. von der projektiven Form des Utopie-Syndroms] Befallene wähnt
> sich im Besitz der Wahrheit und damit nicht nur des Schlüssels, sondern auch der
> moralischen Verpflichtung zur Beseitigung alles Übels der Welt. In der Annahme,
> daß die Wahrheit, wenn sie nur klar und laut genug verkündet wird, alle Men-
> schen guten Willens überzeugen muß, wird er zunächst missionarische Wege
> beschreiten. Führt dies aber nicht zum erwarteten Erfolg, so liegt die Schuld bei
> denen, die verstockt sind und sich der Wahrheit gegenüber schließen. […] [D]aß
> in Extremfällen ihre Ausrottung nicht nur wünschenswert, sondern zur Be-
> glückung der Menschheit einfach notwendig ist, ergibt sich dann fast zwanglos.
> Auf jeden Fall ist es klar, daß die Schuld am Nichterreichen der Utopie nicht in,
> sondern außer ihm zu suchen ist.[34]

In Anlehnung an Watzlawick u.a. schafft sich Schabowski so ein
Erklärungsmodell, mit dem er die Gesellschaftsstrategie der DDR in
einem völlig neuen Licht erscheinen lassen kann. Nicht nur er selbst,
sondern alle in der DDR agierenden politischen Handlungsträger lassen sich damit als Psychopathen klassifizieren, die am Utopie-Syndrom gelitten hätten. Mit dem Einbringen von Lektüre wie Watzlawick u.a. oder auch Melvin J. Laskys *Utopie und Revolution* in seinen

Erklärungsversuchen seit 1993 scheint er seinen vollkommenen Denkumschwung mit Glaubwürdigkeit ausstatten zu wollen. Gegenüber
seinen anfänglichen Analysen sollen spätere Selbstreflexionen durch
gründlichere Belesenheit wohl besser durchdacht wirken (Vgl. Sb,
115). Doch was Theo Pirker bereits 1990 als 'Strickfehler' bezeichnete, offenbart sich hier in ähnlicher Form. In seinen Analysen will
sich Schabowski durchgängig als jemand vermitteln, der sich um das
Offenlegen seiner persönlichen Verantwortung bemüht. Dennoch illustriert das Aufgreifen von Ansätzen wie dem Utopie-Syndrom als
Erklärungsmodell für die DDR-Vergangenheit schlechthin, dass er
sich der tiefen Widersprüche seines Handelns nicht bewusst ist. Wenn
man in Betracht zieht, dass er sich im Lichte der von Watzlawick u.a.
beschriebenen pathologischen Symptome eines Utopisten als Teil
einer am Utopismus leidenden Gesellschaft sehen will, gelingt es ihm
mittels seiner Erklärungsstrategie, individuelle Verantwortung auszu-
klammern.

Folgt man der Logik des Arguments von Watzlawick u.a. in Schabowskis Räson, würde er in seiner Rolle als Parteifunktionär als (tem-
porärer) Psychopath gelten.[35] Damit ist er mit einem pathologischen
Krankheitsbild ausgestattet, was ihn von der Verantwortung für
jegliches Verhalten im Krankheitszustand freispricht. Mit einer solchen Ausgangsposition lässt sich individuelle Verantwortung nicht
verhandeln. Indirekt ließe sich prinzipiell mit dem Erklärungsmodell
sogar die Absolution der gesamten Parteiführung als psychopathische
Opfergestalten ableiten, denn mit seinem Argument unterminiert
Schabowski darüber hinaus selbst kollektive Verantwortung, verlagert
Verantwortung vom Subjektiven (dem Menschen) auf das Abstrakte
(System): 'Das System […] war längst im Begriff, sich selbst zu liqui-
dieren. […] Die Unausweichlichkeit dieses Endes war in der Lehre
selbst angelegt'.[36]

Schabowskis 'Selbstblendungsthese' ist ein Indiz für eine spezifische Verarbeitungsweise, in der er sich aktiv bemüht, Brüche und
Diskontinuitäten in seiner Identität zu überwinden, um eine kohärente
Lebensgeschichte zu konstruieren. In ihrer Studie zur Veränderung
der Selbst-Empfindung oder zur 'diachronischen Erfahrung des
Selbst' fanden James Lampinen, Timothy Odegard und Juliana Leding: 'When they [people] describe how they have changed over time
they say things like, "I have grown" or "I have evolved" […] These
are not literal statements. They are metaphors of continuity'.[37]

In seinem jüngsten schriftlichen autobiographischen Rückblick von 2009 *Wir haben fast alles falsch gemacht* zeichnet sich ein qualitativer Zuwachs ab, der diese Kontinuität von Lebensgeschichte und Identitätsbildung untermauert. Neben dem Wiederaufgreifen von Passagen aus früheren Texten, reflektiert er dort mit zwanzigjähriger Distanz zum Ende der DDR erneut über Schuld und Verantwortung und begreift diese nun tatsächlich individuell. Im Rückblick auf den Gerichtsprozess zu seiner Mitverantwortung bei den Todesfällen an der DDR-Grenze, bekennt er:

> Die Frage, wer dafür verantwortlich ist, hatte nicht nur eine juristische, sondern auch eine moralische Dimension. [...] Wenn man noch einen Funken Anstand besitzt, spürt man sofort, dass es aufrichtiger ist, den schweren Vorwurf dieser Schuld hinzunehmen [...]. (Wh, 42-3)

Die Tatsache, dass er sich allerdings auch in diesem Text erneut auf das Utopie-Syndrom-Modell beruft (Wh, 63-4), um zu begründen, warum ihn zu DDR-Zeiten keine Zweifel gekommen seien, ist ein Indiz, dass er auch heute noch mit Selbsterklärungswidersprüchen und inneren Unsicherheiten kämpft.

Schabowski begegnete den öffentlichen Anschuldigungen von Anfang an vor allem durch öffentlich abgehaltene Selbstreflexionen (z.B. Wh, 51).[38] Den Schlüsselmoment, der ihn einen Platz in der vereinten deutschen Gesellschaft gewährt und ihm eine Art Akzeptanz verliehen habe, identifiziert er in der moralischen Schuldbekenntnis in seinen Gerichtserklärungen von 1996 und 1997, dessen Wortlaut er in den Anhang des Textes von 2009 *Wir haben alles falsch gemacht* stellt. In einem Interview 2011 empfindet er den 'Vorteil', den ihn seine Abwendung von kollektiver hin zu individueller Schuld an den Mauertoten einbrachte, als einen befriedigenden Moment der Selbstreinigung und Selbstbefreiung, der ihm nun gestatte, offen zu jungen Menschen über das DDR-System zu sprechen.[39] Damit hat sich Schabowski heute als noch immer öffentliche Figur eine neue gesellschaftliche Rolle erobert, in der er Einladungen zu Veranstaltungen folgt, Vorträge als 'Vertreter des Systems' der DDR hält und vor Ideologie und Verblendung warnt. Ob dies Teil einer 'peinlichen Selbstvermarktung' ist, wie Frank Hoffmann suggeriert,[40] oder ein Erkenntnisprozess, der auf kritischer Selbstbefragung im öffentlichen Rampenlicht beruht (Wh, 45), sei dahingestellt. Was sich jedoch mit Bestimmtheit sagen lässt, ist, dass Schabowski 'Erinnerungsarbeit'[41] für sich genutzt hat, Werte umzudeuten bzw. neu zu belegen, um mit seiner Lebensgeschichte in einer kohärenten narrativen Identität anzukommen, die ihm erlaubt, sich in die Gesellschaft des vereinten Deutschlands erfolgreich integriert zu fühlen.

Anmerkungen

[1]   Philippe Lejeune, *Der autobiographische Pakt*, Frankfurt/Main: Suhrkamp, 1994, S. 421.

[2]   Ebd.

[3]   Hans Joachim Schröder, *Interviewliteratur zum Leben in der DDR. Zur literarischen, biographischen und sozialgeschichtlichen Bedeutung einer dokumentarischen Gattung*, Tübingen: Max Niemeyer, 2001, S. 4.

[4]   Über die enge Verwandtschaft von Textsorten mit selbst-dokumentarischem Charakter wie Autobiographien, Biographien, Erlebnisberichte, Tagebücher, Briefe Reportagen, Porträts, Interviews, Interviewliteratur und Mischformen siehe zum Beispiel Schröder, *Interviewliteratur*, S. 1-61.

[5]   Siehe zum Beispiel A. Jefferson Singer und Pavel Blagov, 'The Integrative Function of Narrative Processing. Autobiographical Memory, Self-Defining Memories, and the Life Story of Identity', in: Denise R. Beike, James M. Lampinen und Douglas A. Behrend, Hg., *The Self and Memory. Studies in Self and Identity*, New York: Psychology Press, 2004, S. 137-8 (hier: S. 132).

[6]   Jessica J. Cameron, Anne E. Wilson und Michael Ross, 'Autobiographical Memory and Self-Assessment', in: Beike, u.a., Hg., *The Self and Memory*, S. 207-26 (hier: S. 207).

[7]   Schröder, *Interviewliteratur*, S. 19.

[8]   Singer und Blagov, 'The Integrative Function', S. 121.

[9]   Ebd., S. 124.

[10] Dan P. McAdams, *The Person. An Integrated Introduction to Personality Psychology*, Fort Worth, TX: Harcourt College, 2001, S. 643.

[11] Bereits 1990 wird Schabowski von einem Volkskammerausschuss auf Amtsmissbrauch und Korruption untersucht. 1993 beginnt ein Verfahren wegen Wahlfälschung gegen ihn, was 1997 eingestellt wurde. 1995 beginnt der Prozess vor dem Berliner Landgericht bezüglich seiner Mitverantwortung für die Mauertoten, infolgedessen er 1997 zu drei Jahren Haft verurteilt wird, die er 1999 nach der Urteilsbestätigung

durch den Bundesgerichthof antritt. Durch die Begnadigung vom Berliner Bürger-meister Eberhard Diepken im Jahr 2000 wird Schabowski nach nur zehn Monaten aus der Haft entlassen.

[12] Singer und Blagov, 'The Integrative Function', S. 123. Dabei schließe Selbst-reflexion über (narrative) Erinnerungen – 'storied thought' – einen Lebensrückblick ein, in dem Individuen über ihr Leben als Ganzes reflektieren und nicht nur über bestimmte, das Selbst formende Erinnerungen – ebd., S. 126.

[13] Der narrative Verarbeitungsprozess im autobiographischen Gedächtnis richtet sich auf ein konkretes Endziel. Für detaillierte Ausführungen siehe z.B. Dan P. McAdams, 'The Redemptive Self', in: Beike u.a., Hg.,*The Self and Memory*, S. 95-115 (hier: S. 102) und Stefan Granzow, *Das autobiographische Gedächtnis*, Berlin: Quintessenz, 1994, S. 102-25.

[14] Günter Schabowski, *Der Absturz*, Reinbek: Rowohlt Taschenbuch, 1992, S. 94. Zitate im Folgenden mit Seitenangaben im Text nach der Sigle Ab.

[15] Diese Information ist einer persönlichen Korrespondenz zwischen A. James McAdams und der Autorin vom 12. Dezember 2003 entnommen.

[16] Christian Jung, *Geschichte der Verlierer. Historische Selbstreflexion von hoch-rangigen Mitgliedern der SED nach 1989*, Heidelberg: Winter, 2007, S. 250

[17] Günter Schabowski mit Frank Sieren, *Wir haben fast alles falsch gemacht. Die letzten Tage der DDR*, Berlin: Econ, 2009, S. 9. Zitate im Folgenden mit Seiten-angaben im Text nach der Sigle Wh.

[18] Volker Klemm, *Korruption und Amtsmißbrauch in der DDR*, Stuttgart: Deutsche Verlags-Anstalt, 1991, S. 64.

[19] Privatpersonen, die angeben, Schabowski beruflich aus DDR-Zeiten zu kennen, geben sich darüber auf Internetforen oftmals echauffiert. Beispielsweise heißt es in einem Eintrag vom 20. Juni 2008 auf www.ddr-im-www.de: 'Ich habe ihn mehrmals in Berichterstattungen im Sekretariat der Bezirksleitung persönlich erlebt. Wenn er heute heuchlerisch dem Marxismus abschwört so ist das für ihn symptomatisch. Zu DDR-Zeiten war er hart gegen jene, die […] "Verfehlungen" begangen haben. Heute tut er so harmlos, […] er war ein Teufel und ist heute nicht anders.' Unter: http://www.ddr-im-www.de/index.php?itemid=385 (abgerufen am 1. Juni 2011).

[20] Schröder, *Interviewliteratur*, S. 103.

[21] Günter Schabowski, 'Selbstblendung. Über den Realitätsverlust der Funktionäre', in: Karl Markus Michel und Tilman Spengler, Hg., *In Sachen Erich Honecker*, *Kursbuch* 111, Berlin: Rowohlt, Februar 1993, S.111-24. Zitate im Folgenden mit Seitenangaben im Text nach der Sigle Sb.

[22]   McAdams, 'The Redemptive Self', S. 100.

[23]   Günter Schabowski, *Das Politbüro. Ende eines Mythos*, Reinbek: Rowohlt Taschenbuch, 1990, S. 7-13 (hier: S. 7). Zitate im Folgenden mit Seitenangaben im Text nach der Sigle DP.

[24]   Vergleiche hierzu den fast identischen Wortlaut in: Günter Schabowski, *Abschied von der Utopie. Die DDR das deutsche Fiasko des Marxismus*, Stuttgart: Franz Steiner, 1994, S. 12.

[25]   Singer und Blagov, 'The Integrative Function', S. 132; Vergleiche hierzu auch das Konzept der Historikerin Dagmar Günther von autobiographischen Texten als 'kommunikativem Akt', in: Dagmar Günther, '"And now for something completely different": Prolegomena zur Autobiographie als Quelle der Geschichtswissenschaft', *Historische Zeitschrift*, 272:1 (2001), 25-61 (hier: S. 49).

[26]   Hans-Hermann Hertle, Theo Pirker, Rainer Weinert, *Der Honecker muß weg. Protokoll eines Gespräches mit Günter Schabowski am 24. April 1990 in Berlin/West*, Berlin: 1990, S. 74. Zitate im Folgenden mit Seitenangaben im Text nach der Sigle DH.

[27]   Damit meint Schabowski, dass er in Positionen aufgerückt ist, weil ihm durch Umstände wie dem Flugzeugabsturz von Werner Lamberz 1978 oder dem Absetzen Konrad Naumanns von seiner Funktion als 1. Sekretär Vorteile erwachsen seien, die seiner Karriere Auftrieb verliehen hätten. Nach dem Tod von Lamberz und dem daraus folgenden Aufstieg Joachim Herrmanns in Lamberz' Position wurde Schabowski zum Chefredakteur des *Neuen Deutschland* berufen. 1981 rückte Schabowski ins Zentralkomitee und gleichzeitig auch als Kandidat ins Politbüro auf, wo er seit 1984 Vollmitglied war.

[28]   Jeannette van Laak und Annette Leo, 'Erinnerungen der Macht, Erinnerungen an die Macht. SED-Funktionäre im autobiographischen Rückblick', *Deutschland Archiv*, 6 (2008), 1060-7 (hier: S. 1062).

[29]   Antonia Grunenberg, 'Anti-Faschismus und politische Gegenwelten', in: Claudia Keller und literaturWERKstatt Berlin, Hg., *Die Nacht hat zwölf Stunden, dann kommt schon der Tag. Antifaschismus und Neubewertung*, Berlin: Aufbau Taschenbuch, 1996, S. 9-23 (hier: S. 15.)

[30]   Bernd Wittich, 'Initiationen zum Antifaschisten. Folgenreicher engagierter Antifaschismus in der DDR', in: Brigitte Rauschenbach, Hg., *Erinnern, Wiederholen, Durcharbeiten*, Berlin und Weimar: Aufbau Taschenbuch, 1992, S. 180-96 (hier: S. 181).

[31]   Jung, *Geschichte der Verlierer*, S. 250.

[32]   Jessica J. Cameron, Anne E. Wilson und Michael Ross, 'Autobiographical Memory and Self-Assessment', in: Beike u.a., *The Self and Memory*, S. 207-26 (hier: S. 212).

[33]   Ebd., S. 215.

[34]   Paul Watzlawick, John H. Weakland, Richard Fisch, *Lösungen. Zur Theorie und Praxis menschlichen Wandels*, Bern, Göttingen und Toronto: Hans Huber, 1997, S. 73.

[35]   Das heißt solange er der Utopie verhaftet war. Nach dem Lossagen von der Utopie fühlt sich Schabowski geheilt, indem er neue Einsichten über die Utopie gewonnen habe.

[36]   Sb, 111. Daher finden sich in seinen Essays von 1993 und 1994 auch keine Schuldzuweisungen in Richtung Honecker mehr.

[37]   James M. Lampinen, Timothy O. Odegard und Juliana K. Leding, 'Diachronic Disunity', in: Beike u.a., *The Self and Memory*, S. 227-62 (hier: S. 246).

[38]   Siehe hierzu auch Schabowskis Veröffentlichung zu Vorträgen von 2006 in Schabowski, *Der Zerfall einer Leihmacht*, Rostock: ß Verlag & Medien, 2009.

[39]   Rudorff, Dietrich, '"Ich war ein Verblendeter" Ein Gespräch mit Günter Schabowski', *Deutschland Archiv*, 3 (2011)., Online-Ausgabe bei der Bundeszentrale für politische Bildung, unter: http://www.bpd.de/themen/2WKJAJ.html (abgerufen am 1. Juni 2011).

[40]   Frank Hoffmann, 'Erinnerung als Integration. Zum ostdeutschen Autobiographie-Boom seit 1990', *Deutschland Archiv*, 5 (2011). Online-Ausgabe bei der Bundeszentrale für politische Bildung, unter: http://www.bpd.de/themen/DDWQZ8.html (abgerufen am 14. Juni 2011).

[41]   Hoffmann, 'Erinnerung als Integration'.

David Clarke

'Wer schreibt, kann nicht töten': Writing and Life in Reinhard Jirgl's *Abtrünnig: Roman aus der nervösen Zeit*

Reinhard Jirgl's *Abtrünnig: Roman aus der nervösen Zeit* is an aesthetically complex text which explores the function of autobiographical self-reflection through fictional means. Its protagonist and narrator tells the story of his own frustration and failure, a story which appears inevitably to end in violence. However, the structure of the text, which incorporates various Internet-style 'links', ultimately offers the reader two possibilities: to circle endlessly within the novel in the hope that the narrator's story might somehow be read in such a way as to produce a more positive outcome; or, like the narrator himself, to step outside of the story, liberating themselves from a world which ultimately cannot be redeemed.

Dennis Tate's monographs on Franz Fühmann and on autobiographical writing in the GDR have convincingly demonstrated the importance that many critical socialist writers attached to the authentic reflection of their own lived experience in the face of the SED's ideologically distorted version of social reality in East Germany. As Tate points out, GDR cultural politicians were from the outset suspicious of autobiographical writing and, by extension, the attempt to present the 'subjective authenticity' (Christa Wolf) of the writer's own experience where this could not be made commensurate with the Party line.[1] The function which such 'subjective authenticity' was to take on for the writers Tate has analysed cannot simply be understood as a desire for self-expression, although it was that too. Rather, these writers believed that their reflection on their own experience could be a contribution to the socialist project: by revealing socialist society's failings and contradictions through the authentic portrayal of their own experience, leading writers like Wolf, Fühmann or Christoph Hein believed,[2] the ideological carapace of the SED's view of that society could be cracked open, offering the possibility of debate and change. This was, then 'an autobiographical literature in which the political and the personal would be inextricably merged'.[3]

This chapter, however, examines the writing of Reinhard Jirgl, an author whose work, despite his East German socialisation, radically challenges all of the assumptions upon which such 'subjectively authentic' and indeed political writing in the GDR was based. Jirgl's literary project sets out a very different case for turning one's life into literature, which can nevertheless be productively read against the backdrop of the model which Tate outlines. This is particularly the case for the text examined in detail here, Jirgl's 2005 novel *Abtrünnig: Roman aus der nervösen Zeit*. This is not an autobiographical text in the traditional sense: the narrator is not coterminous with the author Jirgl, and their biographies, whilst broadly similar, are certainly not identical.[4] Yet, as in most of Jirgl's novels, we are presented with a figure who narrates their life in retrospect (as, for example in the novels *Abschied von den Feinden* of 1995, *Die Unvollendeten* of 2003 or, more recently, *Die Stille* of 2009), often from a point of defeat or near to death. A significant difference in *Abtrünnig* is that the unnamed narrator is himself a would-be literary author, who is, in fact, at work on the text that the reader of Jirgl's novel holds in their hands. For example, in a scene in which the narrator is introduced to a group of 'KULTURTRÄGER' by his lover Sophia, he reads to them from the text 'Auf Tag & Stunde', an earlier chapter of *Abtrünnig*.[5] The novel is constructed as a series of dated chapters, which appear in chronological order, detailing the arrival of the narrator in Berlin, his attempts to establish a literary career and pursue his love affair with Sophia, and his eventual failure and isolation. The main events of the novel are dated between the late summer of 2000 (15) and the summer of 2004 (518). Beyond this, the main body of the text is sandwiched between a short preface and postscript, which are both dated in the autumn of 2004 from the point of view of an author who has now completed the work we are about to read, or have just finished reading.

The fact that the novel proper begins with a section in the first person told from the point of view of a former border guard working in Frankfurt an der Oder is something of a red herring, in that we can ultimately see this as an act of ventriloquism on the part of the author figure, who is told this man's life story when he meets him later in Berlin (319) and whose murder he later reports (505). Other life stories are also included in the text which the narrator is producing, including that of a writer who worked as a forester in the GDR whilst secretly writing a novel (217-69), a painter whose work, after his death, is destined for the rubbish tip (127-9), and the narrator's uncle, a quiet, bookish man, persecuted by his neighbours (338-56). The choice of these figures, including the former border guard, reflects the narrator's view of contemporary German society and his own relationship to it, to the extent that the reader may begin to question whether they are merely masks for the expression of his own predicament. That predicament, which is also expanded on in a number of undated essays and social observations arranged between the dated chapters, will be familiar to readers of Jirgl's other novels.

Jirgl's central, bleak and unremittingly illustrated thesis on human civilisation takes as its focus the notion of the 'Masse'. Although Jirgl points to the particular conditions of the existence of the 'Masse' in the different societies he has written about, including the GDR, pre-unification West Germany and contemporary Germany, his novels present their existence as a general fact of human civilisation: human beings are portrayed as displaying a natural tendency to persecute any individuals who are different, or who cannot be absorbed into an unthinking herd, which is characterized by its pettiness, its desire to subordinate itself to authority and its sadism towards anyone who falls outside of the norm: or, as the narrator of *Abtrünnig* puts it, 'das Große Ressentiment gegenüber all denen, die *anderes* sein wollen, vor=Allem *anders* denken od nur *anders* sein wollen als SIE' (69).[6] Jirgl's (generally male) protagonists are usually outsiders who observe the workings of the 'Masse' and perceive this dialectic of subservience and cruelty as essentially universal and transhistorical.

The consequence of this position, as Arne De Winde has observed in relation to Jirgl's first published novel *Mutter Vater Roman* (1989), is a tendency to present the history of human society as an endless cycle of brutality, which sometimes expresses itself in war and genocide, but is equally to be observed in the everyday war of human social existence.[7] In Jirgl's most widely received novel to date, *Die Unvollendeten* (2003), which deals with the expulsion of Sudeten Germans from Czechoslovakia in the aftermath of World War Two, this tendency is particularly evident. The major criticisms that have been levelled at the novel have tended to concentrate on the portrayal of a young SS recruit who is witness to a massacre of concentration camp inmates on one of the 'death marches' in the final days of the war, a representation which, it has been claimed, tends to exculpate the young SS man as a victim of historical circumstances.[8] However, more central to the novel is the presentation of the Holocaust, the expulsion of Germans from the Sudetenland, and the ongoing persecution of the powerless in contemporary Germany in terms of an interminable genealogy of cruelty that is so unstoppable that it takes on the character of a natural force. The narrator of this text is the offspring of an expellee family, writing an account of his family's suffering as he lies dying of cancer. At the end of his account, he holds out no hope for an end to this never-ending cycle of tragedy, emphatically rejecting the notion of historical progress:

> Das 20. Jahrhundert, das Jahrhundert der Lager & Vertreibungen, nach soviel Freigelassenheit zu Idiotie u Grauen, vom Blut aus zerissenen Lungen durch-tränkter nächtiger Zeit, darin auch TECHNIK durch Freiheit zu Sklaverei sich steigern konnte; das Neue ist neue Idiotie & neues Grauen mi alter Blindheit Angst & Hoffnung, daraus DIE SCHULD hinaus bis in den-Kosmos & hinein dis in die Gene treibt. ?Nach wievielen Jahrhunderten wird das 20. Jahrhundert endlich zu-Ende sein, und ?Was kommt ?Wann Danach. Aber: Das 20. Jahr-hundert, es hat ja soeben wieder begonnen.....[9]

The 'century of camps and expulsions', then, is not a historical epoch as such, but the eternal condition of human existence, from which there seems little prospect of escape.

This is a vision of human history in which all of the brutality is repeated in the present, offering little hope of escape for the individual who stands outside of the cruel 'Masse' and its relationship with power; a vision which is echoed by the narrator of *Abtrünnig* in his account of the auction of the building he lives in to the vengeful husband of his lover Sophia. Here the rich husband is portrayed as the typical man of the 'Masse' who uses whatever position of power he has within the social order to persecute others, but the narrator's protocol-like account of the auction itself is interspersed with boxes of text which contain accounts of atrocities from a number of different historical contexts, including the Holocaust, the war in Mozambique in the 1970s, the Soviet Gulag, and the Conquistador invasion of Peru (153-8). The clear implication of all this is that the sadistic behaviour of Sophia's husband towards the narrator, who finds himself in the weaker position within the social order of contemporary Germany, is merely the current form of a more general tendency to sadism that characterizes all social relations based on power; a clearly problematic position, in that it denies the historical specificity of the particular events referenced, seeing them all as broadly comparable to conditions in contemporary capitalist society.

Leaving this difficulty aside, however, it is important to note the possible strategies which the narrator's text explores in terms of resisting or at least coming to terms with this general tendency of human civilization. Within the novel contained between the preface and the postscript, two possible approaches are put forward. Firstly, the narrator imagines the possibility of withdrawal entirely from the society which persecutes him. This is the possibility of becoming a 'Genie-aus-dem-Wald' (103), as one of Sophia's rich friends describes him, retreating into total isolation and living only through the creation of his text, much like the forester he writes a portrait of, and to whom he also gives this epithet. This figure, perhaps an idealized projection of the narrator himself, sets about replacing his life with the literary work: '*Meinem Buch künftig des Lebens Ganzes=Ich*' (261). As the narrator becomes increasingly alienated from life in the city, he takes walks in the woods around Berlin and fantasizes about not returning to civilization (427 and 453). As this alienation grows, the narrator's flat, which he is eventually expelled from by Sophia's husband, becomes a hiding place ('Höhle' and 'Versteck', 129) from the rest of human society. He generally expresses a longing for spaces which lie 'außerhalb der Geschichts-bewegungen' (479), although, like his threatened flat, these are constantly under threat from the encroachment of the civilization he despises. Nevertheless, this retreat does seem to represent the possibility of experiencing some kind of individuality beyond the mainstream of society, which reduces each of its members to an 'auffällig konsens-kompatiblen Personeneinheit=ohne Skrupel' (187). To make this retreat in order to experience real individuality is, in the narrator's view, the definition of 'Abtrünnigkeit' and can expect to be met only with hostility from the society of the 'Masse'.

The second possible reaction to this state of affairs is to meet the violent oppression of otherness with counter-violence. The narrator's text actually ends with an explosion of violent rage, in which he murders a stranger (an arrogant representative of the 'Masse') and is put on trial. As the narrator attempts to defend his individuality, he portrays himself as being worn away by the forces of society like a cliff hollowed out by the endless movement of the waves, which could at any moment collapse, and there are frequent intimations throughout the course of his text that such a collapse would result in violence against others.

This impending danger is emphasised through the use of so-called 'Links' within the text, a notion adapted from World Wide Web technology. Jirgl provides the reader with some guidelines as to how these 'Links', essentially pointers which invite the reader to skip to another part of the text, should be used (543), but their function is not always the same, as will be demonstrated below. In this case, however, confrontations between the narrator and the brutality and cruelty of the 'Masse' are frequently interspersed with links forward to the chapter 'Freak Waves. Jähe Wut' (486-97), in which the narrator produces a series of philosophical meditations on the normative pressure applied to the individual, until he begins to feel a 'Ratlosigkeit, die insgeheim anschwellende Wut, die Wut des Auswegslosen inmitten der banalsten Wüste' (495) and explodes into a violent and destructive rage against the contents of his flat. Here the intellectual act of writing as an attempt to come to terms with the hostile society appears to fail, giving way to randomly directed violence.

The implication is clearly that the narrator's attempt to withdraw from the human society which threatens his individuality in order to preserve that individuality in the act of writing is a failing project. The chapter which follows this episode, called simply 'Amok', describes the narrator's final descent into murderous violence, and thus the final failure of his attempt to maintain his independence and identity in this hostile environment. He has lost self-control and run amok, rather than maintaining control over the situation through the medium of writing.

What Jirgl's narrator appears to be recording here is a decidedly elitist version of the 'going postal' which American cultural critic Mark Ames interprets as the consequence of a society which increasingly punishes difference and perceived weakness, encouraging the mass of the population to regard cruelty and indifference to others as the only means of their own personal survival. Such massacres and rampages in workplaces and schools have increasingly become a feature of contemporary capitalist societies since the 1990s, and Germany has not been excluded from this, as school shooting sprees in Emstetten (2002), Erfurt (2007) and Winnenden (2009) have demonstrated. Such real-life rampagers, however, fit the pattern described by Ames much better: the perpetrators are not alienated intellectuals, but rather ordinary frustrated and disenfranchised people, who feel there is no future for them in an increasingly competitive and cold society;

people who do not have the intellectual resources, perhaps, to sublimate their pain in the act of writing.[10]

Having said this, the reader arriving at the postscript to the narrator's text in *Abtrünnig* soon realises that these final violent scenes are not an expression of the defeat of his literary project, but merely a fictive playing out of the consequences of such a defeat: if the act of writing cannot save him, he seems to suggest, then violent rage may be the consequence; and yet, 'Wer schreibt, kann nicht töten' (541). The narrator has succeeded in writing, and the text he offers us, as he had already suggested in its preface, is a way of locking away ('einsperren') 'die Menschen & ihre Geschichten, die nach=mir greifen und mich schrecken' (11), allowing him to go 'befreit in meine Landschaft hinein' (541), presumably into that space 'außerhalb der Geschichtsbewegungen' (479) which he seeks throughout the narrative. There is no real explanation, however, of how the narrator, who describes himself 'eine Zeitbombe' in the preface (11), and who, furthermore, has shown in detail how society has slowly encroached on his independence and isolation throughout the text, is able to stand back from the apparently inevitable path of violent rage and distance himself from his life experience in this way.

Yet the postscript does perhaps represent an attempt to bring together destructive violence and the act of writing, to see them as equivalent rather than alternative. The narrator describes himself moving across an empty landscape, in which his words have literally buried the people and stories 'die nach mir greifen' (541). The completion of the text represents, then, the destruction of the world and the people it contains, which are now banned, as if by magic, in the pages of what has been written. They are destroyed just as surely as a violent crime has been committed, as the gun and ammunition which the narrator describes weighing heavy in his pocket suggest. Clearly, there is no sense in which we can talk of this as a realist ending – the space of 'Existenz' (539) described in the postscript's title cannot literally exist –, but it can nevertheless be understood metaphorically as a justification for turning one's experiences into literature.

In the first monograph to be published on Jirgl's work, Karen Dannemann has argued that, despite the bleak picture offered by the author's texts, his moral insistence on facing the grim realities of human civilization is in fact a means of expressing 'eine humane

Sehnsucht nach dem Ende des Menschenopfers in der Geschichte [...], den Glauben an das immerhin Mögliche: aus der Geschichte zu lernen'.[11] Applied to the narrator of *Abtrünnig*, himself a literary author and thus at least to some extent a stand-in for the author Jirgl himself, this reading would place his text's analysis of the failings of human civilization in line with that of the authors of 'subjective authenticity' discussed by Tate. In other words, his unflinching representation of society's ills as he has experienced them could be seen as a first step to their overcoming. On balance, however, it seems difficult to find evidence for this positive reading in *Abtrünnig*. The postscript offers not the vision of a world transformed by the writer's insights into its problems, but rather an act of self-liberation in which the irredeemable world and his experience of it is banished into a kind of oblivion between the pages of the writer's manuscript, allowing him to step outside its bad reality.

In an essay on memory, Jirgl has suggested that literature should 'hold open' memories of the traumatic horror of lived experience in the face of forgetfulness.[12] Nevertheless, the narrator's transformation of his own life into text in *Abtrünnig* ultimately becomes a willed forgetting, comparable to the kind that Kai Behrens identifies with Nietzsche's view of the function of art, particularly in the early work *Die Geburt der Tragödie* (1872). For Nietzsche, as Behrens argues, the appropriation of experience and its reworking and estrangement in the work of art allows an escape from the constraints of reality that is a kind of forgetting.[13]

Although, on closer inspection, it is by no means possible to find an exact implementation of Nietzschean thought in *Abtrünnig*, there are nevertheless suggestive parallels between the narrator's strategy in Jirgl's novel and the view of art put forward by the philosopher in *Geburt der Tragödie*, a text which Jirgl's narrator in fact cites on one occasion. In *Geburt der Tragödie*, Nietzsche famously introduces the distinction between Dionysian and Apollonian art. For Nietzsche, the Dionysian as it appears in Greek culture has its source in nature as an indivisible force, standing in opposition to the human principle of individuation. According to Nietzsche, the dissolving of the individual sense of self by the Dionysian is experienced by the Greeks in their confrontation with the 'Schrecken und Entsetzlichkeit des Daseins', which can only be overcome through the forms ('die glaenzende Traumgeburt') which art creates.[14] For Nietzsche, Western art and thought after Socrates are increasingly characterised by the turn away from the Dionysian and the vital energy it gives to culture. In this sense, the destructive, anti-individual Dionysian is by no means a purely negative principle for Nietzsche: in fact, it is the force of life itself, which the Apollonian principle of art must harness in order not to become deadened abstraction.[15]

Jirgl's narrator in *Abtrünnig* also finds himself confronted with the 'Schrecken und Entsetzlichkeiten des Daseins', although understood in quite a different way from that to be found in Nietzsche. Here the mechanisms of human civilization threaten to reduce each individual to a man of the 'Masse', that is to say to rob him of his individuality altogether; for those who resist, their attempt to sustain individuality can be fatal, faced as it is with the violent reaction of their fellow human beings to anyone who cannot be assimilated to the dominant normative subjectivity and the values of mass society. So, for Jirgl's narrator, that which threatens the principle of individuation is not a force which can be harnessed in order to give life to the world of representation. Rather, it is a danger which must, as it were, be contained within the work of art in order for the artist to distance himself from it. In Nietzsche's terms, then, the strategy of Jirgl's narrator is distinctly Apollonian.

This reading of *Abtrünnig* echoes Simon Ward's comments on Jirgl's earlier novel *Hundsnächte* (1997), in which, Ward argues with reference to Nietzsche, the text becomes a kind of 'traumhafte Flucht' from the unstoppable processes of contemporary civilization.[16] This understanding of the function of art becomes more explicit in *Abtrünnig*, in which the horror of social existence as experienced by the narrator is, as it were, metaphorically contained within the text as a toxic substance might be sealed in concrete. Unlike the kind of autobiographical writing described by Dennis Tate, this transform-ation of life into writing takes as its starting point the inalterability of the ills it observes in society at large. Writing cannot hope to change them, but only provide a refuge for the writing subject, allowing him to achieve at least aesthetic mastery over them, and thus distance from them.

The irresolvable nature of the problems presented in the text produced by Jirgl's narrator at the level of the social is further emphasised by the use of the 'Links' within the text already mentioned above. Dieter Stolz attempts a reading of these 'Links' and their function which figures the reading process as a kind of training for the reader in the 'Eigen-Sinn' which the narrator so values. Pointing out that none of the links lead directly into the 'Amok' chapter, in which the narrator (appears to) commit a violent crime, Stolz suggests that the 'Links' encourage an anti-authoritarian and anti-linear movement through the text, which will encourage the reader to become 'weniger disponiert für die unkritische Übernahme viereckiger Bildschirm-Horizonte der Informationsgesellschaft'.[17] Such a perspective might invite another kind of Nietzschean reading of the text in which the reader chose to follow the various 'Links' in ever new combinations, circling (perhaps endlessly) through the novel as they recombined its elements in the hope of avoiding the final moment of 'jähe Wut' and its accompanying violent rampage. This would be a reading of the text in line with Gilles Deleuze's interpretation of Nietzsche's eternal return, in which the modern work of art becomes the theatre of a thought experiment, the stage on which an infinite series of 'metamorphoses and permutations' are tried out in order to see whether the subject would be ready to will them eternally. In this theatre, 'nothing is fixed', it is a 'labyrinth without a thread',[18] Deleuze writes, a description which, in some respects, fits Jirgl's maze of a novel very well. However, this would be to see the function of the 'Links' in the texts as essentially affirmative, suggesting that the reader might eventually construct a version of the events portrayed that could be accepted.[19]

It would be more accurate to argue that the 'Links' present us with a maze without an exit. The instructions Jirgl provides for the reader are scant, and it is unclear whether the author would prefer us to return to our jumping off point having read some (but how much?) of the text at the other end of the 'Link', or whether we should continue from that point until we reach the next 'Link', where we could move to another part of the text. The latter method, if followed rigorously, would lead to the text disintegrating into a series of disconnected fragments, and would also lead to a circling through the text which would be endless but, unlike in the positive model outlined above, ultimately fruitless. It is hard to imagine how any recombination of events and thoughts would help to resolve the problems the narrator faces: instead, all that would remain would be an endless going back over the same ground without any prospect of resolution. This is nowhere more clearly illustrated than in the chapter 'Das Geld', where a box containing a text entitled '10 Grundregeln zum Selbst-Loswerden' (136-7) is linked to a passage in the later chapter '1same Spitze', which in turn ends with a reference back to '10 Grundregeln zum Selbst-Loswerden' (290). To follow these links would therefore leave the reader trapped in an endless loop without the prospect of moving forward to resolution. Any such resolution, our fictional narrator's literary strategy suggests, cannot be found within the text and the social world it portrays, but only by stepping outside of the text and the world, enclosing both in a self-contained aesthetic object. Only then, so the bleak conclusion of Jirgl's novel, can narrator and reader place themselves at a distance from a civilization beyond redemption.

Notes

[1] Dennis Tate, *Shifting Perspectives: East German Autobiographical Narratives Before and After the End of the GDR*, Rochester, N.Y.: Camden House, 2007, p. 31.

[2] Tate does not devote an extended analysis to Hein in *Shifting Perspectives*, but my own reading of Hein's literary project is not dissimilar to the model set out by Tate – David Clarke, *'Diese merkwürdige Kleinigkeit einer Vision': Christoph Hein's Social Critique in Transition*, Amsterdam: Rodopi, 2002, pp. 19-51.

[3] Tate, *Shifting Perspectives*, p. 226.

[4] For details of Jirgl's career and background see David Clarke, 'Einführung', in: Clarke and Arne De Winde, eds, *Reinhard Jirgl: Pespektiven, Lesarten, Kontexte*, Amsterdam: Rodopi, 2007, pp. 7-12.

[5] Reinhard Jirgl, *Abtrünnig: Roman aus der nervösen Zeit*, Munich: Hanser, 2005, p. 100. The chapter 'Auf Tag & Stunde' can be found on pp. 39-67 of the novel. Further references to *Abtrünnig* appear in parentheses. The orthography of all quotations from Jirgl's texts appears as in the original. There is no space here to engage with Jirgl's particular use of language, but useful analyses can be found in Arne De Winde, 'Das Erschaffen von "eigen-Sinn"-Notaten zu Reinhard Jirgls Schrift-Bildlichkeitsexperimenten', in: Clarke and De Winde, *Reinhard Jirgl*, pp. 111-49, and Karen Dannemann, *Der blutig=obszön=banale 3-Groschen-Roman namens »Geschichte«: Gesellschafts- und Zivilisationskritik in den Romanen Reinhard Jirgls*, Würzburg: Königshausen und Neumann, 2009, pp. 244-81.

[6] For a further discussion of Jirgl's portrayal of the 'Masse' see David Clarke, '"Störstellen": Architecture in the Work of Reinhard Jirgl', in: Julian Preece et al., eds, *New German Literature: Life-Writing and Dialogue with the Arts*, Frankfurt/Main: Lang, 2007, pp. 143-59. Also Dannemann, *Der blutig=obszön=banale 3-Groschen-Roman namens »Geschichte«*, pp. 292-300.

[7]   Arne De Winde, 'Diese "Geschichte voll der Ungereimtheit & Wiederholung"': Krieg, Gewalt und Erinnerung in Reinhard Jirgls MutterVaterRoman', in De Winde and Anke Gilleir, eds, *Literatur im Krebsgang: Totenbeschwörung und memoria in der deutschsprachigen Literatur nach 1989*, Amsterdam: Rodopi, 2008, pp. 43-76 (here: p. 53).

[8]   On this debate, see Clemens Kammler, 'Unschärferelationen: Anmerkungen zu zwei problematischen Lesarten von Reinhard Jirgls Familienroman Die Unvollendeten', in: Clarke and De Winde, eds, *Reinhard Jirgl*, pp. 227-34.

[9]   Reinhard Jirgl, *Die Unvollendeten*, Munich: Hanser, 2003, p. 250.

[10] Mark Ames, *Going Postal: Rage, Rebellion and Murder in America*, London: Snowbooks, 2007.

[11] Dannemann, *Der blutig=obszön=banale 3-Groschen-Roman namens »Geschichte«*, pp. 324-5.

[12] Reinhard Jirgl, 'Erinnern – ein Meer und seine Form', in De Winde and Gilleir, eds, *Literatur im Krebsgang*, pp. 23-42 (here: pp. 24 and 29).

[13] Kai Behrens, *Ästhetische Obliviologie: Zur Theoriegeschichte des Vergessens*, Würzburg: Königshausen und Neumann, 2005, p. 116.

[14] Friedrich Nietzsche, *Die Geburt der Tragödie oder Griechentum oder Pessimismus*, Leipzig: Naumann, 1907, p. 31.

[15] Nietzsche, *Die Geburt der Tragödie*, p. 160.

[16] Simon Ward, 'Ästhetischer Radikalismus in der Posthistoire: Zum literarischen Bild der Geschichte in Reinhard Jirgls Hundsnächte', in: Clarke and De Winde, eds, *Reinhard Jirgl*, pp. 151-77 (here: p. 167).

[17] Dieter Stolz, '"Das Aufbrechen der verpanzerten Wahrnehmung":Reinhard Jirgls Roman *Abtrünnig* – ein (un)vermeidbarer Amoklauf', in: Clarke and De Winde, eds, *Reinhard Jirgl*, pp. 236-52 (here: p. 250).

[18] Gilles Deleuze, *Difference and Repetition*, trans. Paul Patton, London: Continuum, 2004, p. 68.

[19] Ibid., p. 66.

Andrew Plowman

Experience, Military Fiction and the Shameful Self in Ingo Schulze's *Neue Leben*

This chapter examines Ingo Schulze's epistolary novel *Neue Leben* (2005) in the light of his essay 'Lesen und Schreiben' (2000), in which Schulze disavowed the quest for authentic self-expression defining Christa Wolf's famous essay of the same name (1968). The focus is the novel's treatment of Enrico Türmer's conscription to the GDR's Nationale Volksarmee. Parodying the conscription narrative in Jürgen Fuchs's *Fassonschnitt* and *Das Ende einer Feigheit*, it subverts tropes of military fiction in pursuit of a literary strategy whereby lived experience is fictionalized and stripped of its connection to an individual authorial voice. Türmer's stories about conscription in the literary manuscripts in the novel's fictional appendix further displace authentic experience. However, at the same time they disclose an experience of shame, and possess an excess of affect that threatens to usurp the narratives that *Neue Leben* ostensibly tells.

Concluding the survey part of *Shifting Perspectives: East German Autobiographical Narratives Before and After the End of the GDR* (2007), Dennis Tate lauds Ingo Schulze's *Neue Leben* (2005) as a novel about the 'multiple opportunities for self-reconstruction' opened up 'by the collapse of the GDR'.[1] *Neue Leben*, he claims, confirms the ongoing vitality of a tradition of exploiting the potential of 'autobiographical prose forms' that has shaped both GDR literature and, since 1990, a distinctive eastern German writing.[2] Schulze's novel is, Tate concedes, an unlikely endpoint to a survey launched by a discussion of Christa Wolf's 'Lesen und Schreiben', the essay born out of Wolf's experience of writing *Nachdenken über Christa T.* (1968). Himself the author of a piece on 'Lesen und Schreiben' (2000) that Tate glosses as a 'counter-manifesto' to Wolf's, Schulze is a writer associated with multi-perspective works far removed from Wolf's well-documented striving for what she later termed subjective authenticity.[3] With characteristic earnestness, Wolf, working in the GDR, strove to valorise the human subject and the author's self-expression. In *Neue Leben*, long after the GDR's demise, Schulze more playfully flaunts the 'tongue-in-cheek ambiguity' arising from his novel's multiple layers and from the overlap between its real author and its fictional protagonists.[4]

Notwithstanding Tate's appraisal, *Neue Leben* has to date attracted relatively little close attention. This may owe both to its length at almost 800 pages and to its complexity. Insofar as *Neue Leben* can be described as an autobiographical work, it is hardly straightforward, being an epistolary novel in which elements of its author's biography are refracted through the multiple personas and perspectives noted by Tate. In the foreword, in a gesture reminiscent of E.T.A Hoffmann's *Lebensansichten des Katers Murr nebst fragmentarischer Biographie des Kapellmeisters Johannes Kreisler in zufälligen Makulaturblättern herausgegeben von E.T.A Hoffman* (1819-21), a fictional version of Schulze introduces the letters of Enrico Türmer. Against the background of the events of 1990, Türmer's letters, he claims, draw a compelling picture of Türmer's transformation from a 'Theatermann' with aspirations rooted in GDR culture into a 'Zeitungsredakteur' and a 'glückliche[r] Unternehmer' (a dubious assertion given the mention of the collapse of his enterprise and his disappearance in 1998).[5] The main part consists of Türmer's letters, which date from 6 January to 11 July 1990 and are accompanied by footnotes in which the fictional Schulze highlights details, contradictions and fabrications. The content and tone vary according to the recipients. Letters to Türmer's sister, Vera, foreground the deterioration of his relationship with the actress Michaela following his abandonment of the theatre to help establish a newspaper in the spirit of the GDR opposition group Neues Forum. Letters to Jo, a pastor and a childhood friend, reveal more about the beginnings of the *Altenburger Wochenblatt* (NL, 91), from start-up problems through escalating editorial differences to Türmer's departure to set up an advertising newspaper. The longest letters are to the West German photographer Nicola Hansen, in whom, without reciprocation, he confides. Here, Türmer relates his life story. The final letter, to Nicola, brings the novel full circle. An eye injury that is reported to Vera in the present in the opening letter is recalled as an epiphany in which Türmer recognised that his old life defined by his childhood ambition to become a writer was over. *Neue Leben* closes with a fictional 'appendix' containing Türmer's literary manuscripts, which, in confirmation of the surrender of his ambition, he had used as letter paper. These deal largely with his conscription to the Nationale Volksarmee (NVA).

In notable discussions, Christine Cosentino has considered the work's ambivalent relation to autobiography, while Jill Twark has examined how repetition and narrative retardation result in a frustrating 'simulation of the complex real'.[6] This reading draws on both of these to examine how *Neue Leben* mobilises the tropes of military fiction in its treatment of Türmer's conscription in his letters to Nicola and in his manuscripts. It argues that the subversive handling of tropes of the conscription narrative familiar from Jürgen Fuchs's literary accounts of his military service belongs to a fictional strategy whereby authentic experience is incorporated and the text simultaneously disavows the attributes of a distinctive literary voice. The chapter continues now by reading Schulze's 'Lesen und Schreiben' as the key in *Neue Leben* to a poetics in which Wolf's concept of the 'dimension of the author' yields to a notion of 'style' rooted in the relation to subject matter and mediated through the act of reading. It then analyses the parodic take on the conscription narrative offered by Türmer's letters. It closes by discussing two of Türmer's manuscripts. Whilst these contribute to the layers of fiction in the novel, 'Der Spitzel', paradoxically, discloses at its core an experience of intense shame in which the subject is most exposed and 'Letzte Übung' articulates a related impulse to disappear. Here, *Neue Leben* reveals an excess of affect that threatens to spill out beyond the narratives it ostensibly tells, and illuminates the role of shame in the literary representation of the self.

Schulze's 'Lesen und Schreiben' was a contribution in 2000 to a collection in which emerging writers reflected on the significance of reading for their writing. As observed, Tate identifies it as a 'counter-manifesto' to Wolf, whose own 'Lesen und Schreiben' shaped perceptions about the role of subjectivity and the institution of authorship in GDR literature. However, Schulze's piece is not simply a riposte to Wolf. It is also seeks to rethink aspects of her position in the formulation of an aesthetics which acknowledges both the collapse the discursive system of the GDR and, from the perspective of new conditions, Schulze's roots in that system. As Cosentino notes, the two essays share common features.[7] A confessional tone relates the two writers' personal experience to their respective literary practice. Both writers grasp literature as a practice committed to working through the legacy of a past regime and the psychological upheavals occasioned by the transition from, for Wolf, the Third Reich to the GDR and, for Schulze, from this to the Federal Republic. Both pieces respond to a perceived crisis of narration by invoking literary influences and, more or less explicitly, the example of the author's own work. Where Wolf, however, valorises the literary voice of the author, Schulze renounces it. Rejecting the objectivity claimed by the aesthetic doctrine of socialist realism, Wolf championed literature as a site of memory, depth and imagination that in exemplary fashion could help realise the humanist goal of socialism: the 'Subjektwerden des Menschen'.[8] Underwriting this conception was the 'Dimension des Autors', that is, Wolf's commitment 'wahrheitsgetreu zu erfinden auf Grund eigener Erfahrung' and to develop a voice in her own endeavour 'Ich zu sagen'.[9] While Schulze brings the concept of experience into play, he refuses to couple it to any such voice. His essay starts by relating how his ambition to write emerged out of his childhood reading of Jack London's autobiographical novel *Martin Eden* (1909). In the GDR, he claims ironically, he knew he would be spared the material hardships endured by Martin Eden since this was a state where authors enjoyed privileged status and where 'einige[...] Liedzeilen' could unleash political turmoil.[10] This caricature of the status of GDR writers serves less to parody Wolf than it does the accusations of Western critics who attacked her during the 'Literaturstreit' of 1990 as the figurehead of a 'Gesinnungsästhetik' that elevated political over poetic concerns.[11] Nonetheless, Schulze delineates himself against Wolf when he claims that all literary discourses alter their meaning outside the constellations which produced them and renounces the expression of 'ein [...] ausgeprägtes, unverwechselbares Ich' in his prose (LS, 93). Schulze makes his points first as the reader of philosophical and literary works. From Vilém Flusser he derives the idea of the self as fragmented into different relations to the world. Whilst Wolf is hardly an essentialist, Schulze's concept of the self is yet more decentred, since each act of relating to the world engenders 'ein anderes ICH, denn jedes Sich-In-Beziehung-Setzen entwickelt eine eigene Wellenlänge' (LS, 93). Schulze also invokes Alfred Döblin, who claimed not to possess a unique style, to develop a concept of literary style as 'die Resonanz zwischen [dem Schriftsteller] und seinem Stoff, zwischen Idee und Sprache und der vorgefundenen Sprachstile' (LS, 94). Given the reference to existing language uses, it is no surprise that Schulze grasps literary production as an activity that mobilises qualities of the act of reading '[w]enn die Motive in Bewegung geraten und man im Dialog mit ihnen ihrem Lauf folgt' (LS, 89). Perhaps paradoxically, Schulze also links his disavowal of literary voice to his own writing experience. He claims that his attempts before 1990 to make his military service the centrepiece of a quest for authentic literary self-expression had produced unsatisfactory work. Only when he abandoned this quest in *33 Augenblicke des Glücks* (1995), which he wrote in Russia after he had left his job in the theatre to produce an advertising newspaper there, did he truly discover his talent for writing:

> Das Schreiben war mir erst gelungen, [...] als ich nicht mehr nach meiner unverwechselbaren Stimme gesucht hatte [...]. In St. Petersburg hatte ich wiedergefunden, was meine ureigenste Erfahrung traf: Der Wechsel von einem Gesellschaftssystem zu einem anderen. Ein ICH [...] hatte ich dazu nicht gebraucht. (LS, 92)

Turning Schulze's failure to write into a novel, *Neue Leben* casts this abnegation of voice into literary form. Türmer's autobiographical narrative in the letters to Nicola incorporates in fictional form elements of the biography described by Schulze in 'Lesen und Schreiben'. Like Schulze, Türmer describes his childhood conversion to religion and the influence of London on his ambition to become a writer. If 'Lesen und Schreiben' caricatures a particular post-unification perception of GDR writers, *Neue Leben* further mobilises megalomaniac self-aggrandisement and fantasy in the construction of a narrative voice that Twark identifies as picaresque.[12] Türmer claims that his literary ambition was sparked by a sign from God, following which he started to write as if guided by the Holy Spirit. His narcissism apparent, he continues by relating how he set his heart on becoming a figure applauded by the population and feared by the regime for his plain-speaking: 'Ich würde schreiben, was andere nicht zu sagen wagten [...]. "Wenigstens einer", würden [alle] flüstern, "wenigstens einer, der den Mund aufmacht."' (NL, 146) Further parallels to Schulze's literary career emerge when Türmer describes his plan to author an 'Armeebuch' (NL, 318), a critical account of his conscription that will make his name when it is published in the West. As in Schulze's case, the project stalls, and another dynamic emerges as Türmer follows the author of *Neue Leben* into the study of Classical Philology, the theatre and ultimately the advertising paper business. This culminates in 1989 in the collapse of his literary fantasies and the disintegration of the inflated sense of self that nourished them. Türmer describes to Nicola how he was overcome after the fall of the Berlin Wall by the realisation: 'Mich gab es nicht mehr' (NL, 586). *Neue Leben* shadows Schulze's renunciation of a literary voice in formal as well as plot terms when it couples Türmer's loss of self to the start of his letter writing. Insofar as the letters to different addressees embody, as Cosentino notes, diverse 'Sprechhaltungen',[13] they perform the fragmentation of the unified narrative voice Türmer aspires to into the multiple relations to the world described in 'Lesen und Schreiben'.

The novel's treatment of Türmer's conscription has to date barely received comment. This is a shame, because it illustrates well how Schulze's experience is filtered into a fictional plot that relinquishes the claim to embody a distinctive voice. Significant here is not just how Türmer's narrative in his letters incorporates biographical details, but also how it rereads various literary sources including both school and generic conscription narratives. This demonstrates the feedback from reading into writing posited in 'Lesen und Schreiben' and it highlights the role of the novel's fictional appendix. In a striking *mise-en-abîme*, Türmer's manuscripts, which deal mostly with the NVA, further serve to displace authentic experience in *Neue Leben*. Their protagonists stand in a similar relation to Türmer as he, or the fictional editor Schulze, in turn stands to the author Schulze.

The NVA has recently emerged as an important motif in literary explorations of the memory of the GDR. Established in 1956, it served as the centrepiece of a network of military and paramilitary organisations designed to bind individuals to the GDR state.[14] Introduced in 1962, the year after the Berlin Wall was built, conscription became a basic social experience for millions of young men. For them, volunteering above and beyond the basic eighteen months of service could secure access to prestigious university places and social advancement. If the Stasi provided writers with a privileged *topos* immediately after unification, the NVA has now come to the fore in more differentiated explorations of the remembered normality of life in the GDR. Alongside Christoph Brumme's *Tausend Tage* (2000), Jörg Waehner's *Einstrich-Keinstrich* (2006) or Uwe Tellkamp's *Der Turm* (2008), *Neue Leben* is among many works to engage creatively with the elements of a conscription narrative going back not to the GDR's tradition of 'sozialistische Militärbelletristik', which was associated with Walter Flegel and Horst Senkbeil and supported the cause of 'sozialistische Wehrerziehung',[15] but rather to Jürgen Fuchs's accounts of his military service in the late 1960s and early 1970s. Publishable only in the West, Fuchs's *Fassonschnitt* (1984) and *Das Ende einer Feigheit* (1988) offered an unfavourable image of the NVA which drew on a

wider critical tradition of the representation of the military that included Günter Wallraff's Bundeswehr diaries from the 1960s, Hans-
Hellmuth Kirst's *08/15* trilogy of novels (1954-1955) and even Jaro-
slav Hašek's *The Adventures of the Good Soldier Švejk* (1921-3).[16]

Fuchs's accounts possess a dual significance for Schulze's novel.
What unites *Neue Leben* with them thematically, first, is its subtler
exploration of the experience of conscription as a metaphor for life in
the GDR. If Waehner or Tellkamp present the NVA as a microcosm
of a repressive GDR, Schulze offers a more nuanced picture of the
relation between army and state. In the *Süddeutsche Zeitung* in 2007,
Schulze asserted that GDR society in its breadth was irreducible to the
NVA, claiming 'dass die DDR anders war als ihre Armee'.[17] *Neue
Leben* underlines this in Türmer's failure to make his conscription the
focus of a work that will turn him into a critical writer. To appreciate
this failure, one must consider, second, the novel's parodic reworking
of Fuchs, whose *Fassonschnitt* and *Das Ende einer Feigheit* have
helped to establish a set a narrative *topoi* which has come to dominate
the representation of the NVA. Of course, Fuchs's texts point to universal aspects of military life, such as the rituals of discipline and a
routine of 'putzen, Betten glatt ziehen, marschieren' punctuated by
spells of inactivity.[18] If the NVA appears indistinguishable here from
any other army, Fuchs also explored aspects that were more specific.
His texts deal with his memories of paramilitary education at school,
the ideological pressure to volunteer above the regular term and his
own failure to object for fear of the consequences. They further high-
light the role of the communist party and of political indoctrination,
the suspected presence of informers and a punitive military justice
which saw conscripts consigned to the military prison in Schwedt an
der Oder for minor political offences. What lends his accounts literary
depth is his reflection, in *Fassonschnitt*, on his own acquiescence in
his military socialisation, and his attempt, in *Das Ende einer Feigheit*,
to mobilise 'Schreiben als letzte Gegenwehr' against this in his furtive
note-taking at the time and in the text itself.[19]

Neue Leben offers a striking send-up, even alongside other works'
parodies of Fuchs's accounts, such as Leander Haußmann's novel and
film project *NVA* (2006). Elements of Fuchs's narrative tilt into the
absurd as Türmer's ambition to become a critical author creates
heightened expectations about the army. Letters to Nicola show how
Türmer decided in advance on the NVA as the focus of this ambition.

He recalls how he imagined the novella he was writing whilst still at school as an East German version of Hermann Hesse's *Unterm Rad* or Robert Musil's *Die Verwirrungen des jungen Törleß* (both 1906) in which a young man is broken by his encounter with the totalitarian state as it reveals itself in the military. Türmer sketches the story with pathos:

> Für ihn gab es kein Ausweichen, kein Entrinnen, die totalitäre Macht überwachte jeden Schritt. Schließlich saß mein Held zerschlagen und bleich bei einer Tasse Kaffee in der Küche, seine Mutter – wieder eine deutsche Mutter, die ihren Sohn hergeben mußte – umsorgte ihn schweigend, das Gesicht abgewandt, damit er ihre Tränen nicht sah. (NL, 262)

He also reports 'staging' the unfolding events of his call-up in his imagination to provide material. In order to stylise conscription as the 'Inbegriff des Von-zu-Hause-Abschied-Nehmen' he purposely caught a lingering farewell glimpse of Dresden's 'Canaletto-Panorama mit Hofkirche' (NL, 261-2) when, in a scene familiar from Fuchs, he and the other conscripts left for barracks. What the NVA inspires in Türmer, though, is not fear, but hope. In a parody of the link between experience and self-expression that Schulze rejected in 'Lesen und Schreiben', Türmer relates how he invested in military service his hope of developing a unique literary voice: 'Befehle preisgegeben, geschliffen bei Appell und Sturmangriff, würde ich von selbst einen unverwechselbaren Stil ausbilden.' (NL, 260)

Neue Leben is an ironic work, however, in which such aspirations are undermined. In his letters he cuts a more ridiculous figure than the tragic one he once sought to style himself as. In a parody of Fuchs's failure to object, Türmer relates his refusal to volunteer to become a non-commissioned officer. This pales beside the conscientious objection that forces Jo into a career in the church. By comparison, Türmer's limited refusal appears entirely self-serving, since to object would ruin his literary career. Türmer's account of a school presentation on the aggressive intentions of West Germany's Bundeswehr also sheds unflattering light on his oppositional resolve. Having initially refused to proceed, he backs down and reads a script written by his mother. Türmer retrospectively glosses his reluctant performance as a decisive step towards his ambition – 'Ich war unangreifbar, ich war zum Schriftsteller geworden' (NL, 204). But the embarrassed silence that greets his mother's words suggest otherwise.

Türmer's account to Nicola of his service in a motorised infantry regiment offers many familiar elements. Like Fuchs, Türmer notes the universal tribulations of military life arising from a routine of cleaning and marching. Contrary to his initial 'Angst, nicht alles notieren zu können' (NL, 272), quiet periods allow time for the crucial activity of writing. He also dwells on elements promising insight into the GDR's true character and tells how to this end he would read assiduously the monthly supplements to 'Vom Sinn des Soldatenseins' (NL, 280), the NVA's ideological manual. Just as *Fassonschnitt* invokes the crushing of the Prague Spring in 1968 as an event that shaped Fuchs's memory of conscription, Türmer relates how the imposition of martial law in Poland following the rise of the Solidarity movement fuelled his imagination. The prospect of deployment in Poland in the service of a repressive socialism enabled Türmer to see a nocturnal exercise shortly before his discharge in a sinister light. Türmer tells Nicola the curious incident of how on this occasion he risked the charge of sabotage and consignment to Schwedt for allowing his truck's motor to run to warm his sleeping companions, while he slipped away to relieve himself. Briefly, he claims, he saw himself as 'der glücklichste und freieste Mensch, den Sie sich vorstellen können' (NL, 312).

But the dominant note in Türmer's account to Nicola of military service is bathos as he concedes: 'Die Hölle sah anders aus' (NL, 279). Military life, he observes, was indeed characterised by the meting out of humiliations. But this proves to be 'ein plumpes Spiel' (NL, 279) in which trainers and conscripts securely played out well-defined roles. It was, 'unangenehm, im Schutzanzug und mit Gasmaske zu rennen' (NL, 279). But, in a reversal of the *topos* of relentless indoctrination as a sign of the army's ideological role within the state, Türmer gains weight due to the sedentary 'Polit-Unterricht' (NL, 279). Only once does the NVA deliver the material Türmer craves. A key incident offers an unexpected take on the gesture of observing and writing which Fuchs took from Wallraff's Bundeswehr diaries and which has become a staple element of many NVA narratives. It also turns upside down their protagonists' familiar wariness of fellow conscripts as potential informers. Türmer's own note-taking sees him confronted as an informant by other soldiers. In, as he notes, 'eine[r] Szene, wie ich sie gerne erfunden hätte', he was subjected to a humiliation that he does not explain save to register his surprise 'daß sie instinktiv wußten, wie sie mich am tiefsten demütigen konnten'

(NL, 288). The scene is not what it seems, however. No one, it tran-
spires, would dare humiliate an informer; the informer was actually
Knut, who orchestrated the humiliation. Moreover, in a further twist,
Türmer responds by hiring out the writing skills revealed in this way
to soldiers willing to pay him to write letters. His first commission
comes from Salwitzky, who wants to remind his wife of the sexual
intercourse with her that he misses. Türmer's literary ambitions have
been debased long before he surrenders them.

It is instructive here to consider Türmer's manuscripts in the
novel's fictional appendix. Five of the seven pieces echo incidents in
Türmer's letters that relate to his conscription, and they invite reading
as fragments of his planned 'Armeebuch'. 'Schnitzeljagd' (NL, 661-5)
is set in a school 'Ferienlager' and alludes to the paramilitary training
he underwent. 'Jahrhundertsommer' (NL, 667-72) relates to the letters
Türmer wrote for other soldiers. It describes how a certain Salwitzky's
cries of 'Rosi, du Sau!' (NL, 673) bring his bunk crashing down as he
dictates his sexual experiences. 'Titus Holm. Eine Novelle aus Dresden' (NL, 699-782) resembles the novella that Türmer claims to have
been writing and features the story of his presentation about the Bundeswehr. 'Der Spitzel' (NL, 673-81) is linked to Türmer's humiliation
and 'Letzte Übung' (NL, 783-90) to the manoeuvre before his discharge.

Türmer's manuscripts add another layer in which experience is incorporated into fiction. At the same time, they are curiously revealing,
as 'Der Spitzel' and 'Letzte Übung' especially demonstrate. This is
not, however, of the literary voice that Schulze disavows and Türmer
strives for, but of a more basic condition of human nakedness. In 'Lesen und Schreiben', Schulze identifies as central to his literary practice the insight that his contingent motivation to write dissipates: 'Der
Anlaß verliert sich beim Schreiben. Ideen und Begriffe [...] verbrau-
chen sich als Katalysatoren und sind nicht mehr nachweisbar' (LS, 87-
8). He elaborates by distinguishing the immediate subject matter from
the themes of his work. His work, he claims, would be impossible
without his experience of the transformation of East Germany in 1990.
However, he adds: 'Diese "Transformation" ist aber nicht mein zen-
trales Thema, sondern der Stoff, in dem all die alten Geschichten von
Liebe und Tod Gestalt gewinnen.' (LS, 96-7) These remarks relate to
33 Augenblicke des Glücks and *Simple Storys* (1998), but it is easy to
see how they relate to *Neue Leben*. It in turn requires little effort to

grasp how Türmer's own narratives about the GDR might hinge on issues more universal and fundamental.

If Türmer's letters suggest his narcissism and opportunism, then 'Der Spitzel' and 'Letzte Übung' reveal an affective excess that seeps out through the GDR narrative he seeks to tell. Its core is an intense shame that expresses itself in twin impulses to disclose and efface the nudity of his self. In recent literary studies, shame is theorised as the awareness of a moral nakedness in which the self stands unmediated by the social relations in which identity is normally constructed. Michael Minden, in an essay on Grass, contrasts shame as a trope with guilt. Where guilt is epistemological, having to do with knowledge of what one has done, the condition of shame is ontological. It relates to an uncomfortable sense of who one is that is situated on the threshold of the individual uniqueness of the body and the socially coded world of culture.[20] For Martin Swales, who discusses Schlink's *Der Vorleser* (1995), too, shame is a nexus of affect that comprises a socio-psychological element associated with how one sees oneself and perceives oneself to be seen whilst also being rooted in the body, especially its sexual and excretory functions.[21] 'Der Spitzel' casts Türmer's humiliation as an incident narrated by another soldier, Edgar, who is cleaning the corridor outside the room where it occurs. It illustrates how shame forms a nexus that undercuts Türmer's ambition to situate himself critically towards the GDR in his prose and ensnares him in a concern with (his own) bodily humiliation. Again the contrast with *Fassonschnitt* is illuminating. For all his fear of informers, Fuchs must confront his own actions when he unwittingly passes on information about a comrade.[22] In so doing he positions himself in relation to the symbolic order of the GDR in a narrative that turns on the gap between his critical attitude and conformist behaviour. No such cognitive pay-off awaits Türmer, whose narrative cannot escape the affect generated by the scene of the soldier who is stripped and has his buttocks smeared with boot polish while others try (unsuccessfully) to stimulate his penis. 'Der Spitzel' strives for distance by shifting the narrative perspective toward Edgar outside. But here, physical humiliation spills into the pleasure of furtive observation as Edgar shines the floor – 'klack, klack, klack' (NL, 676) – in a masturbatory frenzy. For Stephen Pattison, the experience of shame, in which the whole person is exposed, generates a desire to disappear.[23] Where 'Der Spitzel' transforms a shameful moment of being publicly seen to be humiliated into a secret, pleasurable act of looking, 'Letzte Übung' stages an unseen disappearance. This manuscript (the only one to feature a protagonist named Türmer) gives the occurrence on the manoeuvre a fantastic twist. As the protagonist steals off, the elements of the milieu crucial to Türmer's ambition to transform himself into a critical writer fall away. He leaves behind his sleeping comrades, his concern that allowing the engines to run may result in disciplinary charges, and the memories of his largely underwhelming military service. In the unspoilt 'Sperrgebiet' (NL, 787) Türmer defecates, sheds his uniform, turns into a wolf and vanishes into the night. The disappearance 'Letzte Übung' stages is emblematic for *Neue Leben* as a whole. While it offers a response to the experience of shame in 'Der Spitzel', it also anticipates Türmer's surrender of his literary ambitions and the final disappearance reported by the fictional editor Schulze.

The author of multi-perspective works and of a counter-manifesto to Christa Wolf, Ingo Schulze is for Dennis Tate an unlikely heir to a distinctly eastern German tradition of autobiographical writing. Taking Schulze's 'Lesen und Schreiben' as its departure point, this reading of *Neue Leben* has explored its strategy of incorporating biographical experience whilst also disavowing the goal of authentic self-expression characterising Wolf's literary project. The focus has been the novel's parodic engagement with military fiction, an aspect that illustrates how, for Schulze, reading informs the act of writing and illuminates the failure of Türmer's literary ambitions. When contemplating *Neue Leben*, it remains valid to point to its convoluted structure. But this alone misses the poignancy of Schulze's literary undertaking and its relation to individual human experience. In and between the layers of text inhabited by its real author and fictional editor Schulze, its fictional protagonist Türmer and his protagonists, the novel indeed performs the dissolution of a unified voice into diverse speech acts and the dissipation of experience into fiction as generic elements come into play. But its paradox is that, at the point where that experience is most implicated in fiction, it speaks of a shameful nakedness that threatens to spill beyond the conscription narrative Türmer seeks to tell – and by extension beyond the story of the post-unification transformations that Schulze ostensibly offers. The heart of *Neue Leben* as a construction of the self is a nexus of affect that is trivially, absurdly, but always painfully human.

Notes

[1] Dennis Tate, *Shifting Perspectives: East German Autobiographical Narratives Before and After the End of the GDR*, Rochester, NY: Camden House, 2007, p. 61.

[2] Ibid., p. 61.

[3] Ibid., pp. 61 and 22.

[4] Ibid., p. 61.

[5] Ingo Schulze, *Neue Leben. Die Jugend Enrico Türmers in Briefen und Prosa. Herausgegeben, kommentiert und mit einem Vorwort versehen von Ingo Schulze*, Berlin: Berlin Verlag, 2005, p. 11. Hereafter NL and page number in brackets in the text.

[6] Christine Cosentino, 'Ingo Schulzes Roman *Neue Leben*: Autobiografie, "wahrheitsgetreue Erfindung", Fiktion', *Germanic Notes and Reviews*, 38:1 (2007), 11-18; Jill Twark, 'New East German Satire: Ingo Schulze's *Neue Leben* as a "Novel of Complexity"', *Gegenwartsliteratur*, 8 (2009), 67-89 (here: 72-6).

[7] Cosentino, 'Ingo Schulzes Roman *Neue Leben*', pp. 11-15.

[8] See 'Lesen und Schreiben' in Christa Wolf, *Die Dimension des Autors. Essays und Aufsätze, Reden und Gespräche 1959-1985*, 2 vols, Darmstadt: Luchterhand, 1987, II, pp. 463-503 (here: p. 503).

[9] Wolf, 'Lesen und Schreiben', pp. 481 and 499.

[10] Ingo Schulze, 'Lesen und Schreiben oder "Ist es nicht idiotisch, sieben oder gar acht Monate an einem Roman zu schreiben, wenn man in jedem Buchladen für zwei Dollar einen kaufen kann"', in: Ute-Christine Krupp and Ulrike Janssen, eds., *Zuerst bin ich immer Leser. Prosa schreiben heute*, Frankfurt/Main: Suhrkamp, 2000, pp. 80-101 (here: p. 81). Hereafter LS and page number in brackets in the text.

[11] Stuart Taberner, *German Literature of the 1990s and Beyond*, Rochester, NY: Camden House, 2005, pp. 1-7.

[12] Twark, 'New East German Satire', p. 72.

[13] Cosentino, 'Ingo Schulzes Roman *Neue Leben*', p. 12

[14] Hans Ehlert und Matthias Rogg, 'Militär, Staat und Gesellschaft der DDR in historischer Sicht', in: Hans Ehlert and Matthias Rogg, eds., *Militär, Staat und Gesellschaft in der DDR. Forschungsfelder, Ergebnisse, Perspektiven*, Berlin: Links, 2005, pp. 1-26.

[15]   Bernhard H. Decker, *Gewalt und Zärtlichkeit. Einführung in die Militärbelletristik der DDR 1956–1986*, New York: Peter Lang, 1990, pp. 1-3.

[16]   See also Andrew Plowman, '"Eine Armee wie jede andere auch"? Writers and Filmmakers remember the NVA', in: Renate Rechtien and Dennis Tate, eds, *Twenty Years On: Competing Memories of the GDR in Postunification German Culture*, Rochester, NY: Camden House, 2011.

[17]   Ingo Schulze, 'Was aber hätte ich getan? An der Ungeheuerlichkeit der Mauer ändert der wiedergefundene Schießbefehl nichts', *Süddeutsche Zeitung*, 14/15 August 2007, p. 11.

[18]   Jürgen Fuchs, *Fassonschnitt*, Reinbek: Rowohlt, 1984, p. 57.

[19]   Jürgen Fuchs, *Das Ende einer Feigheit*, Reinbek: Rowohlt, 1988, p. 111.

[20]   Michael Minden '"Even the Flowering of Art Isn't Pure": Günter Grass's Figures of Shame', in: Rebecca Braun and Frank Brunssen, eds., *Changing the Nation: Günter Grass in International Perspective*, Würzburg: Königshausen und Neumann, 2008, pp. 23-35 (here: pp. 24-5).

[21]   Martin Swales, 'Sex, shame and Guilt: Reflections on Bernhard Schlink's *Der Vorleser* and J.M. Coetzee's *Disgrace*', *Journal of European Studies*, 33 (2003), 7-22 (here: p. 10).

[22]   Fuchs, *Fassonschnitt*, p. 285.

[23]   Stephen Pattison, *Shame: Theory, Therapy, Theology*, Cambridge: Cambridge University Press, 2000, pp. 73-4.

Hannes Krauss

Memories of a GDR-Watcher, oder:
Die westdeutsche Germanistik und die DDR-Literatur

This concluding chapter could be a fragment of the autobiography of an academic. Looking back over a personal preoccupation with the literature of the GDR extending over several decades, it reflects critically on the treatment of the subject in West German literary scholarship – from beginnings in the 1960s still overshadowed by the Cold War down to post-unification studies. The essay calls for a continuing engagement with GDR literature which is mindful of its special social and political significance, but approaches individual works as original contributions to writing in the German language since the Second World War.

Etwa 1968 habe ich die DDR-Literatur für mich entdeckt – und seither bin ich nicht mehr von ihr losgekommen. Für meine Beschäftigung mit dem Thema spielten Kontakte mit britischen Literaturwissenschaftlern eine wichtige Rolle, haben sie doch in mehrfacher Weise zu meiner 'Emanzipation' beigetragen: ihr Wissenschaftsverständnis – weniger hierarchisch als das deutsche – ermöglichte mir erste Veröffentlichungen; auf britischen Konferenzen habe ich gelernt, wie produktiv Zugänge sein können, die frei sind von der Bürde der damals in der westdeutschen Germanistik verbreiteten biographischen Aufgeregtheiten; und auf britischem – sozusagen neutralem – Boden fanden meine ersten Begegnungen mit DDR-Wissenschaftlern statt.

Nach dem Ende der Teilung wurde im deutschen Literatur- und Wissenschaftsbetrieb die Banalisierung oder Dämonisierung der DDR-Literatur populär. Vor einigen Jahren habe ich das zum Anlass genommen, meiner eigenen wissenschaftlichen Vergangenheit nachzuspüren. Dabei gerieten zwangsläufig auch typische Tendenzen des westdeutschen Umgangs mit der DDR-Literatur in den Blick, so dass das Ergebnis meines Rückblicks hoffentlich nicht nur von persönlichem Interesse ist.

Auf den ersten Blick haben meine Überlegungen mit dem Thema dieses Bandes (Autobiographie-Forschung) wenig zu tun. Und doch gibt es, glaube ich, einen mittelbaren Zusammenhang. Kein Forschungsgebiet der neueren deutschen Literaturwissenschaft war so eng verknüpft mit den Biographien derer, die sich damit befassten, wie die DDR-Literatur. Vielleicht kann mein Beitrag verstanden werden als

Bruchstück einer Wissenschaftler-Autobiographie. Er mag manchmal unangemessen privat klingen, zeigt aber, dass nicht nur DDR-Germanisten eine wissenschaftliche Vergangenheit hatten – und kann so möglicherweise zur Versachlichung einer Debatte beitragen, die in Deutschland auch mehr als zwei Jahrzehnte nach der politischen Vereinigung noch immer recht emotional geführt wird.

Zur Genese meines Interesses an der DDR-Literatur

Vielfältig waren die Begründungen (d.h. Rechtfertigungen, Entschuldigungen, Ausflüchte, Selbstbezichtigungen), die nach dem Ende der DDR von westdeutschen Germanisten gesucht wurden, um ihren wissenschaftlichen Umgang mit der Literatur dieses Landes zu legitimieren; ganz ohne Kalkül ehrlich waren nur wenige. Das mag damit zusammenhängen, dass das eigene jahrelange Treiben in einem immer noch von Rache- und Abrechnungsgedanken geprägten politischen Klima kein allzu großes akademisches Prestige verhieß. Es gibt aber auch objektive Gründe: bei kaum einem Gegenstand der neueren Germanistik haben sich literarische, lebensgeschichtliche, politische und ideologische Dimensionen so ununterscheidbar vermengt, wie bei der Befassung mit der Literatur der Deutschen Demokratischen Republik.

Ich selbst bin Ende der sechziger Jahre, im Rahmen von Arbeiten zum *nouveau roman* eher zufällig auf ein paar neuere DDR-Romane gestoßen. Einen *nouveau roman* habe ich darunter zwar nicht gefunden, vieles indes, was mir fremd, weil in meinem Tübinger und Berliner Literaturwissenschaftsstudium inexistent war. Das machte mich neugierig; auch deshalb, weil das, was ich las, manifest von den anderswo erworbenen Vorstellungen (und Vorurteilen) über die Literatur und das Leben in der DDR differierte. Versuche, bei vielleicht übersehenen Spezialisten der Literaturwissenschaft mehr zu erfahren, endeten frustrierend. Analysen, die das Etikett 'wissenschaftlich' verdient hätten, waren rar. Man hatte die Wahl zwischen einer DDR-internen apologetischen Deutung der Literatur als planmäßiger Realisierung von – nur vage als Theorie kostümierten – dogmatischen Programmen und verschiedenen Varianten einer nicht minder ideologiebefrachteten Literaturbetrachtung aus westlicher Sicht, die oft aus der Biographie ihrer Vertreter erklärbar, methodisch aber selten nachvollziehbar war.

Als die meisten DDR-Schriftsteller ihre nach der Staatsgründung übernommene Pflicht, die Massen nachträglich auf die Ziele der angeblich siegreichen Revolution einzustimmen, schon nicht mehr besonders ernst nahmen, schienen für die DDR-Literaturwissenschaft die Prinzipien dieses literaturpädagogischen Großversuchs immer noch zu gelten:

> Letztlich geht es bei allem Für und Wider in künstlerischen, ästhetischen wie politischen Fragen der letzten Zeit um das Menschenbild unserer unmittelbaren, sozialistischen Gegenwart. Wir lehnen ganz entschieden ab, ein verzerrtes, ja geradezu kastriertes Menschenbild, wie es in der Dekadenz gang und gäbe ist, für den Sozialismus gültig anzuerkennen.
> [...]
> Alles, was uns mit künstlerischen Mitteln hilft, den umfassenden Aufbau des Sozialismus in dieser oder jener Weise zu erhellen und einen Schritt voranzubringen, ist willkommen und wird unter dem kritischen Blick von Millionen Lesern oder Zuschauern inhaltlich wie formal zu bestehen haben.[1]

In der Bundesrepublik lieferte Lothar von Balluseks 1956 entstandene, 1963 überarbeitete, in hoher Auflage vom Bundesministerium für gesamtdeutsche Fragen verbreitete Studie über *Dichter im Dienst*[2] zwar partiell brauchbare Zustandsbeschreibungen, zumal in solchen Passagen, in denen auf die Differenz zwischen real existierender DDR-Kunst und den Möglichkeiten einer sozialistischen Kunst verwiesen wurde:

> Sozialistischer Realismus ist nicht mit kommunistischer Kunst identisch, da viele kommunistische Künstler, vor allem die außerhalb des kommunistischen Machtbereichs lebenden, bei aller Parteilichkeit der Gesinnung an ihre Kunst künstlerische Maßstäbe legen und sich solcher Formen bedienen, die unserer Zeit entsprechen oder vorauseilen.[3]

Insgesamt aber blieb das Buch Abrechnung und Aburteilung im Geiste des Kalten Krieges.

Und sonst? Peter Jokostra hatte 1960 in einer Miszelle im *Merkur* am Beispiel einiger Lyriker (darunter Bobrowski und Huchel) auf die spezifischen Probleme des Schreibens 'im zernierten Raum' verwiesen:

> Charakteristisch für die verborgene, verschwiegene und verschüttete Zonendich-
> tung ist die verzweifelte Suche nach einem Ausgleich von Wirklichkeit, also dem
> im Gedicht bewältigten Leben, und der widersinnigen Realität, die lediglich
> Scheinwerte offeriert und in sterilen Postulaten verharrt.[4]

Marcel Reich-Ranicki hatte unter seine 1963 erschienenen deutschen
Schriftstellerporträts[5] auch neun DDR-AutorInnen aufgenommen (u.a.
Seghers, Hermlin, Strittmatter und Fühmann); Jörg Bernhard Bilke
offerierte 1969 in der Zeitschrift *Der Deutschunterricht* einen ersten
informativen Überblick über die Entwicklung der DDR-Literatur und
setzte sich – in einer Beilage zum selben Heft – kritisch mit der nach-
lässigen Rezeption dieser Literatur in Westdeutschland auseinander.[6]
Dennoch kann man mit Fug und Recht behaupten, dass DDR-Literatur
für die westdeutsche Germanistik der sechziger Jahre ein Non-Thema
blieb, das allenfalls in ein paar mehr oder weniger dem Kalten Krieg
verpflichteten Sätzen aufgegriffen wurde. Ironischerweise war es eine
Arbeit des wegen seiner nationalsozialistischen Vergangenheit um-
strittenen Hermann Pongs, die das Gegenteil zu beweisen schien –
allerdings nur vordergründig. Bei Licht besehen bleibt Pongs' um-
fangreiche Studie über *Dichtung im gespaltenen Deutschland*[7] allenfalls eine Kuriosität: die Klage eines Wertkonservativen über den
Verlust der – bei Goethe noch auffindbaren, in der Gegenwartsliteratur schmerzlich vermissten – ideellen Mitte. Seine Diagnose meint den
Osten gleichermaßen wie den Westen:

> Das Verhängnis der Spaltung geht nicht nur quer durch Deutschland, es geht
> durch jeden Deutschen hindurch. Das Vergangene lähmt durch Schuld, und wo es
> Hass hervorruft, verfremdet es die historische Wirklichkeit. Thomas Mann hat das
> Komplexhafte der Zeitneurose im *Doktor Faustus* ins Mythische gesteigert: Satan
> als der große Welt- und Seelenspalter. Was die Wohlfahrtsgesellschaft überdeckt,
> macht die Dichtung radikal offenbar. Inzwischen ist die Mauer hinzugekommen.
> Die Härte des Kollektivzwangs wird unmenschlich. Sie kann auch Dichter
> mundtot machen. Die Flucht ins Ästhetisch-Artistische auf der anderen Seite
> treibt dem Sinnlos-Absurden zu und endet auch im Unmenschlichen.[8]

'Jenseits der Spaltung' spürt Pongs den 'Urphänomenen' der Dichtung
nach. Er versichert zwar, es gehe ihm nicht darum, 'Goethe oder die
Klassik gegen die Moderne auszuspielen', aber letztlich benutzt er die
DDR-Literatur dann doch als Knüppel gegen die – damals in West-
deutschland erst ganz behutsam gepflegte – Adaption moderner
Schreibstrategien. Unzufrieden mit dem Menschenbild von Frisch,
Hildesheimer und selbst Uwe Johnson, entdeckt er Erwin Strittmatter,

Karl Heinz Jakobs, Erik Neutsch und Hermann Kant. Die sind zwar nicht vollkommen – Strittmatters 'Augenblicksmetaphern' beispielsweise erreichen 'weder ins Religiöse noch ins Naturgroße [...] Tiefenschwingungen'[9] – aber letztlich

> gewinnt dann die 'soziologische' Perspektive des Ostens eine unverhofft fruchtbare methodische Bedeutung: Sie zwingt in die Ehrfurcht vor der Ganzheit der Dichtung zurück und schafft gleichgewichtige Gegenkräfte gegen die Flucht ins rein Artistische westlicher Interpretation. Als Ergänzung zur Kontaktarmut im Westen erscheint ein Grundzug mitteldeutscher Dichtung, für den ihr begabtester Dramatiker repräsentativ wird: Bert Brecht. Die von ihm in vielen Abwandlungen geschaffene revolutionierende Muttergestalt wird zum Inbegriff mitmenschlicher Lebenswerte. In ihr wird den Ausartungen des männlichen Prinzips die Ahnung einer Weltordnung entgegen gedichtet [...]. So können beide sich aufeinander zu bewegen. Es ist zugleich der Triumph des dialogischen Prinzips, das paradoxerweise gerade den dialektischen Marxismus Brechts durchbricht. Damit sind Ausblicke gewonnen, vom Geist her die Spaltung zu überwinden auf Gespräche zu, die sich der Weltthematik von Evolution und Revolution ohne Hass und Hochmut öffnen.[10]

Getarnt hinter blumiger Vieldeutigkeit zieht Pongs mit Brecht gegen die Moderne ins Feld; eine Germanistenlist von nachgerade Brechtscher Dimension.

Kurz und schlecht: ideologieunterfütterte Literaturbetrachtung aus beiden deutschen Staaten traf sich – bei allen Kontroversen im Detail – in einer Überbewertung der Inhalte des literarischen Werkes und einer Geringschätzung seiner ästhetischen Dimensionen. Vor dem Hintergrund einer nichtexistenten bzw. trivialen Forschungslage habe ich 1969/1970 auf eigene Faust versucht, die DDR-Literatur aufzuarbeiten – und dabei das Land gleich mit zu erkunden. Nicht nur für mich geriet so die Literatur zum Projektionsraum für Visionen. Die Glorifizierung der frühen DDR-Literatur durch eine aus der Studentenbewegung hervorgegangene 'linke' Literaturwissenschaft ist in einschlägigen Publikationen des Oberbaum-Verlags dokumentiert.[11] Die literarische Entwicklung der DDR in den sechziger Jahren bestärkte derlei Wahrnehmungen. Nicht wenige Autoren hatten nach dem Mauerbau die subjektiv ehrliche Hoffnung gepflegt, in der Konzentration aufs ungestört Eigene endlich sozialistische Kunst in all ihren Dimensionen erproben und entfalten und so auch dem 'richtigen' Sozialismus auf die Sprünge helfen zu können. Und die Prosa-Texte jenes Jahrzehnts – mit einer ganzen Reihe außergewöhnlicher Neuerscheinungen – schienen dies zu bestätigen.

So entdeckte ich mithilfe von Hermann Kant, Christa Wolf, Erwin Strittmatter, Erik Neutsch und anderen die DDR-Literatur – und ein für mich völlig neues öffentliches Umgehen mit Literatur. Meiner Faszination über solche Entdeckungen stellten sich die Debatten um Kants *Aula*, Strittmatters *Ole Bienkopp* oder Christa Wolfs *Geteilten Himmel* als Vorboten der Becherschen Literaturgesellschaft dar. Ich war beeindruckt davon, dass so viele Leser Briefe an Autoren schrieben; ich war beeindruckt, weil offensichtlich in Betriebskulturgruppen heftig über Gegenwartsliteratur diskutiert wurde; ich war beeindruckt von der Intensität der öffentlichen Debatte um den *Geteilten Himmel*. All das schien mir Indiz für die Demokratisierung einer Kultur, die nicht länger im Zeichen elitärer Ästhetik stand. Im Kontext unscharfer Studentenbewegungs-Utopien und genährt durch den öffentlich gepflegten Mythos vom 'Leseland', signalisierte mir der DDR-Literaturbetrieb den Erfolg einer radikalen Bildungsreform. Der Warencharakter der Kunst schien überwunden durch den handfesten Gebrauchswert der Kultur.

'Möglichkeiten des sozialistischen Romans'

Vor diesem Hintergrund entstand 1970 meine Staatsexamensarbeit über 'Hermann Kant *Die Aula* – Möglichkeiten des sozialistischen Romans'. Dieser Roman schien mir in ganz spezifischer Weise repräsentativ für die Literarisierung der Lebensverhältnisse – ja, er versprach sogar, sie mit literarischen Mitteln voranzutreiben. Nach einem Schnelldurchgang durch die DDR-Literaturgeschichte[12] und der Auseinandersetzung mit theoretischen Positionen des sozialistischen Realismus (von Gorki über Trotzki, Lenin, Brecht, Eisler, Lukács und Bloch bis zu Mao Tse-tung[13]) wählte ich schließlich als methodische Basis für meine Arbeit den theoretischen Ansatz von Horst Redeker. Redeker hatte damals – durchaus auf der Höhe seiner Zeit – versucht, die Funktion sozialistischer Kunst in semiotischen Kategorien zu beschreiben.[14] Der semantische Aspekt, unter dem Literatur bislang ausschließlich betrachtet wurde, sei – so Redeker – unzureichend, weil er nur die Relation von künstlerischem Abbild und widergespiegeltem Objekt (von ästhetischem Zeichen und Bezeichnetem) erfasse. Man könne ein Kunstwerk in der Gesamtheit seiner ästhetischen, gesellschaftlichen und psychologischen Dimensionen aber nur dann begreifen, wenn man die Relation zwischen Produzent, Rezipient,

Zeichen und Bezeichnetem, also den pragmatischen Aspekt, berücksichtige. Da sich ein Kunstwerk erst in der Rezeption gesellschaftlich verwirkliche, müssten für den Interpreten materielle 'Struktur und Funktion [...] eine dialektische Einheit'[15] bilden.

Das Kunstwerk errichte eine Modell-Welt, in der die Leser ihre schöpferische Aktivität entfalteten; so gewännen sie 'durch Vorstellung praktischer Erfahrung im Spiel, in der Vorstellungsform der Praxis'[16] Einsichten und Anregungen. Die in 'der Arbeit am Modell'[17] entwickelte Aktivität wirke über die Abbildung hinaus wieder auf die reale Praxis. 'Damit hängt die spezifische erzieherische Funktion der Kunst zusammen, die sich [...] nicht auf das Ablesen von Erkenntnissen reduzieren lässt'. Im pragmatischen Aspekt eines Kunstwerks stelle sich die Dialektik zwischen Individuum und Gemeinschaft dar. Jeder Rezipient erlebe sich im Kunstwerk selbst, genieße seine eigene Aktivität an einem Produkt, das ihm als das eines anderen bewusst sei; der Künstler sei bestrebt, 'das Eigene so zu sagen, dass es auch für andere zum Eigenen werden kann.'[18] Die wichtigste Funktion der Kunst (für Produzent und Rezipient) liege in der geistigen Bewältigung der Wirklichkeit über die Abbildung. 'Durch das Bild wird [...] eine neue, 'verfremdete' Haltung zur Wirklichkeit geschaffen.'[19] Sozialistische Literatur wolle etwas im Praktischen erreichen und verändern: 'Auseinandersetzung um Werke, die aus einer schöpferischen Haltung ihrer Autoren zu unserer Wirklichkeit entstanden sind, die darum echte, offene Fragen aufwerfen,' gehöre – als 'deren gesellschaftliche Umsetzung und "Verwirklichung"'– grundsätzlich zum Kern dieser Bücher. 'Die Literatur wird mehr und mehr zum öffentlichen Forum der geistigen Auseinandersetzung um wesentliche Fragen unserer Gesellschaft.'[20]

Interessant – damals von mir allerdings nicht weiter verfolgt – ist, dass die Bedeutung der Rezeption als textanalytischer Kategorie fast gleichzeitig in Ost- und Westdeutschland entdeckt wurde.[21] Ein frühes Indiz dafür, dass vielleicht doch nie soweit voneinander entfernt war, was jetzt unter großen Mühen zusammenwächst?

Redekers Definition der Literatur als ein Modell, das Erfahrungen im quasi spielerischen Kontext vermittelt, und seine Forderung, bei der Textanalyse nicht nur die Semantik im Blick zu haben, sondern die komplexe pragmatische Dimension eines literarischen Kunstwerks, faszinierte mich. Versprach sie doch einen objektiveren, ideologiefreieren Zugang zu meinem Untersuchungsgegenstand allein

schon deshalb, weil sie die spezifischen Produktions- und Rezeptions-
bedingungen jedes Textes angemessen zu berücksichtigen schien.
Modellhaft-exemplarisch sollte dieses Verfahren an einer Analyse von
Hermann Kants Roman *Die Aula* erprobt werden.

Aus arbeitspraktischen Gründen und aus Gründen einer ebenso
schmalen wie zufälligen Datenbasis konnte mein Versuch, die
pragmatische Dimensionen von Kants Roman – d.h. Produktions-
bedingungen, Textstruktur und Rezeption – in der Analyse zusam-
menzuführen, bestenfalls zur Simulation eines Verfahrens geraten.
Grundlage waren Leserbriefe an den Autor, Ergebnisse einer Umfrage
in Berliner Bibliotheken, Protokolle zweier Diskussionen in Betriebskulturgruppen und eine an der PH Magdeburg entstandene literatur-
soziologische Examensarbeit. So spärlich das zur Verfügung stehende
Material war, so entschieden geriet mir das Fazit der Arbeit: 'Im
Gegensatz zur Sprachlosigkeit moderner bürgerlicher Literatur ist die
aktuelle sozialistische Literatur auf breite Verständlichkeit aus. Sie ist
gesellschaftlich und kommunikationsfördernd'. *Die Aula* stand für
mich in der Tradition einer bürgerlich-aufklärerischen Literatur
(Diderot, Heine, Heinrich Mann), die in literarischen Mischformen die
didaktischen Potenzen der offenen Form und der journalistischen
Sprache nutzte. In vergleichbarer Weise erschienen mir die Debatten
um Strittmatters *Bienkopp* und Christa Wolfs *Der geteilte Himmel*
exemplarisch für einen – nicht länger durch die Kultur-Bürokratie
unterdrückten – Austausch der Schreibenden und der Lesenden.

Alte Interessen – Neue Einsichten

Äußere Umstände (Schuldienst, andere Akzentuierung der universi-
tären Arbeit) zwangen mich, das Thema fast zehn Jahre auf sich beru-
hen zu lassen. Als ich es danach wieder aufgriff, kamen mir zumindest
die Basiskenntnisse über den Literaturbetrieb der DDR zunutze, die
ich 1970 angefangen hatte zu sammeln. Außerdem konnte ich auf ein
sehr viel breiteres Angebot an unterstützender Sekundärliteratur
zurückgreifen. Die durch den Grundlagenvertrag besiegelte Normal-
isierung der Verhältnisse zwischen den beiden deutschen Staaten
schloss offensichtlich auch die Literaturwissenschaft ein. Das Thema
DDR-Literatur war unter bundesdeutschen Germanisten hoffähig
geworden. Obgleich es nicht gerade im Mittelpunkt der Forschungen
zur deutschen Gegenwartsliteratur stand, waren zwischen 1971 und

1981 in der Bundesrepublik eine ganze Reihe wichtiger, zum Teil auch grundlegende und neue Perspektiven eröffnender Arbeiten erschienen. 1970 unterschied Peter Demetz in seiner 'kritischen Einführung in die Deutsche Literatur seit 1945' vier 'literarische Szenen': Schweiz, Österreich, DDR und Bundesrepublik.[22] In den Folgejahren erschienen kurz hintereinander vier Gesamtdarstellungen zur DDR-Literatur, denen – bei allen konzeptuellen Unterschieden – gemeinsam war, dass sie ihren Gegenstand als Faktum akzeptierten und ernst nahmen. Konrad Frankes Buch über *Die Literatur der DDR* verharrte größtenteils noch in deskriptiver Faktizität, hatte aber unschätzbare Qualitäten als Nachschlage-Werk und Kompendium.[23] Werner Brettschneiders Untersuchung *Zwischen literarischer Autonomie und Staatsdienst*[24] strafte den polemischen Titel auf erfreuliche Weise Lügen: auch wenn Brettschneiders Phasenmodell etwas forciert wirkte, hatte er doch als erster westdeutscher Germanist gründlich und sachlich die Literatur der DDR und ihre Entstehungsbedingungen nachgezeichnet. Seine – damals von Behn und Kähler[25] heftig kritisierte – These, die DDR-Autoren hätten sich allmählich von staatlicher Gängelung befreit und ihre Texte seien gesellschaftsneutraler, 'literarisch autonom' geworden, wurde durch die Entwicklung der folgenden Jahrzehnte bestätigt. Hans-Dietrich Sanders *Geschichte der schönen Literatur in der DDR*[26] dagegen befasste sich, dem Titel zum Trotz, vor allem mit den Auswirkungen der DDR-Kulturpolitik und war zudem in einer Weise polemisch, die die Einflüsse des ausklingenden Kalten Krieges nicht verleugnen konnte. Fritz J. Raddatz' *Materialien zur Literatur der DDR*[27] blieben eine Sammlung – kenntnisreicher, anregender – Zeitungs-Essays, die sich nur äußerlich durch Buchumschlag und umfangreichen bibliografischen Apparat als systematische Darstellung gerierten.

Den Beginn einer neuen Qualität der Auseinandersetzung mit der DDR-Literatur signalisierten Manfred Jägers Studien über *Funktion und Selbstverständnis der Schriftsteller in der DDR*.[28] Im Mittelpunkt standen Autoren und ihre Texte; Auswahlkriterium war nicht potentielle Nutzbarkeit im Kalten Krieg, sondern die Funktion für die Leser. Gerade dadurch, dass Jäger Anspruch und Entstehungsbedingungen dieser Literatur ernst nahm, öffnete er den Blick für eine bislang wenig gesehene Dimension der DDR-Literatur: ihre Funktion und Bedeutung auch für westdeutsche Leser.

Jäger durchbricht damit ausdrücklich auf der programmatischen Ebene ein inter-
pretatives Verfahren, das in der differenzierten Deskription literarischer Entwick-
lungen der DDR-Prosa sich bescheidet. [...] vertritt er die These, die DDR-
Literatur werde nur 'in erster Linie für DDR-Bürger geschrieben'. Den Praxis-
bezug zum Erfahrungsbereich des Rezipienten in der BRD versucht Jäger mit der
Hindeutung auf die gemeinsamen Probleme der Leser in der BRD und der DDR
herzustellen.[29]

Voraussetzung für diese – vor allem in Jägers Christa Wolf-Interpre-
tationen artikulierte – Position war eine profunde Kenntnis der
Zusammenhänge und Hintergründe. Heinz Blumensaths und Christel
Uebachs *Einführung in die Literaturgeschichte der DDR*,[30] konzipiert
als Unterrichtsmodell für die Sekundarstufe II, reichte weit darüber
hinaus, und war im Grunde die erste umfassende Einführung in die
DDR-Literatur auf der Basis von Quellen, Dokumenten und Hinter-
grundinformationen. Hervorragend ergänzt wurde sie durch die im
selben Verlag erschienene, von Hans-Jürgen Schmitt herausgegebene,
Einführung in Theorie, Geschichte und Funktion der DDR-Literatur,[31]
eine Sammlung von Einzelbeiträgen, die sich zu einem vorläufigen
Gesamtbild der DDR-Literatur, ihrer kulturpolitischen Voraussetzungen und ihrer gesellschaftlichen Funktionen zusammenfügten.
Ähnliches leistete auch das Bändchen von Peter Uwe Hohendahl und
Patricia Herminghouse, das Vorträge eines Symposiums mit amerikanischen und deutschen Germanisten zusammenfasste.[32] Der unauf-
geregte Blick von außen hat auch in der Folgezeit manches zur Versachlichung der Diskussion beigetragen.[33] Bis weit in die achtziger
Jahre hinein waren es vorwiegend Symposien außerhalb Deutschlands, auf denen sich west- und ostdeutsche Germanisten über Gegenwartsliteratur austauschen konnten. In der DDR selbst begegnete man
einschlägig interessierten westdeutschen Kollegen in der Regel mit
einem Misstrauen, das nur teilweise als Spätfolge der Knüppelger-
manistik des Kalten Krieges erklärbar war.

In der zweiten Hälfte der siebziger und zu Beginn der achtziger
Jahre spiegelt sich ein neues, seriöseres Interesse an der DDR-Literatur in einer ganzen Reihe von Dissertationen wider. Besonders hervorzuheben ist Manfred Behns breitangelegte Untersuchung zur Rezeption der DDR-Literatur durch die bundesrepublikanische Germanistik;[34] daneben Spezialuntersuchungen von Gottfried Pareigis, Volker
Gransow, Eberhard Mannack, Jochen Staadt, Manfred Bock[35] sowie
ein von Karl Lamers herausgegebener Sammelband.[36] Hans-Jürgen
Schmitt legte mit Band 11 der Hanserschen *Sozialgeschichte der*

deutschen Literatur eine neue Gesamtdarstellung vor;[37] auch das sehr präzise Einleitungskapitel von Peter Weisbrods *Untersuchungen zum literarischen Wandel in der DDR*[38] kommt einer kompakten Gesamtdarstellung nahe. Und, *last but not least*, das bis heute gültige Standardwerk Wolfgang Emmerichs.[39]

Biografische Zäsuren und neue, kontroversere und dadurch auch anregender gewordene Forschungen zur DDR-Literatur haben schließlich dazu beigetragen, den 'Rauchvorhang' meiner eigenen Projektionen vor dem Untersuchungsgegenstand zu zerreißen. Im Rahmen eines Vorlesungsprojektes zur deutschen Nachkriegsliteratur an der Universität Essen wandte ich mich Ende der 1970er Jahre noch einmal Hermann Kant zu. Meine Mutmaßung, Kants Romane signalisierten den Beginn der Literaturgesellschaft, hielt einer exakten – sozialgeschichtlich unterfütterten – Textanalyse nicht länger stand. Eine Konfrontation seiner Texte mit realsozialistischen Schlüsselideologien enthüllte bei genauem Hinsehen den apologetischen, herrschaftssichernden Charakter dieser Literatur. Besonders stark trat das Legitimatorische von Kants Schreiben in seinem zweiten Roman *Das Impressum* zutage, aber auch meine wohlwollende Einschätzung der *Aula* musste ich revidieren. Damals von mir enthusiastisch gewertete Leserurteile waren offenkundig weniger Ausdruck eines neuen, sozialistischen Lektürebewusstseins als Indiz für undistanziert-identifikatorische Lektüre. Die unterstellten kommunikativen Vorzüge des Textes funktionierten nur solange, wie die Leser mit den ihnen unterbreiteten Kommunikations- und Mitgestaltungsangeboten prinzipiell übereinstimmten. Abweichende Erfahrungen, abweichende Zukunftsperspektiven gar, wurden implizit diffamiert durch einen Gestus, der den Erzählerstandpunkt für unwiderlegbar gut, weil historisch richtig ausgab, und der so die scheinbare Modernität des Textes als Ornament und Staffage decouvrierte.

Mittels einer Art sozialhistorisch gestützter Immanenz, wie ich meinen methodischen Zugriff provisorisch nennen will, konnten die in der Examens-Arbeit von 1970 aus einer forcierten Adaption rezeptionsästhetischer Theorien abgeleiteten Thesen zum sozialistischen Roman überprüft und revidiert werden. Nicht mit dem endlich Literatur gewordenen Programm einer demokratisierten Kultur hatten wir es hier zu tun, sondern mit einer aus den Besonderheiten der DDR für ihre LeserInnen entstandenen Literatur. In der *Aula* werden, wie in kaum einem zeitgenössischen Roman sonst, die Entstehungs-Bedingungen eines kulturellen Biotops – das in den Folgejahren mehr und mehr zum künstlich beatmeten Gewächshaus verkam – thematisiert. Hier wird die Herkunft der realsozialistischen Funktionsträger aus der jüngsten deutschen Geschichte erklärt – und so zugleich ihr Privileg im sozialistischen Alltag gerechtfertigt. Kants Werke schreiben die Geschichte der Funktionselite der DDR; das ist eine authentische Leistung, aber keine neue Literatur.

Zu einem neuen methodischen Zugriff

Jene in der frühen westdeutschen Forschungsliteratur gepflegte Kalte-Kriegs-Animosität gegen DDR-Literatur, die mich einst zu wohlwollendem Enthusiasmus provoziert hatte, und ebendieser hatten sich im Lauf der Jahre gegenseitig neutralisiert. Jetzt konnte an ihre Stelle eine – näherungsweise – vorurteilsfreie Betrachtung treten, in deren Zentrum der Text stand. Nicht als Objekt antiquierter Philologie, sondern als Anlass für genaues Lesen, dem sich die zahllosen – im hermetischen Literaturbetrieb der DDR besonders wichtigen – intertextuellen Referenzen genauso erschlossen wie jene Bezüge zur zeitgenössischen westdeutschen Literatur, die einer ausschließlich auf den Spezialfall DDR-Literatur fixierten Betrachtungsweise verborgen geblieben waren.

Was mich interessierte, war eine Art deutsch-deutscher Komparatistik, die gleichwohl die Besonderheiten ihres Gegenstandes mit reflektierte. Den Anfang bildete eine 1981 begonnene, nicht abgeschlossene und nicht publizierte Untersuchung über 'Aussteigerfiguren' in der neueren DDR-Prosa. Sie zeigte, dass in den siebziger Jahren die Unangepasstheit zu einem wichtigen Handlungs-Movens literarischer Figuren geworden war. Gerti Tetzners *Karen W.* (1974), die den Widerspruch zwischen ihren eigenen Hoffnungen und den Anpassungsstrategien ihres Lebensgefährten nicht länger hinnimmt und in einem schmerzhaften Erfahrungs-Prozess neue Lebensperspektiven sucht, Klaus Schlesingers Kotte (*Alte Filme*, 1975), der – weil ihm Kraft zur radikalen Alternative fehlen – wenigstens am Wochenende aus dem gewohnten Trott ausbricht, vor allem aber Jurek Beckers Karl Simrock (*Schlaflose Tage*, 1978), der planmäßig, radikal und rücksichtslos (gegenüber sich und anderen) Alternativen zum gesicherten Alltag als Familienvater und Lehrer sucht und praktiziert – sie alle sind, wie auch Plenzdorfs Edgar Wibeau (*Die neuen Leiden des jungen W.*, 1972), typische literarische Handlungsträger der 70er Jahre. Ihre strukturelle Verwandtschaft zu den Nonkonformisten-Figuren der westdeutschen Literatur der fünfziger und sechziger Jahre (bei Gerd Gaiser, Wolfgang Koeppen, Heinrich Böll oder Martin Walser) ist unübersehbar. Dennoch sind sie genuine Produkte einer Gesellschaft, deren Paradoxien das Etikett 'real existierender Sozialismus' präzise benennt. Rudolf Bahro hatte diese Paradoxien in seiner Studie *Die Alternative*[40] beschrieben und dort die These von einem 'überschüssigen Bewusstsein' formuliert, das diese Gesellschaftsformation mit der zunehmenden Spezialisierung der Individuen erzeuge: Bewusstsein, das nicht funktional eingebunden sei in den gesellschaftlichen Reproduktionsprozess und deshalb auch nicht durch den Arbeitsprozess absorbiert werden könne, sondern das Potenzen freisetze, die sich teils als 'kompensatorische Interessen' (z.B. in der für die späte DDR charakteristische Freizeit- und Nischenkultur) artikulierten, teils aber auch als 'emanzipatorische Interessen'. Wenn Beckers Hauptfigur mit ihren geplanten Ausbrüchen den Zentralgedanken Bahros nachgerade zu illustrieren scheint, so ist das weniger ein Beleg für philosophische Einflüsse auf die Literatur als ein Indiz für jene gesellschaftskritische Dimension, die gute DDR-Literatur spätestens seit den siebziger Jahren auszeichnete.

Mit dieser Entwicklung korrespondierte eine wachsende Bedeutung der DDR-Literatur auf dem westdeutschen Literaturmarkt und eine rapide anschwellende Zahl einschlägiger literaturwissenschaftlicher Veröffentlichungen. Bis heute aktuell sind Wolfgang Emmerichs Studien;[41] sie nehmen Texte, Entstehungs- und Distributionsbedingungen gleichermaßen ernst. Mit Einzelinterpretationen, die eingebettet sind in eine präzise Beschreibung der Kulturpolitik, gelingt ihm das Kunststück, einer Literatur, die jahrzehntelang im öffentlichen Bewusstsein nur als Politikum wahrgenommen worden war, als Literatur gerecht zu werden. Emmerichs Methode schließt Einsichten in die landestypischen Bedingungen der Erzeugung und Verbreitung dieser Literatur nicht aus, verhindert aber, dass die Texte hinter vordergründiger politischer Neugier verschwinden. Sein Verfahren, einzelne Werke aus ihren Entstehungsbedingungen heraus zu erklären, hat auch mich bestärkt in meinen Versuchen, die literarischen Qualitäten der DDR-Prosa aus sich selbst und ihrem Kontext heraus verstehen und nachzeichnen zu wollen – und sie so in Schutz zu nehmen vor einem auch in den achtziger Jahren noch populären und nach dem Ende der DDR neu in Mode gekommenen soziologischen Scheininteresse an Literatur.

Aus dem Gesagten ergibt sich, dass eine verlässliche Gesamtdarstellung der DDR-Literatur im heute immer noch andauernden Vereinigungswirrwarr nicht weniger problematisch wäre als sie es im Klima des Kalten Krieges war. Es müssen wohl noch einige Jahre ins Land gehen, um Verletzungen vernarben zu lassen und Verwerfungen zu glätten, bevor ein angemessenes Bild jener Literatur gezeichnet werden kann, für die ja nicht nur ihre vormoderne Biederkeit charakteristisch ist, sondern auch ihr für die zweite Hälfte des 20. Jahrhunderts außerordentlich hoher Rangplatz im gesellschaftlichen Alltag. In der Zwischenzeit sollten wir die Zugangsmöglichkeiten zu Akten und Archiven weniger zu spektakulären Enthüllungen nutzen als zur Sammlung und Addition von Einsichten. Bausteine zu einer Gesamtdarstellung können solche Arbeiten insofern sein, als sie – mit durchaus exemplarischem Anspruch – Themen- und Problemkreise fokussieren und helfen, bekannte Fakten in komplexeren Zusammenhängen neu begreifen.

Anmerkungen

[1] Erwin Pracht, 'Probleme des künstlerisch-realistischen Schaffens', *Deutsche Zeitschrift für Philosophie*, 11 (1963), 956-77 (hier: 976 und 974).

[2] Lothar von Balluseck, *Dichter im Dienst. Der sozialistische Realismus in der deutschen Literatur*, Wiesbaden: Limes, 1963.

[3] Ebd., S. 134.

[4] Peter Jokostra, 'Zur Situation der Dichtung in Mitteldeutschland', *Merkur*, 149:7 (1960), 680-687 (hier: 682).

[5] Marcel Reich-Ranicki, *Deutsche Literatur in West und Ost*, München: Piper, 1963.

[6] Jörg Bernhard Bilke, 'Auf den Spuren der Wirklichkeit. DDR-Literatur: Traditionen, Tendenzen, Möglichkeiten', *Der Deutschunterricht*, 21:5 (1969), 24-60.

[7] Hermann Pongs, *Dichtung im gespaltenen Deutschland*, Stuttgart: Union Verlag, 1966.

[8] Ebd. S. 5.

[9] Ebd., S. 418.

[10] Ebd., S. 6.

[11] Vgl. Autorenkollektiv soz. Literaturwissenschaftler Westberlin, *Zum Verhältnis von Ökonomie, Politik und Literatur im Klassenkampf. Grundlagen einer historisch-materialistischen Literaturwissenschaft*, Berlin (West): Oberbaum Verlag, 1971, S. 184ff.

[12] Gelesen habe ich u.a. Romane von Bruno Apitz, Marianne Bruns, Karl Heinz Jakobs, Erik Neutsch, Brigitte Reimann, Max Walter Schulz, Anna Seghers, Erwin Strittmatter und Christa Wolf. – Uwe Johnson, den ich ebenfalls damals las, zählte ich zur westdeutschen Moderne.

[13] Texte der Expressionismusdebatte – sowie Ernst Bloch und Hanns Eisler: *Die Kunst zu erben* (1938); Bertolt Brecht: *Volkstümlichkeit und Realismus* (1958); Maxim Gorki: *Über sowjetische Literatur* (1934); W.I. Lenin: *Parteiorganisation und Parteiliteratur* (1905); Mao Tse-tung: *Reden zur Literatur und Kunst* (1942); Leo Trotzkij: *Literatur und Revolution* (1924).

[14] Horst Redeker, *Abbildung und Aktion. Versuch über die Dialektik des Realismus*, Halle/Saale: Mitteldeutscher Verlag, 1966.

[15] Ebd., S. 81.

[16] Ebd., S. 78.

[17] Ebd., S. 85.

[18] Ebd., S. 94.

[19] Ebd., S. 115.

[20] Ebd., S. 125.

[21] Vgl. Hans Robert Jauss, *Literaturgeschichte als Provokation der Literaturwissenschaft*, Konstanz: Universitätsverlag, 1967.

[22] Peter Demetz, *Die süße Anarchie. Deutsche Literatur seit 1945. Eine kritische Einführung*, Frankfurt/Main, Berlin: Propyläen-Verlag, 1970, S. 13-69.

[23] Konrad Franke, *Die Literatur der DDR*, München: Kindler, 1971.

[24] Werner Brettschneider, *Zwischen literarischer Autonomie und Staatsdienst. Die Literatur der DDR*, Berlin (West): Erich Schmidt, 1972.

[25]   Manfred Behn, *DDR-Literatur in der Bundesrepublik Deutschland. Die Rezeption der epischen DDR-Literatur in der BRD 1961-1975*, Meisenheim am Glan: Hain, 1977, S. 78ff. und Hermann Kähler, *Der kalte Krieg der Kritiker. Zur antikommunistischen Kritik an der DDR-Literatur*, Berlin (Ost): Akademie-Verlag, 1974, S. 92.

[26]   Hans-Dietrich Sander, *Geschichte der schönen Literatur in der DDR. Ein Grundriss*, Freiburg: Rombach, 1972.

[27]   Fritz J. Raddatz, *Traditionen und Tendenzen. Materialien zur Literatur der DDR*, Frankfurt/Main: Suhrkamp, 1972.

[28]   Manfred Jäger, *Sozialliteraten. Funktion und Selbstverständnis der Schriftsteller in der DDR*, Düsseldorf: Bertelsmann Universitätsverlag, 1973.

[29]   Behn, *DDR-Literatur in der Bundesrepublik Deutschland*, S. 103.

[30]   Heinz Blumensath und Christel Uebach, *Einführung in die Literaturgeschichte der DDR. Ein Unterrichtsmodell*, Stuttgart: Metzler, 1975.

[31]   Hans-Jürgen Schmitt, Hg., *Einführung in Theorie, Geschichte und Funktion der DDR-Literatur*, Stuttgart: Metzler, 1975.

[32]   Peter Uwe Hohendahl und Patricia Herminghouse, Hg., *Literatur und Literaturtheorie in der DDR*, Frankfurt/Main: Suhrkamp, 1976.

[33]   Vgl. die von Ian Wallace herausgegebene Zeitschrift *GDR Monitor*; Dennis Tate, *The East German Novel*, Bath: University of Bath Press, 1984; James H. Reid, *Writing Without Taboos. The New East German Literature*, New York, Oxford, München: Berg, 1990.

[34]   Manfred Behn, *DDR-Literatur in der Bundesrepublik Deutschland*.

[35]   Gottfried Pareigis, *Kritische Analyse der Realitätsdarstellung in ausgewählten Werken der 'Bitterfelder Wegs'*, Kronberg: Athenäum, 1974; Volker Gransow, *Kulturpolitik in der DDR*, Berlin (West): Spiess, 1975; Eberhard Mannack, *Zwei deutsche Literaturen? Zu Günter Grass, Uwe Johnson, Hermann Kant, Ulrich Plenzdorf und Christa Wolf. Mit einer Bibliographie der Schönen Literatur in der DDR (1968 - 1974)*, Kronberg: Athenäum, 1977; Jochen Staadt, *Konfliktbewusstsein und sozialistischer Anspruch in der DDR-Literatur. Zur Darstellung gesellschaftlicher Widersprüche in Romanen nach dem VIII. Parteitag der SED 1971*, Berlin (West): Spiess, 1977; Stephan Bock, *Literatur Gesellschaft Nation. Materielle und ideelle Rahmenbedingungen der frühen DDR-Literatur (1949-1956)*, Stuttgart: Metzler, 1980.

[36]   Karl Lamers, Hg., *Die deutsche Teilung im Spiegel der Literatur. Beiträge zur Literatur und Germanistik der DDR*, Stuttgart: Verlag Bonn Aktuell, 1978.

[37] Hans-Jürgen Schmitt, *Die Literatur der DDR*, München: Hanser, 1983.

[38] Peter Weisbrod, *Literarischer Wandel in der DDR. Untersuchungen zur Entwicklung der Erzählliteratur in den siebziger Jahren*, Heidelberg: Groos, 1980, S. 1-23.

[39] Wolfgang Emmerich, *Kleine Literaturgeschichte der DDR*, Darmstadt, Neuwied: Luchterhand, 1981; erweiterte Neuausgaben Leipzig: Kiepenheuer, 1996 und Berlin: Aufbau, 2000.

[40] Rudolf Bahro, *Die Alternative. Zur Kritik des real existierenden Sozialismus*, Köln, Frankfurt/Main: Europäischer Verlagsanstalt, 1977, S. 407ff.

[41] Wolfgang Emmerich, *Die andere deutsche Literatur. Aufsätze zur Literatur der DDR*, Opladen: Westdeutscher Verlag, 1994.

Dennis Tate: List of Publications

1. Authored Monographs

Shifting Perspectives: East German Autobiographical Narratives Before and After the End of the GDR, Rochester, NY: Camden House, 2007.

Franz Fühmann: Innovation and Authenticity. A Study of his Prose-Writing, Amsterdam: Rodopi, 1995.

The East German Novel: Identity, Community, Continuity, Bath and New York: Bath University Press/ St Martin's Press, 1984.

2. Edited Volumes

Twenty Years On. Competing Memories of the GDR in Postunification German Culture, ed. with Renate Rechtien, Rochester, NY: Camden House, 2011.

German Life Writing in the Twentieth Century, ed. with Birgit Dahlke and Roger Woods, Rochester, NY: Camden House, 2010.

Dislocation and Reorientation: Exile, Division and the End of Communism in German Culture and Politics. In Honour of Ian Wallace (German Monitor, 71), ed. with Axcl Goodbody and Pól Ó Dochartaigh, Amsterdam: Rodopi, 2009.

Views from Abroad: Die DDR aus britischer Perspektive, ed. with Peter Barker and Marc-Dietrich Ohse, Bielefeld: Bertelsmann, 2007.

Heiner Müller: Probleme und Perspektiven (Amsterdamer Beiträge zur neueren Germanistik, 48), ed. with Gerd Labroisse and Ian Wallace, Amsterdam: Rodopi, 2000.

Günter de Bruyn in Perspective (German Monitor, 44), Amsterdam: Rodopi, 1999.

Geist und Macht: Writers and the State in the German Democratic Republic (German Monitor, 29), ed. with Axel Goodbody, Amsterdam: Rodopi, 1992.

Günter de Bruyn: Märkische Forschungen (Manchester New German Texts), Manchester: Manchester University Press, 1990.

European Socialist Realism, ed. with Michael Scriven, Oxford and New York: Berg, 1988.

3. Journal Articles and Book Chapters

'Introduction: The Importance and Diversity of Cultural Memory in the GDR Context', in: Renate Rechtien and Dennis Tate, eds, *Twenty Years On. Competing Memories of the GDR in Postunification German Culture*, Rochester, NY: Camden House, 2011, pp. 1-19.

'Schicht um Schicht – The Evolution of Fred Wander's Life Writing Project in the GDR Era and Beyond', in: Birgit Dahlke, Dennis Tate and Roger Woods, eds, *German Life Writing in the Twentieth Century*, Rochester, NY: Camden House, 2010, pp. 164-78.

'Brandenburg as a "Spiritual Way of Life"? Günter de Bruyn and the Appeal of Living "Off the Beaten Track"', in: David Clarke and Renate Rechtien, eds, *The Politics of Place in Post-War Germany: Essays in Literary Criticism*, Lewiston: Mellen Press, 2009, pp. 197-215.

'"Von der Fröhlichkeit im Schrecken": Fred Wander's Celebration of Dislocation', in: Axel Goodbody, Pól Ó Dochartaigh and Dennis Tate, eds, *Dislocation and Reorientation: Exile, Division and the End of Communism in German Culture and Politics. In Honour of Ian Wallace* (German Monitor, 71), Amsterdam: Rodopi, 2009, pp. 197-208.

'"Böhme[n] am Meer", "Bohemien mit Heimweh": Franz Fühmann's Competing Identities and his Tribute to "Tonio Kröger"', in: Nigel Harris and Joanne Sayner, eds, *The Text and its Context: Studies in Modern German Literature and Society. Presented to Ronald Speirs on the Occasion of his 65th Birthday*, Oxford: Lang, 2008, pp. 289-301.

'Das Ende des "Literaturstreits" und die Rehabilitierung der autobiografischen Prosa ostdeutscher Schriftsteller in der Berliner Republik', in: Peter Barker, Marc-Dietrich Ohse and Dennis Tate, eds, *Views from Abroad: Die DDR aus britischer Perspektive*, Bielefeld: Bertelsmann, 2007, pp. 53-64.

'Angelsächsische Forschungen: Günter de Bruyn in der englisch-sprachigen Welt', in: Lothar Jordan, ed., *'Und doch gleicht keines der Dörfer dem anderen': 80 Seiten von und zu Günter de Bruyn*, Frank-furt/Oder: Kleist Museum, 2006, pp. 41-6.

'War as a "God-damned Crusade": The Continuing Significance of Stefan Heym's "The Crusaders"', in: Dirk Göttsche and Franziska Meyer, eds, *Schreiben gegen Krieg und Gewalt: Ingeborg Bachmann und die deutschsprachige Literatur 1945–1980*, Göttingen: V&R Uni-press, 2006, pp. 119-30.

'"Ich wer ist das" – Dropping the Mask of Ambiguity? The Autobiographical Thrust of Heiner Müller's Late Writing', in: Hermann Rasche and Christiane Schönfeld, eds, *Denkbilder. Fest-schrift für Eoin Bourke*, Würzburg: Königshausen und Neumann, 2004, pp. 266-76.

'"[...] vielleicht nur für Franz geschrieben": Volker Braun's Intertextual Tributes to his Special Relationship with Franz Fühmann', in: Rolf Jucker, ed., *Volker Braun in Perspective*, Amsterdam: Rod-opi, 2004, pp. 71-90.

'Travelling on the S-Bahn: German border crossings before and after unification', in: Peter Wagstaff, ed., *Border Crossings: Mapping Identities in Modern Europe*, Oxford: Lang, 2004, pp. 81-104.

'Uwe Johnson's Awkward Legacy: A Sympathetic Secret Policeman of the Pre-"Stasi" Era', in: Paul Cooke and Andrew Plowman, eds, *Writers and The Politics of Culture: Dealing with the Stasi*, Basing-stoke: Palgrave, 2003, pp. 25-40.

'Ein nicht anerkannter britischer Durchbruch: Franz Fühmanns Beitrag zum Erfolg des Films "Der Schwur des Soldaten Pooley"', in: Brigitte Krüger, ed., *'Dichter sein heißt aufs Ganze aus sein' – Zugänge zu Poetologie und Werk Franz Fühmanns*, Frankfurt/Main: Lang, 2003, pp. 201-17.

'The End of Autobiography? The Older Generation of East German Authors Take Stock', in: Martin Kane (ed.), *Legacies and Identity: East and West German Responses to Unification*, Martin Kane, Oxford: Lang, 2002, pp. 11-26.

'Border Crossings and Walls in Heads: German Culture since Unification' (inaugural lecture, April 2001). Occasional Paper 13, European Research Institute, University of Bath, at: http://www.bath.ac.uk/eri/pdf/op-tate.pdf (accessed 2 August 2011).

'A Pioneering Work of Autobiographical Fiction or a Travesty of the Biographical Facts? Stephan Hermlin's "Abendlicht"', in: Wolfgang Müller, Christine Cosentino and Wolfgang Ertl, eds, *Bestandsaufnahme: Deutsche Literatur zehn Jahre nach der Vereinigung* (*glossen*, 10, 2000), at: http://www2.dickinson.edu/glossen/heft10/tate.html (accessed 2 August 2011).

'"Mehr Freiheit zur Wahrheit": The Fictionalisation of Adolesencent Experience in Christoph Hein's "Von allem Anfang an"', in: Bill Niven and David Clarke, eds, *Christoph Hein*, Cardiff: University of Wales Press, 2000, pp. 117-34.

'Changing Perspectives on Günter de Bruyn: An Introduction', in: Dennis Tate, ed., *Günter de Bruyn in Perspective* (German Monitor, 44), Amsterdam: Rodopi, 1999, pp. 1-8.

Contributions to the *Encyclopedia of Contemporary German Culture*, ed. John Sandford, London: Routledge, 1999. Consultant editor and author of forty-five entries, including 'Berliner Ensemble', 'Günter de Bruyn', 'Censorship: GDR', 'Deutsches Theater', 'Drama: GDR', 'Franz Fühmann', 'Christoph Hein', 'Hermann Kant', 'Der deutsch-deutsche Literaturstreit', 'Georg Lukács', 'Myth', 'Ulrich Plenzdorf',

'Prose fiction: GDR', 'Publishing: GDR', 'Socialist Realism', 'Writers' Congresses: GDR', 'Writers' Union of the GDR'.

'A History Full of Holes? France and the French Resistance in the Work of Stephan Hermlin', in: Helmut Peitsch, Charles Burdett and Claire Gorarra, eds, *European Memories of the Second World War*, New York and Oxford: Berghahn, 1999, pp. 55-66.

'The Spectre of the Apocalypse in the Work of Franz Fühmann', in: Axel Goodbody, ed., *Literatur und Ökologie* (Amsterdamer Beiträge zur neueren Germanistik, 43), Amsterdam: Rodopi, 1998, pp. 257-70.

'Fühmanns heimliche Odyssee: Die Rezeption von James Joyce in seinem Werk', in: Brigitte Krüger, Margrid Bircken and Helmut John, eds, *Jeder hat seinen Fühmann: Zugänge zu Poetologie und Werk Franz Fühmanns*, Frankfurt/Main: Lang, 1998, pp. 185-96.

'Keeping the Biermann Affair in Perspective: Repression, Resistance and the Articulation of Despair', in: Robert Atkins and Martin Kane, eds, *Retrospect and Review: Aspects of the Literature of the GDR 1976–1990* (German Monitor, 40), Amsterdam: Rodopi, 1997, pp. 1-15.

'Günter de Bruyn: The "gesamtdeutsche Konsensfigur" of Post-unification Literature?', *German Life and Letters*, 50:2 (1997), 201-13.

'Delusions of Grandeur and Oedipal guilt: Franz Fühmann's Greek Experience as the Focus of his War Stories', in: Hans Wagener, ed., *Von Böll bis Buchheim: Deutsche Kriegsprosa nach 1945* (Amsterdamer Beiträge zur neueren Germanistik, 42), Amsterdam: Rodopi, 1997, pp. 389-405.

'James Joyce and Socialist Realism: Modernist Awareness and Ideological Constraints in GDR literature', in Hilary Chung et al., ed., *In the Party Spirit: Socialist Realism and Literary Practice in the Soviet Union, East Germany and China*, Amsterdam: Rodopi, 1996, pp. 141-9.

'Unexpected Affinities: Johannes Bobrowski's "Boehlendorff" and Franz Fühmann's "Barlach in Güstrow" as Landmarks in the Early Evolution of GDR literature', in: John Wieczorek, ed., *Johannes Bobrowski (1917–1965)*, Reading: Centre for East German Studies, University of Reading, 1996, pp. 37-52.

'Writing in the Shadow of Auschwitz: The Moral Imperative at the Heart of East German Literature', in: Graham Bartram, Maurice Slawinski and David Steel, eds, *Reconstructing the Past: Representations of the Fascist Era in Postwar European Culture*, Keele: Keele University Press, 1995, pp. 118-34.

'The Failed Socialist Experiment: Culture in the GDR' (with Axel Goodbody and Ian Wallace), in: Rob Burns, ed., *German Cultural Studies: An Introduction*, Oxford: Oxford University Press, 1995, pp. 147-208.

'"...natürlich ein politischer Roman". "Märkische Forschungen" im Kontext der Honecker-Ära', in: Heinz Ludwig Arnold, ed., *Günter de Bruyn* (Text und Kritik, 127), Munich: edition text und kritik, 1995, pp. 84-91.

'Trapped in the Past? The Identity Problems of East German Writers since the "Wende"', in: Hans H. Jahn, ed., *Germany in the 1990s* (German Monitor, 33), Amsterdam: Rodopi, 1995, pp. 1-16.

'Undercover Odyssey: The Reception of James Joyce in the Work of Franz Fühmann', *German Life and Letters*, 47:3 (1994), 302-12.

'"Neue deutsche Literatur": The Forum of the Divided Nation', in: Rhys W. Williams, Stephen Parker and Colin Riordan, eds, *German Writers and the Cold War*, Manchester: Manchester University Press, 1992, pp. 47-64.

'The Sufferings of "Kamerad Fühmann": A Case of Distorted Reception in Both German States', in: Arthur Williams, Stuart Parkes and Roland Smith, eds, *German Literature at a Time of Change 1989–90*, Berne, Frankfurt and New York: Lang, 1991, pp. 285-98.

'Franz Fühmann: A Neglected Legacy', in: Martin Kane, ed., *Socialism and the Literary Imagination. Essays on East German Writers*, Oxford, New York and Munich: Berg, 1991, pp. 91-105.

'Subjective Authenticity in Franz Fühmann's Early Prose Writing', in: Margy Gerber et al., eds, *Studies in GDR Culture and Society. Selected papers from the Fifteenth New Hampshire Symposium on the German Democratic Republic*, Lanham, MD and New York: University Press of America, 1991, pp. 135-50.

'Max Schwedenow, the Identikit Romantic? Günter de Bruyn's "Märkische Forschungen"', in: Howard Gaskill, Karin McPherson and Andrew Barker, eds, *Neue Ansichten: The Reception of Romanticism in the Literature of the GDR* (GDR Monitor Special Series, 6), Amsterdam: Rodopi, 1990, pp. 27-40.

'The Socialist Metropolis? Images of East Berlin in the Literature of the GDR', in: Derek Glass, Dietmar Rösler and John J. White, eds, *Berlin – Literary Images of a City*, Berlin: Erich Schmidt, 1989, pp. 146-61.

'The "Other" German Literature: Convergence and Cross-fertilisation', in: Keith Bullivant, ed., *After the Death of Literature: West German Writing of the 1970s*, Oxford and New York: Berg, 1989, pp. 176-93.

'Joachim Walther: An Update', *GDR Monitor*, 20 (1989), pp. 81-2.

'"Breadth and Diversity": Socialist Realism in the GDR', in: Michael Scriven and Dennis Tate, eds, *European Socialist Realism*, Oxford and New York: Berg, 1988, pp. 60-78.

'Introduction' (with Michael Scriven), in: Scriven and Tate, eds, *European Socialist Realism*, pp. 1-10.

'The Novel in the GDR', in: Keith Bullivan, ed., *The Modern German Novel*, Leamington Spa and New York: Berg, 1987, pp. 3-18.

'Franz Fühmann als Lyriker und Förderer der Lyrik in der DDR', in: John L. Flood, ed., *'Ein Moment des erfahrenen Lebens' – Zur Lyrik der DDR*, Amsterdam: Rodopi, 1987, pp. 51-72.

'Beyond "Kulturpolitik": The GDR's established authors and the challenge of the l980s', in: Ian Wallace, ed., *The GDR in the 1980s* (GDR Monitor Special Series, 4), Dundee, 1984, pp. 15-29.

'"Ewige deutsche Misere"? GDR Authors and Büchner's "Lenz"', in: Graham Bartram and Anthony Waine, eds, *Culture and Society in the GDR* (GDR Monitor Special Series, 2), Dundee, 1984, pp. 85-99.

'Rediscovering Marx: The Coming of Age of East German Literature', *The Crane Bag*, 7:1 (1983), 13-16.

'Not Just an Irish Obsession? The Sense of Place in the Work of Seamus Heaney and Johannes Bobrowski', *Irland: Gesellschaft und Kultur*, 3 (1982), 304-17.

'Socialist Realism as an Agent of Protest: Stefan Heym's "Five Days in June"', *Times Higher Educational Supplement*, 11 February 1977.

'Community Under Scrutiny: The Short Story in Contemporary East German Writing', *Atlantis*, 6 (1973-74), 26-36.

Contributors

Peter Barker taught German Studies at the University of Reading until 2004. 2005-8 he was Senior Research Fellow at the University of Reading, and Director of the Centre for East German Studies 2002-6. He has published on the political history of the GDR, the PDS, and transformation processes in eastern Germany. His research on the Sorbian minority in Brandenburg and Saxony has been published in, among others, the monograph *Slavs in Germany: The Sorbian Minority and the German State since 1945* (2000).

David Clarke is Senior Lecturer in German at the University of Bath. He studied at the Universities of Leeds, London (UCL) and Swansea, and has taught at the Johannes-Gutenberg-Universität Mainz and Nottingham Trent University. He is the author of a book on the East German author Christoph Hein and has also published on GDR literature, contemporary German literature, German film, and cultural memory. Most recently, he edited the volume *Remembering the German Democratic Republic: Divided Memory in a United Germany* (with U. Wölfel, 2011).

Christine Cosentino is Professor II of German at Rutgers University. She received her PhD at Columbia University. She is co-founder and co-editor of the online journal *glossen*, a journal on contemporary German literature, film, and art. She is the author or editor of several books and numerous articles in U.S., Canadian, and European journals, primarily on the literature, cultural policies, and history of the GDR. She has also published on literature in the Federal Republic and unified Germany, as well as on Expressionism and lyric poetry.

Owen Evans is Senior Lecturer in Film and Television in the Media Department at Edge Hill University. He has published on GDR literature, German film and European cinema, including monographs on Günter de Bruyn and German literary biography, and recent articles on *Das Leben der Anderen* and *Sophie Scholl: Die letzten Tage*. He is co-founding editor of the international journals *Studies in European Cinema* and the *Journal of European Popular Culture*, and co-founding director of the European Cinema Research Forum (ECRF).

Axel Goodbody is Professor of German Studies and European Culture at the University of Bath. He studied German, French and English at Trinity College Dublin and the University of Kiel. He has published on Romantic and modern German literature, with a special focus on representations of nature and environment, and ecocritical theory (most recently *Ecocritical Theory. New European Approaches*, ed. with Kate Rigby, 2011). He was a founding member of the European Association for the Study of Literature, Culture and Environment, and its President 2004-6. He is Associate Editor of *Ecozon@. European Journal of Literature, Culture and Environment*.

Ute Hirsekorn completed her PhD on autobiographical texts of the GDR political elite in 2008 at the University of Nottingham. She is currently a Teaching Associate in the German Department in the School of Cultures, Languages and Area Studies, University of Nottingham. Her research interests include political autobiography and memoirs before and after German unification, and East German autobiographical texts after 1989. Her most recent publication is 'Thought Patterns and Explanatory Strategies in Life Writing of High Ranking GDR party Officials after the Wende' in Dahlke et al., *German Life Writing in the Twentieth Century* (2011).

Sara Jones completed her PhD at the University of Nottingham in 2008 with a dissertation on GDR cultural politics. In 2009, she was awarded a 3-year Leverhulme Early Career Fellowship to carry out a project analysing memories of the Stasi in different cultural artefacts. She is currently Research Fellow at the University of Birmingham, working cross-College in the Departments of Political Science and International Studies, and Modern Languages. She is author of *Complicity, Censorship and Criticism: Negotiating Space in the GDR Literary Sphere* (2011), and co-editor of *Writing under Socialism* (2011).

Martin Kane is the author of a study of George Grosz and Ernst Toller, and has written widely on postwar East and West German literature. He has edited three volumes of essays on the repercussions of the Wende – the latest being *Legacies and Identity. East and West German Literary Responses to Unification* (2002) – and translated works on Michael Schumacher (2003), the history of the SPD (2006), Karl Marx (2007) and agro-biodiversity in China (2011). His most recent scholarly publications have been on literary representations of the life and work of Ferdinand Lassalle.

Hannes Krauss studied German literature and history in Tübingen und West Berlin. He taught in secondary schools, before taking up a post as lecturer at the University of Essen in 1973. He retired in 2011. He has been a guest lecturer in Bergen, Edinburgh, Turin, Warsaw, Providence (USA) and at a number of Russian universities. His research focuses on contemporary German-language literature and the literature of the GDR. He has published studies of the work of, among others, Jurek Becker, Günter de Bruyn, Wilhelm Genazino, Christoph Hein, Brigitte Kronauer, Hans-Joachim Schädlich, Hans-Ulrich Treichel, Fred Wander, and Christa Wolf; also on GDR literature, modernism and the literature of German unification. He is editor of the reader '*Vom Nullpunkt zur Wende…*' (with A. Erb, 1994, 1999).

Georgina Paul is Fellow and Tutor in German at St Hilda's College, Oxford. She has published widely on the literature of the GDR and of GDR writers post-1990, on contemporary women's writing in German and on contemporary German poetry. She is co-editor (with Helmut Schmitz) of *Entgegenkommen. Dialogues with Barbara Köhler* (2000) and author of *Perspectives on Gender in Post-1945 German Literature* (2009). She is currently editing an essay collection on Barbara Köhler's 2007 Odyssey cycle, *Niemands Frau* (forthcoming 2013).

Helmut Peitsch is Professor of German at the University of Potsdam, holding the chair of Literature of the 19th and 20th centuries. Before moving to Potsdam, he was Professor of European Studies at Cardiff University (1994-2001) and Visiting Full Professor at New York University (1992-94). He was Lecturer at the Universities of Berlin, Leeds and Swansea. Recent publications include: (with Charles Burdett and Claire Gorrara) *European Memories of the Second World War* (2006), *Nachkriegsliteratur 1945-1989* (2009), (with Helen Thein) *Walter Boehlich: Die Antwort ist das Unglück der Frage. Ausgewählte Schriften* (2011), and *Walter Boehlich – Kritiker* (2011).

Andrew Plowman is Senior Lecturer in German at the University of Liverpool. His main research interests are autobiographical prose and German literature and film before and after unification. His recent publications include the volume *Divided but Not Disconnected: German Experiences of the Cold War* (2010, co-editor). He is currently completing a monograph study of the representation of the Bundeswehr in German culture after 1955.

Heinz-Peter Preußer taught at the Free University of Berlin and the University of Osnabrück, before moving to Bremen. His work ranges across modern and contemporary literature, aesthetics, media and film studies. Publications include *Mythos als Sinnkonstruktion. Die Antikenprojekte von Christa Wolf, Heiner Müller, Stefan Schütz und Volker Braun* (2000) and *Letzte Welten. Deutschsprachige Gegenwartsliteratur diesseits und jenseits der Apokalypse* (2003). He is (co-) editor of the volumes *Krieg in den Medien* (2005), *Kulturphilosophen als Leser. Porträts literarischer Lektüren* (2006), and *Amazonen. Kriegerische Frauen* (2010). Since 2006 he has edited the *Jahrbuch Literatur und Politik*, most recently Volume 6: *Alternde Avantgarden* (2011).

Renate Rechtien is Lecturer in German Studies, Department of Politics, Languages and International Studies, University of Bath, UK. Her main research interest is East German literature before and after unification, with a special focus on the writing of Christa Wolf. Her recent publications include *The Politics of Place in Postwar Germany: Essays in Literary Criticism* (co-edited, 2009), *Cityscapes of the German Democratic Republic* (special number of *German Life and Letters*, ed. 2010), and *Twenty Years On. Competing Memories of the GDR in Postunification German Culture* (co-editor, Camden House, 2011).

Joanne Sayner is Lecturer in Cultural Theory and German Studies at the University of Birmingham. She is author of *Women without a Past: German Autobiographical Writings and Fascism* (2007). Her research specialisms include the politics of memory in post war Germany, feminist theory, and autobiography. She is currently completing a book on antifascism in the former GDR entitled *Reframing Antifascism: Memory, Genre and the Life Writings of Greta Kuckhoff*.

Ricarda Schmidt is the author of *Westdeutsche Frauenliteratur in den 70er Jahren* (1982) and *Intermedialität bei E.T.A. Hoffmann*

(2006). She has published essays on Christa Wolf and other GDR writers, and (co-)edited *Heroes and Villains* (2002), *Literarische Wertung und Kanonbildung* (2007), and *Patterns of Knowledge in the 19th Century* (2010). Recent articles on Kleist include '"Odd Bodies": Kleists Körperdarstellungen' (2010), 'Performanz und Essentialismus von Geschlecht bei Kleist' (2011) and 'Die Penthesilea-Rezeption in der Moderne' (2012). A co-edited volume on *Violence in Kleist* is due to appear in 2012. She is Professor of German at the University of Exeter and principal investigator of an AHRC-funded project on *Kleist, Education and Violence. The Transformation of Ethics and Aesthetics.*

Index

SABINE FISCHER-KANIA / DANIEL SCHÄF (HG.)
SPRACHE UND LITERATUR IM SPANNUNGS-FELD VON POLITIK UND ÄSTHETIK
Christa Wolf zum 80. Geburtstag
2011 · ISBN 978-3-86205-029-1 · 274 S., kt. · EUR 27,—

CAROL TULLY (HRSG.)
ZEUGEN DER VERGANGENHEIT.
H.G. Adler – Franz Baermann Steiner. Briefwechsel 1936–1952
2011 · ISBN 978-3-86205-385-8 · 365 S., kt.. · EUR 36,—

MICHAEL EWERT / RENATE RIEDNER / SIMONE SCHIEDERMAIR (HRSG.)
DEUTSCH ALS FREMDSPRACHE UND LITERATURWISSENSCHAFT
Zugriffe, Themenfelder, Perspektiven

2011 · ISBN 978-3-86205-093-2 · 193 S., kt. · EUR 40,—

MARTIN LIEBSCHER / CHRISTOPHE FRICKER / ROBERT v. DASSANOWSKY (Eds.)
THE NAMEABLE AND THE UNNAMEABLE
Hofmannsthal's *Der Schwierige* Revisited

2011 · ISBN 978-3-86205-030-7 · 219 S., kt. · EUR 22,—

HILARIA GÖSSMANN / RENATE JASCHKE / ANDREAS MRUGALLA (HRSG.)
INTERKULTURELLE BEGEGNUNGEN IN LITERATUR, FILM UND FERNSEHEN
Ein deutsch-japanischer Vergleich
2011 · ISBN 978-3-86205-095-6 · 466 S., kt. · EUR 47,—

IUDICIUM Verlag GmbH
Hans-Grässel-Weg 13 · D-81375 München
Tel. +49 (0)89 718747 · Fax +49 (0)89 7142039 · info@iudicium.de
Bestellungen richten Sie bitte an Ihre Buchhandlung oder an den Verlag.
iudicium **Das Gesamtverzeichnis finden Sie im Internet unter www.iudicium.de**

TOMISHIGE, YOSHIO / ITODA, SOICHIRO (HG.)
AUFFÜHRUNGSDISKURSE IM 18. JAHRHUNDERT
Bühnenästhetik, Theaterkritik und Öffentlichkeit
2011 · 978-3-86205-019-2 · 215 S., Farb-Abb., kt. · € 96,—

GEILHORN, BARBARA
WEIBLICHE SPIELRÄUME
Frauen im japanischen Nō- und Kyōgen-Theater
2011 · 978-3-86205-036-9 · 258 S., geb. · € 29,—
(Monographien, hg. vom Deutschen Institut für Japanstudien, Bd. 48)

ÁROKAY, JUDIT
DIE ERNEUERUNG DER POETISCHEN SPRACHE
Poetologische und sprachtheoretische Diskurse der Edo-Zeit
2010 · 978-3-86205-249-3 · 283 S., kt. · € 30,—
(Iaponia Insula. Studien zu Kultur und Gesellschaft Japans,
hg. von Irmela Hijiya-Kirschnereit, Bd. 24)

TAMURA, KAZUHIKO (HG.)
SCHAUPLATZ DER VERWANDLUNGEN
Variationen über Inszenierung und Hybridität
2011 · 978-3-86205-348-3 · 254 S., kt. · € 23,—

HINDINGER, BARBARA /
LANGNER, MARTIN-M. (HG.)
»ICH BIN EIN MANN! WER IST ES MEHR?«
**Männlichkeitskonzepte in der deutschen Literatur vom Mittelalter
bis zur Gegenwart**
2011 · 978-3-86205-021-5 · 347 S., kt. · € 36,—

IUDICIUM Verlag GmbH
Hans-Grässel-Weg 13 • D-81375 München
Tel. +49 (0)89 718747 • Fax +49 (0)89 7142039 • info@iudicium.de
Bestellungen richten Sie bitte an Ihre Buchhandlung oder an den Verlag.
iudicium   **Das Gesamtverzeichnis finden Sie im Internet unter www.iudicium.de**

Multilingual Europe, Multilingual Europeans

Edited by
László Marácz and
Mireille Rosello

Multilingualism is a crucial if often unrecognized marker of new European identities.

In this collection of essays, we observe how a plurilinguist and pluricultural political entity practices and theorizes multilingualism. We ask which types of multilingualism are defined, encouraged or discouraged at the level of official policies, but also at the level of communities. We look at speakers of hegemonic or minority languages, at travellers and long-term migrants or their children, and analyse how their conversations are represented in official documents, visual art, cinema, literature and popular culture.

The volume is divided into two parts that focus respectively on "Multilingual Europe" and "Multilingual Europeans." The first series of chapters explore the extent to which multilingualism is treated as both a challenge and an asset by the European Union, examine which factors contribute to the proliferation of languages: globalisation, the enlargement of the European Union and EU language policies. The second part of the volume concentrates on the ways in which cultural productions represent the linguistic practices of Europeans in a way that emphasizes the impossibility to separate language from culture, nationality, but also class, ethnicity or gender. The chapters suggest that each form of plurilingualism needs to be carefully analysed rather than celebrated or condemned.

r o d o p i

Orders @ rodopi.nl—www.rodopi.nl

Amsterdam/New York, NY
2012. 323 pp.
(European Studies 29)
Bound €67,-/US$87,-
E-Book €61,-/US$79,-
ISBN: 978-90-420-3528-7
ISBN: 978-94-012-0803-1

USA/Canada:
248 East 44th Street, 2nd floor,
New York, NY 10017, USA.
Call Toll-free (US only): T: 1-800-225-3998
F: 1-800-853-3881

All other countries:
Tijnmuiden 7, 1046 AK Amsterdam, The Netherlands
Tel. +31-20-611 48 21 Fax +31-20-447 29 79
Please note that the exchange rate is subject to fluctuations

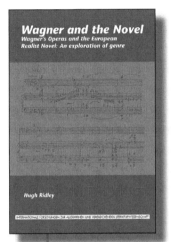